I scrambled for a better foothold and snapped my radio back on. Al was there, bless him! "I'm trying to get clear, Al, and make it to the top of the hill for a pickup.... See you God knows when."

I snapped off the radio and glanced around me. I froze. Ten feet away I was looking up the business end of a semi-automatic rifle held by a grinning, nervous young North Vietnamese soldier. Another soldier, standing to his left, held a wicked-looking sword, like a samurai. I had had it. Grimly, I hung on to the vines with one hand and raised the other in surrender.

There I was, Major Larry Guarino, age forty-three, husband, father, twenty-three-year fighter pilot, veteran of two other wars, now a prisoner of war in North Vietnam.

God Bless
Ron Byrne

A POW'S STORY

2801 Days in Hanoi

Col. Larry Guarino

IVY BOOKS • NEW YORK

Ivy Books
Published by Ballantine Books
Copyright © 1990 by Larry Guarino

Library of Congress Catalog Card Number: 90-93137

ISBN 0-8041-0691-6

Manufactured in the United States of America

First Edition: October 1990

AUTHOR'S NOTES AND ACKNOWLEDGMENTS

This is a memoir focused on the ninety-two months which I spent in the jails of North Vietnam as a prisoner of a Communist enemy. Though they were signers of Geneva Conventions concerning prisoners of war, the Vietnamese chose to exempt themselves from those agreements and treated us as common criminals were treated a hundred years ago.

While incarcerated I recalled, many times, events of WWII, and it was as though my flying adventures of those earlier years in China and French Indochina were plotted along a course which would carry me to a predetermined destiny some twenty years later.

Soon after our repatriation in the spring of 1973, I began to assemble a great amount of reference material that I would need for my writing when the time was right. It was impossible to keep a daily log of events or records of any kind because of the severe conditions of captivity. After writing only a few chapters, I found the work and the recollections entirely too stressful, and I dropped the project. Fourteen years later, at the urging of several friends who were historians, I again began to write what they felt would be an important historical document.

The process of collection and writing has taken several years, and as I progressed through the writing of this book I found it necessary to call upon my former POW friends to verify the accuracy of certain incidents, and they were most obliging. My thanks are extended to Colonels Jim Kasler, Ed Hubbard, Richard Keirn, George Day, and Ron Byrne. If there are slight inaccuracies they are not such to deter the story line; this book is as complete as I could possibly make it.

I have taken the writer's option of using pseudonyms in those instances where it appeared to be in the best interest of all concerned. Conflicts that arose between myself and several others were brought out because there are important lessons to be learned from those incidents, all of which were part of the history of our incarceration.

Up to the year 1969, we numbered not more than three hundred and seventy in the North Vietnamese prison system. If every one of that number were so inclined, then there could be three hundred and seventy separate stories about our experience at the hands of the Communists. I think readers would be rather surprised at the differences of opinions we had among us; therefore, I would point out that this is my memoir, my personal recollection, my view of how it was and what was happening to us.

Very valuable assistance and encouragement was provided to me by Mrs. Pat Robson, a history buff and a dear friend whose early comments presented a challenge to my fighter-pilot mentality and got me off top dead center into serious writing. Dr. Wayne Thompson, at the Office of Air Force History, was responsible for giving helpful direction and checking the book for historical correctness.

The difficult secretarial chores and final recording of the written material on the word processor was done dependably, precisely, and affectionately by both Louise and Carl Alles of Satellite Beach. Carol Jose, of Indialantic, Florida was the final editor before reaching the publisher's office. All of these people have most deservedly earned my sincere thanks and respect.

This memoir and whatever success it may achieve, is dedicated to two very important people in my life.

To Evelyn: my wife and friend for forty-seven years, who carried on and brought up our four sons single-handed during my absence of eighteen of our first thirty years. Evelyn has that never-quit attitude befitting a real fighter pilot. All of her suffering and hard work was done with great love for me, her family, and also for the United States Air Force. She has established standards, she never faltered!

To Colonel Ronald E. Byrne Jr., my friend and cell mate for forty-four months under extremely cruel conditions. Ron had a sometimes very difficult person to live with, but he was more than up to it. His optimism had much to do with my mental survival, and on more than one occasion, I know he saved my life. There can be no closer friends than two men who have suffered together. Thanks for everything, Ron.

L.G.

SOUTHEAST ASIA

Chapter One

THE LAST DIVE

Monday morning, June 14, 1965
Korat Royal Thai Airbase, Thailand

I rolled over in my sack and peered at my watch—its green dial showed 4:30 A.M. Christ! Time to get up and at 'em. It was still dark when the air strike orders for the day, and the pilot and aircraft assignments, were posted by the operations duty officer. Bad weather over most of North Vietnam had forced cancellation of many missions to targets that were considered very important by the Joint Chiefs of Staff. For the third day in a row, a dual air strike was laid on to try to recoup. I was to lead twelve F-105 Thunderchiefs, carrying the maximum load of 750-pound demolition bombs. The target was a control center near the Thanh Hoa bridge. It was so hotly defended, the air force and the navy had already lost more than a dozen aircraft. The second target, a sprawling supply-and-ordnance depot at Son La, forty miles southwest of Hanoi, was covered by eight more 105s and four F-4 Phantoms.

The orders carried the usual bad-weather warnings and instructions that, should one of the target areas be closed down due to weather, all twenty-four of the mission aircraft would proceed to the target with the more favorable conditions.

My flight call sign was "Teak Leader," and as mission commander of the Thanh Hoa strike with the twelve F-105s, my individual call sign was "Geronimo." Lieutenant Colonel Bill Craig, Commander of the 44th Fighter Squadron, was the mission commander of the force going to Son La. Bill was just winding up his tour of duty in Southeast Asia, and in two weeks I would be assuming command of the squadron upon his departure.

1

The alternate target instructions on the ops order made for a long and complicated pilots' briefing. Takeoff time was getting close as we raced to the personal equipment section to pick up our gear. I put my G suit on, then checked my snub-nosed Smith and Wesson .38. I charged out the door, carrying my 'chute, helmet, bag of maps, mission data cards, and target photos.

I spotted my aircraft down the flight line by its last three numbers—220. It was a sleek, silver beauty and mighty impressive with eight 750-pounders hanging on it. My faithful crew chief, Sergeant Rush, greeted me with a smile and helped me place my gear. We gave our three-million-dollar baby a walk-around check. I had a lot of respect for Rush—he had earned my absolute trust. I first met him on a boondoggle trip to Hawaii the year before. He was a conscientious, hard worker who knew his airplane inside out. As I signed the bird off on the maintenance form, I saw a pickup truck approaching with our intelligence officer at the wheel. He told me my mission was scrubbed due to weather, and to divert my twelve aircraft to Bill's target in the Son La area.

I walked over to Bill's aircraft for a last-minute chat, and I saw that it was a dullish, cloudy day with rain squalls in all directions. I was not feeling my best . . . something was bothering me. Could have been the close one I had a few days before, when I had an oxygen failure at thirty-five thousand feet. I had fibbed a little when I told Captain Unitan, our flight surgeon, that I felt perfectly okay to fly.

Bill Craig was all strapped in and smiling at me as I climbed the ladder to his cockpit.

"What's a matter? You feelin' okay?"

"Sure," I said, "but there's something awfully wrong about today. I don't like it! I don't like the way the mission was planned or laid on, and the briefing was all screwed up."

"I know, I know! I don't like it either, but we have to be flexible and do the best we can anyway."

I took my right glove off and stuck out my hand, "So long."

Bill's eyebrows lifted in surprise. "What do you mean 'so long'? I'll see you right back here on the ground in two hours!"

"Oh sure." As I backed down the ladder, I had a feeling that Bill thought I was getting weird. After we started engines, I got word that two of my twelve birds were out of commission, so we pressed on with ten.

We taxied to the arming area, near the end of the runway. There, armorers and ordnance men made a last-minute check and removed the safety arming wires from the bombs. While they were doing this, I called up the KC-135 air-refueling aircraft, to make sure they were in the rendezvous area. I told them that we would be up there shortly to join them, for air refueling.

The F-105 burned a lot of fuel during a maximum-weight takeoff and climbout, so whenever we could arrange it, we topped off our tanks by air refueling. We figured our flight plans to have plenty of fuel during the air strike and for return to base, just in case some emergency situation arose that might require our staying over enemy territory longer than we had planned.

Lining up on the runway, we ran up our engines. Everything checked out. I looked over to Charlie Hart, my wingman, and as the sweep-second hand passed the mark, we tapped our afterburners and got the usual sudden swift kick in the ass of power that made the bird leap forward. After takeoff, we made a right to the course heading. We picked up the tankers on radar, received their directions, and made it on up to the rendezvous point at eighteen thousand feet.

It was pretty well socked in, but I managed to get a brief sighting of the tankers, and swinging in behind them, I kept them in visual contact. We were brought in very close by voice instructions from their boom operator. Because the tanker pilots were flying on instruments, the leader wisely chose to maneuver to provide some separation between the tankers to avoid collision. It took about twenty minutes before the last man called in "topped off." I asked the tanker pilots to shove up the power and climb out in a turn to clear us straightaway to the target area, which they did.

Charlie and I pushed the power up and headed out to the target, but again, because of the weather, we were unable to rejoin the squadron. From there it took us about thirty minutes to make it to the target area, flying in solid weather all the way.

We made a straight on-course weather penetration, cross-checking our position on radar as we broke out of the overcast at ten thousand feet in light rain. I could see smoke, fire, and plenty of shooting from the ground near the target. Captain Turk Turley had gotten there first and had taken charge. Three F-4 Phantoms were circling the target, calling the mission leader for permission to bomb first and leave the scene because they were already sweating low fuel. The Phantoms were supposed to be giving the F-105s area cover against a possible intercept by enemy MiG-17s. Several 105s had already been lost to MiGs, so they were definitely a threat to be considered. We were pretty pissed off at the request to bomb first and leave us without cover, but Turk had no choice but to give them the okay. They selected a big-gun site on the floor of the valley, and obviously rushed their attack because they missed badly, their bombs impacting about three hundred feet short of the gun.

Keeping the target area in sight in a left turn, I noticed that the metal skin was peeled back from the top of my left wing, which meant I had taken one or more hits. Normally hits in an aircraft (even with explosive shells, as long as no critical part of the airplane is hit) go unnoticed by the pilot taking the hits. Turley called, "Move out to the west—another flight is cleared into target." The antiaircraft gunners scored more hits in my wings and my left outboard bomb rack. "Christ!" I thought, "they're throwing up everything they have!" They were shooting like crazy. The damage I had taken should have warned me to abort the mission. On any other day, my judgment would have been a lot better, but that day my below-par condition was costing me.

The visibility worsened as we edged in to pinpoint a spot in the supply area that Turley was describing to us. Headquarters people were mighty critical about where our bombs landed, so we wanted to do it right! We approached from the west, making a rolling, diving turn to the north, zeroing in on the bomb run. The people manning the guns on the ground had some very distinct advantages over the attacking aircraft. There was no element of surprise at this point during the attack because many other aircraft had already been there. The ceiling was seven thousand feet, and we had to assume that the ground gunners knew the exact ceiling: that was probably the reason I was hit so many times before making my bomb run.

You put a guy in a duck blind, and even if he is the worst shot in the world, if enough ducks are stupid enough to fly over him close to his gun barrel, sooner or later he's going to luck out and hit one. It was impossible to set up a steep dive angle, because once that big bear of an F-105 heads downhill, it needs a couple of thousand feet for a pullout. There was all kinds of stuff coming up at me, and the air looked a dirty brown. I had a split second to wish that I had taken time, back on the ground, to set up my toss bomb computer so I could make a radar run and get an automatic release from any dive angle, but I hadn't done it, so now I had to depend on Kentucky windage, eyeballs, and then reach up my rear end for the solution to the problem of exactly when to punch the pickle button to get rid of the bombs.

Impossible to get a good dive angle! Last split-second thoughts:
"This is stupid—I'm going to be very low—ground's coming up
fast—feel like I'm in a tin can and someone is jabbing holes in
it with an ice pick—now pickle, suck back on the stick, hard
rolling turn—oops—just caught a big shell in my belly—tap the
burner, evasive action!"

The explosive force of the enemy shell slamming into the
belly of my F-105 fighter bomber shook me and the aircraft. I
leveled my wings and headed west, making the radio call that
I'd been hit. My cockpit began to fill with smoke. I flipped the
air-conditioning lever into the "vent" position to try to clear the
smoke out. Suddenly my rudder went full travel, and I was into
a wild yawing series. My bird went into a wing roll, and things
were looking pretty grim. I called my flight: "I might have to
punch out, keep an eye on me . . . I'm making it away from the
target at about five thousand feet and heading 270 degrees."
Somebody replied, "Roger, got you." The F-105 was now gy-
rating wildly, and I was afraid that if I waited any longer, I
wouldn't be able to grab the ejection handles, because of high
G forces. I decided I'd better bail out while I could. I radioed,
"So long guys, see you tonight." Taking a deep breath, I pulled
the ejection handles, and the rush of air told me the canopy had
blown. This was it. I squeezed the triggers and was catapulted
into the air. I tumbled briefly, then heard a loud pop and felt the
jerk as my 'chute opened and filled with air.

I looked down and saw there was now nothing but air between
me and enemy territory. I looked up at the orange and white
canopy of my 'chute, thinking, "Good God! This can't be happening to me! It only happens to other guys." Luckily, I still
had my helmet on. I grabbed the chin strap and yanked it tight
for head protection on landing. I held on to my riser straps and
tried to think clearly and get oriented. I noticed I'd lost my
watch—probably from the force of the ejection. Damn! I'd been
wearing that Zodiac for twelve years. As I drifted down, I saw
one of our F-105s in a tight turn close by. He had me spotted
and I gave him an "okay" wave-signal. Now I hoped he would
move away so that the enemy would not be able to pinpoint my
descent. I breathed a sigh of relief when he disappeared.

As I looked below, I could see nothing but green jungle. Off
to my left was a range of hills. Drifting lower, as I came about
even with the tops of the hills, my body began a wild oscillation
from side to side, and I was helplessly swung up almost as high
as my 'chute. Though I'd come close a few times in my years of

flying fighters, this was my first bailout. Pilots don't like to jump out of airplanes that are still working—they say bailing out after being hit is kinda like practicing dying, "you gotta do it right the first time!" I was alarmed at this unexpected wrinkle in my otherwise smooth descent, and I grabbed my front risers and pulled down hard so I'd drop faster, hopefully into steadier air and out of the strong currents that were causing me problems. Sure enough, the 'chute steadied down. As I came closer, I tried to scan the terrain and get myself ready to land. I was sure I'd end up in deep jungle and knew that one of our choppers would soon pick me up. But when I got down to several hundred feet, I realized with a jolt that I was going to land at the very edge of a small village!

It was too late to do anything about it. As my feet touched the ground, I grabbed my 'chute-release rings, yanked hard, and the 'chute blew away. My knees slammed into my chin and I felt my teeth slice through my lower lip. I could see smoke rising from the center of a circle of a dozen grass and bamboo huts mounted on bamboo poles above the ground. The village was definitely inhabited! Hurriedly, I scrambled for my survival gear. Suddenly I had a very strange and strong sensation, so powerful that I was compelled to stop packing and look up to my right. As I live and breathe, I saw Jesus Christ standing there, a vision, or an apparition, over one hundred feet tall. It was as real as anything I have ever seen. I thought fleetingly of all the close calls I had had in my life. Was this what He had been saving me for all these years? Looking down at me He said, "Larry, today I am going to show you something!"

"Lord, how I know you are!" I thought. Turning away, I grabbed my stuff together to try to make it out of there.

I got rid of my 'chute harness, then tossed emergency rations from my parachute seat pack into a canvas bag. I wondered why nobody drew down on me, since I'd landed barely ten feet from one of the village huts. I figured that the villagers had seen me coming down and had withdrawn to keep me under surveillance from a safe distance. I put out a call on the two-way survival radio: "Hello Vampire Squadron, this is Geronimo, on the ground." I got an immediate response. I guessed by the voice that it was my buddy, Al Vollmer. What a twist of fate this was! Our positions were now reversed from a few months ago, when I had capped him after his bailout over the Ban Ken bridge in Laos. I reported minor injuries, but otherwise okay so far. Al came back: "You'd better get moving. We've got you covered.

Help is on the way!'' I looked around me and hoped it wouldn't be long in coming. I started to run up a nearby hill. I had gotten only a few yards when I remembered I'd left my plastic water bottle back in my 'chute harness. Damn! I doubled back, snatched it out, and gurgled down a couple of big swallows. What a relief! My mouth was dry as desert sand from the tense situation I found myself in, still expecting a bullet to rip through my drawers at any moment. Moving back up the side of the hill, which was planted in corn, I slipped and slid around in the mud in my worn, slick-bottom boots. About two hundred yards up, I came up against a wall of jungle, and it *was* a wall. It was as though the jungle had been shoved back by the villagers just enough to scratch out a space for living and a small, barely tillable area.

It stopped me as surely as if it had been made of bricks. I couldn't crawl over, or under it, so I moved to the left, puffing from the effort, tiring rapidly, praying that the chopper would hurry the hell up and pluck me out of there. I hunched down close to the ground, moving along the edge of the jungle. I came upon a fast-moving little stream, and gratefully slipped down into it to snatch a breather. I had to hang on to the vines growing from its deep sides to keep from being carried away by the force of the current. As I hung there, trying to gather some energy, bird calls pierced the silence, but I had not seen any birds. I felt real alarm, as the skin on my neck started to prickle. I scrambled for a better foothold and snapped my radio back on. Al was there, bless him! ''I'm trying to get clear Al, and make it to the top of the hill for a pickup. But I'm bushed. And these goddamn slick boots don't help any. I keep slipping and sliding around. I don't know if I can make it. For God's sake, tell them we need better flight boots! Cleated bottoms!'' Al told me to hang in there and try to get to the top of the hill again. ''Okay, I'm leaving . . . see you God knows when.''

I snapped off the radio and glanced around me. I froze. Ten feet away I was looking up the business end of a semiautomatic rifle held by a grinning, nervous, young North Vietnamese soldier. Another soldier, standing to his left, held a wicked looking sword, like a samurai. I had had it. Grimly, I hung on to the vines with one hand and raised the other in surrender. They moved in, and as the end of the gun barrel came to within six inches of my nose, I thought, ''If that son of a bitch shakes any harder, it will be all over for me by accident.'' He seemed more frightened than I was. I spoke to him softly, hoping to calm him down. His buddy reached for my holster and relieved me of my

.38. Six more armed men and two women—one of whom was carrying a rifle—closed into a tight circle around me. No doubt they saw me coming down and had played it very cautiously. They motioned me out of the stream, and somehow I managed to scramble up the side. Tying my arms tightly behind me, they picked up my gear and pushed me toward the village. When we got there, they pulled me into a hut that was apparently the home of the village elder. He was an old, placid sort of guy, with a long, narrow white beard. Pinned on the wall behind him was a picture of Ho Chi Minh, and they looked like twins. He sat cross-legged on the wooden floor and stared at me curiously for a long time, saying nothing. The soldiers came up and spoke to him in their native tongue. He said something in response, and must have given his permission, because then they grabbed me and hustled me off back to the heavy brush. They sat me there, under cover, until some official-looking type came up and took inventory of everything I had on and was carrying. Another woman came up to me and offered me a drink of water. None of the people seemed angry, only very curious about me. The girl with the rifle sat across from me, and her eyes never left me. She was fairly tall, husky, good looking, and much larger than the other Vietnamese women. I may have been the first real westerner she had ever seen—one of the "Yankee imperialists" she had read or heard about from childhood. She was face-to-face with the enemy of her people, as she had been taught to believe, but she was in control of herself and allowed no emotion whatsoever to show.

I was glad I had landed a good distance from the area we had bombed before my bailout. I knew from other wars that an aircrewman's life is up for grabs once he's in the 'chute. It's impossible to predict what may happen. To the peasants, a foreigner who has been contributing to their misery, for whatever reason, is an evil snake descending on them by parachute. Some will treat the captive just like they would a snake: stomp him, kill him with any weapon handy—gun, knife, rock, or bamboo spear—out of hatred or open hysteria. So far, I knew I had been very lucky. I was still alive and relatively unharmed. I had hope. After a while, they walked me down to the village again and did some more chatting among themselves.

Then a senior-looking guy, obviously a man of some official authority, arrived. He berated the others, pointing to my arms where they were tied, I guessed not nearly securely enough to suit him. He directed that the ropes be cinched up tighter behind

me on both arms and wrists. The official then took my handkerchief, pretended to wipe my face—and swiped it. They began
to march me around in a wide circle to throw off any rescuers.

Suddenly, we heard the sounds of aircraft nearby. My captors
looked frightened, and my hopes soared briefly, knowing that
Al was still around waiting to direct rescue aircraft. Vollmer had
no way of knowing I was already tied up like a sausage and it
was probably too late. The man in charge gave orders to get me
out of sight, and I was roughly shoved into the brush again.
They had put my reversible survival hat on me. It was made of
soft, water-repellent poplin, olive drab on one side and orange
on the other—I had it on orange side out. The planes came
booming in, and I prayed for a miracle. I knew it was my buddies in F-105s, wondering where I had gone and why I didn't
come up on the radio. The rain started down again, and through
it, just below the cloud layer, I saw a C-123 rescue-director
aircraft. Then along came a squadron of SPADs—propeller-
driven single-engine air force or navy A-1s, I couldn't tell for
sure. Then two rescue choppers, right over my head, going
across the village and right over the spot where I had first landed.
All the village militia was out by now, perhaps twenty of them.
They stood, under cover, up and down the path, and every man
was firing as fast as he could. One of the SPADs came down to
fifty feet or less, right down the path near me. Dipping his
wings, he looked right and left. I stood up and shook my head
so he'd spot the hat. I swear the pilot looked right at me. As he
zipped by me, something flew off his drop tank—a piece of
metal, or a fuel cap. Somebody scored a hit on him, but as the
Vietnamese shoved me back down, the SPAD pilot didn't seem
to be in any trouble, and figured he hadn't seen me at all, since
he never made another pass. The rescue aircraft stayed around
for twenty or thirty minutes, but as the rainfall became heavier,
they slowly withdrew. Then all was quiet again. There I was,
Major Larry Guarino, age forty-three, husband, father, twenty-
three-year fighter pilot, veteran of two other wars, now a prisoner of war in North Vietnam.

Chapter Two

THE CAPTURED YANKEE AGRESSOR

The senior man talked to a few of the soldiers . . . they concluded that it was safe to get me back on the road. We resumed our trek, meeting many Vietnamese villagers. Some stood and stared, while others rushed on, hardly daring to steal a peek. We walked at a fast clip. The main idea was to get me far away from my touchdown point, so that rescuers would not be able to locate me and do some shooting or bombing in a desperation move to save me. The country was mostly rolling hills and green jungle. The terrain was flooded in many areas and cut with small and large streams due to heavy seasonal rain.

We came to a deep, very fast-moving stream. One of the soldiers tied a rope tether around my neck and indicated that I was to cross the stream. I hoped he wasn't serious, but he prodded me with his gun, and I had no choice. He held the end of the rope and stood back with the others to see if I would make it across. Once in the swift water, I hesitated again. They made it clear that I had to cross, so I squatted lower, and now in water up to my chin, I inched forward on slippery rocks. Choking in the fast water, I knew I was a goner if I slipped. The Vietnamese weren't at all concerned. Miraculously, I made it across the fifty-foot-wide stream. I was completely bushed and flopped down on the bank.

Quite a crowd had gathered to watch my stream crossing. Now I had an escort of ten soldiers plus a brown-shirted guy whom I took to be a political cadre or officer. They kicked me back up to my feet and marched me up and down some steep, muddy slopes. I fell to the ground and motioned that my wrists were badly cut from the wet ropes. That was a mistake, because the brown-shirted one had them pull the binders tighter! The day had darkened in steady rain.

They prodded me along until we came to another fast stream. "This has got to be it, I can't make it across another one. I guess drowning is the way I'm going out," I thought. Again I felt the strong presence of the Lord with me as I stepped into water up to my chin. Again, the watchful peasants hovered on the banks. Cautiously, laboriously, I inched my way over slippery boulders toward the far side. It seemed a miracle that I had made it again, as I scrambled up the bank on the other side. I was reaching the end of my strength and endurance. Continuing along, I came to a very steep slope covered with slick yellowish mud. I tried to climb it, but it was a disaster. I slipped, rolled, and tumbled in the yellow-orange slime. They forced me to rise again and again and continue the climb. As I was puffing my way up, I made the remark, half-aloud, "Was this the way it was when You were making Your way up that hill?" He replied, "Something like that, only you don't have that heavy thing to drag along with you." And so it was for the next hours—I felt that the Lord was with me and never left my side, though my faith was tested often in the bad days, and years, that followed.

That evening we came to another village. The people gathered around me, pointing and staring. The political man made me walk over to an angled log fence. He made me lie back against the logs and began what I figured to be a public denunciation of me, jabbing his finger toward me, while his voice rose louder and louder. Soon the villagers were all excited, and some got worked into hysteria at the antics of this political cheerleader. They picked up rocks and started stoning me. I ducked and turned as best I could, trying to avoid serious injury, but I was knocked senseless when a couple of them hit me square on the head. Some of the people grabbed at me, tearing at my clothes. Luckily the soldiers intervened and hustled me away. That was a close one, and I was glad to be on the march again, away from there.

As night fell, they walked me through narrow paths. Often we had to cross bridges that were only rough, slippery logs. It was still raining hard. My boots had no traction at all, and it was amazing that I didn't slip and fall. The log bridges were three to ten feet above streams or deep ditches. Had I fallen, I would have broken some bones.

We came to another village and the mob scene, starring me and the politico, was repeated. He played his part well, shaking his fist at me and yelling louder and louder, until the villagers (who at first were only curious) became excited, then hysterical;

then the rock-throwing and body attacks started again. Some of
the people got their hands on me and pulled my hair and tore at
me, and again the soldiers hustled me off. This went on far into
the night. . . . I lost track of how often. I moved through it like
a robot. Finally they brought me into the last village and made
me climb a ladder into a hut, which sat up off the ground on
poles. There was a meeting going on. A woman was tending a
small fire, and she gave me a tiny cup of tea, holding the cup
for me as I drank. The hut was a large, one-room family shelter
that looked like it could accommodate fifteen to twenty people.
My hands and arms, still tied tightly behind me, had gone from
painful to dead numb. Climbing first up then down the bamboo
ladder was slow and torturous, but having no choice I somehow
managed it.

We resumed our march in the black of night. The man behind
me worked a hand-actuated flashlight. He tried to show me the
way as I crossed over more log bridges, but most of the time the
light quit at the halfway point. My luck continued, however,
and I didn't fall. The night seemed endless.

It was close to midnight when we came to a small town with
masonry buildings; the biggest one had the hammer-and-sickle
insignia on the face of it. There were a lot of soldiers around,
and I saw some type of weapons-carrier vehicle there. A Vietnamese who spoke some English came over and asked me if I
was seriously injured. I replied that I was not, but I could no
longer feel my arms and hands. He didn't understand or else
just ignored my predicament. I was ordered into the back of the
vehicle, along with eight or ten soldiers, and we rode off down
a bumpy road. Because of the rain, the soldiers pulled a protective tarp over their heads. I was at the very back of the vehicle,
and the tarp ended at about the middle of my head. As the steady
rain collected on the tarp, it ran over the edge and poured down
my neck. I was shivering with cold. All the soldiers had guns,
and for a while they kept busy oiling them. Then, one by one,
they fell asleep, and the guns clattered against one another as
we bounced over the pothole-ridden roads. Suddenly I felt an
arm slide around my shoulders as the soldier next to me began
to cuddle me. I wasn't sure whether he was trying to help warm
me or what, but I felt some alarm. Then, with his right hand,
he began to touch me and feel for my breast pockets and ex-
plore. Finally he began to unzip my flying suit, and I realized
what he was up to. Jesus! I began to kick and holler and woke
up another soldier who was directly in front of me. He got the

idea and chewed out the masher, which diverted him for a while; but when the man in front of me fell asleep again, the masher made a comeback. I raised another ruckus and woke several soldiers, who quickly realized what was going on. They yelled at him, and he quit bothering me. However, he didn't remove his arm from around my neck, and I didn't complain, because it offered me some protection from the rain pouring down my neck. By then I was sitting in two inches of water.

The vehicle stopped from time to time. Some of the soldiers got out, and others replaced them. Early the next morning, most of the soldiers took off. Only the driver and two soldiers stayed with me. By daylight, I could see that the armored vehicle was like an old U.S. Army weapons carrier, except that it had a machine gun permanently mounted on the left rear. Up front the windshield was armor-plated with only two thick glass ports to look through. There was nothing visible to indicate its origin.

The driver pulled into a walled compound and made some contacts. A woman came out, carrying a bowl of rice and a foul-smelling vegetable, which I later named "swamp grass." It smelled like sewage and tasted worse. . . . I gagged on it. Even so, I managed to swallow a little, but when she offered more, I turned my head away. Another woman, carrying a baby of about a year old, came to stare at me. She shook her fist at me and yelled. I clucked my tongue at the baby and it giggled. The woman angrily slapped the baby's mouth. Then she took its fist and began to smash it in the face. She was showing the infant that I was something very evil and hateful. This type of mother-child scene occurred several different times that day. It was easy to make the children smile and giggle, but the mothers always took the same quick and angry corrective action.

The soldiers drove me out of the compound and parked in the dirt road. A large mob quickly gathered. The soldiers, particularly the driver, seemed proud of me, because having me in their custody gave them real status. Another local authority came up and began to denounce me. The mob began screaming and shouting and pushing closer, shaking their fists. The soldiers, worried about losing control, clicked the bolts back on their rifles in a warning gesture. But the throng continued to press forward, and several grabbed me, trying to pull me out of the truck. The mob was out of control, the driver realized we were losing it, and I was starting to sweat the outcome. Jumping behind the wheel, he shoved it into gear. I could hear the fenders banging heads, but the driver didn't care who he hurt as he yo-

yoed the vehicle back and forth, plowing his way through the crowd.

We drove away from the town, and after an hour or so we came to soccer field. We drove into the middle of it and stopped. Again a large crowd gathered. A very thin old lady began the denunciation; the rocks flew until the driver had to move out again. This scene was repeated several more times that day. The reason for this exercise was to teach the people to hate the "Yankee aggressors" and to whip them into a fighting frenzy. It seemed to be working.

By that night, I was near total exhaustion. I hadn't eaten or slept for two days, and my head was bleeding from rock cuts. My soaked boots were full of mud and stones, and I was caked with mud right down to my undershorts. I was totally demoralized. I was moved into a smaller vehicle, like a Jeep. I was taken over to the side of the road to take care of my toilet; however, I was unable to move my arms, much less my fingers. One of the guards held my penis, sort of routinely . . . as though it belonged to him. Back in the Jeep I realized that I was no longer tied, but I still couldn't move my paralyzed arms. They removed my shoes and spread my legs apart, tying my feet to the corners of the front seat. As they started to tie my arms back behind me, I pleaded with a new man, who seemed to be the officer in charge, not to tie my arms behind me again. He finally acquiesced and seemed satisfied to tie my arms across my chest in X fashion, very tightly. This gave me some relief, because I was worried about permanent physical damage. A guard got in on either side of me, and on the all-night ride the one on my right beat my ribs continuously with his fists. He was a pipsqueak and couldn't hurt me much, but the little bastard did succeed in turning my side black and blue.

Early in the morning we stopped, and I was blindfolded and left in the truck for a few minutes. One of the soldiers came back and completely enshrouded me in a blanket, so that no one could see me. Soon I was gasping and struggling for every breath. I began to pray for help, but I didn't think that the Vietnamese knew that I was going down for the count. I wasn't sure that they gave a damn either. Suddenly I felt a cool breeze blowing across me. From where? "How could that be?" I wondered. I felt that I had again been handed a miracle—fresh air to breathe when I was certain that I was a goner. I didn't understand it then, nor do I now.

Later they pulled the blanket away from my face and lifted

the blindfold. The guard fed me a hard-boiled egg, which I wolfed down. He cut up a small green peach with a penknife and poked pieces of it into my mouth. When we got underway again, I could hear us splashing through water, then I could feel that we were in flat country, which I correctly guessed was the delta area leading to the city of Hanoi. In another hour or so, traffic sounds told me that we were in a big city. The pavement became smooth under the wheels. Then I heard the clanging of steel doors. The vehicle moved forward a few yards, stopped; the doors clanged again behind us, and a soldier came, untied me, and beckoned me out of the vehicle. I moved stiffly and laboriously made my way out. I hurt everywhere. Sraightening up, I came face to face with an angry Vietnamese who immediately launched into a tirade in English—calling me a "dirty murdering aggressor." He screamed, "You have come here to kill us! You have come here to murder us! You are going to pay for your crimes! You are going to pay for your crimes! You criminal! Where did you take off from? Where did you take off from?"

I tried to look derisive and mustered my own anger.

"Who the hell are you? Go and get me an officer, I'm a major in the United States Air Force, and I want to be treated like one. I have rights as a prisoner of war."

"Prisoner of war nothing! You are no prisoner of war. You are a criminal of war, that's what you are, and that's the treatment that you're going to get! Where did you take off from? You took off from Korat, didn't you?"

"No, I took off from Da Nang." I stood up to my questioner as well as my condition would permit. Little did I know that I was facing "the Rabbit," the most hated of the prison interrogator-torturers. I would get to know him very well.

Periodically during my long journey, I had thought about how to answer the question they would surely ask about my launch base. At that time our bases in Thailand were still a carefully guarded military secret, despite the fact that the U.S. media had already blown the cover. I had decided I would give only misinformation, and that's what I did.

"You'll be very sorry you came here to bomb my people!" the Rabbit screamed. Then several guards took me by the arms and dragged me to a cell block that I later learned the prisoners called "New Guy Village."

Chapter Three

HOA LO THE CITY JAIL

I was shoved into a cell. I looked around me. It was about seven feet wide by sixteen feet long. Against the far wall was a wooden bench, with a set of rusty old iron leg stocks set up to hold four people. I judged that the jail was fifty or sixty years old. There was one arch-shaped window seven feet up from the floor, with a double set of iron bars across it. I could see out by climbing up on one of the benches, but there was nothing to see but another wall, six feet away. It was about sixteen feet high, topped with broken glass. Steel angle irons, strung with barbed wire, protruded from the top of the wall.

My clothes were filthy and thick with mud, so I was glad to get out of them. In a few minutes I was handed a pair of thin blue-and-white striped cotton pajamas. I was allowed to keep only my shorts, T-shirt, and socks.

I noticed that in the center of the heavy steel cell door there was a tiny peep that the guard could open from the outside. Across the outside of the door there was a two-inch steel bar for extra protection. It was secured with a hasp lock after the door was closed. I was taken to a young Vietnamese interrogator who was called "the Owl." He was a little fellow, very thin, with a sallow complexion and deep-set black eyes. He ordered me to sit on a small, low wooden stool that was hard as stone.

I disliked the Owl at first sight. He stared at me for a long time, then asked me my name, rank, and serial number, which I gave him. When he asked my unit designation, I refused to answer. He asked several times, his temper rising as I gave no answer. Then he calmed down, and began a singsong recital:

"We know all about you, you're from the Forty-fourth Squadron, Okinawa. The other squadrons in your wing are the Twelfth and the Sixty-seventh Squadron. You are part of the 313th Air

16

Division in the Eighteenth Fighter Wing. We know all about you, and *all* of your people! We only ask you to check your attitude, to see if you have a good attitude." I knew that he didn't know anything of any substance. The information he had just recited so smugly was printed on my personal gear and parachute . . . as it always is in peacetime. At this early stage, we hadn't yet taken precautions to prevent the enemy from gaining this information. He continued asking me questions of a military nature, such as my position in the squadron, and how many combat missions and flying hours I had. I remained silent. "Sooner or later you will give us all that information!" he remarked snidely. "You will show a good attitude, so you can be humanely treated!" Owl leafed through my wallet. He examined a white business card. "Who is this?" he demanded, holding up the card. I saw it was a card from a Bangkok Cab Company with the driver's name.

"That person is a taxicab driver."

"Why do you keep his name?"

"So if I go to Bangkok on a shopping trip and I need a taxi, I'll know who to call."

He squinted, stood, and pointed a finger: "No! You lie! This man was your intelligence associate in Thailand. You worked hand-in-hand with him. You are an intelligence officer! You have come up here to spy on us!" It was such an incredible accusation, I jumped up, too:

"Are you *serious*? Could you actually think that I flew up here and bailed out of a multimillion-dollar airplane just to check on what you guys are doing? Really!"

He yelled for the guard and sent me back to my cell.

I was tired and lost track of time. Suddenly the cell door opened, and the guard came in with food. It was in a type of Asian mess kit, a series of little pans, one on top of the other, held together with flat steel bands. My first meal consisted of three thin slices of pork, a baked potato, green beans, soup, two square slices of bread, very much like our American bread, and half a small loaf of French bread. I was amazed at the amount and quality of the food. I downed as much as I could, patted myself on the stomach, and thought, "If the food is like this all the time, I'm going to have trouble keeping my weight down." I tried to lie down on the steel cot in the corner. It had three rough, uneven, two-inch-thick boards for a mattress. It was impossible to get even slightly comfortable. I knew I was soft from easy living.

At the next interrogation, the Owl was persistent in his questioning, and I refused to answer, repeating name, rank, serial number, date of birth, consistent with the Code of Conduct of the American fighting man. He launched into a lecture on the "crimes" I had committed against his people. I yawned and showed a bad attitude, which angered him all the more. Finally, in a huff, he sent me back to the cell block. I was escorted by an old guard, "Stoneface," who never cracked a smile. In my cell I found a second set of pajamas, an enameled tin cup, and a mosquito net. My toilet, a one-gallon tin can with a wooden top, sat in a corner.

I knew I was getting in deeper, although they had not yet gotten rough with me. I prayed, paced the floor a little, then tried to get some sleep, but the cell lights were on all night and outside the building, a loud radio program played continuously.

The next day Stoneface showed up again and took me out to the "bath" building, a filthy old shower building with a typical French toilet that reminded me of World War II in French Morocco and Algeria (where I found that the French colonials didn't use sit-down toilets, but preferred to step on cement footprints and take careful aim through "the bomb sight"). It was all in nasty condition, and there were several large green scorpions crawling around the dump hole. The showers weren't working, but a tiny stream of fresh water trickled from a spigot. I managed to wash, my first cleanup in four days, and my morale took an upswing. Strange as it seems now, at that point I still considered my capture a great adventure. I was sure I would soon be freed by my buddies, and I wanted to do everything that was expected of a professional officer during this brief captivity.

I was taken for another visit with the Owl. This time he didn't ask me any questions but gave me a long lecture about the history of the Vietnamese people. After three or four hours of this (and a numbed behind), I was taken back to my cell and fed another meal similar to the one I had the day before—sliced pork and green beans. Again I was amazed at the good quality of the food. Stoneface came around with my flight suit, made me put it on, and then a photographer popped in and took a couple of shots of me.

Later that day, the Owl acted a little friendlier. He asked me if I knew Captain Harris, a member of my fighter wing. I said that I did, and asked him how Captain Harris was.

"Oh, he's fine."

I tried to keep looking at Owl so he wouldn't realize that my

mind had drifted. Smitty Harris's name took me back to Korat,
about four days before I got "smoked." It was a squadron pilots' briefing. After the usual bits of flying safety were covered,
I went to the rostrum to give my views of the war and our part
in the war. Competition between pilots as to who had the greater
share of combat sorties was getting to be annoying. To pacify
the slow-comers, I said, "There is no particular rush to get your
missions in. There is going to be enough time in this action for
everyone to fly fifty missions—one hundred missions—possibly
three hundred, or even five hundred missions." At that point,
Bill Craig interrupted me, saying he didn't necessarily agree
with me, he felt that there was a good chance that the war could
be over in a couple of months. I reminded Bill that I had been
in Southeast Asia since 1961 and had observed the slow buildup
of American forces throughout Southeast Asia, along with the
total radar-and-communications environment. I pointed out that
there were a lot of new faces and high-powered, high-priced
help over from the United States. There were also many new
fighter operations both in South Vietnam and Thailand. With all
that activity, the idea of a short war didn't make sense to me.
There were very good reasons to believe we were in for a long,
long stay. Some of our politicians had already stated that, if it
was necessary, we would stay in Southeast Asia for the next
seventeen years! I felt no one on our side really understood what
a tough old guy Ho Chi Minh was. Our bombing didn't scare
him, it only made him madder. He threw out the French after
they had occupied his country for a hundred years.

I wound up the briefing by telling the pilots to plan on a very
long war, and by all means to take every possible measure to
avoid capture. I referred to Captain Smitty Harris of the 67th
Fighter Squadron, who had already been captured. "I pity
Smitty," I said, "because anyone captured could very well be
a 'play toy' for the Chinese for the next fifty years." It was a
thought I didn't like to recall, now that I, too, was in Hanoi, but
those were my feelings at the time.

The Owl yelled, bringing me back.

"What are you doing?" He realized I was far away. I answered quickly.

"I'm listening, go ahead." He composed himself, then ventured one or two more military questions, which I brushed off.

"Do you know many black people?" he asked.

"Yes, I do."

"They are always a happy, singing people, always smiling. I think you call them niggers."

"No, I don't call them niggers. Usually whites refer to them as 'colored.' "

"How about Eskimos? Have you ever been to Alaska?"

"Yes, I have."

"Do you know your government bought Alaska from the czar, who stole it from the Eskimos?"

"I think it was considered a legitimate land sale."

"And do you know how much you paid for it?"

"I think fifteen million dollars."

"No, only ten million!" He looked pleased with himself.

"Well, you have to remember that it happened a long time ago, and real estate was very cheap at the time." He went on with more political hogwash, then sent me back to my cell.

I paced the floor and took stock of my situation. They had started out tough, but hadn't touched me yet. . . . So far, so good. Apparently they didn't feel any urgent need for military information, or they would have worked me over for it. I hoped that the Vietnamese authorities would continue in this line, because so far the treatment wasn't bad. Why did they waste so much time on Vietnamese history, and that childish line about "showing a good attitude?"

During the night I lay there, stiff and half-asleep. The door clanked open, and an elderly, kindly civilian Vietnamese guard came in, carrying a folded blanket. I didn't get up from the cot. Silently he came over, lifted my head gently, and slipped the blanket under it as a pillow. He looked at me sadly, went out, and closed the door. I couldn't figure the gesture, and though I appreciated the kindness, I thought they might be going all-out on a grease job to get me to talk out of appreciation for small favors.

The next day, the Owl lectured again, and as he spoke, two gray rats came through a hole in the wall and played about his feet. He didn't seem alarmed or even mindful of it. Occasionally he would kick them away. I was flabbergasted. The punch line of the lecture was, "Your president should keep all of your people home and not send them to foreign lands; he must stop interfering with the business of the Asian people; he should spend the people's money not on airplanes and bombs to kill our innocent people, but to clear up his rat-infested slums."

As he rambled on, another Vietnamese came in the room. He was tall, handsome, and I judged about forty-two years old. Owl stood up until told to sit by this man, who was obviously very senior in rank. He wore a uniform but showed no rank or insignia. I continued to sit on my tiny stool, and Owl picked up the lecture again. The senior said nothing but studied me closely.

I was dismissed, returned to my cell block, and the guard motioned me to pick up my *cuom* (meaning food). It sat on a shelf in the hallway of the cell block. This food was a big change from the first week. One bowl contained old dried rice with dirt over it and the other a conglomeration of green weeds with a fuel-oil smell. I thought they were trying to poison me and didn't touch the nasty stuff. Later, I was taken to the Owl again, who sat smugly, looking proud of himself. He proclaimed in his loud, irritating, singsong voice, ''And now you have been punished! That is nothing compared to what you are going to get if you don't show repentance for your crimes and a better attitude!''

That night, while my stomach roared, I planned my tactics for the next set of interrogations; then I prayed for guidance and deliverance from my enemies. As I sat on the edge of the steel cot, my eyes fell upon something written on the cell wall directly in front of me. I leaned over, and my heart gave a leap as I read the words ''Look under table.'' What table? There was no table here; it must mean under the bench with the leg stocks. I scurried over, dropped to my knees, and checked out the underside of the rack, but found nothing. Maybe there was a table and it had been removed from the cell? Frustrated, I sat down again, but every few minutes I got up and checked the bench. Suddenly I got the idea. Picking up the small stool in the corner, I looked carefully at the top. Scratched into the grain faintly with a pencil was ''look under.'' I quickly flipped the stool over. There, stuffed into a crack of the wood, was a tightly folded note. Turning my back to the door, I picked up the toilet bucket and held it in front of me as a fake in case the guard peeked in. ''Hi,'' I read. ''About six weeks here before move. Food pretty good. No torture. You will be contacted. Keep your eyes and ears open. Pray and put trust in God. Yank.''

Chapter Four

PROPAGANDA AND BRAINWASHING

During the next week I didn't eat any of the food, convinced that it was contaminated. I did drink all the water I could. Walking and praying became my main pastime. There were plenty of ants on the floors and walls of the cell and a couple of small mice to keep me company. At night the mosquitoes were fierce. The cell was filthy by our standards, but then the thought came to me that it might very well be the best I'd ever see in North Vietnam! At least it was big enough to get some walking exercise, and there was plenty of light during the daytime.

Looking carefully at the walls, I found the name of a fellow American, Ron Storz. There was also a calendar scratched out, indicating that he had moved out just two days before I moved in. He probably left that morale-boosting note under the stool.

I worried about my wife, Evelyn, and our four boys, though I was consoled knowing the air force would take good care of them. My main concern was how I could do the very best job possible in the time I'd have to spend as a POW, figuring I'd lose at least a year of my life, perhaps even more. . . . What an awful thought! It got so I was even listening for the sounds of helicopters coming to get me out of Hanoi! "Okay, okay this is a great experience guys, but ten days is plenty! I want out of here!"

The next time out for interrogation I met "the Dog." He was the senior-looking official who had come in while I was with the Owl. He had not spoken before, but now he spoke English, and quite well. He lectured me about the incorrect position of the United States government in the war, and how we had no right to interfere in the domestic problems of the Vietnamese people. He went on for three or four hours! Finally he let me go. In the hallway near my cell, I found the same slop waiting for me, a tiny bowl of hard, dirty rice and more stinky swamp grass. I refused it, much to the annoyance of Stoneface.

On the night of June 25, I heard the sounds of doors opening. A few minutes later, I whistled "Anchors Aweigh." Got an immediate reply from Lieutenant Junior Grade J. B. McKamey, U.S. Navy. Talking through the wall, I learned that he'd been shot down two hundred miles south on June 2 and had a really hairy and arduous trip to Hanoi. J. B. Had no unusual news about the war, since he had been "smoked" before me, but he did give me one news item that shook me up. "I heard that Alvarez, [the first pilot shot down, in August of '64] has been executed by firing squad."

The next day I beefed about the food again to the Owl. He said, "That's the way it will be, until you learn to cooperate, like the other Americans!" I got mad and said, "Well, I'm not gonna cooperate, I've given you my name, rank, and horsepower, and that's all you get! Now I wanna eat!" But the slop kept coming. For the first weeks I didn't notice any change, but suddenly the weight virtually fell off me.

When McKamey was out to interrogation, I would get lost in thought. It was like departing the world altogether, as I mentally fingered the beads, thinking about Evelyn and our four boys, my lost opportunities, and my lost command. All of it was extremely depressing. Insidiously I'd slipped into a phase of self-pity . . . just about the worst indulgence there can be for a POW. When I came back to the present, my chest was wet and I was standing in water. I think it was my own tears.

It had been more than a week since I had eaten anything, and food was now foremost in my thoughts. Nervous tension wiped out any nature's call I may have had, and I was still carrying whatever I ate in Korat on the morning of my shootdown.

The next time out, I saw the Dog, who seemed extremely nervous, actually trembling, as he continually looked toward the door of the quiz room.

"Now I am going to ask you some things and I want you to answer loudly and clearly, do you understand? Loudly and clearly! Give your name, rank, and serial number." From his manner, it seemed apparent that this session was being recorded in some way. Also, I figured from his jitters, his personal health and welfare may have been at stake.

I did as I was asked, adding my birthdate, which was April 16, 1922, Easter Sunday.

"Now tell me how you were shot down."

"Okay. I took off from Da Nang and flew up here. When I got close to the target my engine just crapped out."

"Say that again," Dog said "Again!"

Dog didn't know what the hell I was saying. In a sweat he pleaded, "Tell me again how you were shot down."

I repeated the same thing, and the session was abruptly halted.

An hour later the Dog called me back; he was still highly pissed. "And who told you Americans that you could appoint yourselves as the international gendarmes? Who asked you? Who gave you the right to speak for people all over the world? Who gave you the right to tell us what we can or what we cannot do? *You, you* Guarino, you think you can go anywhere, do anything, and that people are going to be afraid, just because you are an American!"

Later I reflected on the Dog's mood and comments. Isn't it amazing that when foreigners think of us—meaning "us" from the United States—they think of all of us as Americans. They don't seem to notice whether we are white, black, brown, or yellow, or whether our names end with vowels or *-ski* or whatever; to them we are all the same, Americans. Never does a man feel so "American" as when he is out of his own country. It's pathetic that only in our own country, many of us still choose to identify ourselves by groups, whether by ethnic background, religion, or color.

Toward evening of the same day, I met another interrogator, a little fellow, very young, possibly in his middle twenties, who was playing the part of the Nice Young Kid. He stared at me for a long time before he spoke, and he watched his words carefully. He told me things about himself, and about his girlfriend, who was also in the army. They could not marry for a long time, because he knew the war would last a long time. The army would not allow her to marry, or give her an assignment where they could be closer together. From time to time, he would ask me questions about myself, but I would smile back, and as politely as I could, I refused to answer. He told me I was going to be there a long time and I should try to cooperate so the Vietnamese people would tolerate me.

After several meetings, the Nice Kid finally came up with a choice bit of advice that I labeled as just another lie by an interrogator, even though it made a hell of a lot of sense. He studied me for a long time, as I sat with numbed rear end. "You know . . . if you refuse to answer questions about your aircraft and your weapons . . . they will be angry . . . but not too angry . . . ! If you refuse to answer questions about your organization or your politics . . . they will be angry . . . but not too angry. . . . But . . . if you refuse to answer just personal things about yourself and your family . . . then they are going to be very very angry! You are probably going to be here for a long, long time; you must try to get along as best you can!" The Kid was telling me that I could go just so far with a hard line against them and that sooner or later the hammer would fall.

The Kid then talked about how bad it had been under the French, and he asked me if I knew much about the French occupation. I said I knew a little and that I knew the French called the native people "Annamites." That was the wrong thing to say. His eyes turned to very narrow slits, and it was the only time I ever saw him genuinely angry.

"Annamités [he pronounced it in the French, something like Ah-nah-mee-tays]. We hated that name! It means 'peace-loving people.' They made it sound like we loved our existence, as if we loved the French. We *hated them*; we did not want to be their slaves. We were *not* the 'peace-loving people'; we fought, we fought to throw them out!"

That night I thought about how it was twenty years before, and it seemed like yesterday. I was getting my first inkling that everything a person sees or hears goes down on a kind of tape in one's brain. To recall almost anything that happened in the past, intense concentration is needed to play back the mind tape. It's all there, and it's truly astounding what volumes the mind retains. This instance is one that I had not given a thought to since '44. Here's how it played back.

It was at Chengkung Airbase in China, the home of the Sixteenth Fighter Squadron of the U.S. Army Air Corps. There was excitement on that day of November 1944 when we got the order to go out on our very first combat mission in our new P-51C Mustangs. The mission was to escort a dozen four-engine B-24 bombers to destroy the railroad bridges north of the city of Hanoi, in the land then known as French Indochina.

Twenty of us were on the mission. Toward the close of the briefing, the intelligence officer, Captain "Pappy" Turner, added a review of survival tactics. He made a very unusual closing statement. "Gentlemen, if you are shot down, or have to bail out or crash-land in Indochina, remember this: Avoid detection, if you can, until you can get your bearings. Then, try to be picked up by Frenchmen. If you can't, continue to evade. As a last resort . . . capture by the Japanese may be better than being caught by the Annamites. . . . Don't be taken by them. . . . They hate our guts."

Not only did they hate our guts, but they hated the French, too, as the Kid had just illustrated.

Another interrogator called "the Eagle" was primarily interested in information of a technical nature, mainly weapons and aircraft. He had a noticeably flat head, his fingers were brown from chain-smoking, and even though he tried to act calmly, I could tell his nerves were frazzled. He said he knew all about flying, because he had been a MiG pilot. He wanted me to feel that all of us pilots are big buddies, and we can talk freely together, as members of the "fraternity of pilots."

I went along with the gag and asked him if he had flown a MiG-17. He replied that he had only flown 15s. "How do you navigate to target?" he asked. "Simple," I replied. "How do you navigate in your MiG?" He shrugged his shoulders and said, "You know, it is easy for us." I said, "I do the same thing you do, I just fly kind of dead reckoning. Just take up a heading and fly toward the target—that's all." I don't think he knew what I was talking about; he was a fake and didn't have the slightest idea of what airplanes were all about. I realized I could fabricate in dealing with this fellow, and I did.

He told me that earlier I had admitted that I was from Da Nang. I denied it, replying that I must have been in shock when I said that. . . . But a little while later I appeared to give in to him, saying, "Well, okay, I did take off from Da Nang." He seemed relieved to get that admission, although he would rather that I had said Korat.

I refused to answer every question after that. After about an hour of my stubborn silence, he completely lost his cool and screamed at me in Vietnamese. He rushed over and gave me one helluva clout across the face, which sent me sprawling across the floor. It was easy enough to do. . . . It was tough to keep balanced on the tiny stool anyway. He worked himself into a frenzy and kept on yelling, finally stomping out.

The next day I saw him again. He seemed to be trying to avoid another confrontation with me, though he behaved like he was still nervous as a coot.

He spread out a map on top of the quiz table, and I could see that it belonged to one of our fighter pilots. It had a circle drawn around Hanoi, which I knew was the possible range of surface-to-air missiles. The map also had lines drawn from targets in the Hanoi area back to bases in Thailand, with the compass headings and mileages inscribed.

"You know your side slowly escalates the war against us, each day a little closer to Hanoi. Do you think they will bomb Hanoi?"

"Nah."

"How close do you think they will come?"

"Draw a circle around Hanoi, maybe thirty, forty miles." I had no idea of what our side was going to do.

"So you think this area will be a sanctuary?"

"Sure."

"Do you know that yesterday the B-52s attacked North Vietnam for the first time; so why do you think they did that?"

"Well, that's simple. . . . It's retaliation."

"Retaliation for what?"

"Retaliation for shooting me down. They're not going to let you get away with that." The truth was, I wanted very much to believe the B-52s came up just for me. Every man who gets shot down eventually gets around to thinking that no one in the world is as important as he is, and in my case, I believed that the United States Air Force would go all out to get me out of that jail. I was still expecting a chopper to come into the prison courtyard to pick me up! It was just a question of time until I would be sprung from there. I didn't know how they were going to do it, but I knew that any minute it was going to happen. How silly can you get?

"Escalation war," rather than all-out war, was an invention of the times, and something our side set into motion especially for Vietnam. From all indications it came from Defense Secretary McNamara, on recommendation of his staff of whiz kids, and the idea was also supported by presidential advisors. "Escalation" was supposed to show Hanoi that U.S. action against them was controlled and measured in direct proportion to the amount of pressure exerted or number of atrocities that Hanoi perpetrated on South Vietnam.

However, someone apparently failed to realize that this kind of slow intensification of military activity is similar to a boxer telegraphing his punches. North Vietnam had a good feel for what to expect from us, and the "measured" action by our side allowed them the time they needed to improve their air defense system and to establish more lines (and alternate lines) of communications and supplies. It also gave the propaganda ministry of North Vietnam the tools they needed and the time to prepare their people mentally, get them "psyched up" as it were, for the next step-up in bombing pressure.

It had now been fifteen to twenty days since my last real food. I was spending most of my time in prayer, conserving energy in place of exercise. I had cranked out five thousand Our Fathers and seventeen thousand Hail Marys. "Food . . . food . . . food. . . ." It had priority in my mind over everything, including fear of my captors. I continued to hope that my refusal to eat would cause them to improve the food—but they didn't care, and the same filthy slop appeared day after day.

I never saw the Owl again, but interrogations continued with the Eagle and the Dog, and now the Rabbit was brought in. I was holding my ground, but they were making heavy threats of serious punishment. I had been told in survival lectures: "When you think they are going to torture you, leak some innocuous personal information." The trouble with that is, some guys will anticipate punishment a lot sooner than others. The real truth is, you don't ever know they are going to torture you . . . until they do!

The Nice Kid hadn't helped me any with food, but he did give me a couple of books to read. One was *Letters From South Vietnam*, a collection put together by the Viet Cong. These "letters" were supposedly written by people who were militarily active against the government of South Vietnam. We named them the "Super Gook Stories." One of the letters told of a young man's personal experiences against American soldiers as they roved around the south in their tracked armored personnel carriers. Every time he fired a single shot from his Russian AK-47, anywhere from two to six Americans fell down dead! The young Viet Cong was thrilled with his work, expressing regret only because his younger brother was not able to participate in this easy slaughter.

Throughout the book there was plenty of commentary by Lord Bertrand Russell. I doubt if a man ever lived who hated the United States more than that leftist s.o.b. The book was a load of poisonous invective against the U.S. No matter how well-intentioned, how humane, or how generous our efforts around the world were, Russell vilified all of it, and it really tweaked my beak! I hated him.

Another book was *Dien Bien Phu Victory*, the story of how the Viet Minh army of Ho Chi Minh, under General Vo Nguyen Giap, shellacked the French at that turning-point battle in 1954. The underlying lesson that the party wanted to get across to the reader was: Whatever our claims of losses inflicted upon the enemy, they are only very modest claims. The proof of this can be seen in the losses that were voluntarily reported by captured French officers. Therefore, you should believe *everything we say*.

Well, here is a real example of how much of their bullshit could be believed. When I jumped out of my bird on the fourteenth of June, I went up on their scoreboard as the 320th "kill" over North Vietnam. But at that time it was not possible that in all of Laos, North, *and* South Vietnam that more than fifty fixed-wing aircraft had been downed; so there was more than a six hundred percent exaggeration rate there.

There were three pamphlets I found interesting. Each was a case file of a court trial that had been held in Hanoi. The accounts were of legal action taken against "participants in commando raids." Each file was fully documented, with photographs of the court proceedings, individual photos of each commando-team member, and photographs of layouts of the equipment that they carried with them. The Asian commando teams were usually made up of ten men.

The charge sheets were identical: "Illegal penetration of the borders of North Vietnam, with the intention of spying and sabotage." All of the Asian commandos' equipment was shown as American-made military issue, and included handguns, small automatic weapons, flare pistols, parachutes or rubber boats (depending on the entry methods), supplies of U.S. food rations, medical supplies, radio equipment, maps, charts, and a supply of local currency.

The captured commandos were dressed exactly like me, in blue-and-white striped pajamas. They looked scared to death and with good reason. In every case the final sentence against the team leader was death by firing squad. The remaining team members received jail sentences from twenty-five years down to twelve. A few very youthful team members, who had doubtless readily confessed and showed a willingness to cooperate, were given "light" sentences of eight to twelve years. It was intended to scare me, and it did.

At my next interrogation, the Nice Kid stared at me for a long time. He ran his fingers nervously through his hair. Finally he spoke.

"And what do you know about Vietnamese culture?"

"Not very much."

"Of course. That's because we do not have a culture. We

never had time to develop one. Since the beginning of our history we have struggled to gain independence. Did you know the Chinese occupied our country for one thousand years? Then came the French, and we have finally thrown them out, and now we have the Americans.''

Stoneface came in, stood at attention, and pointed at me, beginning a tirade that lasted until the Kid put up his hand.

"My man says you are very impolite; you refuse to stand for him in your cell, and now you refuse to sit correctly.''

"Why do you listen to him? He is old and has not earned even one stripe. You are an officer. Don't you have the training to figure these things out for yourself? I think you should throw him out of here.''

"You do not understand our way. You see, ours is a people's army. If we officers do not allow the people to tell us, then how will we know if we do things wrong?''

My hunger was overwhelming, and I could smell McKamey's lunch pail from two cells away. He would read off the daily menu to me while I drooled and got weaker by the day.

Captain Smitty Harris from the 67th Fighter Squadron and navy pilot Phil Butler's group hid notes in the toilet area. I read them then destroyed them without leaving a reply, because I still didn't feel I knew enough to risk replying. I was sure the guards were searching my cell for notes, because oftentimes I was left in the bath area for extended periods. I figured that they also saw the note under the bench, but chose to leave it as though they were not on to it.

On the seventh of July I was taken to interrogation again, and this time was met by *six* Vietnamese. One of them looked to be a high-ranking civilian. The Nice Kid was trembling as he interpreted for the non-English-speaking group. Two crude wooden airplane models, one an F-105, the other an F-104, were on the table in front of them.

I listened to a blast in Vietnamese by the civilian, and then the Kid translated it to me: "You came here to murder us and were caught red-handed! You are a criminal and do not deserve the humane treatment! And now you must tell us all about your aircrafts!''

"I told you I'm not gonna do that.''

The civilian spoke once more, and the Kid turned to me, almost imploring. "For the last time, will you tell us about your aircrafts? You are going to be severely punished!''

"No.''

The civilian left looking very upset; he was soon followed by all the others. I was left there alone. "If they're doing this to scare me, it's working real good. . . . I'm definitely scared."

That night around nine, Stoneface came in carrying a couple of hammers. He had two armed soldiers and a woman with him. After motioning me to the back of the cell, they proceeded to knock the steel cot apart and carry it into the hallway piece by piece.

They made me put the skeeter net up over one of the bunks that had the heavy leg stocks. Then Stoneface pointed to the bunk, and I got up on it. He lifted the heavy iron crossbar, put my right leg into it, then brought the bar down and clamped it shut, using an antiquated iron-and-brass padlock. The stocks were rusty, and the hinges creaked and squealed; the crossbar was three-quarters-of-an-inch thick by three inches wide and shaped to accommodate the ankles. I couldn't believe that these people, signatories of the Geneva Conventions, were using leg stocks. But they sure as hell did.

It was hot as blazes, and up on that narrow slab of boards I was soon slick with greasy sweat. Wallowing in self-pity I asked, "Why did this have to happen to me?" (Doesn't everyone ask that when disaster strikes?) "Why, why . . . ?" Tasting my own salty tears, I began to seriously doubt my mental and physical toughness. Like most fighter pilots, I was once convinced that, other than in some very rare and fleeting moments of stark terror, I was practically fearless. Now, looking down at my legs in the irons, I asked myself, "What's the big deal? All they're doing is restricting your movement and starving you." And the starvation was largely my own choice. There was food, rotten though it was. I had to admit that the punishment was mild compared to what they *could* do if they decided to get really rough.

The full realization of the debilitating effects of captivity itself had not yet set in, and wouldn't until later, when I had absorbed far more punishment.

The takedown of a man's spirit begins the very second his feet touch the ground in enemy territory. It's one thing to be zipping around the skies in a supersonic aircraft ducking anti-aircraft shells or missiles. Apart from a close one now and then, you are always a short time from home base and the good life. Shot down, however, you come to a dead stop, zero miles per hour, in the silent jungle (if you're lucky) or soon in the hands of the enemy. They don't look like us, they don't think like us, their society is 150 years behind ours. You quickly learn that this is a very different ball game. It's their ballpark, and their umpires, and their book of rules. They can call 'em any way they want; they can do anything they want to you; there's no way to appeal for help. The International Red Cross is outlawed by the Communists as a lackey of the Western powers. They don't give a damn about Geneva agreements concerning treatment of POWs—they don't give a damn about Geneva anything. They sign documents because it looks good for world opinion (just as the Russians, Chinese, and North Koreans do). But honor them? No chance!

The prisoner's morale and fighting spirit are quickly squelched, because he knows he has nothing going for him. Then the threats start, and they never let up. Next come the minor, but extended punishments: solitary confinement, poor food, and very little of it. While you're wondering how to extricate yourself from your predicament, you come to the edge, just the edge of understanding that a human being, physically and mentally, is a very fragile piece of work. Already the pressures were wearing me down, but I didn't realize that it was the entire experience so far, not just the new experience of the irons, that was bringing me close to a mental breakdown. Fear of what might come next was also a factor in mental debilitation.

The next morning, J. B. asked what all the hammering had been about, and I told him that I was getting into some really "deep kimchi." He told me he didn't understand why they were being so decent to him, because they hadn't asked him any questions, but lectured him constantly about the Vietnamese people and their struggles. I believed that the V looked at the young lieutenant as someone who had been "badly misled," so they were taking it upon themselves to "educate" him.

"God, Larry, I feel so bad that they are all over you," McKamey said. "What we need here is a couple of nice fat commanders or lieutenant colonels. Then the V would be so excited about it, they'd probably get off your butt. Maybe somebody like Colonel Risner. I read about him in *Time* magazine."

Lieutenant Colonel Robinson Risner was the commander of our sister squadron, the Sixty-seventh, back at Kadena, Okinawa. He was also a very good friend of mine. Robbie was a war ace in Korea and had recently distinguished himself in missions over North Vietnam. He had been shot down and rescued in April of '65. His picture appeared on the cover of *Time* magazine, and he was the latest and best-known American hero.

The Communists knew all about him, too, and were very anxious to get their hands on him.

When J. B. said that, I got real nervous. "Shush up on that J. B. If these people ever catch Robbie, they'll skin him alive. He's my personal good buddy, and he's the last guy I'd want to see up here!"

The food continued to be terrible. Once they perched a small dog's skull on top of the dirty rice. I had asked the Dog why the cook insisted on serving up such slop. He answered, "The cook wants you to know that he hates you."

"Tell him I'm very impressed." I was getting so weak, it was difficult for me to sit up. Stoneface would make me change legs daily in the irons. Sometimes he'd take me out to the toilet and sometimes not. I kept my bucket close so I could manage to pass water. Believe it or not, my Korat food was still with me, and on my first Sunday in irons, I was suddenly hit with tremendous stomach cramps. No matter how loudly I yelled, no guard came to let me out of the irons. I didn't figure out how to use the toilet bucket while in the irons until days after the initial seizure of cramps had passed. The inability to handle even the most basic needs is, in itself, a terrible infliction of torture.

About July 12, just before J. B. McKamey was moved out, he said a very touching thing to me. "Larry, I haven't cried since I was a kid when my dog died. But today I got pretty choked up thinking about you, in irons, and starving, too." J. B. tried to leave food in the toilet area, but I always got there too late. The stuff spoiled too quickly in the heat. A couple of times I saw some good-looking food in the dump hole, but it was covered with scorpions, and I could only wish.

I was seized with suspicion of my fellow officers. Why was McKamey being treated better? How was it that I could hear four of my fellow Americans talking and giggling together—had they all sold out to the V? I was angry and saddened, and no matter how much they tried to communicate with me, I refused to have anything to do with them. Of course, I was dead wrong! It was simply the first of many examples of various levels of treatment toward different prisoners and not for any reasons that ever made sense to us. Using apparently random selection played us into their hands. With it, they knew they were creating just exactly what they had accomplished with me already: sowing the seeds of distrust of my fellow officers.

God, I was hungry! More than thirty days had passed, and I had eaten very little, though I had been drinking all the water I needed. Once in a while I'd get a couple of tiny pieces of pig fat. Finally they replaced the hated swamp grass with boiled pumpkin; I could handle half a small bowl of that, which was like eating water anyway.

My imagination about food went wild. I could hear the V dumping buckets out in the back alley. It was probably their toilet buckets, but to me it smelled like my favorite dessert, toasted pound cake with vanilla ice cream and sliced peaches! Sitting there that night in the irons, covered with slick sweat, I looked back over my shoulder, and up in the night sky I beheld a beautiful sight. A great big yellow full moon. I could see the face of the man in the moon, the only friendly face I'd seen in five weeks, and I was poignantly reminded of the old songs we sang as Evy and I drove around Branch Brook Park with Larry Tobia and the gang in Larry's old '31 convertible Chevy:

More tears . . . more self-pity. Poor Evy . . . and me, too.

Chapter Five

MEETING JERRY

On the twentieth of July I heard "Anchors Aweigh" whistled through the cell windows. I called, "Hello, Yank."

"Yeah."

"What's your name?"

"This is Jerry Denton, U.S. Navy. Who are you?"

"Guarino, major, Air Force."

"Oh . . . yeah, I've heard of you; the Vietnamese released your name as captured."

"No kidding? Well that's great news, Jerry." That meant that Evy knew I was alive, and Hanoi would sooner or later have to be accountable for me.

"What kind of airplane were you flying, Jerry?"

"Ha, ha . . . That's what *they* would like to know." Denton's voice had strength and confidence. "Wow, this guy is gonna be tough, just what I need, a guy with big brass ones to bolster my sagging morale," I thought.

"I'll bet you're from Canoe U." (U.S. Naval Academy.)

"That's right! How are they treating you?"

Looking down at my skinny body, my leg locked in stocks, I felt it best not to moan about my predicament like a crybaby. I needed Jerry to stay tough for both of us, so I answered, "Oh, they aren't treating me too badly."

"Well don't worry," Jerry said, "We'll hack 'er."

"Yes sir, we'll sure hack 'er."

"How many men have been repatriated so far?" he asked.

I couldn't believe my ears! "Never heard of *anybody* being repatriated."

"How's the mail been coming through?"

"Don't be ridiculous, Jerry. We don't get any mail up here."

"Well, don't worry about it, we'll hack 'er."

Jerry and I talked and sang. He liked me to whistle for him. The Rabbit gave us hell about communicating. I told him we had to speak to one another; there wasn't anything else to do there. Then he said, emphatically, "You are absolutely forbidden to speak or make any sounds; you must only sit and ponder your crimes against the Vietnamese people!"

A few days later, returning from interrogation, Denton said, "Larry, these guys are really after me. What have you been telling them to satisfy them?"

"I don't tell them anything."

"How do you avoid answering their questions?"

"Well, just don't answer. Give your name, rank, and horsepower." Jerry said okay, he'd stick with it.

The next day he asked again, "Larry, you must be doing okay with them. Can't you at least give me a hint?"

"Well, whatever you do, I wouldn't tell them anything about your family. There's no telling what these bastards are liable to resort to, or what they can get somebody back in the States to do for them. The Dog has already threatened me with that."

"Oh, Lord." Jerry sounded worried." "I've already told them all that. Can you give me any other tips?"

" 'Fraid not, Jerry. I told you I'm not doing so good either. I haven't eaten for almost six weeks now, and I've been locked in these stinkin' leg blocks for over two weeks."

"Leg blocks! What do you mean?"

"You know, stocks. Don't you have stocks in your cell?"

"No. You mean you're in stocks?" He sounded incredulous.

"Yeah, sure am!" I could just feel Jerry's morale slipping right down the crapper. He had no idea of the shape I was in because I hadn't told him. As I said, I needed Jerry tough for both of us, but I think my revelation pulled his plug.

Jerry was doing things about the same way I did in the first weeks of capture. We both wanted so badly to do a good job that we overdid it. We wanted to tell them to go to hell or where to shove it. I even ridiculed some of the juvenile line of propaganda patter that they tried to use to convince me of our "wrongful thinking." We Yanks start out very tough and sometimes even feel guilty if we *aren't* being tortured! No need to rush it. . . . They'll get around to it in their own time. It's probably a good guess that had we the opportunity to start over again, we would have saved ourselves a lot of grief by using our heads instead of our emotions. Denton was wilting, so we tried to cheer one another up with meaningless chatter.

A few days went by. "Larry, I've been thinking about it for three days, but can't figure it. How do you take a crap in irons?"

"Aw heck, that's a long story. You don't want to hear it."

"Yeah, I'm really interested. How in hell do you manage it?"

I went through a laborious explanation of how it was accomplished, even though I had only done it once.

"Now what the hell did you want to know all that for?"

Jerry sure popped a surprise on me that time. The V had moved him into a cell that was one closer to me and was also equipped with leg stocks, but Jerry hadn't even mentioned it. Guess he didn't want me to think he was a sissy either.

Getting out of the irons and getting some decent food were my first priorities. I told myself that no matter what any interrogator might say, I had to stay in control and exercise great patience. My next time out was with the Rabbit. He stared for a long time, and I stared back, for the first time realizing why he was called "the Rabbit." Hunched over the table, I saw that his ears stuck way out, his cheeks were puffy, and his lower lip was slightly split. He did kinda look like a rabbit!

He reminded me that I'd been there a long time without any of "my fellows" to speak to, and that he understood I must be very lonely.

"I know it is very difficult to be alone. . . . It is natural for all creatures to be together, even de cows, de horses, too. . . . Yes, even de chickens."

When he said that, even though I had been determined not to, I blew it wide open. I blurted, "Chickens! Chickens get lonely? How do you think of shit like that?"

He jumped up and slunk toward the door, giving me angry side glances.

Then it was Dog's turn again. Once he had asked, "Have you ever been in this part of the world before, perhaps during the war against the Japanese? Did we fight a common enemy?" I denied it at first, but now, desperate to get something to eat, I figured I'd leak a little WWII war story, so I said, "Matter of fact I was here in '44 and did my part in helping you to oust the Japanese from your country."

The Dog then talked about Ho Chi Minh's forces entering Indochina from South China toward Hanoi along the Lang Son railroad. I kept my mouth clamped shut because that was exactly the area that my China squadron worked over with our P-51 Mustangs. A lot of the targets we were assigned were were to help the French in Indochina. I got the uncomfortable feeling that most of the people we shot up then weren't Japanese at all, but Ho Chi Minh's Viet Minh. The French got us to do their dirty work for them!

Dog closed out the subject with, "It was such a long time ago, no need to worry about it now." I couldn't dismiss it that easily, even though my attempt at a reasonable discussion with him didn't even earn me a good-conduct banana.

Back in the irons again, my mind drifted back to my China days. In March of '45 we were informed that the Vichy French government in Hanoi was no longer getting along with the Japanese, and that there had been some fighting. We couldn't guess why the French would rock the boat so late in the game, but perhaps rocking the boat was what it was all about. The news coming out of Europe was that the jig was up for Germany. Perhaps the Vichyites thought the timing was right to oppose the Japanese actively and get a more influential position among the Allied powers in the settlement of the war. Whatever the reason, it was a tragic miscalculation, because the Japanese dealt with them ferociously.

Several dozen French legionnaires, escorting French women and school children, arrived at Poh-sei, our little air base on the South China border. We learned that French people were bugging out from all over the Hanoi area on any available conveyance, even on foot.

One sergeant, whose name was Jacques, told us that he didn't understand the sudden upheaval in Indochina, but in his opinion the French were all washed up down there, that between the Japanese and the Indochina Communists it was time to get the hell out of there. It sounded to me like the legionnaires were a bunch of deserters, and Jacques hadn't the slightest concern for anything other than his personal safety.

The next day our first scheduled mission to help the French was a flight of Mustangs to bomb an old monastery, now a barracks housing Japanese soldiers. The target was Mission Michet, located near Lang Son.

We took off, with Al Johnson leading the flight and Dick Drake on his wing. My wingman was Bob Wardle. We carried a pair of five hundred-pound delayed-action bombs and a full load of ammo. The Mustang K was a delight to fly. You felt like you could whip the whole world in it. I don't know if our painted shark noses scared anybody, but they looked really hot and made us feel great. Our skip-bombing mission was a smashing success, and Mission Michet was history. We made a couple of strafing runs to make life just a little more miserable for the Japanese and then headed back to Poh-sei. A couple of hours later we got a report that said we had killed five hundred Japanese soldiers.

On our next mission we tooled off to look at an area well south of the river in flat terrain near the Liu-chow peninsula. We came upon a gathering of thousands of what looked like Chinese, all dressed in blue. . . . A strange sight, no vehicles, no weapons, just a mob of people milling about, and we couldn't figure out what they were doing. We made a couple of low passes but didn't fire a shot. I pondered that sight for many a day. I didn't know then, and really never knew until Dog informed me, that South China was the mobilization area for Ho Chi Minh's Viet Minh forces!

Here I was, locked in irons in a Hanoi prison cell, and I suddenly realized that what the Dog was telling me dovetailed perfectly with what I had seen with my own eyes in South China twenty years earlier—part of Ho Chi Minh's early organization of his cadre for a Communist Vietnam!

Denton's voice brought me back.

"Larry, I've got ants all over me."

"God! How'd that happen?"

"They gave me a piece of fish with some kind of sweet sauce on it. I picked it up with my fingers, and when I finished, I wiped them off on my mosquito net." Inevitably the ants had swarmed in. Poor Jerry!

Stoneface took me out to the toilet area. On the way he pointed to a long, thick wooden slab, motioning me to pick it up to move it. It was a piece of black Asian wood, heavy as cement. I tried to lift it but was unable to keep it balanced, and I fell over backward, barely getting out of the way as it slammed to the ground. My heart was pounding and so were my ears. I tried but couldn't lift it up. Stoneface was trying to figure out if I was as bad off as I looked. He locked me in the toilet and left me there for a long time. I found a note from Smitty Harris. It read, "For God's sake Larry, please answer us." I wet a burnt match tip and told him what had happened before I had been shot down: "Smitty your wife's okay, with friends, baby boy born." I left the note in the same hiding place I had found the other. Back in the cell, I decided to show Stoneface the scar from my navel to my sternum. Most of my stomach had been removed in January of 1961 because of a massive internal hemorrhage caused by stomach ulcers. If there was the slightest strain of sympathy in Stoneface, I'd soon find out. Maybe he'd pass the word and get me something decent to eat.

Rabbit called me out, looked at my scar, and said, "Is your side so desperate that they send people up here without a stomach?" He left the room for a moment, and when he did, I swiped a pencil from a stack he had on the table.

Once in the cell, I told Jerry what I did. He asked me to hide the pencil in the toilet so he could cut it with a razor blade he'd found. He wanted to put out some poop for the boys, since he was the senior man.

It had been so long since I had eaten, my head was spinning, and I was too weak to sit up. My mind was doing funny things. The chipped paint on the far wall, to me, formed a very clear picture of the Sacred Heart of Jesus, thorns and all, and I talked to Him all the time. Looking back I suppose it was nutsy as can be, but at the time it was very meaningful.

Smitty Harris, who was in a large cell with Bob Shumaker, Phil Butler, and Bob Peel, sent a message to us explaining a code that could be used to communicate by tapping walls, should it become necessary. Harris said that he got the code by accident in a casual discussion with a survival-school instructor who said it had been used in Sing-Sing Prison. Neither Smitty Harris nor any of us realized that this would be the most valuable life- and mind-saving piece of information contributed by any prisoner for all the years we were there. The tap code alphabet was arranged in five rows and five columns, leaving out the letter K and using a C in its place when needed. The system used only dots (or single taps), with no dashes like the Morse code.

Columns

1 - 2 - 3 - 4 - 5

Rows: 1 . . . A - B - C - D - E
2 . . . F - G - H - I - J
3 . . . L - M - N - O - P
4 . . . Q - R - S - T - U
5 . . . V - W - X - Y - Z

The first tap denoted the row, the second tap, the column. Each letter needed two sets of taps. For example letter A:

1 tap (first row), slight pause,
1 tap (first letter in row).

Letter *H*:

2 taps (second row), slight pause,
3 taps (third letter in row).

I was learning just how industrious a fellow Denton was. With the cut-up piece of pencil, he wrote on a piece of toilet paper what was tantamout to an operations plan. He then hid it in some iron scrollwork in the toilet building. When each of us in New Guy Village got the chance, we looked at it. Jerry's plan described the "situation" and the need for planning escapes. I felt that putting this sort of thing on paper was much too risky and was entirely unnecessary. Everyone knew the Code of Conduct as well as Jerry did. I told him so, but he still thought it was necessary for him to publish directives.

With my piece of the pencil, I wrote a morale note, similar to the one I had found earlier. I hoped it would have a good effect on the next guy to occupy my cell. I added a last sentence to the note to cool the Vietnamese, should they discover it:

"Hello—The Vietnamese don't treat you too badly. Put your trust in God and pray. A couple of weeks here while you are interrogated. Don't worry, just do your best. The Vietnamese are basically a hard-working and decent people. *Friend Yank*." I know the V read it, but the last sentence kept them off my butt, because it showed that at least I had respect for them. They never removed the note while I occupied that cell.

In a message from the Harris group, I learned I was the eleventh man captured, and there were now about twenty of us in Hanoi.

The combination of poor physical condition, demoralizing environment, and the uncertainty of how long we would have to endure imprisonment, had me frantic. How long? How long? Our politicians had said we'd stay in Southeast Asia for the next *seventeen years* if necessary! The Nice Kid said that Ho Chi Minh had stated many times, "We will fight for five, ten, twenty years or longer!" What horrible thoughts! We had to find better things to think about.

My mind drifted from one wild thought to another. Immobilized, losing track of time and place, I felt separated from my actual being. I remember floating about in thin clouds dreaming of a lot of buddies I had lost in the past.

The clanging of the steel cell door opening jerked me back to consciousness. Stoneface pushed the door open, and in walked the Rabbit himself. Standing close to the stocks he said, "Even though you still do not show repentance of your crimes toward the Vietnamese people, because of your sickness, we decide to show you the humane treatment, but only for a time [holding up his index finger as if to caution me]. The guard will take you out of the irons and give you food. Continue to ponder."

He left, and Stoneface let me off the slab, pointing to my stomach, meaning, "That's the reason you're getting out." I kept my mouth shut. Feeling relieved, I sat on the floor and stared at the Sacred Heart of Jesus.

Mealtime came, and the food was edible. I went into a wolfing mode, practically inhaling every scrap of food in two tin dishes. There was bread, pumpkin soup, and a side dish of boiled squash, with bits of smashed chicken and bones. It had a layer of grease on it, but to me it was as delicious as dinner at the Waldorf. It didn't occur to me that forty-seven days of practically no food would shrink my stomach. I was like a little kid just finishing three chocolate ice-cream sodas!

Naturally I got sick immediately, with severe stomach spasms followed by the inevitable acute case of diarrhea.

Even so, at each mealtime I tried to eat as much as I could. I stayed sickly for a week, spending most of the time just lying on the cool cement floor. Rabbit called me out once, but I could barely stay upright on the wooden stool, so he sent me back.

Toward the end of August, I was feeling better. It had rained heavily in July and August, the height of the rainy season, and I learned that the Vietnamese backed off on interrogations because the guards didn't like to get wet taking the POWs back and forth. It was always peaceful when it rained; nobody bothered you, and the sound of falling rain was therapeutic to my troubled mind. To this day, I am especially fond of rainy days.

Chapter Six

THE BLACK WALL

The last night in August, as I lay on the floor staring at the ceiling and watching the geckos chase flies, Stoneface came in and motioned for me to roll up my gear in a rice mat. Then he tucked it firmly under my arm, blindfolded me, and led me out of the cell. It was very dark in the passageways and in the yards he led me through. I was able to see just a bit by slipping the blindfold off one eye. We were going through an area with what looked like machinery. My heart quickened its pace; I was scared. It may have been Phil Butler who said there was a section of the camp that had implements of torture. My imagination took off.

It was a long walk, and I suspected Stoneface was trying to confuse me by walking me in circles. Finally, he pushed down the blindfold and I looked up over a steel door and saw the letter *L*; cell block L was my new home. Inside I could see three or four cell doors. He took me to the last one, opened it, then pushed me inside. He pointed at little strings up in the corners over a cement bunk and made me understand that I should put up my mosquito net, which I did. Stoneface put his finger to his lips, meaning, ''Be absolutely silent.'' He locked the door, opened the peep grate, then left.

The mosquitoes were swarming. I quickly got under the net, then looked at my cell-home. It was about seven feet square, with two cement bunks, one on each side wall. A twenty-inch-wide by seven-foot-long space between them was all the walking space there was. The cell was like an elevator shaft, going up about twenty feet. A pair of narrow windows, covered by wire mesh, began about sixteen feet up from the floor. A dim bulb burned during the hours of darkness. I lay down, trying not to touch the net with any part of my body, because the bloodsucking mosquitoes were quick to jab me when I did.

Just outside pigs were snorting and flopping around a wet yard, and water was running constantly; I couldn't see anything, but heard it all night. Once I got up, went to the peephole, and yelled, "Anybody here besides me? Answer me if you can hear me." No response. I didn't get much sleep that night—I was too concerned about what might happen next.

The next morning I heard the time chimes, which sounded everyday at six A.M., twelve noon, and six P.M. I tossed back my net and waited. Some sort of work area was close by—I could hear people banging on sheet metal, then filing or sawing at its edges. The screeching sounds were loud and greatly amplified by the shape of my tubelike cell. The sounds bounced around the room and pounded my ears hour after hour. The noise of the pigs increased. They snorted, squealed, grunted, passed gas, passed water. I could even hear them defecating! "Is this awful racket going to be constant?" I wondered. "Don't know if I can stand this for long." It was absolutely nerve-racking, and my nerves weren't up to a whole lot.

A new civilian guard brought food, and as he set it down on the far bunk, a horde of hungry ants rushed out from under the block mounts of the leg irons and swarmed into the tin plates. Jesus! I quickly rattled the plates on the cement, and they jumped off. I put a piece of fried bean curd out near the blocks for them to munch on as I ate the bread and bean curd.

While eating, I was startled by two lightning-fast brown rats who darted around the cell and between my feet, looking for food. They had come in under the door, which had about a three-inch gap at the bottom.

The guard beckoned me out to dump the remaining food into a bucket, and I noticed several things. The leg irons, when used, would be locked in place by sliding an iron bar through a slot in the wall from outside the cell. When pushed all the way in it would then lock the top and bottom halves of the stocks together.

All around the base of the outside corridor there was a six-inch channel cut into the floor. When prisoners locked in the stocks had to go, they sat in it until attendants or other prisoners came in to flush out the cells with pails of water. The mess would run through the channels and out to the yard. Although Hanoi was ninety miles from the sea, its elevation was zero. It was always in danger of flooding during the rainy season, and the city was literally floating on excrement.

Just outside the corridor was an exercise yard, except it was almost impossible even to walk out there, because the ground was ninety percent covered with huge rat turds. I didn't think the brown rats could take credit for that; the mess was much too large. There was also an open fifty-gallon cistern for holding bath water, which came in through a bamboo pipe. I could see the bottom of the stone tank easily and the water looked clear and clean.

I had more visitors to my cell. Arriving under the door were two huge scorpions, exactly like the ones that hung around the *"bo*-dump." One of the most important words in Vietnamese, *bo* means toilet bucket. The *bo* is a very important part of Vietnamese culture, and the Vietnamese understand, very well, anything connected with shit. We could never use the street expression "they don't know shit, man," because they did! The scorpions came in with raised stingers, but when they sensed my presence, they backed out into the cement channel where the pickings were presumably better.

The light was turned off from the outside at daylight. Even during the daytime the cell was very dim because the small, high windows did not allow much light. Examining the cell only increased my anxiety. Men had remained in this narrow confinement for years; one calendar from the '50's indicated the inmate had stayed for nine years! God, how terrible! Lying on my side facing the wall, I read scratched in the wall, *"Mia Maria"*—"My Mary"—put there by a suffering, lonely man like me. God only knew how long he lasted.

Mosquitoes by the hundreds lived under the cement bunks, where it was very damp. I sat swinging my legs and swatting mosquitoes until my hands were swollen. Suddenly, I saw a huge gray-white web-footed rat poking his head under the door. He was so big he couldn't get under the door to enter the cell! He sniffed about, showing me inch-long white fangs, then swirled his tail under the door, still trying to get in. His tail was over an inch thick! No doubt, this rat and his friends were the producers of the huge turds that covered the outside yard. What a disgusting and frightening creature! My heart pounded so, it was difficult for me to breathe, even as I told myself to calm down and take it easy.

The file, rasping on metal, always continued until darkness set in. The water kept flowing, and the pigs kept up their racket twenty-four hours a day. I thought I'd really go over the edge.

A couple of difficult days went by, and then one morning, just at daylight, I woke up screaming at the top of my lungs. I had just seen Evelyn crying as though her heart would break. Even in my awful loneliness I could not bear the thought of Evelyn crying for me, a world or more away, and there was nothing I could do for her. As my tears streamed down, I got the cold shakes, even though I was sweating. I wrapped a blanket around me. Then the goddamn far wall started to move toward me, and it turned black. "For God's sake, what are these people doing to me?" I wondered frantically. "They're going to crush me with that wall! Can I go through that blackness? No, don't do that! You'll never come back if you go through there! Hold that wall back!" I braced my legs against the far bunk and yelled in total panic. Just then, I saw the friendly guard who had given me the blanket that night in New Guy. He was standing just outside, looking through the peep. His eyes were filled with tears; they were running down his face. He stuck his fingers through the bars of the peep, meaning for me to touch him. I did, and his touch, the touch of another human being, was reassuring. He stayed for a long time, but eventually he had to leave to take care of his duties. I was again desolate and frantic, but at least no longer claustrophobic.

The nice guard came several times. Knowing I was in danger of losing it altogether, he tried to encourage me. Once he pointed to the other bunk, meaning soon I'd get company. Another time he held up five fingers, meaning five more sleep downs before a move. Another time he motioned down, down with both hands, then put his face against two clasped hands, meaning lie down and sleep. He tried his best for me, and I hated to see him depart the cell block, but sooner or later he had to tend to his other duties.

Still on the verge of panic the next day, I found I could write a message with the aluminum spoon handle on the bottom of the enameled tin plates. I don't know what good it possibly could have done except to scare the hell out of any American who may have seen it, but anyway I wrote, "L.G. close to God in stockyards. Panic. Bad bad place."

That afternoon I rolled up both cotton blankets and piled them up on the stocks. I stood on them on tippy toes to see what I could see out the high window. The walls looked a foot and a half thick, but I could also see the branch of a tree with leaves on it. Standing there until late afternoon, near dark, I asked God for rain, which I felt somehow would calm me down.

I stared up at the branch, saying, "Please God make it rain, just a little rain.'' I said it so often it sounded like a simple little poem. Then I heard music with it, music that I can still vividly remember almost twenty-five years later. Without question, I was nutty as the proverbial fruit cake.

A little bit of rain God, for me this evening,
A little bit of rain for me tonight.
A little bit of rain will sweep the dark clouds from my mind,
So I can think again of Mother and brothers and all the wonderful
  things I've left behind.
A little bit of rain God for me this evening,
A little bit of rain for me tonight,
A little bit of rain will mend a lonely broken heart.
There'll be tomorrow, a happy day with loved one's caresses.
Never more to part, never more to part, never more to part.

In the very dim light of early evening, the tree branch was visible, dead still. Then my heart leaped. The branch was moving! Just a little at first, then swinging wildly. The wind was blowing up, and I cheered it on. "Come on baby, let's have it, I know it's coming, let's have it." There was a ferocious lightning bolt, then a clap of thunder, and it started to come down, not just a little shower but a genuine tropical deluge. I felt fantastic. . . . I could ask Him for a favor and He actually did it for me! I was so relaxed, I was finally able to lie down and get some badly needed rest. It rained most of the night, and I slept.

Often the sounds of women screaming at the top of their lungs superseded all the other horrible sounds. Sometimes it went on for hours, and it only added fuel to my own frantic worries. My God, they torture their own women, too! What kind of people are these Vietnamese? I was horrified. What could these women possibly have done? Were they political prisoners? Do they punish routine offenders by flogging or torture? It would be many years before I got the answers to those questions. Like everything else in North Vietnam, it was never what it seemed.

One night, while leaning against the wall, I heard a bumping on the other side. My heart pounded with excitement! I listened hard for the tap code but could not make anything out. There was a man in the next cell all right, but then he wasn't trying to tap or communicate, he was just playing a game. I couldn't imagine how long that poor soul had been in that horrible confinement. The game he invented was to knock the wall with his head in a cadence like—bump, bump . . . bump, bump, bump.

Then the guy on the other side of the wall was supposed to imitate the bump cadence and repeat it. The game continued until someone made an error, then it started all over again. Painfully simple. Going over to the open peep I called, "Hey over there, I know you're there, answer me." Sure enough I heard the words, *"allo allo."* Then, softly he started to name big cities of the world: "Shang-hai, New York, Son-Fron-cis-co, Yoko-hama, Liver-pool." All the cities he named were sea-ports. This fellow was definitely maritime; maybe he was a sailor hauled off the docks in Haiphong. I questioned him some until I realized he spoke no English. I never did find out what his native tongue was. He spoke a few words of Spanish, French, Italian, even Chinese, and he mixed them up.

We were quiet for a while. Then he came through with a beauty: he sang all the Spanish words to "Siboney," how about that! He really picked up my morale . . . someone to talk to, a fellow sufferer. Then he asked me to sing by saying, *"Mon ami, chante, chante, por favor!"* He called me "my friend" and asked me to sing in French, then used Spanish to say "please." I sang him my rain song, and when I finished he applauded loudly, and I was very pleased.

Another night we heard fireworks or maybe the sound of distant bombing. Siboney (his new name) called from the peep, "Mon ami, mon ami." He was very excited.

"What's up, Siboney?"

"Boom Boom, *Meigua, Meigua feigei.*"

Lordy, I hadn't heard those words since my China days! *"Meigua feigei"* means "American fliers"! Siboney was telling me that it was bombing going on out there by American fliers! It was exciting to think that our side was bringing the war right to the outskirts of Hanoi.

Siboney never learned any English, but when I sang the rain song, he'd sing along with the melody using "la-las." He got a great kick out of it, and mentally it was very good for both of us. At times when I felt really down I tried to explain that I didn't feel like singing, but he would ask so pathetically, *"Mon ami, por favor, por favor,"* and I couldn't refuse him.

I still had a stub of pencil and a couple of blank pages from the story books the Nice Kid had given to me. I wrote down all the words of my song.

As I carefully stood in the yard amongst the rat dung, I noticed soapy water coming down the drain channel from under another building. I called, "Anyone over the wall?"

"Yeah it's me. . . . Al."

"Al who?"

"Alvarez."

My God, I was in touch with our number-one shootdown, Lieutenant Junior Grade Everett Alvarez! I remembered when the news reported his capture on the fifth of August 1964. Captain Ed Skowron said, "The Commies have captured a Navy pilot, they've got someone to play with, and I sure feel sorry for the poor bastard. We'll have to watch the news for the next few days. The Commies will have him making all kinds of phoney statements. They have ways." So he hadn't been executed as McKamey said back in New Guy. He was here!

Alvarez asked my name. I asked, "Do you think we'll ever get out of here?"

In reply, he sang, "California Here We Come!"

"What a guy he must be," I thought. "He's been here over thirteen months, and he still has lots of hope."

Though the exact number of days I spent in cell block L was confused, later I was able to confirm that the stay was less than two weeks. Two weeks? More like an eternal nightmare.

It was a couple of hours into darkness when I heard the cell door opening. The Eagle stood there. He pointed to my rice mat and said, "Roll up, and prepare yourself! You move tonight." Again I was blindfolded and led over a circuitous route.

Eagle pushed me up against a vehicle, and my heart was pounding so that he may have heard it. He said, "Do not worry, you will not be harmed. You go to a new place."

"Will I see my friends there?"

"Mmmmmmm. Do you know Quincy Collins?"

"I may have heard his name."

"He says he knows you from Japan. He has a broken arm, but the people have taken good care of him. . . . He says he can play the piano, and other things."

"I heard he has some talent." Quincy had been one of my very capable duty pilots up at Itazuke in the 80th Squadron. He certainly was talented. He could sing, dance, recite comical monologues, and play a number of instruments. He was a North Carolina boy, a graduate of the Citadel.

Eagle made me climb into a small Jeep-like vehicle, and soon I was joined by others. Alvarez, Hayden Lockhart, and Navy Lieutenant Phil Butler. Phil knew I was completely clanked up and reached over and squeezed my hands reassuringly, and it felt good, I needed that! He said, "Don't worry Larry, our side is hitting them hard all over, including Hanoi!"

That startled me, but I said nothing. Didn't Phil know that we were in Hanoi? Did he think we were somewhere else? Was he just saying all that to make me feel better?

Even though blindfolded, we were able to peek out just enough to see the moon and stars, and we knew we were driving west into the hillier countryside, we figured about thirty-five miles. We stopped and were led into a compound with a number of buildings, but it was dark and difficult to get things into perspective. Alvarez and I were put into a cell together! I had company, and more than that, I was the first American Alvy had seen up close for thirteen months! We were so excited we chatted like a couple of magpies. It was dead quiet, so our voices carried right to the ears of the Rabbit. He came down and shined a flashlight through the barred window directly into my eyes. "Quiet! or you will be severely punished!" When he saw Alvarez with me, he must have decided that he still wanted Alvy in solitary, so he sent the turnkey down, and Alvy was moved to another cell around the other side of the same building.

There were no lights—it was pitch black. I lay down on the wooden bed boards to rest, but hardly slept a wink. At daylight, the loud crowing of a rooster startled me. He stood right outside the window and was the biggest damn chicken I'd ever seen.

The cell windows had no glass. They were barred and rigged with shutters, which were open. My cell was in a four-cell building, in the southwest corner of a nine-building walled complex. Each cell block was walled off so we couldn't see each other over the twelve-foot-high walls.

The inside of each cell was similar. Most were set up for two-man occupancy. The inside walls were sharp, lumpy cement. They were so rough it was tough to tap without skinning the knuckles. The walls went up about eight feet, and from there the ceiling was domed like a church. The bed boards and the floors showed very little wear. Off the ends of the bed boards was a three-by-seven-foot walking space. My guess was that the buildings were pre-WWII. All were well grounded with tall lightning rods. The outside terrain sloped down rather steeply toward the east.

The parade began. One at a time, each American carrying his toilet bucket, closely followed by a guard, came through my front yard. The rule of absolute silence was not yet strictly en-

THE BRIARPATCH

IN THE LOW HILLS
40 MILES WEST OF
HANOI

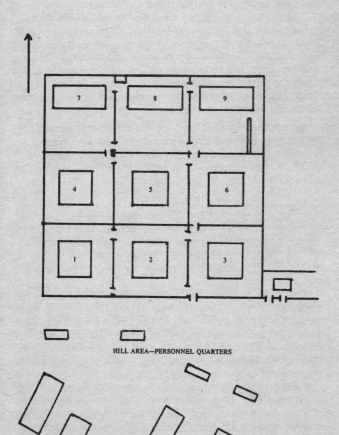

HILL AREA—PERSONNEL QUARTERS

forced, so as they passed me they greeted me and identified themselves.

"Hi, I'm Ron Storz. Larry, isn't it great to be close enough to talk?"

"Got your note Ron, it helped me a lot." I was impressed by Storz, a tall, blond, and very handsome young fellow.

"Hi, Larry, do you remember me? Smitty Harris from the 67th."

"Gosh Smitty, I'm sorry, I didn't recognize you."

"It's this damn beard; haven't shaved for a couple of weeks."

Here came Bob Shumaker, then Phil Butler and others. The last man down was my good friend from the 12th Squadron, Bob Purcell. "Percy" was prematurely silver-haired. It was a heartbreaking sight to see him slipping along in his bare feet down the steep, gravelly path while trying to control a rusty toilet bucket that had no handle, was overfilled, and spilling over his hands. I felt sick for poor Percy.

"Hi, Larry, old buddy, how's the number one wop in Hanoi?"

"Much better now, Percy, but on the ropes for a while."

All the *bos* were simply dumped into a corner of the yard; there wasn't even a hole in the ground. This was the typical Vietnamese way. They threw garbage or human waste in one place until it piled up so high they couldn't walk around it. Then they would move it and start all over again. However, there was one point of sanitation they always maintained. Because all of Asia had suffered from plagues that killed millions in the early 1900s, Asians learned that all drinking water must be filtered and boiled. The water they brought us for drinking purposes was always very hot.

The guards were very raggedly dressed soldiers, and not of the civil jail system. One of them had only one slipper. Most of the foot gear was rubber shower clogs, the soles made of old tires. The guard who was in my compound most of the time was nicknamed Horrible. His face was severely pockmarked, and the hair was patchy on his scarred skull. Once he took off his cap, pointed to his head, and said, "Cholera."

I was having a hard time keeping my mind occupied. I decided I needed a tough "think project" to exercise my mind.

My first "think project" was to store canned peaches, my favorite. I had to size up all the wall space and erect ten-inch-wide shelves, ten inches apart. Then I had to figure out how many jars of peach preserves I could stack on the shelves. I was

BRIARPATCH
EACH BUILDING 4 CELLS

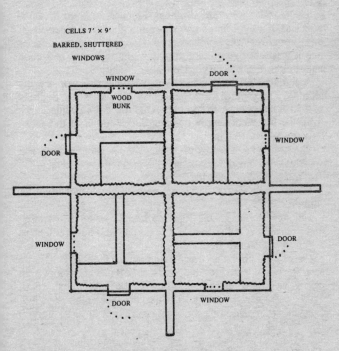

CELLS 7' × 9'
BARRED, SHUTTERED
WINDOWS

WINDOW

DOOR

WOOD
BUNK

DOOR

WINDOW

WINDOW

DOOR

DOOR

WINDOW

SHARP LUMPY CEMENT INSIDE WALLS AND
EXTENDED OUTSIDE WALLS BETWEEN CELLS
TO STOP PRISONERS FROM COMMUNICATING

amazed at how many jars of peaches you could fit into a seven-by-nine-foot cell!

On Sunday someone suggested that at a given time we would conduct church services, together, but of course in our separate cells. We recited the Lord's Prayer, then sang "The Star-Spangled Banner." We finished with the Pledge of Allegiance. I doubt if there was a dry eye in the house, and I'm sure that our thoughts were nearly identical, mainly that as military officers of the United States, we wanted to do a job that our people would be proud of. We had great pride in our country, and in each other. Our bond was already close, and through the difficult years ahead it would become even closer.

The next day we heard airplanes. I looked up to see the business end of an F-4 in a bomb run coming at us. Instinctively, I dived for cover. The bombs landed close by. Someone hollered that it was a bridge or dam they were out to bust. The Rabbit later told us that our planes were after a schoolhouse!

A couple of RF-101s whizzed by, taking pictures at very low altitude. On another day, September 15, we saw a flight of F-105s coming in close to attack. "Those are *our* guys," the former F-105 pilots announced with pride. After the raid, I called down to Smitty Harris.

"I've got some very strong feelings today about Risner, and your assistant ops officer—what's his name? Ray something."

"You mean Ray Merritt?"

"Yeah, Ray Merritt—I'm real worried about those two for some reason."

I thought about Robbie Risner a lot. He was a dear friend, and I prayed to God as hard as I could that he'd never end up as a "guest" in North Vietnam.

(What I did not know was that in fact, the flight of F-105s we saw was being led by Robbie, and that he'd had his canopy shot off and was joined up by Ray Merritt for the flight back to Korat. Truth is stranger than fiction! The next day, September 16, 1965, Lieutenant Colonel Robinson Risner and Major Ray Merritt were *both* shot down and captured!)

The Briar Patch camp was difficult to support because of its distance from the city. There was no electric power. The food was mostly rice, pumpkin soup, and once in a while, a piece of duck wing so tough it couldn't be chewed. Fortunately, we were only there for a week.

One night we were told to roll up our gear for a move. We

boarded a bus and rumbled back toward the city to a new camp just outside Hanoi. The Vietnamese name for this place was Cu Loc, but soon we would give it a name that would stick.

Chapter Seven

THE ZOO

The guards put me by myself into a corner room of an old empty building. I dumped my gear on the bare floor and set up my mosquito net over the rice mat as best I could. A few minutes later Shumaker's group and a few others were also put into the same building.

The next morning I took stock of the situation. This place was no jail and had never been used as one before. If the intention was to use it as a jail, then plenty of modifications would be needed to make it secure. The windows were simply boarded over and nailed from the outside. The doors were louvered and padlocked shut. It was easy to peek outside by pushing the doors out because the padlock allowed some slack.

The Shumaker–Harris group was a couple of rooms away and chatted with me to keep up my morale. We guessed about twenty of us were there. I asked Shu how come they were joined up, while some of us were solitary. "What is it that you tell the interrogators so they don't get too upset?"

Shu said when the situation got tense, they leaked out some innocuous personal information. I told Shu that I felt that I was holding a line against the V that wasn't even there. Shu and Butler said they understood why I felt that way, and that I had the lonelies, but after all, we were in the kettle together and they would do anything they could to keep up my morale. They probably made a better judgment call than I did, and avoided heavy punishment by backing off, giving answers to trivial questions.

Peeking out to my left, I could see an antiquated swimming pool. This was a typical French-built complex, stuccoed brick buildings with clay-tiled roofs, just like in French Morocco. The camp toilet, next to my room, was the *bo*-dump for everyone. So, when out of hearing of the guards, each man on the way to the dump spoke to me through the boarded window on the hall side.

I drew a cross on the far wall and spokes around it to show rays of illumination. This was my praying place. I was strangely obsessed with thoughts of Robbie Risner, greatly fearing for his safety. One day I moved from the cross to the front door for my afternoon peeking session. I pushed the doors out and looked at the building beyond the pool, where several guards were unlocking the door. A tall American emerged who wore only white shorts, and I could see that he had a beautiful suntan. I gasped! Good God Almighty, it was Robbie Risner! I was furious. I felt let down, disappointed as I rushed over to the cross and demanded, "What are you doing to me, Lord? Didn't I ask you not to bring Robbie up here? Don't you know what they are going to do to him?" A few hours later another American was escorted to the *bo*-dump from the room next to Risner; from his deep voice I thought it was Phil Butler. He walked rapidly and widened the gap between himself and the lollygagging guard. Once next to my side window he called, "Larry, I've got big news, Colonel Risner is at Heartbreak!" (Heartbreak was a section of the main city jail with small cells, similar to the Stockyards cell).

"Wrong!"

"What do you mean wrong?" He was taken aback.

"He's here, in the room right next to you!"

"What?"

The next day I spotted Robbie leaving his building, heading my way. "Larry, can you hear me?"

"Yes, what the hell are you doing here? Didn't you learn anything the first time you got shot down?" I don't know what the hell I meant by that remark, except that I was really upset. Maybe I thought that Risner and God had teamed up just to piss me off.

"I couldn't help it. I was doing over 550 on the deck when I got hit." Now I had Robbie apologizing!

"I saw Evy just before she went home. She was doing great. Don't worry about her. Larry, do you pray?"

"Do I pray? You're damn right I pray! What else have we got in here?"

The guard hustled him away. The next day he continued. "Just before I came here, I saw the secretary." He meant the secretary of defense, Robert McNamara. "He said he thought the war would be over by next April, but I think it'll take until

June. You know this guy Rabbit? He talks to me for six hours a day. He says that soon I am going to be able to speak to General Giap about the treatment of our men.''

''Robbie, be careful with the Rabbit. He's setting you up, getting you to talk. He's a very dangerous guy, and he knows all about you.''

I figured that when Robbie got smoked the first time, he should have played it a little cooler and got himself a headquarters job. He was the kind of man anyone would admire; didn't drink or smoke or use bad language. A great competitor, and a hot stick man who could really move an airplane around the sky. Very few men could put him down in air-to-air competition. I don't know why his personal welfare meant so much to me, but it surely did.

Before Risner was hustled away, I made one more comment. ''Rob, I think that if these people don't make a major change by October, we'll drop a nuke on them.''

''Oh, I don't think we will ever do anything like that.''

Here I was, thinking that a nuke was the only sure way to alter the course of the war. Wasn't I one of the people who wouldn't vote for Goldwater because he threatened to do just that? Yes I was, but that was before we realized we were actually going to fight a land war in Asia, something we had been warned never to step into by a lot of brilliant generals.

There were a lot of men and women doing various jobs to bring the camp up to prison status. They moved us from cell to cell every few days so the workers could do their jobs. They were installing two-foot-high brick stanchions on which to mount the bed boards. Iron bars were installed in the window spaces. The French doors in my cell were eventually removed, replaced by very heavy wooden doors with peep holes big enough to pass water jugs through. The inside electric boxes and light switches were moved to the outside, and all of the perimeter walls were raised and topped with barbed wire. The entire project lasted into the following spring.

Interrogations continued, and we decided to quit using that word, shortening it to ''quiz,'' or, if tapped through the wall, simply ''QZ''; ''QZR'' for interrogator. We made maximum use of abbreviations.

In October, I was in the center room of the same building. I had Airman Arthur Black in the room on my left and Commander Bill Franke on my right. The guards were still slack, so we talked through the now-barred windows, which also had closed, louvered shutters on the outside. We were discussing what we should call the camp. Scotty Morgan came up with a beauty. He called out, "This is the first time I've ever seen animals visit a zoo to look at people."

The Zoo became our official name for the camp, with the individual buildings named Barn, Stable, Chicken Coop, and Pigsty, which was my building.

Captain George Hall, my friend from the 15th Reconnaissance Squadron, was now opposite me in the end room of the Pool Hall building. George had gone back to the States at the end of June to pick up and ferry back a replacement RF-101. He was on the same flight with Evelyn.

"So how was Evelyn doing, George?"

"She seemed to be doing fine. Was headed to McGuire Air Force Base in New Jersey."

"Did she look happy?"

"No Larry. She didn't look happy." That was a dopey question! From that news, I figured Evelyn would go to her mother's in Belmar, New Jersey. After she got herself together, she would probably move to Florida, because the two older boys were in college there, and she would want to be close to them.

The prison camp of North Vietnam was getting to be "the" place to meet old friends!

The word came across that Jerry Denton had come to the Zoo and was in a cell near Risner.

Jerry still had his pencil, and soon an operations plan was passed to George Hall. While we cleared the area for guards, he read it aloud to all of us in the Pigsty and the Stable. The Plan contained the following:

1. Follow the Code of Conduct.
2. Communicate by all means available.
3. Don't try to escape without outside help.
4. Don't antagonize the guards.
5. Learn all POW names and locations (each building number and room number was included).
6. Collect and save matches, wire, nails, rope, and paper.
7. Complain about the food, clothing, no exercise or church services.
8. Church services on Sunday would be signaled by whistling of "God Bless America."
9. Maintain a listening watch. Sleep when the V sleep.

THE ZOO CAMP

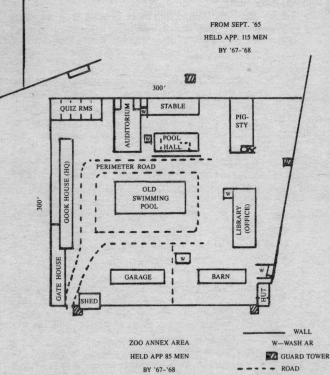

FROM SEPT. '65
HELD APP. 115 MEN
BY '67–'68

300'

QUIZ RMS

AUDITORIUM

STABLE

W

PIG-STY

POOL
HALL

W

GOOK HOUSE (HQ)

PERIMETER ROAD

300'

OLD
SWIMMING
POOL

W

LIBRARY
(OFFICE)

GATE HOUSE

W

GARAGE

BARN

W

SHED

HUT

ZOO ANNEX AREA
HELD APP 85 MEN
BY '67–'68

——— WALL
W—WASH AR
▨ GUARD TOWER
- - - ROAD
→ ⊢ ENTRANCE

I was appalled that Robbie had teamed up with Denton to publish a document that, if discovered, would result in retaliation by the V. It really wasn't a question of "if," but rather "when."

My neighbor Bill Franke and I had a lot of voice discussions, while leaning against our common wall and speaking through the closed shutters. Once in a while we got caught, but the guards didn't do anything to us. Bill, an F-4 squadron commander, was a very common-sense guy, and did not believe in making waves that would provoke the Vietnamese.

When George was finished reading the plan, I said, "What do you think, Bill?"

"I think that if the V find that piece of work they are going to kick some ass. Your boy Risner likes excitement, doesn't he?"

"I think Denton's influence is very strong there, Bill. How about let's tell 'em to destroy it?"

We called over to George to dump the writings into the *bo*; everyone now knew the content—no point in keeping a hot item like that for the V to discover. But George was reluctant to destroy the orders of the senior ranking officer. Instead, he passed the document to the Shumaker group. One of them called to say he didn't think the V would find it because "they would never inspect your personal things." That's how naive we were at that time!

In the meantime Art Black and I drilled a hole through our common wall, using the wire handles we took off the water jugs. We had a dime-size hole through the six-inch wall. We took turns stepping back and grinning so the other guy could take a good look. Then I passed Art a load of toilet paper that I'd been hoarding. We made a temporary plug out of bread, hoping the V wouldn't notice the hole.

Art said that a recent quiz with Rabbit was just a bull session, sort of man-to-man. They talked about Art's family and other seemingly innocent chatter. Art said that Rabbit got around to the virtues of socialism. Art thought he did well by asking questions that seemed to stop Rabbit in his tracks. I was alarmed at that and warned Art that he was underestimating Rabbit.

I suggested that the safest route would be to act ill-informed, not too bright, and not attract attention to one's self; to run in the middle of the pack, so to speak. The V could be convinced that the individual behaving thus might not actually know very much, possess no leadership qualities, and therefore pose no particular threat to the security of the camp.

At the end of the month the V searched the cells. Dummkopf the turnkey spotted the soft spot. He went to Art's cell, and I saw a crowbar come poking through the hole. Dummkopf had found the crowbar in Risner's cell, where Robbie had also done some concrete modifications! Dummkopf was livid. He slapped the hell out of Art and me, but lucky thing for us he was a little guy and didn't know how to deliver a punch American-style, or he would have really hurt us. Of course they also discovered the operations plan. That discovery put them about two years ahead of us. They took it and used it as a checklist against us. We taught them the business. They looked for all the things we were directed to collect. They removed all number placards from buildings and rooms. They ignored our complaints, and we were strictly forbidden to communicate with each other. They moved Risner back to Heartbreak, convinced his charisma and leadership was dangerous to them.

In a few days the V came around with a pile of papers and a bowl of sticky rice, which they used as paste. They stuck a notice up on the inside of the shutters, where we could see it all the time. It was a demoralizing official directive signaling that the future would be even bleaker.

Chapter Eight

THE CAMP REGULATIONS

The directive on our walls read:

All U.S. aggressors caught red-handed in their piratical attacks against the Democratic Republic of Vietnam are criminals. While detained in this camp, you will strictly obey the following:

1. *ALL CRIMINALS WILL BOW* TO ALL OFFICERS, GUARDS, AND VC IN THE CAMP.
2. *ALL CRIMINALS MUST SHOW POLITE ATTITUDE* AT ALL TIMES TO THE OFFICERS AND GUARDS IN THE CAMP, OR THEY WILL BE SEVERELY PUNISHED.
3. *ALL CRIMINALS WILL ANSWER ANY QUESTION* ORALLY OR *WRITE ANY* STATEMENT OR *DO ANYTHING DIRECTED* BY THE CAMP AUTHORITY, OR THEY WILL BE SEVERELY PUNISHED.
4. *CRIMINALS ARE FORBIDDEN TO ATTEMPT TO COMMUNICATE* IN ANY WAY, SUCH AS SIGNALS, TAPPING ON THE WALLS, ATTEMPTING TO COMMUNICATE WITH CRIMINALS IN THE NEXT ROOM.
5. WHEN IN THE BATH AREA, *DO NOT ATTEMPT TO COMMUNICATE* TO ANY OTHER CRIMINALS IN THE NEXT AREA, OR YOU WILL BE SEVERELY PUNISHED.
6. ANY CRIMINAL WHO ATTEMPTS TO ESCAPE, OR HELPS OTHERS TO DO SO, WILL BE SEVERELY PUNISHED.
7. *ON THE OTHER HAND CRIMINALS WHO* FOLLOW THESE CAMP REGULATIONS AND WHO *SHOW A*

GOOD ATTITUDE BY CONCRETE ACTS WILL BE
SHOWN A HUMANE TREATMENT.
SIGNED: CAMP AUTHORITY

There were six others, much like the first seven.

The Vietnamese dreamed up these regulations to put continuous pressure on the prisoners. Regulations made it simple for
the camp authorities to trump up false charges. The overall intention was to make each POW pay, either by giving information, or participating in some way in the Vietnamese propaganda
programs. As one interrogator said, "Ho Chi Minh has decreed
that each criminal must do his fart (he couldn't pronounce the
letter *P*) toward helping us in our final victory!" The Vietnamese also hoped this ongoing program of humiliation, intimidation, and punishment would create informers out of prisoners
who couldn't take the pressure. They always liked to have an
excuse for punishment. Not that they needed one, but it seemed
to make them happier to exclaim, "You have broken the camp
regulations, you must be punished!" The camp regs were the
lever and the excuse.

As if that wasn't enough to steepen the nosedive in morale,
Hobnail, the new and strict turnkey, came to each cell with more
instructions. Throwing open the shutters, he pointed first at me,
then at himself. He stood at attention, then went into a deep
bow. He was telling us that from now on we would bow anytime
we met any Vietnamese, just like it said in the new regs, and
they meant to enforce it.

Leaning against the bars nearest to Bill Franke, I asked him
what he thought of this latest humiliation. Bill was a very prac-
tical man, who believed we should adopt methods of dealing
with the V that could result in less punishment for all of us,
should we find ourselves in prolonged incarceration. He said,
"We may even have to kiss their asses before we're through, but
that's okay too, just as long as someday we all get the hell out
of here alive."

By pretending they didn't understand what the V wanted, some
of our people tried to resist the bowing. Others gave a short head
jerk, and still others gave a deep waist bow with arms hanging
to the floor. Bob Purcell told them that he only bowed before
Jesus Christ. That got him six months in solitary. Eventually the
Vietnamese decided "no bow, no chow." The bowing order
was repeated over and over. Some POWs were pushed into a
bowing position by the guards. The Vietnamese won that one.

In November, the weather turned cool. We each had two cotton blankets, and Bill Franke commented that three blankets wouldn't be too much, if we could get them. A number of Vietnamese appeared on the front porch carrying rolls of blue-colored electric wire.

"Whaddya think Bill? Are they going to wire up for electric blankets?"

"Don't think so, but its going to be a long, hard winter for sure."

We found out that the wires were for the new loudspeaker system that would pipe in a heavy daily ration of propaganda, one-sided news items, jewels of Vietnamese history and the Vietnamese struggles against imperialism, and threats of punishment from the camp commander from his post in the headquarters building.

Two or three times a day we heard the VOV, Voice of Vietnam. The announcers were a man named Van Tuong and a woman named Tu Huong (pronounced Van Toon and To Whom). Every broadcast included the latest count of American planes shot down and accounts of Viet Cong victories in the south over U.S. forces and the "Saigon Puppet Troops." In every program they usually used a part of Ho Chi Minh's famous, "Fight for five, ten, twenty years, or longer," statement. At first, they used many taped quotes from Lord Bertrand Russell, and other Communist sympathizers. Later they included statements from visiting Americans.

This radio broadcast was really directed to Allied troops fighting in South Vietnam, but they didn't have the skills necessary to effectively hit the morale of opposing troops. While praising the bravery and ingenuity of the Viet Cong (VC), they held to ridicule the "cowardly and heartless" efforts of the U.S. Army and Marine Corps. That could only have a counterproductive effect—it would anger our troops and spur them to a greater effort.

Thereafter, the attack of the VOV was against the U.S. leadership both in the field and in Washington. Our men were exhorted to turn against their officers, throw down their weapons, and "cross over to the other side" where they would be "joyously welcomed as brothers in the fight against imperialism." They spoke of one American who had already done so, and was now leading the VC against his former comrades.

The speaker system, or camp radio, was referred to as "the Box," "the Bullshit Box," then later "CBS," meaning "Camp

Bullshit System," which, in my opinion, produced about the same quality of information as CBS back home.

The news by Van Tuong was read out of *Nhan Dan*, the *People's Daily*. That was the government paper, which of course held one hundred percent to the government's propaganda line and was the only paper available to the people. It was printed only in Vietnamese, and we got pieces of old issues to use for toilet paper.

The other publication we got, printed in English, was the weekly *Vietnam Courier*, the *VNC*. This locally produced paper carried political statements and items not normally put out over the Box. It made for good between-the-lines speculation.

Americans associate the word "propaganda" with Goebbels, Hitler, and the Nazis. Since 1940 the word has had, in our country, a dirty connotation; no one wants to resort to the use of it. Too bad for us. Other people use the word freely, whenever appropriate, and in the correct sense. The literal meaning is "the spreading of doctrine, our way of thinking, our point of view." There is nothing wrong with it. We spread our propaganda through government sources such as the Voice of America, and our own media sources. We *should* be telling the American people, and everyone else in the world that "this is what we stand for, this is the way we look at it, this is the American way." (Too often today, our media repeats the propaganda of hostile nations as though it were indisputable truth.)

Rabbit called me out to "check my attitude."

"Your Risner, he is a very clever fellow, isn't he?" I didn't like the sound of that remark. "Clever" probably meant sneaky to the Rabbit. I answered innocently, "Gosh, I don't know if I'd use the word clever for Colonel Risner. He's just a nice person, a good family man, and very religious, too."

"You know he calls us gooks. He says we live in a gook house."

"Gosh, I find that difficult to believe. He is such a considerate person."

"What else do you know about him?"

Knowing full well that the Rabbit had his copy of *Time* magazine, which I'd read a couple of times, I told him what he already knew for sure.

"Well, I know that he is younger than I and that he has a wife and several sons. Also he is an American Indian, I think from Oklahoma."

"What else?"

"He is known to be a great fighter pilot and a decent human being. Everyone likes him because he is such an honest person and, like I said, you have to admire him for his faith in God." Rabbit seemed satisfied. He knew it was approximately the truth from what he'd already read in *Time*. What I didn't want to do was get caught in an outright lie. That would hand Rabbit an excuse to put it to me, and as we understood by then, it pleased them to have an excuse, however unnecessary.

I spoke to Robbie just before he left the Zoo. I told him exactly what I had said to Rabbit, and he replied it was "okay, didn't hurt me any."

The *bo* dumping procedure became a routine. The turnkey made us push the *bos* out on the porch, then appointed one prisoner to carry them, two at a time, to a large open cesspool out behind the Pigsty building. I got the job only one night. The dirt path was slimy from the spillover of the *bos*, and the cesspool was something I'd never seen the likes of before. A square acre of floating feces. Ron Storz inherited the chore from me, and it did have one thing on the plus side—it gave him an excellent opportunity to talk to some prisoners who were difficult to reach. Storz did a great job, pretending he was talking to the guards, while passing information.

One afternoon the turnkey had us put the buckets out in the middle of the porch. Suddenly orders were being shouted, and the guards picked up the *bos* (something they would never do!) and stashed them out of sight. Franke muttered, "I think we've got important visitors." We could hear doors opening in sequence, then somebody yelling, first in Vietnamese, then in English.

My cell door was opened. Several guards stood at attention, then an important-looking, dumpy man wearing civilian clothes and dark glasses followed the Dog into the cell. "Get back, get back against the wall!" Dog commanded. Then he stood at attention and was actually trembling in fear of the arrogant civilian who strode around, saw my cross, my ten commandments, and calendar. He ranted in Vietnamese, then Dog did the translating.

"Do you know what you have done? Do you know what you have done?" Dog shouted fiercely.

"Me? Hell, I haven't done anything! I've been locked up here for five and a half months."

"You! You! You!" he screamed, "Pah-tic-ally you! Pah-tic-ally you!"

"What the hell are you talking about?" I demanded. Dog now stood quivering against the side wall. When the civilian took a breath, Dog translated, "You have come and murdered our children, our wives, our families! You have come to kill the Vietnamese people!" The civilian lost his cool. They were both yelling at the same time. Dog was sweating and dripping spittle as he yelled, apparently trying to win the approval of the VIP.

Over all the hollering, from a few cells away, I heard Alvarez's voice, frantically calling for his *bo*. "*Bo, bo, bo,* I need my bo fast!" Everybody left my cell and converged on Alvy's cell. They flung open his doors and Alvy said, "I told you I needed the *bo!*"

The excitement quieted down abruptly. After the doors were bolted, I asked Bill Franke what was going on. "Get this Larry, and pass the word. Alvarez couldn't hold it! He shit on the floor! When the V saw it there, they stuck up their noses and disappeared. Maybe they respected the call of nature above all else. Haven't we already said that they very well understood shit?" The word spread around the cells and may have been the only laugh I would have for the next three years.

"Lordy Bill, what could have prompted that harangue?"

"I'd have to say that finding the ops plan kicked the whole thing off. They are scared to death over our ingenuity, the number of surprising things we're capable of doing. They overreacted and considered it a major security problem. They figured they had no choice but to report our 'dark schemes' to higher headquarters."

One night in November, I was called out to the Rabbit. He spoke very, very softly. He said he found my copy of the song about "Rain." "What would you do with that?"

"Maybe I can get Burl Ives to sing it."

"What will you do with all the money you will make?"

"Donate it to the Vietnam War Relief Fund."

Rabbit took my copy of "Rain" and also a checker board that I had drawn across the covers of another book they had given me to read. Although Rabbit had to know I had a pencil, he didn't mention it. (The guards examined me so closely after that, I decided it was too dangerous to hang on to it any longer.)

He inquired about my health. Then he said I would meet a very important member of his government that night, and above all I must answer all his questions truthfully and respectfully. He told me to return to my cell and "prepare yourself."

An hour later they took me to a small room in front of the auditorium building. Soon a man came in. I never found out who he was, but he was silver-haired and in his seventies. He wore a black, high-collared, woolen Communist party coat. He was charming, and seemed quite worldly, and spoke excellent French and English. He didn't ask hard questions, but treated me very gently. He said he merely wished to meet an American pilot. He spoke about his country and how poor his people were. He inquired very lightly about my family. Toward the end of his visit, he asked two final questions. One was, "What do your young fighting men believe in?" I replied, "They believe in freedom, democracy, peace, equality, and the hope for a good life, the same things that your young people believe in."

"We know that you place the importance of the dollar above all else."

"I don't think that's true, but people who don't like us say that."

"But how do you make them fight? What do you tell them?"

"Well we do the same as you do—point to past accomplishments with patriotic pride. We also use motivational techniques, just as you use those slogans that we see on your tin cups. You know, *Quyet Chien*, *Quyet Thang*. What does that mean?"

"It means resolve to fight, resolve to win."

"There you are. That's what I mean."

The visit was mostly social, and I behaved respectfully toward him.

Red Berg moved in next door with Art Black. He tap-called me early one morning, around seven o'clock, saying, "Larry, listen. We're leaving this morning."

"What are you talkin' about?"

"We're going home," he replied. The camp radio had been in operation for a couple of weeks by that time. Berg continued, "You notice we have not heard anything about anybody getting shot down the last few days. It's because there is a cease-fire." This was just one of the many hundreds of yo-yos in morale we were destined to have. When one guy gets something in his head, he affects everybody else's morale.

"What do you mean, Red?"

"Have you heard anything about a shoot-down the last three days? No! It's because the war's over! They've been negotiating."

A couple of days before that, a new prisoner, Jim Bell, a navy RA-5 pilot, had told us that they were negotiating seriously on the outside. He got us all excited. In fact, we all started making shopping lists! I had a fabulous list of fifteen or twenty items, and everybody was doing it! We were talking about Hong Kong, what we were gonna get on our way home, where the PXs are, and all that crap. Red was all charged up, and thinking about it, dreaming about it, and he said with conviction, "We're goin' home, we're goin' home, the trucks are gonna be here before eight o'clock, before eight o'clock!"

I got on my knees and peeked outside through a crack.

"Hey, listen, I'm lookin' out the window here. I see a couple of peasant broads building another wall and puttin' some barbed wire back here. If we're goin' home, how come they're still buildin' the camp?"

"Don't pay any attention to that. They just let the contract and they can't stop it." Red wasn't joking. He had heard about contracts around the air force bases, and he knew you can't stop a contract once the union gets hold of it; the project goes ahead. So Red was saying that in this Commie country, there was no difference; they had union problems, too! So never mind the camp being built up around us—'cause we're goin' home today!

The only thing I got out of that conversation was that there was at least one guy in North Vietnam nuttier than I.

One of the guards was called the Green Hornet because he wore a forest green French paratrooper's uniform. He was very verbal, and you could hear him coming from a long way off—he sang, whistled, or talked to himself. He had a new rifle, which he proudly showed me. I admired it, then stuck out my hands to take it for a close inspection. He stepped back alarmed, with an expression like, "are you crazy?"

Another guard opened the shutters. He had his rifle slung high on his right shoulder. His head was heavily bandaged, and blood was visible seeping out through the very top of the wrappings. I pointed and asked, "How'd that happen?" He explained by gestures. A week before, the order had come out for all soldiers pulling guard duty to have bayonets in place. They were going all-out to intimidate us. Well, one of his buddies had his rifle slung high on the shoulder, bayonet and all. As they were chatting, his friend dropped his cigarette, then bent over to pick it up, and the bayonet came forward and stabbed the guard in the head.

Even a change of *bos* was an indicator. On the seventeenth of

November, the turnkey replaced my little *bo* with a larger, newer one. Franke said, "Larry, you are getting a cell mate. They don't waste big toilet buckets on singles."

About nine that night I saw the Rabbit in a quiz room. He sat and stared, then said only, "Now try to obey the camp regulations." He sent me back. The cell door was open, and by God, standing there in the center of the cell was my friend Ron Byrne from the 67th Squadron! I was so glad to see him I wanted to kiss him, but trying hard to keep in check, I held it to an embrace. This was the best thing so far.

"Boy am I glad to see you, buddy!" he exclaimed.

"Well, I can't say I'm thrilled that you're here, but I'm sure glad to get you for my cell mate," I replied. Six months alone was a very long time for an outgoing person like me. The guard gave a half smile and locked the door. The last I had seen Ron was the night before I was shot down. He had ferried a 105 to Korat from Kadena, and that night we went to Mass together.

"I was shot down in August," he said sadly. "I've been over at Heartbreak." We flopped down on our bunks and whispered for hours about our families. If happiness exists in such circumstances, that was the happiest night I'd had in six months.

A couple of days later, Ev Alvarez was joined up with air force captain Tom Barrett, after seventeen months in solitary. What a happy day for Alvy!

Christmas was coming, and the guards were very strict with us. They were briefed daily and had a big meeting once a week so they would know how much pressure to exert on us. There were many little ways to harass us. They'd let the food sit on the floor of the porch for an hour or two, until it was cold and covered with ants. They'd limit our eating time to five or ten minutes. They'd slam the doors on your heels. They'd visit your cell every couple of minutes, so you'd have to bow, and bow, and bow. They knew that bowing really torqued us. They'd accuse us of communicating and call the duty officer, which would result in a quiz and more pressure. The simplest of their spiteful measures, such as the withholding of toilet paper, soap, toothpaste, or needed items of clothing, bugged us terribly.

Bill Franke messaged, "Are you two through kissing yet?" Ron and I were so excited, we had neglected Bill. We told him that soon he would be joined up. He answered, "Don't think so. They'll never join up O-5s or higher." (An O-5 is the pay-grade used by all American military services to indicate the rank of lieutenant colonel (air force, army, marines) or full commander (navy). O-6 designates a colonel or navy captain.)

The Dog said snidely, "Ga-reeno, had you not come to bomb our people, you could be driving around Kadena with your wife and sons. Well, perhaps in a year, or two years, you can go back." The V didn't know any more than any of us how long the war would last. "Surely there's no way we could be here for *two more years*!" I thought, horrified at the mere idea.

"Do you want to write a letter home, Ga-reeno, to tell of the humane treatment you are getting?"

"No thanks," I replied. "Don't know where my family is now, so I'll wait until I get a letter from home first."

Frenchy called me out to check my attitude. What was happening to me was repeated with others. Frenchy spoke English with a very strong French accent. He was in his mid-forties, and the same rank as Dog. He started out many words with a double *O*—"And oowhat oowould you like for Christmas?" I didn't know what he wanted me to say. Obviously, he had something in mind.

"On the occasion of your Christmas celebration, oowhat oowould you like from the good heart of the humane Vietnamese people?" It was like charades.

"Oowhat is your most fervent desire, your most fervent oowish?" The light finally dawned.

"Well, I would like very much to have a letter from home."

At these December meetings, and from then on, Dog and Frenchy wore their rank insignia with their uniforms—three stars over a bar, equivalent to a U.S. Army captain. The Rabbit had one star on a bar, a junior lieutenant. The uniforms of all of the soldiers were considerably improved. The footgear remained rubber flip-flops or at best, canvas sneakers.

On the fifteenth of December, 1965, Frenchy handed me a letter from Evelyn! It was the most beautiful letter I had ever read, and the finest Christmas gift of my life.

1 Nov 1965

My Dearest Larry,

What a beautiful fall this has been. Everywhere I've been visiting has brought back the most pleasant memories of things we have done together. Just a simple drive to Asbury Park reminded me of our first time there, how terribly sick you became and how I didn't know what to do to make you forget.

There is no doubt how much I loved you right from the start.

Visiting Rita and passing Branch Brook Park, the trees all in such beautiful reds and yellows. Can you remember the many hours we spent there. I guess I was never really aware of all the beauty around us. I wonder if children growing up are aware of it, I'm sure I wasn't then.

The boys have been very good about writing often. I'm especially proud of Tom who seems to be working very hard. He said he got an A in his mid-term math exam—how about that? Allan is doing fairly well also. Ditto our young sons. Had to make a Jack-o-lantern for Jeff, though I know it didn't compare to the nice ones you've made . . .

Hope that if you can write you will tell me what to do about car, where to live, etc. Have been prolonging it in hopes there would be no need to make the decision.

How very lucky I am to have saved all those beautiful letters you wrote me. Even if I didn't have them I would be reminded constantly how good you have been to me. My dearest Larry, how I love you! You have really taught me so much . . . I want to tell you over and over that I love you! . . . Everything I do—I feel you beside me, helping me, and I want you to feel the same. My Larry, I love you.

Your Evy.

Chapter Nine

THE HANOI MARCH

Ron and I read Evy's letter over and over, then read it through the walls for anyone else who wanted to hear it. It was a tear-jerker, especially since it arrived at the most sentimental time of year. A few days later, Ron received his first letter from his wife Jo, with all the latest news about their four sons. We were ecstatic.

My cell mate, Major Ronald E. Byrne, had attended the Merchant Marine Academy at Great Neck, Long Island, and later graduated from Oklahoma State University. He flew F-86 Sabres in the Korean War. He was brought up in a Catholic family and served as an altar boy. He knew the entire Mass in Latin. He was a most devout and totally decent human being. It was a fantastic stroke of good luck for me to get him as a cell mate. I was concerned to see that he had dropped twenty pounds or more since the last time I saw him, but I probably looked just as bad to him. Often, I'd raise up from my wooden bed board to look over at him to see if he was still there, that it was real, that I had someone to talk to.

The V were setting a holiday pattern in avoiding harshness during holiday seasons. During the interrogation periods, which were shorter, they did most of the talking, telling us that their treatment of us was "very humane," even though we were "criminals."

On the twentieth of December, Dog called me in. Eventually he got around to talking about the good heart of the people again. Then, after a pregnant pause, he asked, "Would you like to write a letter to your family?" I thought about it for a long time before answering. I knew that the price of writing a letter home would probably be a requirement that I include some of the "humane treatment" crap. I finally decided that that would be a small price in order to give Evelyn some word of me and some reassurance.

After handing me writing materials, Dog told me to first write down the return address. He dictated:

"To U.S. Criminals Caught Red-Handed." That was enough! I threw down the pencil. "I'll never write if I have to use a return address like that! I'm sure it will panic my wife, and maybe cause her a heart attack!"

Dog got very nervous and left for about fifteen minutes. When he returned he said, "Very well, now we'll write again." The return address was softened to: "Camp of Detention of U.S. Pilots Captured in the Democratic Republic of Vietnam." I accepted that and wrote my letter. I felt good as I wrote, just like I was talking to Evelyn. My morale inched up a notch.

From: Lawrence Nicholas Guarino
Address: Camp of Detention of U.S. Pilots Captured in the
     Democratic Republic of Vietnam.
To: Mrs. Evelyn Teresa Guarino (wife)
Address: 321 12th Ave., Belmar, New Jersey USA

            20 December 1965

My Dear Wife, Sons and Beloved Parents,

It is wonderful of the Vietnamese people to allow me to write a letter home on the occasion of Christmas and our Holy Season! . . .

I want you to press on in life as usual, work, school or whatever it might be, for nothing can help except your continuous strong prayers for the end of the war . . .

The few minor health problems which I've had have been attended in timely fashion by a medic in charge. The guards and officers have treated us fairly and we are adequately clothed and housed. We eat twice daily and are supplied with plenty of fresh water . . .

. . . bless Father McIntyre for getting us back to church. I went to communion last on 6 June and Mass on 13 June, so my slate was very very clear before coming here. I'm glad it was because He has taken wonderful care of me along with the humane treatment given to me by the Vietnamese people. It seems to me that these people are determined to fight for their country . . .

I hope that all of you attend Mass regularly or more, and that your prayers are for the end of people's suffering, both ours and theirs as well as the pilots in the detention camps and all of their anxious families. Possibly some not as lucky as I have been injured in bailout or wounded. As you know, when ejecting from a fast aircraft it is easy to be hurt.

Evelyn my Darling. I want to hear all about you. Don't let down, always dress well and keep smiling. Use your own judgment in problems such as cars, housing, etc. as I am not in position to fully appreciate your problems so please feel free to settle them in your own best ways. . . .

My adoration of all of you continues as always and as high as heaven itself. I love you all too much! Please follow the instructions below so your return letter will not be delayed. . . .

That is most of which has been on my mind and I hope it eases your worry. Hope you had a good Christmas and that God grant next year will be a happier one. Evelyn Dear I know you are with me, I feel it.

> My deepest affection to all,
> Larry (Dad)

Before I got "killed," I had never heard of the Democratic Republic of Vietnam, only North Vietnam. "Killed" was a new expression I adopted, because when a plane is shot down, it is recorded as a "kill" on their scoreboard, and being captured by Communists was just as bad as being killed.

After I finished my letter, Dog looked it over and was pleased with it. "Soon you move to another room. You will be surprised at what you see." The V always used the word "room" instead of cell and "rooms" instead of cell block. He continued, "And now, because things go so well for us and we now have the support of the entire world in our struggle . . . for the very first time in Vietnamese history, all, [he repeated this emphatically and rather emotionally, finger pointed to the sky] *All*, of our people will have *some* meat to eat for Christmas."

He said "some meat." When we Americans think of meat, we think of a standing rib roast, an eye of round, a twenty-ounce steak, a roast turkey. It's difficult for us to get a handle on the thinking of very poor people because most of us are spoiled rotten, more or less from childhood. What Dog actually meant by "some meat" was that each Vietnamese would get a tiny crosscut of pig fat and be very grateful for it. And for that, Ho Chi Minh would get big-time credit for years to come, just the way the Chinese were always blessing Chairman Mao.

The next day, Dog called both Ron and me out at the same time. "Would you like to see a Catholic priest on the occasion

of your holy day?'' That was a surprise. We looked at one another and nodded affirmatively.

"Very good. You and Cormier will be taken to see the priest."

We knew he meant Staff Sergeant Arthur Cormier, a para-
medic from the helicopter crew of pilots Bob Lilly and Jerry
Singleton, shot down in November as they were trying to pick
up A-1 pilot Dick Bolstad. All were now "guests" of Hanoi!

A couple of nights later, they came for us. We were blindfolded and taken to Hoa Lo, into room twenty-four. We sarcas-
tically called Hoa Lo, the city jail, the "Hanoi Hilton." Calling
it that was a mistake, because a lot of Americans, with no (or
at best only sketchy) knowledge of what was really happening
to us, believed that we were actually being held in comfort in a
Hilton hotel! We asked Art how the war was going. "No change,
maybe in two years," he answered.

On hand were a number of guards, a photographer, the Rabbit, and old Father Ho Than Bien, the patriarch of the Catholic
Church in North Vietnam. There was also one other man there,
who never took his eyes off the old priest. Ron and I decided
that he was the priest's personal "keeper." They gave us a few
pieces of candy to munch on while we waited. We wondered
what the next act was going to be.

Father Ho Than Bien was white-skinned and silver-haired. He
had not shaved for a few days and had silver stubble all over his
face. He looked part French. He spoke French fluently and soon
learned that we did not, so he used his "keeper" as interpreter.

Ron asked the interpreter if he could assist the priest with the
Mass. Father Ho accepted, and was surprised to find Ron so
fluent with the Latin ceremony.

Then the Rabbit snarled, "Ga-reeno—now you confess your
crimes to the priest! Tell him how many times you have come
up here, how many missions you have flown! And you, Byrne!''

I looked at Rabbit and said, "Just a few."

Ron answered, "Just one."

We figured we were in for a quiz-spiked church service. Father Ho pressed on with the mass. The photographer took a
couple of shots as we were given Holy Communion. Right after
that, we were returned to the Zoo.

We were moved into the center cell at the rear of the Pool
Hall building, which had ten cells. Some of the little cells had
green and white tiled floors. Our cell had two wooden sleeping
boards on cement stanchions, bare walls, and a toilet bucket.
There were no windows at all, except for two rectangular air

ports five inches by nine inches, about ten feet up the wall. It was dark, depressing, and claustrophobic, but the Dog termed it "a nice surprise." He must have thought it was real neat! The latest news on the Box was that both sides had agreed on a three-day holiday cease-fire.

Christmas Day was heartbreaking. They brought a delicious meal of potato soup, (*with* potatoes!) salad, bread, vegetables, and real, fresh turkey! We ate every speck, but my eyes were filled with tears all day, and Ron wasn't doing well, either. We were full of family thoughts. The lesson, once again, was a painful one. The one luxury that a captive cannot afford is self-pity. But it takes time to get the hang of it, because you have to change your normal pattern of thinking.

The days following Christmas were unusually quiet, and the guards didn't bother us. They left the door peeps open for hours. We stuck out our heads and talked to others on our side of the building, and also across to the Stable. My bunk was on the left side of the cell, and my wall neighbor was Ev Alvarez.

Lying in our bunks at night, Alvy and I tapped to one another. He told me about his wife, Tangee, and how high his spirits were because Tom Barrett, his new cell mate, figured the war couldn't last much longer. I told Alvy how much I admired him for being in solitary so long and sticking with it, continuing to be patriotic and loyal. I asked him how he was able to keep up his morale so well, for so long. He replied, "It's not bad now. I get very heartening messages from my neighbor." (He meant me. That lifted *my* morale.)

Several rumors circulated through the walls. The first was that there were now about sixty Americans in captivity. The second was much more exciting. It was believed, from some slip of the tongue of one of the English-speaking Vietnamese, that the cease-fire had been extended to negotiate an end to hostilities! A week later fifteen of us, all early shoot-downs, were loaded on trucks and taken downtown for mug shots, several poses for each man. While there, we were given some chocolate caramel candies. Morale climbed. This must mean the war was ending soon!

A few days later, right in the Zoo, they set up a production-line medical checkup of the same fifteen of us. They checked vital signs, heart, lungs, eyes, ears. They took lab samples—blood, urine, and stool. The stool collector was a mean little guy, nicknamed Dum Dum. He handed each man a small jar through the peep, saying, "You must make stool in this jar, undahstan?'' Dum Dum probably got his name from someone who thought he was dumb. I decided that he was really named after the soft-nosed bullets that do tremendous tissue damage, collapsing on the way through a man's body, opening huge holes. The dumdum projectile is against Geneva Conventions, like many other weapons, including napalm and gas. Dum Dum wore a single bar, the lowest rank officer of their army. He was a very dangerous man, whose English was minimal. Every time he opened his mouth it was a threat. He spoke only "torture English": "You must confess, you will be beaten! You must obey, you get the irons! You never go home!" Unfortunately, we were to see a lot of this hateful little man, and he made good on most of his threats.

The people who examined us were medical corpsmen. There were a few doctors, too. The fellow who was doing the ear check looked in my ears, and before I knew what was happening he stuck a wire into my ear, (presumably to remove some wax) and punctured my eardrum! Within two days it had infected, and it was very painful. When I called for *bac si* (doctor), miraculously the camp medic came around and gave me some pills, which cleared it right up.

Soon the Box confirmed that a cease-fire was in effect! We were wild with anticipation of being freed. But everything that goes up, sooner or later comes down.

The North Vietnamese position was that all U.S. and foreign forces must leave immediately, so the North Vietnamese could proceed with the "reunification" of the north and south. The American position was that the north must immediately desist in its assistance to the Viet Cong and withdraw all forces into the north. The two sides were worlds apart. Toward the end of January, Ho Chi Minh's answer came over the Box.

"Did you get all that Ron? What did he say?"

"Ho Chi Minh just told Johnson to pound rock salt up his ass!"

End of negotiations—hang on for the nosedive again!

Another important lesson we learned, over time (a very long time), was to avoid wild excitement over news items that may have little or no substance. To remain intact at all, the ups and downs of morale had to be managed to mild oscillations over the long haul. We were trying to do that, without even realizing it. In all the cells with two or more people, one man usually was the optimist, while the others were pessimistic. The pessimist knew his role was just that, and he really wanted the optimist to be right, even though he, the pessimist, would decry the optimist's opinions as "utter stupidity." And so the game went on. Unfortunately, the pessimist was usually right.

One evening, the Vietnamese came and signaled Ron to dress, with a hand chop across the wrist, meaning, "long sleeve pajama, something special tonight." We thought he was just going out for a night quiz, but he was gone for four hours, and I got really worried. When he returned, he was physically and mentally exhausted, and glad that his evening's performance was over.

He had been taken to meet a delegation of three Americans, who represented no one but themselves, and whose visit was strictly in defiance of U.S. State Department policy, which forbade travel to North Vietnam. As Ron gave me the details of the meeting, I occasionally asked questions, to get the story straight in my own mind.

As usual, Vietnamese officers and guards were there through the entire session. Ron was made to sit on the little wooden stool, while his inquisitors, fellow Americans, sat comfortably behind a table. The first man was Professor Staughton Lynd, from Yale University. Lynd said very little during the entire time, and as the complexion of the meeting became evident, he looked more and more uncomfortable, because he realized he was in way over his head. Ron figured that he was well intentioned, but somehow got sucked into this Vietnam trip in some very bad company.

The second was identified as Herbert Aptheker, at that time the leading Communist in the United States. He asked Ron a lot of questions about the causes of the war, and my buddy gave the usual answers to most of the questions, and hemmed and hawed around those he wanted to keep from answering. Some of the questions became difficult for Ron to field without pissing off the V, who watched him like hawks, but surprisingly, Aptheker took the hint and backed off, moving to a new subject. He wasn't unduly harsh in his of questioning of Ron, nor was he cruel in his comments when Ron faltered. He seemed content to let the third man of the group take charge and run it his way.

The "take-charge guy," the youngest of the three, was Tom Hayden, who, in Ron's opinion, was the meanest and most vindictive person he had ever had the misfortune to meet.

"Larry, I don't know who he is, but he has to be one of the most rotten people that we have running around loose in our country."

"Jesus, Ron, how bad *is* he?"

"He has locks on hate. . . . He hates everything America stands for."

"Such as?"

"Well, count 'em up. He hates our military system. . . . Hates our political system. . . . In his words he is 'antiestablishment.' I've never heard that one before."

"He probably invented it. Do you think he's a Communist?"

"Well, if he isn't, he sure loves 'em and supports them."

"Maybe he's just a chronic malcontent. You find them in every society."

"He was very agressive with me, wouldn't let up, tried to get me to agree that we are *criminals*, who fought in a criminal war! I tried every which way to avoid saying anything incriminating, but he dogged me unmercifully. I was just praying I could get out of the mess without having the V land on me hard afterwards." He shook his head in disgust.

"I think you did one helluva job tonight, buddy. If the V were after revenge, I don't think they would have let you come back— they would have gotten to you real quick. What kind of man can this Hayden be? A man who comes to Hanoi and harasses his own American pilots! Taking potshots at prisoners is like shooting fish in a barrel! He knew he had you by the balls, and he squeezed 'em. Only a completely rotten, filthy coward would take advantage of our situation."

"He's one dangerous guy, Larry! But you had to be there to see it, to believe it could happen. He holds all of us personally responsible for the war against these people. He is a sick and bitter man, and he had me so furious and upset, I almost threw up in his face."

"Like I said, he has to be the worst kind of yellow son of a bitch alive, to pull shit like that on a helpless prisoner," I said, fury rising in me at the thought of what this guy was doing to us. "Maybe someday our turn will come. You did good to evade his bullshit without ending up in irons, or worse."

In February we heard that Red Berg had had a recent session with a delegation of East European Communists. They gave him a very bad time, highlighted by the question, "If your president told you to go out and drop a nuclear bomb on us, would you do it?" They pressed hard for the answer, which Red tried to avoid. They finally forced an answer, and he told them he would do what his president and commander-in-chief ordered. That made them angry, and one of them retorted ominously, "You are a dangerous man. We must take care of you.'' Of course it threw a scare into Red, but he never heard another word about it.

We knew things would get a lot rougher. We spent time planning phony answers, and phony statements. We needed a fairy tale to give them, one that covered our lives, and our flying experiences in the war, a story that couldn't be busted by the V cross-checking with our friends.

From the first day of my captivity, I had constant anxiety over what to do, or say, if the interrogators got around to probing for nuclear secrets, for the Russians. I wasn't sure about the navy, but I knew that every air force tactical fighter pilot was highly qualified in nuclear operations. We knew the latest weapons, the loading procedures, and the techniques used to deliver the weapons to the targets.

Many of us had pulled duty tours at bases that were set up primarily for retaliatory strikes in case one or all of the ''big three'' (Russia, China, and North Korea) decided to jump the gun and launch nuke strikes against us.

Depending upon each individual's position in the overall scheme of operations, it was also very possible for him to have considerable knowledge of the General War Plan, and the special procedures for relaying and confirming launch orders, directly from the president, down to the pilots and aircrews who would carry out the orders. It was also possible that some of the pilots had memorized long lists of targets, by name and location, in all three of the adversary countries.

This hot subject caused all of us plenty of sweat, so much so that we wouldn't even discuss it when tapping through the walls. Ron and I whispered to one another, and decided that it was up to each of us to develop his own front lines (and secondary lines) of defense, if tortured for this information.

Then Ron wisely said, ''Let's not borrow trouble, Larry. No sense torturing ourselves with worry—wait until the problem raises its head. With luck, maybe it will never come up.''

Why was it that the V never touched on this area of questioning? They may have felt that nuclear military operations were worlds away from their own problems, and that it was best to put interrogation efforts in areas that would be more productive and beneficial to them. They often said they would gladly accept all the materiel assistance and moral support they could get from their Communist allies, and from any other country sympathetic to their plight. "But, [and this was a very big "but"] *with no strings attached*!"

Their friends would probably have relished the opportunity to obtain some of that information. However, the Vietnamese did not want to be run over by any of the three "biggies" and chance losing control of their prisoners at the whim of their allies, so they kept a tight rein on the prison camps and strictly limited the visits of their "friends."

We heard that new shoot-downs were getting immediate torture for information. Apparently the latest world news, and what they perceived to be fading possibilities to negotiate the war's end, encouraged them to move ahead full speed to get what they could from their captives.

The format of the interrogations had developed into a pattern. The Vietnamese were questioning in four categories:

First category: *Military information* of a timely nature, had first priority. The V had learned, from POW admissions under torture, that a list of targets to be struck was published thirty days in advance. They probed to find out if the prisoner under interrogation knew the target list, or any part of it. Getting this information would enable them to improve their antiaircraft capabilities, evacuate unnecessary personnel, and even move out essential supplies or technical equipment, depending on the type of target. The quest for information about aircraft and new armament capabilities was continual. Weapons delivery techniques and flight tactics were also important to the V, because knowledge of these tactics would help them to devise defensive methods to reduce the effectiveness of the air-strike missions. Intelligence about newly installed electronics, and electronic countermeasures, was also of great military value to them.

Second category: *Personal information* on the new captive. This included his chronological biography, from birth to present. A complete family history was considered important, because a personal file provided many useful tools to the interrogators. They could employ threats of harm to the prisoner's family and try to coerce him to write propaganda letters to unions, church groups, or fraternal organizations. Study of a number of files could provide a cross section of the personal psychology of the pilots and aircrews. The Vietnamese wanted to know what motivated us, and what made us tick. They made it obvious they hoped to discover a pattern of personality weaknesses that could be exploited.

Third category: *Political information* about the knowledge

and political affiliations or beliefs of the captive. Of use to the
V were possible prior connections with political parties, including any personal relationships with leading politicians. The V
looked for possible disagreement with party policies and national policies. Exploitation occurred in every case when the
prisoner admitted any connections or personal friendship with
politicians.

Fourth category: *Prisoner secrets.* These were usually ob-
tained from the captives who had been incarcerated for a while
because they would have that information. The Vietnamese
would start these interrogations with the usual excuse that camp
regulations had been violated. Widespread torture was always
blamed on the prisoners, "for breaking regulations," especially
those prohibiting communications. The V wanted full knowledge of the prisoners' command structure, i.e., who was the
camp senior ranking officer, and who were the cell block seniors. The policies of the senior officers, and the programs of
resistance against the camp authorities, were items that the Vietnamese considered extremely important to camp security. Communicating between prisoners particularly upset the authorities,
because they soon learned that, with communications between
cells and cell blocks, the prisoners were able to organize, pass
policies and orders, and keep abreast of what the V were doing.
Communications would make it possible to encourage men being tortured to hang tough, and maintain a respectable level of
resistance against exploitation. The Vietnamese were constantly
trying to upgrade their knowledge of the many methods of communication that had been devised. As time passed, they learned
most of our methods, but they still couldn't bring prisoner communication to a complete halt. They became so spring-loaded,
so hypersensitive about it, they tortured one man for supposedly
communicating by using a controlled technique of pissing into
his toilet bucket!

A formal, neatly typed questionnaire suddenly appeared at
interrogations. It was very technically oriented, and most of us
believed that it was impossible for the Vietnamese to have come
up with it. Dog handed it to me, and truthfully I had never even
heard of the electronic countermeasures and the new weapons
it described. Dog did not believe my claims of total ignorance,
but even though he showed great anger, he moved to a new
topic.

"And now, since you are one of the oldest men here, very
wise and intelligent, I ask you to write a story to discuss the

psychology of the American fighter pilot.'' He pushed pencil and paper toward me. I was aghast, and I showed it by an outburst that took him by surprise.

"Psych—psych—what the hell is that? I can't spell it, and sure as hell don't know anything about it! I told you I'm a passed over [i.e., not selected for promotion] reserve officer, and I followed a captain up here. I can't help you with anything like that. Don't even ask.''

He countered with heavy threats of punishment, and shouted, "On top of that I want you to write your complete personal biography from the time you were born to the time you were captured, and if you refuse you will be punished immediately!''

Of course I refused, and damned if he didn't have the guards haul my skinny little ass to the empty cell at the left rear of the auditorium building. It was five feet by nine feet, a very dark and nasty little place that later was dubbed the Ho Chi Minh Room.

By night, I lay on the bare floor trying to protect my toes against the mosquitoes by pulling my pajamas over my feet and holding them in place by pushing my feet against the door. For two days, I got no food at all. On the third day, they gave me a half cup of soup and a small piece of bread. After a week, I was taken out for interrogation again, and agreed to do a biography. I printed each word, but Dog wouldn't accept it until I wrote in longhand. He showed me a foot-high pile of "writings by your fellows.'' I looked at some, and they were a howl. They wanted stories? They got stories—fairy tales!

In my "masterpiece,'' I told about my father being a member of the peasant working class, and of his labors in a factory run by the imperialists. I also mentioned my grandfather's primary job as a bootlegger, a maker of boots. I told about how the bankers had seized our home and threw us out into the streets. How I struggled as an uneducated officer, and how I was ill-prepared for the war. I wrote that I flew up north following a young captain to the target area because I was merely qualified to fly cross-country flights without weapons. I added that my hearing and sight were below standard. Dog was pleased, and I was pleased that he didn't push for the formal questionnaire, or the psychology thing. They took me back to my old cell, and it was good to be with Ron again.

Several nights later, they came for me and took me to a place I'd never seen before. It was a large building with a wide, high staircase out front. Dog came in and told me that soon I would see a western journalist, and he reminded me to be polite and truthful. I waited in a small side room. A pretty Vietnamese woman with a small child came in and handed me a bottle of beer and some biscuits. I saw another American with a crutch go limping by. I guessed correctly that it was navy pilot Ray Vohden.

My turn came, and I went into a long living room set up with a chair for me, and some couches on the sides. There were lights and cameras everywhere. The cameraman introduced himself and shook my hand warmly. He was a handsome guy, and I was looking for some kind of secret message . . . but no dice. Instead he gave me a look that said, "You poor bastard, I wouldn't want to be in your shoes."

Then, in came the head man with his wife. I announced myself formally: "Major Larry Guarino, United States Air Force." He gave me the phony name of Graham, but I had already recognized him from some of the propaganda books we had been given, which contained his picture. He was Australian journalist Wilfred Burchett, alias "Wellfed Bullshit" to us, who wrote the Communist side of every story, beginning with the Korean war. He introduced his wife, and I stood up while he did. She was blond, French, in her thirties, and good-looking, but rather overweight. She sat down heavily in an overstuffed, western-style chair and her knees were way up. I peeked and thought, "Not bad legs for a porky little broad."

Burchett asked my name, rank, and serial number, and where I took off from. I answered, "North Vietnam."

"Now see heah," he said as he ordered the cameras to cut for a new start.

"Sorry," I said, "slip of the tongue."

Burchett went on with the usual happy horseshit that I was a criminal. I answered that I was not, but a genuine prisoner of war. Burchett then condemned American agression, and I replied that it was an honorable intervention against Communist incursion. "Do you support your president?" he asked. I answered, "He is my commander-in-chief, and I obey his every order." He translated a question from his wife: "How do you justify killing of women and little children?" I answered, "We never would willingly do anything so repugnant as that, but during wartime it's quite impossible to avoid, altogether, the loss of civilian life. That, unfortunately, is one of the abhorrent built-in features of war." They then returned me to my cell at the Zoo.

A couple of nights later, I was again taken out, but to a different location, a municipal building with a large meeting room, where I sat by myself in the quiet for a long time admiring the floor, made of beautiful inlaid tiles. Finally Dog came in and said, "Tonight you meet a western woman. She is very old. You must be talkative, but above all be very, very polite."

Indeed she was old. She introduced herself as Helga Cook, a British woman. I introduced myself again, very formally, while standing: "Major Larry Guarino, United States Air Force." Dog didn't like that, but screw him. She asked me to sit. She wore thick glasses and spoke through very crooked teeth. She grasped the pencil in her right fist and scribbled just a few words on each page of a pad, trying to keep eye contact so I wouldn't notice she was taking notes. After going through the usual crap about the "criminal" war (and there was no doubt she supported communism), she extolled the virtues of the socialist system as though it were heavenly. "Americans are very afraid of the word communism, aren't they?"

"We could say they are apprehensive in that connection."

"Yes, Americans aren't ready for communism, not just yet anyway," she said with a crooked grin. Continuing with her lecture, she then pointed out that the Vietnamese had "correctly replaced God with science." Thinking about all the filth I'd seen in the country so far, I couldn't get excited about the V being a technically and scientifically oriented nation. Mrs. Cook departed after she had taken Evelyn's home address and said that she would "get in touch to tell her how well off" I was.

These events with Burchett and Helga Cook took place in March, 1966. Later in the month, Dog gave both Ron and me our second letters from home.

My letter told me that Evelyn had moved from her mother's place on the Jersey shore to Cocoa Beach, Florida. She wrote about the complications of the move. Before dismissing me, Dog said, "Your wife doesn't ask about your treatment. She is much more concerned about her *things*! Her home and her furniture are very important to her. Someday, we too will have all those things."

"For the sake of your family I hope that you will have all those things, but I do not think that in your lifetime you will see that." I said that as gently as I could; I felt sorry for him, knowing that his people would never enjoy the good life as we know it (and have taken it for granted). So many of our people have lost their way and do not appreciate our freedoms and the material things that are available to us.

In the latest interrogations, monstrous threats were woven into the discussions. Rabbit and Dog used the line routinely. They said their treatment of me depended entirely upon my attitude, and how well "I was able to get along." Should my attitude reflect resistance to the authorities, then as punishment they would keep me prisoner, even after cessation of hostilities, for twenty years, or even for my entire life.

When I asked how they could do this, since I was known to be a captive, the answer was always the same: "We don't give a damn what your people know or believe about you. We can do anything we please! There is *nothing* that your country can do! You think because your country is big and rich, they can tell us what to do? Your country is nothing! We, and we alone, will determine whether you should be kept here to pay for your crimes, and if you should be allowed to live! I repeat, there is *nothing* your country can do!"

These threats, or others with the same gist, were made not only to me, but also to most of the prisoners through the years, as we all resisted the efforts of the QZRs to exploit us.

In the first week of April of 1966, we heard that Jon Reynolds and a couple of others in the Pool Hall building were being starved because they would not give biographical information. Bob Purcell talked the situation over with Jerry Denton. Bob figured that he could get up into the attic, scoot across to the very far end of the building where Jon was, and punch a hole in the ceiling near the spot where the electric light wire went through. Even when it was explained to me, I couldn't visualize how Percy could climb up to the high ceiling, open an access panel, and get into the attic. But the irrepressible Purcell did it, and dropped food and water down to Jon and the others for at least a week before he decided it was too dangerous. A few days later, the V put the hungry men back on regular rations.

The V tried to make it appear that there was a popular movement for trials, stemming from the people themselves, which we knew was a crock. It was a long-range, carefully orchestrated proposition to test outside reaction should they decide to move forward with public trials for us. According to them, it was not without precedence, and they pointed out the legal and historical examples of the sentencing of Nazi war criminals at the Nuremberg tribunals immediately following WWII. Ron and I figured the threat was "scare tactics," but the Vietnamese had special reasons for keeping the possibility of trials in the news for our friends and families back in the United States. The V knew very well that the western press would report this story as big news.

During the period when we were pressured to write biographies, some prisoners who resisted were taken back to Hoa Lo and tortured until they agreed to write.

In the spring of '66 an interesting story passed through the walls. One of our pilots was shot down and captured by one of the minority peoples of the north, the "hill tribes." The pilot had a rather serious injury and received very little medical care, probably because there was little or none to be had. He was kept in a hut, in a small village, for several days, and during that time all of his clothing, including his boots, was taken from him, with the exception of his undershorts, which were badly torn.

The captors were able to see the pilot's sometimes exposed genitals, and they were astounded. Inasmuch as Vietnamese men are much smaller than the average male westerner, their reproductive organs are also much smaller, comparing more in size to our six-to-eight-year-old male children. The pilot involved was (so we heard) particularly well endowed.

He noticed that he was getting a lot of gaping visitors and began to fear that they were thinking of maiming him permanently. At night, there were meetings by the campfire, and people came from surrounding villages, literally from miles around, to view this phenomenon! The pilot feared the worst. The ethnocentricity and nomadic life-style of these minority groups restricted them to their own group, and therefore the bloodline may have run a bit thin over the years. Maybe the American pilot—big, strong, with fair skin—was a welcome stranger. An enemy to be sure, but a man from out of the sky, a man of great accomplishment and from an advanced society. What was there to lose? So they brought a lovely young woman to the pilot's hut, and by sign language informed him they wanted her to have his child. The pilot could not (and would not) do their bidding, not only because of his painful wounds and his debilitated condition, but also because he feared that once the deed was accomplished, his genitalia might be amputated and mounted on a stick in front of the tribal long hut, for viewing by generations to come! It was a story that was probably embellished, but brought a chuckle or two into our grim existence.

In addition to the spreading of their propaganda by way of the printed news and the radio system, the Vietnamese now used one of the bare cells in the Pigsty as a reading room. There was another in the "Library" building. A couple of prisoners would be taken and locked into these reading rooms and told to read pamphlets, books and magazine articles containing the views of countries that supported them, from Russia and Eastern Europe to Africa and Cuba.

A new junior officer shared the library responsibilities with Dum Dum. We named him Spot, because he had a white spot on the left side of his chin. Spot took Ron and me to the reading room and told us to read, then discuss the books and articles between us. We did that, and agreed that the level and quality of their propaganda pitch was ludicrous. As we talked, we saw the two duty guards saunter by the open shutters of the side windows. Then the door opened. Standing there was a former turnkey, and another fellow who had already earned the reputation as a mean s.o.b., even though he had only been in camp a short while. He reminded us of the typical wise guy who hangs around the local drugstore looking for trouble. He handed his rifle over to the other guard, who was noticeably fearful. Then the Hipster walked in slowly, speaking in his own tongue. He was giving us a chewing out for talking, and he had appointed himself to punish us. Ron stepped back, and the Hipster stood squared away with me. I saw it coming. Blocking his first blow, I danced around the cell while he threw a lot of wild punches. Surprising the hell out of Ron (and me even more!) he didn't land a single punch! Ron hollered, *"Bao Cao!"* (the approved method of calling for the duty officer). Spot showed up in a flash and demanded to know what was going on. We told him we were following his orders to discuss the reading material. The other guard must have given the same story, and damned if Spot didn't take our word and let us off without punishment! Spot was probably severely criticized later for going against one of his own, because thereafter no Vietnamese ever took any American's word for anything. We were always wrong and punished "according to the mistake." Ron tapped the story to the guys in the building, praising my boxing ability and my surprising agility.

In April, a surface-to-air missile (SAM) site near Hanoi was hit, and the V were torqued off and became very vindictive toward us. From then on, whenever the bombs came close, we became kicking posts.

In May, they came around and gave us about a fourth of a cup of coffee, then opened our shutters "to help you to hear better."

They played tapes of the battle of Dien Bien Phu. The guards patrolled to be sure we were sitting and listening intently, as we had been instructed. They were going to teach us Vietnamese history whether we liked it or not. It was reminiscent of the early days of Castro's takeover of Cuba. His troops and police had to insure that all citizens were listening to his six-hour tirades against imperialism and his extolling of the new socialist order.

Groucho, our crabby turnkey, was very suspicious of us. He knew we were up to something, but he couldn't nail it down. We had found about a dozen brass washers on some window hinges that had been left in place after the windows were replaced by steel bars. We played "pitch a penny" on a blanket to break up the monotony when we weren't communicating through the walls or just talking between ourselves. We had also torn apart a propaganda book and drawn a chessboard. We used the washers and pieces of paper as chessmen. Whenever we heard the door opening, we quickly threw the stuff under the bed boards until the guards left.

One day Groucho caught us. He pretended to lock the doors, waited about five minutes until he figured we had gotten underway with our "dark schemes," then suddenly burst in on us. He grabbed the chess set, crumpled it, threw it up on the boards, and jumped up and down on it, screaming. The scene was out of Rumpelstiltskin. Groucho was like the angry dwarf, jumping up and down in rage and frustration. He was probably yelling something akin to "You stupid Yankees, don't screw with me, I'm way ahead of you." No other punishment followed, though we weren't sure what rules we had broken. Maybe the one that we were only supposed to sit and "ponder our crimes."

Groucho was very consistent in his attitude and methods. In June, a squadron of F-105s came to the outskirts of the city to bomb an oil storage tank farm. In the middle of the bombing I received an urgent call from Mother Nature. Crawling out from under the bed boards (our required position during raids), I dropped my drawers and sat on the *bo*. Groucho opened the shutter to look in. He couldn't believe his eyes. His look could have meant, "Look at that son of a bitch taking a crap during all this bombing." He probably thought my attitude was gross insubordination, but I felt the bombs were friendly and wouldn't hurt us. After that, we were all issued shirts with black numbers painted on the backs.

Once again Groucho brought us coffee. Standing there in front of the door, he broke into what was supposed to be a great big smile. He showed two rows of broken and dirty teeth and made a sound like, "huh-huh, huh-huh-huh." We thought it was an act that he was ordered to perform for us. Ron looked at me and said seriously, "Larry, I think we're in really big trouble. Something is up." The Box continued on about the "people's demand for the air pirates [us] to be brought to justice," and informed us that in an oil tank raid, pilot Murphy Neal Jones had been captured. Jones was one of my pilots at Itazuke, Japan, in '63 and '64, and I was sad to hear that he was joining us.

The sixth of July was different. We were made to bathe at the wrong time and were hurried in everything we did. The guards looked in on us often, with somber expressions. At two P.M., they fed us greasy cabbage and a banana. "Ron, I think you're right, there are some strange goings-on today. Maybe they are going to take us to some kind of an exhibition." Ron answered, "Yeah, and I think *we* are going to be *it!*"

The guards came with strings and made us tie on our rubber clogs and told us to take our little washrags with us. We heard trucks driving around the camp perimeter road. We were taken out, blindfolded, to the trucks. We slipped the blinds and tried to identify each other, but there was so much excitement, between the chatter and the guards telling us to quiet down, that the only name I caught was Jerry Coffee. After a short ride, we were in a public park. We were off-loaded and made to sit on a blacktop road. It was dark by then, so they removed the blinds, and the Rabbit started his spiel.

"Now today you will see the hatred of the Vietnamese people! Now I give you final warning! Do not look to the left, do not look to the right. . . . Do not look at any Vietnamese in the eye, or it will be very dangerous for you! We will try to protect you, but if our people want to kill you, they can kill you! We will not harm a Vietnamese who tries to harm you. Many have lost their children or other relatives to your bombs. They are angry! Again I warn you, do not look around, only look down!" We were shackled together in pairs, about forty-eight of us, sixteen from the Briar Patch, and the rest form the Zoo. We walked toward a small traffic circle outside the park. Alongside each prisoner, on either side of the column, were guards with fixed bayonets. The city police were supposed to support the soldiers and keep control of the crowds along the route.

The two POWs up front, Bill Tschudy and Al Brudno, were followed by Risner and Alvarez. Ron was on the right side of the column, with Bob Shumaker in front of him. I was on Ron's left, shackled to him, with Smitty Harris directly in front of me. A Vietnamese with a megaphone was acting as cheerleader. When we hit the intersection, he raised his fist and started a chant, and the throng responded as expected. Ron said, "Right on cue!" They started out slowly, but the yells quickly picked up in volume and intensity. I thought at first that it was a propaganda stage play for the world to see, and that the party had complete control of their people and we were perfectly safe. However, after about five minutes of the march, I thought, "If this show was phony, they forgot to tell the guards about it." *They* were scared shitless! The guards walked hunched over, bayonets carried very low and outside. The people started screaming for our blood. The streets and the sidewalks were jammed with humanity crying and pulling out their hair. Complete hysteria set in. The crowd surged forward to beat at us with stones and rocks. Bottles flew, and the guards ducked. Later reports said that over two hundred thousand people were in the streets, and I believe it. Amid all the shouts in Vietnamese, occasionally some familiar words were heard in English: "Yankee, you die," and one that *I* could dig, "Mockna-Mara sunna-bitch, Mockna-Mara sunna-bitch."

Groucho the turnkey was next to Smitty. Every once in a while, Groucho turned to warn my terror-stricken guard to be careful with his damn bayonet. Sure enough, the next time we got jammed up, my guard's bayonet jabbed Groucho's ass, drawing blood. Groucho turned and slapped my guard in the mouth a few times but had to continue on, clutching his wound. Along the route were flatbed trailers with huge spotlights mounted on them, pointed directly at us. There were dozens (maybe even hundreds) of Caucasian press people running up and down the columns taking point-blank mug shots.

I saw a man holding a seven- or eight-year-old child, whose fists were poised. He actually threw the kid over Groucho's head, and he landed right on Smitty, his little fists flailing away as he fell to the ground.

As we rounded a corner, people pressed in again; a civil policeman tried to hold them off. One woman hit Ron with her shoe. The policeman pushed her away, but she came right back, this time swinging at *him*. She picked the wrong cop to fool with! He swung a roundhouse punch from the heels and caught her right on her tits. You could almost hear the air go out of them, and his blow lifted her two feet off the ground. She took off on the run, rubbing her boobs.

We were being pelted with all sorts of stuff. Suddenly a Caucasian—a tall, skinny guy with several cameras hung around his neck—ran up to me, waving his fists and shouting, "You will be executed, you will be executed!" I gave him a short, uncomplicated answer: "Fuck you!" Occasionally Spot would order, "Look down!" We would obey for a few moments, but we had to look around. Spot was in a complete panic. This was clearly far more than he had bargained for.

We walked over a mile, maybe two miles like that before arriving at Hanoi City Stadium. There, the mob swarmed over us, totally out of control, as we inched our way toward the narrow, double-door opening. The pile of people stalled us even as the small opening scraped the hysterical mass off our backs. Ron and I, shackled together, were being pulled apart and were afraid our arms would be ripped off. There were people between shackled pairs, flailing at us. I looked at Ron and said, "Man, this is hell, ain't it?" My sense of humor had not completely deserted me. We finally managed to squeeze through the gates into the safety and relative quiet of the inside of the stadium. We sat on the cinder track while first-aid people did a little patch-up work on guys who were hurt. Our men up front had taken some bloody injuries. Our section, farther back, was pretty lucky. There were no serious injuries other than bruises from the stone-throwing and punches.

When we finally got back to the Zoo, we were almost glad for the safety of the stinking hellhole. Then the Rabbit put out a few more tidbits. "You have seen the hatred and the determination of our people. You now have two ways to go. First way: you can cooperate with us and help us toward our complete victory. If you do this, you will be shown humane treatment and our people will continue to tolerate you. Second way: you can continue to resist and support the U.S. ruling circles, and things will become extremely difficult for you."

After we were taken off the trucks, some prisoners were taken back to their cells; others were taken to torture cells for "processing." A few were tied, still blindfolded, to trees inside the perimeter road. The grass was high and the mosquitoes feasted on them, but that was minor. As the guards walked by, they would deliver a kick to the groin. Pop Keirn was left there for almost two days. His testicles were kicked bigger than tennis balls. Some of us, still shackled together, were left to sit in the road until two or three in the morning.

Those selected for the dubious honor of participating in the march seemed to be people the V thought were healthy enough to make the walk. The exception was seriously wounded Murphy Jones, who was exhibited to the masses on a rack-body truck. The march was the "spectacular occasion" for reasons that the Vietnamese would soon be explaining to us.

I was separated from Ron and taken to a quiz room by several guards, who roughed me up on the way in by twisting my arms high behind me and punching my ribs. Once in the room, they removed the blinders, and I bowed before four senior officers sitting at a table. One said, "Would you like to do that again?"

"I wouldn't like to, but if we must, we must."

"Do you know why we have done that?"

"No."

"For many reasons. First we wished to demonstrate to our own people that the U.S. agressors can be defeated. Also we encourage the American people to stampede to Washington to demand an immediate end to the war. Thirdly, we want to show you the determination of our people to encourage you to cooperate or . . . suffer! So what do you think?"

I spoke very slowly. "I understand your point of view, but I think you've made a mistake. . . . You are going to be very surprised at the reaction you get. . . . It's not going to work anything like you hope for. . . . You don't understand our people at all."

"What do you mean?"

"I mean that our people are going to be very angry at what you have done."

"No, your people are going to demand end to the war. And now what is your decision? Will you help us or not?"

"No, I won't help."

He made threats, discussed it in Vietnamese with the other officers, then said, abruptly, "You are free to go back to your room."

The next day, the walls came alive with speculation about what our government's response to the outrage of the Hanoi spectacle would be. It was like the days of ancient Rome, when returning armies paraded their captives and their booty before the people and their Caesars. Civilization hadn't come very far, but then who can speak of "civilization" while we still make wars upon each other? Even so, the world of civilized nations has its rules, even in warfare. We never thought the American people would take this one lying down, but time would prove us wrong, again!

Of course, I had some very definite ideas on the course of action that the United States should have taken as soon as the news broke.

The American people, and everyone else in the world, needed to be fully informed of this latest violation of Geneva agreements by the North Vietnamese, signatories to those agreements. Coverage in all media was essential to expose those violations, especially the public display, humiliation, and intimidation of prisoners of war for propaganda purposes.

That forced march called for retaliation with all available B-52s and tactical-strike aircraft. Preservation of lives, including ours, should have had low priority. It was necessary to show the Communists, and the world, that the United States could still unleash its power, and any atrocities against its people, like the Hanoi march, would invite that response without exception. To get respect in this world, you have to make people respect your power, and your willingness to use it when sufficiently provoked. Unfortunately, you can't get respect by being reasonable and nice, because "niceness" is interpreted by our adversaries as weakness, and that is why we are spat upon by so many other nations when we try to be nice, reasonable, and generous.

On the morning of the eighth of July, we heard tapping on the back wall, and so we asked the guys in the front cells to keep watch for guards. Ron got on the wall, then called me to say it was Pop Keirn and he urgently needed to speak to me by voice. To comm (communicate) by voice, it was necessary to press your lips to the wall and talk rather loudly. You also had to wrap a blanket around your head to muffle outside sounds, leaving an ear open to hear a warning that a guard was approaching. It was difficult, hot, and claustrophobic, and it was hard to think with a blanket over your head, but it worked.

Pop had just been released from a quiz room, where he had taken the rope torture right after his testicle-kicking experience. I could tell he was in very bad mental and physical shape, and completely demoralized.

"Larry, I want to turn myself over to you, as my senior officer, for future action. I think I did something very serious against our code. I signed a confession, admitting I was a criminal. I'll abide by whatever decision you want to make." My God, poor Pop! My heart went out to him. I think that at that moment, seeing one of my buddies so completely smashed in spirit, I was as totally unglued as he was.

"Pop, stop the bullshit! You haven't done anything wrong. You were just one of the first they picked on. There isn't a guy in this camp who isn't proud of the way you've conducted yourself. You've done a great job! We are next, and we're *all* going to get it. Do you think you can get yourself back together? [Two strong affirmative knocks came back.] Great, Pop. Do you think you can get some rest and make a comeback? [Two strong affirmative knocks on the wall.] Atta boy, Pop! Now get some rest!" I dropped the blanket and swabbed off my tear-soaked face. We messaged the news to the other guys.

That evening, the guards came for me, Ron, and Red Berg. They took us over to Hoa Lo and put us in separate cells in the Heartbreak Hotel section.

Chapter Ten

RETURN TO THE PATCH

1966

My cell in Heartbreak was interesting. There were two names on the wall I'd never heard before: Hillyer and Dupre. Later, when I got the opportunity to put these names into the system, no one else had ever heard of them, either. (Even after the war, none of the services claimed these names as missing in action.) Could they have been there since the days of the French?

My wall-banging finally got the attention of two men in the next cell. They were recently downed navy pilots Len Eastman and Paul Galanti. I taught them how to communicate using the tin drinking cup. It was a method somebody had just thought up: Find a good spot on the wall, place the bottom of the cup there, put mouth into cup, place hands tightly around rim to seal the gap, then speak into the cup. The guy on the other side puts the open part of the cup against the wall, one ear on the flat bottom, and listens. Works great—just like the "telephones" kids used to make.

After I finished briefing them on the prison situation, they told me that they had been interrogated and had done some writing. They did not take torture before writing, because Ken Spiker (another navy type) had either given them some erroneous information or they had completely misunderstood his messages. At that stage of the game, they probably misread the instruction. They thought that Spiker was quoting Risner, telling them not to take torture for phony confessions. They both felt terrible about it when they heard how many guys were going through the mill. They assured me they would take a much harder stand, now that they understood resistance was the game.

The cell door opened quietly, and a man stood there gazing

at me for several minutes. He was a different-looking person, whom I took to be possibly a Pakistani, because of the shape of his face, his eyes, and his color. But as long as he was in Hanoi, he was one of "them."

"Ga-reeno."

"Yes."

"I understand that you have many problems here. That you are always in very serious trouble. May I come into your room?"

"Sure, have a seat." He jumped up on the other cement bunk.

"I have been studying your case."

"Really?"

"Yes, and I think I know what your problem is."

"What is my problem?"

"It's your attitude."

"Honestly?"

"Yes, it's your attitude that keeps you always in trouble. You do not get along well here. If you like, I think I could help you very much."

"It's okay with me." I kept rolling with the character.

"So, from time to time, I would like to come to your room to visit with you, and to help you. Do you mind that?"

"Hell no, I don't mind, I can always use some company."

"Very well. I will see you soon." He seemed very pleased that we had gotten on so well. I never saw him again.

That night, carrying only our tin cups, we were individually taken across the street to a very large office building. We heard later it was the "Ministry of Justice"—a better name for it was the "Torture Palace." We were put into separate rooms. The one I was in had only the bare essentials: stool, desk, chair, and the usual low-wattage light bulb overhead.

Rabbit was the master of ceremonies. "Do you want to make your choice? Which way will you go?" I refused to pick up the pencil. Rabbit wasted no more time, because he was operating a torture production line. The guards shoved me to the floor and tied my arms behind me with coarse ropes. As I lay on my side, blindfolded, a guard jumped on the point of my shoulder while another hauled in on the ropes. Using my tin cup in the center of my back as a pulley, they exerted maximum pressure with the ropes, pulling my arms back until my shoulders nearly touched. The pain was excruciating, and my sternum felt like it would split apart. Through my thin pajama shirt, the friction from the ropes burned me. I cried out, and someone stuffed a wet rag into my mouth. The torturers were young and very enthusiastic, yelling and laughing as they went about their work. Again they jumped on my shoulders and tightened the ropes. I heard a loud snap in my right shoulder and felt the skin on my arms stretching, ready to split. . . . I didn't know my body could take that kind of punishment. They wrapped the ropes around me like I was a sausage about to be grilled. The ropes went around my neck, down my back, and tied either to my feet or my arms, I couldn't tell, because in just a few minutes part of me had gone numb from circulation loss. The pressure on my Adam's apple made it almost impossible to breathe, and I had to turn sideways to suck in a breath.

"You are the only one who resists us," the Rabbit said, lying as usual. It was impossible for him to tell the truth about anything, including the time of day. Even as he spoke, I could hear other Americans screaming from somewhere down the long hallway. I knew I wasn't the only one resisting.

Suddenly, I was left alone to flop around on the floor, still trying to turn my head to a position that would keep my windpipe open. "God, if Evelyn knew what I'm going through, she'd die!" Somebody jerked the rag out of my mouth and took off running. It must have been the "duty" rag, the only available rag in the building. They wanted to quiet down another Yank who was screaming louder than I. There was no feeling in my arms or hands, but my chest and shoulders burned in pain. I lost track of time. I started to rationalize my position. Last September, Risner had put out the word not to take so much punishment that insanity or crippling injury would result. How much was that? How do you know when you're there?

Then I asked myself, "Does the United States Air Force, or my country, expect me or want me to die this way, being pulled apart on a dirty floor in a faraway land? Is this what they want me to do, rather than write a stupid statement saying that I am a war criminal?" I figured that going out that way was dumb; it was time to knock it off. Rabbit came in again. "Do you surrender?"

"Yes."

"Good, now I let you stay there a while longer so next time you know you cannot resist us."

The son of a bitch left me writhing there. Finally he came back with the guards. They did something to me, maybe adjusted the ropes so I could breathe easier. They propped me up on the stool. More time passed, and I felt a worse burning sensation than before. I yelled, "Why are you doing this, I told you I surrendered!"

Rabbit said, "We aren't doing anything to you, we have already removed the ropes." Then I realized that the extreme pain was caused by returning circulation. "I still think you cling to your old ways, but at least you have submitted." Apparently getting a prisoner to submit was an acceptable victory to the Rabbit.

It took a very long time to feel my fingers, and my shoulders hurt like hell. A guard brought water for my cup.

"Now I want you make a concrete act, show repentance for your crimes, and write your true feelings about the Vietnamese people."

It was some time before I could hold or manipulate the pencil, and I wrote very badly. The letter was to the Congress of the United States:

Dear Congress,

During the past year that I have been a captive, the camp commander has given me the opportunity to study the four-thousand-year-old history of the Vietnamese people. I have seen that these poor people have always been exploited. First by the Chinese, then the French, and now by the Americans. And now I ask you to stop immediately and for all time the bombing of these innocent people. . . .

Rabbit came in with a tape recorder, accompanied by another Vietnamese whom I'd never seen before, a civilian who also spoke English. Since the writing was so poor (it looked like the writer had just been tortured), Rabbit figured a voice message might be more effective.

I spoke into the machine softly and extremely slowly. Rabbit interrupted. "What are you trying to do, are you trying to bush around the beat? You think I don't know what you do—you speak like you are in a church. Speak up! Like you are convinced! Sound happy!"

"No, no!" the other guy contradicted. "That's good, nice and slowly."

Rabbit's face turned crimson, and I realized that his comrade was far superior in rank or position. Rabbit was torqued and frustrated, but he kept his mouth shut and slunk out of the room. I felt I'd won the round because of the superior's inexperience in dealing with Americans.

In the wee hours, back at Heartbreak, I was rejoined with Ron. Our stories were almost identical. Red Berg tapped from next door, "God, I can't go through another night like that." I tapped back, "Sure you can, Red." My answer surprised me—it was as though I was mentally preparing to accept torture as a regular routine.

The next day we were taken back to the Zoo and told to sit on the floor to await their next move. Late in the afternoon, we were loaded into trucks to make the forty-mile-drive back to the Briar Patch camp west of Hanoi.

With the new arrivals, there were now a total of fifty-six Americans at the Briar Patch, and some had been there since December '65. The top man was Frenchy, who made his first appearance at the Zoo before Christmas of '65. Frenchy's chief interrogator and director of torture was the Bug. There was also a skinny old guy nicknamed Fish. He threatened a lot, but he wasn't too difficult to deal with. There were also a couple of young junior officers who handled details. Ron and I were put in building two, room A.

For the first few days, not much happened. The turnkey gave us hoes to cut weeds, and it was good to be outdoors for a change. In all of 1965 I had gotten only an hour outdoors. So in 1966, with the year over half gone, I had been outdoors for about two hours, and it was the same for everyone else.

The food was rice and pumpkin soup without pumpkin. Sometimes there was a second "dish," a couple of pea-sized pieces of fish, but mostly it was just fish bones, total quantity about four tablespoons. We got our two ceramic water jugs filled daily.

On July 25, Frenchy started a determined, all-out campaign to get us to pump out phony confessions and other propaganda items. "And now all of you must do all that you are told! You are cree-mee-nals! *Cree-mee-nals!*" he screamed. "It makes no matter what you say, what excuse you use, sooner or later you must admit that you are cree-mee-nals! You must also condemn the U.S. government and beg the forgiveness of the Vietnamese people! You have come up here to kill us! We have caught you red-handed! Now *you* suffer, as we have suffered, and our families have suffered! Also, now *your* families suffer! *You* suffer! *We* suffer! *Everyone* suffers!" Frenchy dearly loved that word "suffer"; of course everything he said was heavily accented, like "suffaire." This ranting went on for at least thirty minutes at a time, three times a day. Frenchy's tirades were always followed by the Communist version of the news, hot off the Hanoi wires.

One of the "quiz kids" came and opened the shutters (we were always kept in darkness in the lumpy-walled cells). He had trouble with English, mixing up his *p*s and *f*s, and he repeated a statement we'd heard before. "And now President Ho Chi Minh has declared that each of you must do his fart! You will answer these questions!" He threw in a pencil and paper with five ridiculous questions. He didn't care what we wrote, as long as we wrote. I can only recall two of them: "Do you admit you are a criminal?" and "What do you think of Bertrand Russell?" They wanted to train us to write when they told us to write.

We refused to write, so the Duck was summoned. Duck was a tall, skinny, high-ranking enlisted man. He had a long neck and ducklike face. He was all business, did exactly what he was told. He pushed up our sleeves and, with our arms behind us, clamped on a pair of adjustable ratchet handcuffs. He placed them high on the forearms, and then squeezed them right down to the bone, with so much pressure that he grunted from the exertion.

The cuffs burned like hell, cut us and numbed us, and after thirty minutes of pain, we scribbled some dopey answers. Ron said, "Wasn't that stupid of us to go through that?"

"Yeah, probably. They're trying to train us, and we're trying to train them."

From time to time, we were reminded that there was still a lot of war going on all around us. We could hear our aircraft on bombing strikes close by. Once in a while, they'd fly right over the top of us, pop their afterburners, and go straight up. "Thirty minutes from here to the Officers' Club—Ron, what a deal, huh?" One day, while washing at a cement tub in front of our cell door, we heard afterburners go, and looking to the north, we saw a ridge of mountains. The Red River flowed just west of that ridge and north into China. Up they went, about a dozen sleek silver F-105s, to about sixteen thousand feet, where they rolled over into a dive to hit whatever target they were after. The guards tried to force us back into the cell, but we dragged our feet and managed to take in the whole show.

The pilots in those beautiful airplanes were on a Rolling Thunder mission to a target near the Red River. Near the target they used a pop-up maneuver, coming in right on the deck to a positive checkpoint before tapping the burners for the fast zoom to a perch altitude, from which they commenced their dive-bombing run. I bet they scared the hell out of all the defenders around the target, because a fast, low approach just about guarantees complete surprise. They were flying pretty close to Hanoi, so you had to assume that they were in a missile-defended area. But according to the questionnaires we were getting, and from what the newest shoot-downs told us, our planes had had some neat new electronics installed. The pilot now got an instrument indication whenever his aircraft had been picked up on enemy radar. Even more than that, he got a reading when a missile had been launched, and he knew from which direction it would approach him. Once he got a visual sighting of the telephone pole–like missile coming, he could take evasive action. Must have been an exciting and fun game, once you got the hang of it. I wondered if the new pilots were like all other pilots I had known in the other wars . . . eager as hell to get up there and at the enemy. Or maybe some of them didn't relish getting shot at, and would rather be back in the States in the training command.

On the fourth of August they put me into building eight at the north end. I was in handcuffs, arms behind me, but the cuffs were not tightened. I sat all night getting "preconditioned." By then my body was so skinny and flexible, I discovered I could squat, step through my arms, and get my cuffed arms up front. Then I tapped to marine Howie Dunn and Lieutenant Shankel, USN.

I told Howie that in my last letter from Evelyn she told me that my oldest son was in flight training. Howie thought it was great. His message was, "Let's hope we can all do a good job up here." The next day, Duck put me into a little corner building on top of which was an unmanned guard tower. I was blindfolded and still in cuffs, and now they were tightened so I couldn't get them forward, but by rubbing my face against the wall I could slip my blinds and peek through a crack. I saw two guys shaving: Bruce Seeber, an old buddy of mine from Alexandria, Louisiana, and Rob Doremus, who was Bill Franke's GIB (guy in the back seat). The last I saw Seeber, he was tall, blond, and very youthful-looking. Now both men had deep, dark circles under their eyes, and they looked ten years older and like they had been through hell.

That night I sat on a little stool in a quiz room in building eight. It was pitch dark. Duck lit a couple of candles on the desk, and in walked the Bug. He sat down and raised one eyebrow, his face near the candle flame, trying to look fierce and threatening. Even though I thought he was a bit of a ham, he actually *did* look fierce and threatening. He said, "It is time you write the three things the Commander asked!" When I refused, he signaled the Duck, who squeezed down the ratchet cuffs until the cutting pain made me cry out. Then they both left me there.

Now in unbearable pain, unable to stand it or think rationally, I did something crazy—something that I found out Bob Shumaker and others also did: I ran across the room and smashed myself head first into the stone wall, trying to knock myself out. I didn't want to kill myself that way, but I think I wanted to be unconscious for a while, so maybe they'd let me alone. Then I thought, "If I keep banging my head this way, and live, I'll bring on a brain tumor." So as the irons continued to burn the hell out of me, and no relief came, in my frantic need to end the suffering I got another brainstorm. There was a deep hole chopped into the cement floor. It was about coffin size, almost eight feet deep. I thought, "If I jump off, and just catch my chin on the edge, I could break my neck. But then, if I miss, I might just paralyze myself or break my legs. Then I'd be worse off than I am now. To hell with that!"

Eventually, of course, the Bug collected the bullshit from me, and I wondered where they were going to store all that crap. They must have ended up with a warehouse full of it from all of us.

Several days later, back with Ron, we were both very weak and shaky. I felt my nerves were unraveling. My buddy Ron, the eternal optimist, was holding up better than I was. A news item on the Box let us know that Americans were fighting all over South Vietnam, and President Johnson said he thought the war could end in eighteen months or two years.

"What do you think, Ron?" Pasty-faced and worn-looking, he held out his hands, like a priest, and with eyes closed he whispered, "If so, we have a chance, we have a chance."

Torture and deprivation took their toll. We were losing weight rapidly, and our ribs stuck out like keys on a piano. Neither of us could have weighed a hundred pounds. Ron looked like a poor soul out of Buchenwald in World War II.

Airmen Black and Robinson tapped a pathetic query to us: "*Must* we take torture every time we go out?" Ron looked at me, the SRO, for the answer. I was too weak to tap an answer myself.

"Tell them to do their best and try to minimize what they do. Try to bullshit their way out of it."

That's what we were *all* trying to do. As far as I ever knew, not a single man of the fifty-six of us escaped torture. Every man got it at least once, and some of us over and over again.

Communicating was difficult, because our trips to the well for bathing or washing clothes were on a sporadic schedule, depending on how angry at us they were. We noticed about fifty extra guards around the camp. These men were not the half-assed interior guards we were used to. These were well-trained regular soldiers, infantry and artillerymen, by their insignia.

One day, Frenchy opened the cell door. He stood with three young artillery officers, probably on a boondoggle tour from a nearby antiaircraft artillery battalion. One of them spoke. Frenchy translated, as Ron and I stood at what semblance of attention our condition permitted.

"He wishes to know how long you have been here." We both looked terrible—heavily bearded, ragged, and obviously under-fed.

"Tell them eighteen months."

"They want to know if you regret your crimes against our people."

We weren't in the mood for that bullshit, and I answered, but softly, so the visitors wouldn't catch it if Frenchy didn't want them to.

"Camp Commander, please, tell them whatever you want to."

Frenchy acted real cool, and without changing expression he answered all their questions. When they departed, Ron said, "Larry, Frenchy likes you. I can tell by the way he looks at you that you have gotten on his frequency. I think he knows you're the oldest guy here, and he identifies with you. You notice he doesn't torture you."

"No, he gets the Bug to do it."

On the sixth of August, the Vietnamese started something new. Right after the morning meal, about 6:30, they came and tied our arms behind our backs, not tightly, but into a slipknot arrangement, so the ropes could quickly be tightened up. Everyone in the camp was tied the same way. Frenchy came and opened the shutters.

"And how are you?"

"Bad, Commander, look at us. I think you are starving us all to death."

"Yes, the food is very, very poor, I know. And now I think your fellows know that you are here [he was pointing to the

sky], but we are ready for them. So from now on, when you
hear *Kang Kang Kang . . . Kang Kang Kang . . . Kang Kang
Kang*, you quickly stand in front of the door and the guards will
instruct you.'' Now what the hell . . . ? Ron and I looked at
one another.

"Well, Lar, whatever this means, what the hell can we do
about it, anyway?'' Ron whispered.

"Yeah, no sense worrying,'' I answered.

That afternoon we heard some excited guards calling to each
other, so we climbed up on Ron's bed board and pushed the
window shutter just enough to get a peek-gap. We saw a soldier
carrying a fifteen-foot pole with a model of a helicopter atop
the pole. They were having a target-tracking training period,
that is, sighting their weapons on a model of a moving helicopter. So that's what it was all about! They were expecting a raid!
We knew then that our people must have our positions plotted!
We prayed for rescue.

Ron and I excitedly shared what we thought the rescue plan
should be. We figured one napalm run across the hill would
pretty well take care of the whole detachment, except for just a
few of the soldiers on guard duty within the prison compound.
A couple of flights, maybe eight birds, would be needed to quiet
the antiaircraft batteries, so the rescue choppers could come in.
It was really only a dream, but even so, it could have been done
fairly easily, and we spent a lot of time praying it would happen.

Suddenly, the gong was sounding: *"Kang Kang Kang! . . .
Kang Kang Kang! . . . Kang Kang Kang!"* We stood by the
door; the turnkey opened it, turned us around, yanked up the
ropes tightly, and made us leave our rubber clogs in the cell.
Barefoot, we were ordered out to the yard. They made us run,
out through the compound gate, in single file. There was a guard
between each pair of prisoners and between the Americans who
were in solitary, so we couldn't talk during the run-out. The
guards were the bayonet-wielding regulars we had seen brought
in to supplement the prison guards. Once outside the wall, we
entered a long narrow pathway that was cut into a hill, from five
to eight feet deep. There were soldiers and even officers standing
on the ramparts above. They ran us as fast as we could go. Red
ants swarmed up our legs, inflicting bites all over us. I was
quickly winded and stumbled badly, but still they rushed us on.
Once in a while they slowed us down, and we saw that some
prisoners were led off the main path to a smaller tributary. Again
we ran until Ron and I were also stopped and led off the main

THE BRIARPATCH

IN THE LOW HILLS
40 MILES WEST OF
HANOI

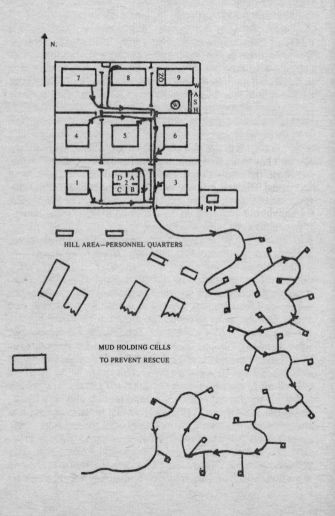

HILL AREA—PERSONNEL QUARTERS

MUD HOLDING CELLS
TO PREVENT RESCUE

path. We had gone about fifty feet down a side path when they stopped us. There was a four-foot heavy wooden door with a cement step and frame around it. A heavy iron bolt secured it. We were blindfolded, then pushed through the door. Once inside, we were standing in six inches of water. We felt around and knew we were in a hole dug out of soft mud. If a bomb landed, we would drown in mud. The Vietnamese were determined to defeat any rescue attempt, even if it cost them the lives of all their prisoners!

It's impossible to describe what despair we felt at that point. We stood there in the water, which Ron was convinced was urine, and believed our lives were over. The cream of the navy, air force, and marines about to go out, barefoot, drowned in the mud in a hole in a Vietnamese prison camp, instead of dying with our flight boots on in the cockpit of a fighter plane.

If we could have thought more clearly, we'd have known that it wouldn't happen that way. The first warning the V would get would be bombs or napalm coming in, probably at night. They wouldn't have time to think, let alone get us out of our cells and into those trenches—they'd be too worried about saving their own asses! The first guys we would ever see opening our doors would be our own army or marine compatriots! But who could think straight? The exercise worked in another way—it destroyed what little morale we had left.

We were kept in that mud hole for several hours before we were dragged out and returned to our cells. Later, we heard that a few POWs were kept there for days at a time, to soften them up for writing exercises. They finally took off the arm ropes on the twenty-ninth of September and quit the daily run-outs, so they must have believed the possibility of a rescue raid had diminished.

While I was at the Briar Patch, the dream of rescue was almost overwhelming. That our people must know our exact whereabouts placed that dream well within the realm of possibility. It was a good fantasy to occupy my thoughts.

The next few months were very difficult because the guards constantly tried to catch us communicating. They'd come sneaking around the extended outside walls and pop open the shutters. One of us was always on steady lookout for them, but even so, we had close calls. Catching us communicating gave them an excuse to torture us and get written stuff like "letters to your fellows in South Vietnam" or "letters to the Bertrand Russell War Crimes Tribunal." That was something supposed to be conducted by the rotten old bastard in the near future, in Norway according to the Box.

Once we actually saw a steer walk through the compound! "Maybe we'll soon get something decent to eat." They did slaughter it, and with no refrigeration, the meat had to be eaten right away. That night, when they brought our soup and rice, there was the unmistakable aroma of beef! We started salivating before the key even opened the door. Unbelievably, both our bowls held a fist-sized chunk of beef! We lit into it, and for the first time since the previous Christmas, our taste buds sprang into action. It was so delicious we couldn't contain ourselves, and we cried into the soup. "God Ron, this stuff actually has taste!" Mealtimes always raised our hopes. It was as though food comforted us, telling us that, "things aren't too bad—maybe something good will happen—it can't go on like this forever." When food becomes the only thing that picks your spirits up, you know you've sunk to the lowest level possible—animal survival. (Fortunately, we did not know we still had almost seven years to go.)

Ever since we became cell mates, to counter the despair we felt, Ron and I had established a nightly routine. Every night before we crawled into the sack we'd say, "Okay, what have we got going for us?" Then we would enumerate every possible positive detail, until we had a checklist of good things. Of course, during the worst of times, we had to dig pretty deep, even inventing things in our favor.

"Okay, let's count 'em up."

"Let's see, well for one, the American people have never liked long wars—it goes against our way of loving to do things in a hurry. Two, we can tell from the Box that fighting is going on all over South Vietnam, and with the numbers of men and the superiority of our equipment, it eventually has to go in our favor. Three, the V will anticipate that and try to negotiate peace while they can still make some gains at the peace table. Four, our wall neighbor, Ralph Gaither, says that they are discussing Laos at Geneva. If that's the case, then they've got to be discussing Vietnam. [Later Ralph admitted that he only "thought" Laos was being discussed at Geneva.] Five, they would already have killed us if they didn't think we were going home someday. Six, we noticed that they don't say anything about trials anymore. Johnson probably sent a secret message to Uncle Ho telling him to back off or else." Seven, eight, and nine were just as thin, but we reasoned that it all added up to plenty in our favor, and we went to bed with an improved attitude and a smidgen of hope for a better tomorrow.

There was no time outside the cells except for the walk to the well about twice a week. If we wanted to exercise, one of us had to walk on the bed boards, which were thirteen inches apart. At the end of the beds was a three-by-seven-foot walking space, three steps each way. One of my pastimes was to step on the hundreds of little ants on the floor, but when upset, those little guys could send up an acid cloud strong enough to make your eyes tear. Also, we had a huge ant colony—I mean tens of thousands of ants—living in holes at the bases of some of the wall lumps. Occasionally they'd come out and slowly migrate to another section of wall. We were very careful never to disturb them.

Sometimes, when there was nearby bombing or an alert sounded, they made us jump into a four-foot-deep hole cut under my bunk. We hated that, because there were many biting spiders in there.

The V also added a new wrinkle. In the moments the shutters were open, or during the rare outside periods, we saw that they were using a crude version of barrage balloons. They appeared to be from eight to twelve feet in diameter, tethered with ropes, not cable, and floated aloft at altitudes between two and six thousand feet. The turnkey told us, through sign language, that if our aircraft hit the lines or the balloons, they would explode. From the handling methods, we doubted if any high explosives were used, but it was good for Vietnamese morale. From our limited view, we sometimes counted as many as forty-two balloons.

Cruelty was the standing order, and our turnkey took every opportunity to make our lives more miserable, beating one or the other of us almost daily. During haircuts, he would use the clippers to grab the hair on the back of our necks and just rip it out, while the armed guards laughed. One day, I had enough. I jumped out of the chair and ran back into the cell. Thereafter, I called the key filthy names every time he opened the door. Finally he learned what the words meant, and beat the hell out of me. I had to back off.

He usually gave us just the end of a shaving brace, with the blade. One day while I was trying to shave, he decided to beat on Ron. We always took turns jumping in to distract the bastard, whenever he beat on the other one. This time, I knocked a stack of tin plates down to the cement, and the enamel on them chipped. That really honked him, because the plates would rust quickly. He turned to hit me, which gave me a very deep cut on my left thumb with the razor blade.

I couldn't stop the bleeding, so later, one of the decent soldiers opened the shutters and looked at it. He got a handful of grass and chewed it, put it on my thumb, wrapped a leaf around it, and tied it with a weed. It healed up beautifully, except that a hard piece of dirt or small stone had gotten into it, and soon I had infection draining around the thumbnail. It fell off, and because of my poor physical condition and malnutrition, it didn't grow back again for five years!

Peeking through door cracks, we could see the guards leading blindfolded, tied prisoners, tethered by ropes around their necks, up and down the gravelly hill, a version of blindman's bluff. One of the guys was George McKnight. They'd put him into a hole in the ground and placed an old wooden door over his head as he squatted there with ants biting the hell out of him. They were conditioning him for a writing exercise. They did that, and other terrible things, to Storz. He was left in rusty handcuffs for so long they couldn't be unlocked, but had to be sawed off. Having to see other guys suffer was one of the hardest parts of captivity for us, but there was nothing, absolutely nothing, we could do about it. To intervene required outside help, and there was none of that forthcoming.

At that time, we had one small comforting personal possession each—Ron had a set of rosary beads given to him by Father Ho Than Bien the year before. He also gave a set to Art Cormier, but had none for me, so instead he gave me a tiny gold religious medal. We were able to keep these things for a couple of years before they took them from us. Ron was good with the beads. I often told him that he missed his real calling, should have been a priest—he was just too nice a guy to be a fighter pilot! I meant that as the highest possible compliment. Standing there, with his now-silver beard, his black pajamas, holding the beads, he looked like he just stepped out of a monastery. "God almighty, Ron, how can these bastards hurt a guy who looks so saintly?"

"I don't know, Larry, they ought to know I wouldn't hurt a fly," he replied, looking toward heaven, giving me his most cherubic grin.

By late November, the north wind had picked up and it was cooling off fast, coming into the Christmas season. The harsh treatment eased off somewhat, because it was time for the V to swing into their "good guy" role. A few letters came into camp.

Evelyn made the mistake of mentioning that our son, Allan, was taking flying instructions in reserve officer's training at the University of Florida. Fish tried to get me to write to Allan to refuse to go into service. But it wasn't tough to outmaneuver Fish verbally, even though he put the press on me for a few days.

There was only one time that Fish came close to punishing me. He threw what looked like a business card on the table.

"And what does that mean to you, Ga?"

I picked it up, examined it, and realized that this joke card had been sent to a POW to pick up his spirits. It was a fun thing, but that wasn't the way the Vietnamese took it. The card read in part "Batman and Robin [the dynamic duo] combine with friends, the world over, to combat the forces of evil."

"Well, this card is meant to be funny." I said.

"Funny . . . What is funny?"

"Funny, you know, it's sort of like comical, a joke, meant to make people laugh." No change of Fish's stern expression.

The Vietnamese had no appreciation of western humor, jokes, expressions, or gestures. Fish obviously took the card to be some sort of black scheme.

Finally he spoke. "I tell you, Ga, I tell you what we think. We think it is an international Officers' Club. They want to get people together to oppose us, but we will defeat them all."

"I'm not explaining this very well," I said. "It's only an innocent attempt at humor."

"Humor . . . humor . . . Do you mean humoresque?"

"Yeah, that's right, humoresque." Lucky word! Fish's copy of *Webster's* probably went back to 1850. He had learned a brand of antiquated English. He dismissed me, shaking his head negatively. He still wasn't convinced, but he did let me off.

In December they started playing Christmas carols on the Box and also a song called, "Puff the Magic Dragon," which I'd never heard before.

Individually they took us up to a building on the hill near their own quarters. They told us we could sing or yell or make any noise we wished while in that room.

Al Brudno came over the Box with a Christmas announcement. First, he read the routines to be followed on Christmas Day, then added, "So you see, gents, the Vietnamese plan to make a BFD out of it—you know what that means, a Big Fine Dinner." Of course Al meant that as a jab, because in the language of fliers, BFD could only mean "Big Fucking Deal."

They replaced some of the cruel guards with some nice kids.

Once the shutters opened, and standing there was a young woman, so beautiful that we both gasped. She was a soldier carrying a gun. Her teeth were like white pearls, her skin was olive, and her eyes were huge, black, and wet-looking, like a young doe. The regular guards tried to get close enough to touch her accidentally. She asked about our families with sign language, and we answered as best we could. She was the first decent-looking woman we had seen in more than a year, and it was like a Christmas gift just to be allowed to stare at her for a minute.

Around Christmas Eve, the temperature dropped into the thirties. Stiff with cold, we huddled under our thin cotton blankets. The only hope we had was for a decent meal on Christmas Day, but even so we all got on the wall to say "Merry Christmas" to one another. We were a quiet, heartbroken group, but before we turned in, I sent my message to Art, Robby, Bob Peel, and Ralph Gaither: "There are a lot of places I'd rather be than here, but as long as I have to be here, I'm proud to be with a bunch of guys as tough as you people are. In the future we'll be proud . . . God Bless you."

Christmas dinner was turkey and vegetables, very good, but not much of it. We then went back to the usual routine as we faced 1967 thinking, "It's got to be better—it can't continue this way."

Chapter Eleven

A YEAR OF DUM DUM

1967

January was a miserable month. The evening meal was eaten in darkness, and it was a race to get it down, because huge cockroaches swarmed all over the food as soon as the dishes were set down on the boards. We had to peel them off our arms and shoo them out of the tin dishes. We got into bed right after eating and listened to the Box. Sleep was almost impossible, because of the cold. It also gave us a constant urge to urinate. From eleven at night, we were up every half hour. By morning, the bucket was brimming. Whenever we got up, we did twenty-five leaning push-ups against the wall to get our hearts pumping and improve our circulation. The hardness of the boards had callused our hipbones, tailbones, knees, and ankles.

The Box came on with a story taken from part of one of President Johnson's speeches. It said that Americans were fighting a "guns and butter war." Our politicians wanted our people to look the other way, pretend there was no war, believe that they wouldn't be inconvenienced by any serious involvement. This guns and butter attitude was, for me, the deepest stab in the gut yet—delivered by our own politicians!

"How the hell are we going to win this war unless we get the participation of every American?"

"According to the reports of fighting, this thing *has* to be wound up in a few weeks!" Ron said.

"Hell, these people still have airplanes!" I countered, "Whatever happened to the first rule of air warfare—complete air superiority? We should have powdered their airfields by now! We shouldn't even let them taxi an airplane! Our generals know that, but the politicians are into it. This damn thing will never end.''

Fish called me out for a bullshit political lecture. After about twenty minutes of harangue, he cocked his head sideways, assumed an angelic expression, and said, ''Tell me, Ga-reeno, do you like to come out here to talk to me?'' I thought to myself, ''Hell it's better than freezing my ass off in the goddamn cell, just as long as you don't try to make me do anything!'' So I answered, ''Oh sure, I don't mind.''

''Truly?''

''Yeah, truly.'' Can you imagine that little son of a bitch trying to romance me? Could he possibly have entertained the slightest thought that I swallowed any of the crap that he was pumping out? Then he sent for Ron, and now the two of us sat before him.

The hard-line position of Ho Chi Minh, which we'd heard a thousand times or more, was that there was only ''one legitimate government'' in South Vietnam, the ''sole legal representative of the people,'' and of course that was the National Front for Liberation, alias the Viet Cong.

Fish picked up the discussion about the Front, then said, ''Of course, that is wrong because there are two sides; that's the reason they are fighting.''

Ron and I looked at one another. ''Yeah, that's the way we look at it. We're sure glad to hear you say that.''

Then he says, ''And that word 'legal'—of course, there's *nothing* legal about it. It hasn't been voted on by anybody.'' We couldn't believe our ears. The North Vietnamese (we thought) were finally moving away from their uncompromising hard-line stand! They must be getting ready to negotiate! We went back to our cell back slapping, shaking hands, and just ecstatic about what Fish had just told us. It seemed to be incredibly good news.

We hadn't been back fifteen minutes, not even time to pass the news through the walls, when the shutter flew open and there stood Fish. With a big smile, he said, ''Let me make just one small correction, Ga. There is only *one* legal government, of course, and just *one* party!'' The shutter slammed closed. Another hard landing, right on our heads! After he dismissed us, Fish ran into Frenchy, who must have asked about the lecture. On hearing, Frenchy's reaction was, ''You dumb shit, that's not the party line!'' So Fish had to run back down the hill to our window and say, ''Listen guys, scrub all after 'Hello' and let's start all over again on that pitch.''

By mid-January, we were back to near-starvation. Sitting on the boards, Ron's thin shoulders were all bones, his buttocks had evaporated, and he could not have weighed over ninety pounds. He said I looked worse, but I couldn't believe that. No one but the V saw us, and later, when our health was way down, we were kept isolated, away from friendly eyes. There was only one time we may have been seen, when returning from the well. We had to stop in front of the window of Chuck Boyd and Jerry Driscoll, which was mistakenly left open. I couldn't even carry a small pail of water, and every few feet I had to stop to rest. My heart pounded so that Ron had to pick up the pail. I was holding up my shorts because I couldn't tighten them enough on my skinny body. If Chuck or Jerry saw us, they wouldn't have recognized us, even though Boyd knew me from the Philippines. He was the one who passed the news, in April of '66, that I had been promoted to lieutenant colonel.

Finally, I was so sick I couldn't get up anymore. Ron called for the medic. Fish also came down, as Ron was trying to pick me up off the floor. I figured it was all over for me, and really didn't give a damn. Fish sat on the bed and checked my pulse for a long time. Then they brought a can of sweet milk, a Russian product, to put on the rice. Fish got us about four extra blankets. Ron took care of me, and the V sent in extra food. In one week we got 150 bananas—they were the only things I could hold down! Several times they brought a bowl of sticky rice with chopped green onions. I couldn't eat it, but Ron did, and he also had some of the bananas. But even with extra food, Ron didn't seem to gain an ounce.

Late in January they took down the Boxes, and we realized that they were shutting down the Briar Patch, hopefully for good. We were moved back to the Zoo on January 27, 1967, into the building called the Library, where we got a larger cell, with two bunks. We had to adjust to the new cell. There were no windows, and the small overhead bulb was on day and night. The little daylight we saw came from a small crack under the door. Our cell was at the end of a long hallway. That night we lay on the boards, under our mosquito nets, listening to the latest reports of Vietnamese victories all over the south and shoot-downs of our guys over the north. Suddenly, the announcer went on another tack, talking about hopes for peace with the comment, "And to show the good heart of the Vietnamese people, we have given armistice."

Armistice! I bolted upright, wide-eyed.

"Ron, did you catch that?"

"Not sure, what did you get?"

"They said they've given armistice. I think they've quit the war!"

This seemed to dovetail with all the talk we had heard from the English-speakers back at the Patch. But as we prayed to heaven that what we thought we'd heard was true, we should have known that when the Vietnamese translate something to English, it loses a whole lot in translation.

The next day we banged the wall and got the attention of Ed Hubbard and Don Waltman. They had interpreted the broadcast the same way we did. They told us there was a new guy next to them, whom they eventually got to the wall and taught to communicate. He was navy Lieutenant Commander Richard Mullen. He was extremely happy to get in touch, because the V had been really putting the screws to him to get him to say that his mission was to attack schoolhouses.

On our other wall was Dan Doughty, an RF-101 pilot and a really fantastic guy. Dan spent literally hundreds of hours lying on the floor, peeking under the door to make sure the hall was clear of guards so we could communicate without getting caught.

Early in February, the V went on an inspection binge. The guys would bang the letters *RS*, meaning room search. All our gear was inspected, sometimes twice a day. We were worried about it, because we still had a pencil I copped. One day they came in, made us strip naked, then stand nose to the wall, arms extended as high as we could reach. It was freezing cold, and we could feel our fingers going numb as our hearts worked to keep up circulation. They carefully searched our clothing, feeling all the seams, trying to discover anything . . . a nail, a stick, a pencil, anything to show we were hatching a scheme. Ron had put the pencil in his mouth. They told us to stay against the wall, then left us for a while. Ron whispered, "Larry, we better get rid of it, they're going to find it." He quickly snapped the pencil in half and we each chewed a piece, swallowed the wood, and spit the lead into the *bo*. We had barely finished when we heard them coming back. We leaped back into position just as they stormed in, clearly furious. They made us bend over, poked at our rear ends, then turned us around and searched in our mouths, making us roll our tongues around to be sure we concealed nothing. Ron had outguessed them, in the nick of time! They were obviously disappointed at not having gotten anything on us. Finally they left us, and shivering with cold, we pulled our clothes on and fell on our hard bunks.

Several times we were quizzed by the Flea. He just talked and never asked us to do anything, but he was a show-off, with a definite flair for acting. When he came to the cell, the key would open the door and stand aside. Flea would stand there with his coat draped capelike over his shoulders. He wore an oversize pair of very dark sunglasses. He'd stand there silently a while, for effect, before speaking. He said his visit was to please the key, who had made a complaint about our behavior. This time it was because the key noticed that I was letting my mustache grow again. Flea made me shave it off, but occasionally I would grow it, just to test them, to see if I could get away with it. That annoyed Ron, because it drew attention. Unfortunately, I didn't always follow my own advice of "keep a low profile."

Ed Hubbard messaged that the guys were resisting going out to see delegations. We were dumbfounded. It was our experience that the V didn't ask—they simply came, blindfolded you, and took you wherever they pleased. I didn't think that was a problem, because they had never tried to get me to use their dictation and I could say anything that was on my mind, as I did with Burchett. However, there was a new twist to going out now—first they rehearsed the "selectee" on exactly what he was to say. If he refused, they would torture him until they were satisfied he saw things their way. But in all the years they did that, the results were mixed, and sometimes even made the V look stupid.

One day, Dum Dum came to our cell. It had been a year since we last saw him, and the change in his appearance was remarkable. He was thinner, black circles rimmed his eyes, and his complexion was sallow. He was a nervous wreck, and we surmised that the incessant bombing near Hanoi had made its mark on him. He was terrified, and we figured he was more likely to use us as his kicking post than ever before. We knew he didn't understand English very well, but he was able to fake it with his seniors, many of whom were not conversant in English either.

He explained that the reason he came to our cell was to find out if we wanted to see the Catholic priest on Easter Sunday. We got our wires crossed—Ron said "yes" and I said "no," so that night they came to get us and took us back to Hoa Lo. First we went into New Guy courtyard, then into the "Blue Room," infamous with the prisoners, who knew it as a torture place. After a while, the old Catholic priest, Father Ho Than Bien, showed up, with another Vietnamese we had not seen before to act as interpreter. There were some bananas and pastries on the table, and a drink of sweet tea. We had a long talk with the priest through the interpreter. Nothing was discussed other than family and religion. The priest came over to us and gave us absolution, and from his purse he gave us Holy Communion. While we knelt to receive Communion, the door popped open, and a guy stuck his head in and took our pictures.

I knew very well that whenever something good like that happened, the V were going to get some mileage off you, someway. But it was a trade-off, especially for Ron, who was deeply religious, and we both needed those brief minutes of comfort to calm our troubled minds.

In the next cell, Bob Lilly and Dick Bolstad replaced Hubbard and Waltman. They were very optimistic about our chances of release in the not-too-distant future. They gave us a lot of strong reasons for their opinions, which in our minds were both believable and helpful. The V probably put these two together hoping for a major conflict between them, from which the V might reap some benefit. They may have thought that Lilly would feel sorry for himself, and resent Bolstad for his capture, since Lilly was shot down in his chopper, in the act of picking up Bolstad. But the Viets were disappointed—Bob and Dick became very good buddies.

One day in late April, I was exercising by running in place when the camp medic peeked in and accused me of communicating by pounding my feet on the floor. He went running for Dum Dum, who told me that I was "very bad, Ga-reeno, you are always breaking the rules, and must be punished, now you get the irons!"

Slug came in with the portable leg irons, which consisted of a pair of heavy ankle braces held in place by a three-foot-long crossbar, three quarters of an inch thick. A padlock kept the irons secure. Slug told me to get up on the bed and spread my legs. He put the irons on, then securely fastened each ankle with ropes to the corners of the boards. He made me put my arms behind me and clamped them together with the standard pair of ratchet handcuffs. He also told me I'd be in them for ten days without letup.

Ron looked on helplessly, and when they left I said, "Am I being tortured for something they want?" Ron answered, "That's what we're going to find out."

It wasn't too bothersome for the first three or four hours, but then the sitting on my skinny tailbone and being completely immobilized started to get to me. My right shoulder, which had been injured in my previous session at the Torture Palace, began to pain severely. "I don't know if I can take ten days of this, Ron," I said miserably. It was just punishment—no confession, no writing, nothing but punishment.

Slug goofed off on me immediately. He was supposed to loosen my hands during mealtime, but he didn't, he made Ron spoon-feed me. Also, I was supposed to be freed for toilet, but I wasn't. Ron had to stick an enameled pot under me so I could pass water. I don't ever remember having to do any more than that.

At night it was impossible to sleep because I couldn't lie back, and when I tried to lie partly on one side, the cuff ratchets would accidently close up tighter. After three days of this, I was a wreck. I yelled for the guards to let me out, but Slug came and beat my face. I kept my mouth shut during his blows so I didn't lose any teeth, but he split my lips and knocked me senseless a few times.

Slug continued to refuse to let me out of the irons for toilet, so I started yelling again. Then I faked panic and passing out. Another guard came in to investigate. He grabbed me by the hair and punched my mouth. I flopped around, and he continued to hit me, but then he did go fetch Dum Dum, and they had to open up the cuffs and let me off the boards for two hours.

Dum Dum was meaner and more spastic then we had ever seen him. We heard that any time the air alert warning sounded, Dum Dum raced around the camp screaming hysterically, out of control.

By the fifth day, I was almost out of my head. Bob Lilly tapped the wall to ask Ron if he knew the secret of opening the cuffs. Bob said he would put a jimmy wire in Ron's soup bowl, out on the porch. We didn't know how Bob could figure which bowl Ron would pick up, because it was strictly a random selection from about ten bowls. Ron set a bowl in front of me, but I couldn't touch it, because often during punishment I wasn't able to eat or keep food down. Ron scarfed up both his and mine. I was watching him, in a daze, as he ate. Suddenly he stopped. "Listen Larry!" Slowly he moved the spoon on the bottom of the bowl. I heard a tiny metallic "clink." "I've got it!" he whispered excitedly, and dipped up a bent wire! The luck of the draw was one thing. The luck that Ron chose to eat both bowls of cabbage soup was another. If he hadn't, the precious jimmy wire would have been tossed out with my soup. He stashed the wire, and at the first opportunity got on the wall to find out from Lilly how to use it.

Poor old Dan Doughty lay there for two hours, clearing for guards, while Ron experimented with the cuff lock.

"It's so easy when you finally get the hang of it," Ron said triumphantly, and I felt the cuffs pop open!

He showed me how and made me practice until I could do it easily, even though my hands were behind me. Whenever I needed a break, I popped the cuffs, leaving the one on my left hand in place. Then I'd lay back, with a blanket over my chest and the skeeter net over me, to make it hard for anyone at the door peep to see what was happening. Our ears were sharply tuned to the unlocking of the door. I could quickly get my hands behind me and snap the cuffs back on, muffling the ratchet sound by coughing or hacking. Twice we nearly got caught, but it was sure worth the risk. Even though my hips were locked in position, I could sleep at night, with one eye open to be sure, but that was enough for some rest anyway.

On the tenth night, Slug came in and let me out of the irons. What a relief! We took it easy for a few days, and thanked Lilly, Bolstad, and Dan Doughty for giving us the clue on the handcuffs, and for doing all that clearing for us. I think my brains would have spilled out if it weren't for them, and Ron, too.

In early May, the camp radio came up with a message, and a voice, we hadn't heard before. The Box said that the camp authorities were directed by the Board of Officers at the Political Bureau (which was in overall charge of the treatment of prisoners) to give us this instruction. It came across like this, and I think I remember the exact words, because I heard it so often.

"The springboard of our policy of treatment toward the U.S. criminals stems from our standing policy of communistic humanitarianism, which is a system of education rather than punishment. We will take a reasonable time to educate you, because we know that there are many things that you do not understand. We expect you to listen attentively; we expect you to try to learn and to show a good attitude. If you do show a good attitude, demonstrated by concrete acts of goodwill, and you obey all the orders of the camp authorities, then you will be given a deserved treatment. . . . However, if after a time you make excuses and pretend not to understand, and you show a bad attitude, then you show us that you still cling to your old ways, and you will be severely punished."

This policy of "communistic humanitarianism" was not invented for the POWs. It was the standard policy of treatment toward their own people as well. Play ball with the party or get your skull crushed in! Here was a policy that held no promise for individual rights and freedom, the dream of all people, but instead threatened punishment for nonconformity to a dehumanizing system. It was a dirty blanket thrown over the heads of the people, to extend absolute control over them, depriving them of their individuality and eliminating personal initiative to strive for a better life. Ho Chi Minh's dictum was "criticism and self-criticism," a self-purging system. The main vehicle for application of the system was the monthly meeting, during which the men and officers were free to criticize one another, to point out each other's mistakes, wrong thinking, materialistic thinking, bad attitudes, or selfishness. The accused must always show a good and proper attitude, by admission of mistakes or wrong thinking and promise to make amends and conduct himself (or herself) in accordance with the will of the people. The young people, in particular, would willingly play the game because they wanted to be "on the team." Remember what the Nice Kid told me about "his man" being free to criticize him for allowing me to show bad behavior? Remember Castro's six hour speeches as he explained this same policy to his own people, while educating them in the new way? He was saying, "Listen, learn, and cooperate, or else!"

What we found out through the wall was that we were all pretending to have great difficulty in understanding the Vietnamese policy of treatment. After all, we'd tell them, we've lived in a capitalistic world all our lives; this new policy is so different from anything we've known, it will take a lot of thinking, and time. Like all programs the V started, they pushed it for a while then lost interest in favor of something else.

Later in May we were moved into cell number one of the Barn.

Dum Dum came to the cell and told us he was giving us another criminal to live with, but first Byrne must write, "I promise to permit the camp regulations," whatever the hell that meant. Ron looked over at me quizzically, and I said, "Write what the man says Ron, permit the regulations," so Ron said, "Okay, I permit the regulations." Dum Dum screwed everything up, and we never figured out how he lasted so long with his superiors.

Then the door opened, and standing there was Fred Cherry,

the first black American captured. We had a new and welcome roommate! We both knew Fred from the 35th Squadron at Itazuke. His left shoulder and ankle had been broken in the bailout from his F-105. His ankle appeared okay, but his shoulder had no muscle tissue left and looked like a wire clothes hanger. Fred told us that after capture he had had practically no medical treatment, and for months was out of his head. Navy man Porter Halyburton had been moved in with Fred, and it was doubtful if Fred could have survived without Haly's care. On the night of the Hanoi March, we had seen an ambulance come into the Zoo to pick up Fred for removal of more rotting flesh from his shoulder. They cut him, and scraped his bones, without any anesthetic! He was horribly treated by the Vietnamese doctors, who had also entered into the antagonistic spirit of the march. . . . They wanted Fred to suffer.

Ha, the turnkey, brought us a canary, and was disappointed because we weren't all that enthusiastic about having a pet. At that point, Ha's attitude changed—not because of the canary, but because the camp commander wanted to turn on some heat. The food ration was always meager and of very poor quality. Once or twice a week, we got a tip of the spoon with a meat paste, like liver; there was always the thin pumpkin soup and sometimes a kind of tasteless squash, like okra, that I called "slickum."

They dreamed up three new programs for us to participate in. Randomly selected POWs were asked to "send home for dollars." Ray Vohden tapped through that Dum Dum had asked him to do that, so we assumed that the V were starting an extortion program to get the families to send a hundred dollars a month, to "insure good treatment." But somewhere along the line, the V figured out that people on the outside wouldn't like the sound of that, so they modified it to twenty-five dollars.

Whenever any money came in from the families, the V "bought" candy, oranges, bananas, and so forth to give to the POWs. That is, they kept a book on these "expenditures," and actually told each guy how much he had left in his personal kitty! This was a move to get the prisoners to accept special favors, which was against the Code of Conduct. Most of our guys knew what was up, so after accepting some of it, they would throw it into the *bo* cans or try to pass it to someone else. The V managed to convince a lot of guys that "everyone was doing it." This program had been going on for a year before I found out that some of our people were actually getting goodies.

These men were as solid as anyone, but they just got sucked in and had a hard time backing out. When I heard they were dumping a lot of good stuff into the crappers, I sent out the word: "since it's already here, just hide the stuff in the wash area for someone else, it will be a welcome change."

The second program was for us to write a camp magazine. You can guess the kind of articles they wanted written—antiwar feelings, appreciation of the "new way of life," a reflection of attitudes that might make the POW a useful citizen (for the Communists) in the future. This one was so ridiculous that I couldn't believe that anyone would be drawn into it, but at Christmas of '68, during the "good guy holiday treatment," we were shown through a room with creations of the prisoners, mostly featuring art work, but sure enough there was a camp newspaper entitled the *New Runway*.

The third program was to "volunteer" to go downtown to work. In this one, you were supposed to repair damage in bombed-out areas of the city, so the Vietnamese people in the streets could see that there were Americans who repented their crimes, and in so doing they would be entitled to better treatment. I never heard of anyone volunteering for this one. By and large the V met with no appreciable level of success, so they set out to find out why. They didn't believe that each man figured out for himself that he didn't want any part of these deals. They decided to find out who was running the resistance against everything "worthy and productive" in their 1967 "springtime of victories."

Earlier, Ron had guessed that I was the senior man at the Zoo. The communication between buildings was limited, so we never knew for sure. Now Ron said again, "Larry I think you're 'it' again, you're the SRO."

On the fifteenth of August, Dum Dum called me out. "Gareeno, will you now admit that you are the senior officer and the ringleader against us?" I answered, "Hell no!" It didn't matter what I said. They made Ron, Fred, and me roll up our gear, then took us to the Hut, a small isolated building against the outside wall in the southeast corner of the camp.

The Hut was a three-room rectangular building. The rooms were joined by large archways, and the floors were big cobblestones. It looked like this building was originally used for carriages or livestock. Two rooms were usable; the archway to the northernmost room was blocked by French doors, nailed shut because the north room was damaged and the window was open, with a lot of bricks missing. We were put in the center room, which had three sleeping boards. The good one was against the nailed-up French doors, where lots of peep cracks allowed a view out through the broken window to the corner of the Barn. You could easily see the key or guards approaching the Hut from there. The front doors of the cells were still the old louvered French doors.

Slug put Ron next to the nailed doors. First he put on the leg irons, locked them, then tied them tightly to the corners of the board. Next, he used a set of hand irons to lock Ron's hands behind him. These were not ordinary ratchet handcuffs, but very small wrist clamps with no adjustments and no ratchets. Instead, they were screwed closed with a wrench. There was no slipping out of these cuffs except with a wrench.

The mosquito nets were in place and thrown up out of the way. Slug then fastened me into place. Two guards tied Cherry's feet down, but when they tried to bring his arms around back to clamp him, I hollered, "Don't let them do it Fred, don't let them!" A guard punched me on top of the head with the hand irons. I knew that they would shatter more of Cherry's already-splintered shoulder bones and cause more complications, maybe even kill him. The guard saw that Fred's arms wouldn't go back. I hollered again, but Fred just sat there dazed. I wanted him to scream his damn head off! The guard who was trying to tie him got pretty excited, but he saw that tying Fred wasn't going to work. Dum Dum came back to take a look, then had Fred returned to the cell in the Barn. Dum Dum said Ron and I would stay that way until we made a "full confession of our crimes."

Back in '65, we had each been given a Chinese folding paper fan, which on their inventory sheet was called an "antihot device." We always had them with us. They came in very handy; on that day we grabbed the wooden handles with our teeth and used them to jostle the mosquito nets until the sides fell down almost into place. Then, continuing to push with the fan, and blowing, we got the nets over our tied legs and feet, into a fair position, with perhaps just a dozen or so mosquitos inside. A lot better than feeding hundreds of them! It was a hot and miserable night, even more so when my net slipped off a hook and fell across my face, nearly suffocating me. There was no sleep for either of us in that painful position, and we were worn out when they came to let us out the next day. We were hoping we could catch some sleep during the daytime, but a constant stream of guards came to the Hut to make us bow and beat on us, so

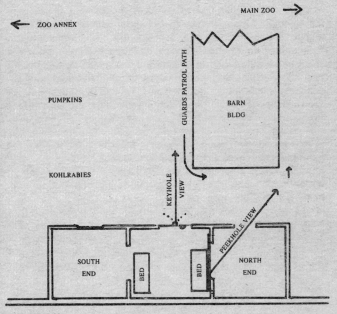

MAIN ZOO →

← ZOO ANNEX

PUMPKINS

BARN
BLDG

GUARDS PATROL PATH

KOHLRABIES

KEYHOLE VIEW

PEEKHOLE VIEW

SOUTH
END

BED

BED

NORTH
END

OUTSIDE WALL

THE HUT
OR GYM

N →

rest was impossible. And that was exactly the idea: to deny us sleep altogether. Late in the afternoon, the turnkey said, *"Lei va cuom,"* meaning, "Get in the irons." We would hear those words hundreds of times. Somehow we endured the first week, and every night we still managed to play our old game, "What have we got going for us?" Then we prayed together, hoping for a miracle.

We were dumbfounded when Dum Dum came and told us that we were to write letters home. Here we were being tortured, and he wanted happy letters to the home front! He dictated mine to me, but I didn't object, hoping that the letter might be one way to trade out of the irons. The letter was mixed propaganda, in stilted English, with questions that showed Dum Dum's real concern about how long the war would last. I knew Evelyn would see right through it, and so would anyone in the air force who read it.

To: Mrs. Evelyn Theresa Guarino
Address: 880 South Orlando Avenue
            Cocoa Beach, Florida 329311 USA
                                        21 August 1967
Dearest Wife Evelyn,

It has been a very long time that I am here, however I am in good health.

They like to compare the war in Vietnam with the American Revolution of 1776, and President Ho Chi Minh with George Washington, and they also have a Declaration of Independence Day.

Since coming here I have been given the opportunity to study about the country from 4000 years back to the present time and these people have certainly had their share of invaders.

Lately we hear a lot about the struggling black Americans in almost 100 American cities which involves 22 million black Americans and has caused the greatest racial issue of all times. If you can let me know the story particularly the issues of the visits of the delegations and how they are received at home and the effects of their visits and publicity on the war. Also, the story on the racial issue and how widespread it is and if you think the news indicates any effect on the Vietnam War. Other than that all is just fine.

                                        Your loving husband,
                                        Lawrence

The Box continued blasting us endlessly with all kinds of information about the behavior of our "fellow Americans" that our morale didn't need. A visitor to North Vietnam, a famous American doctor named Spock (whom we prisoners swore we would curse to his deathbed) made speeches about how appalled he was about America's involvement in the war.

Then we heard from a black guy named Stokely Carmichael, chairman of an organization called the Student Nonviolent Coordinating Committee, who made speeches telling all blacks to turn on their officers and go AWOL. His speech went something like this: "No Vietnamese ever raped my mother; No Vietnamese ever made my sister a whore; What's a nigger doing in Vietnam?" That was good for fifty replays. Each night after the Box news, they would play some melancholy violin music, followed by reading the latest list of Americans killed in South Vietnam. This list was probably gotten from the American press, or a recent copy of the army or air force or navy *Times*. Before reading the list, the announcer quoted Senator Gruening of Alaska as saying, "I do not think that these men have been killed in a just cause; I feel that they have given their lives on behalf of an inherited folly." That quote was used over and over for two solid years.

One of the most pathetic pleas ever was that of an American father who had lost a son in the war. He was crying as he made it. He said his son's life was "wasted" by our government, and that we were in Vietnam, a country with a culture four thousand years old, trying to tell them how to do things. Anytime you hear an American using that "four thousand year" bullshit, you know he has been fed a healthy dose of Communist propaganda. Senator Fulbright (to us "Halfbright") made the statement, too.

We were locked in irons for stretches of about sixteen hours at a time. During the day, camp personnel would peek in to tease me, "Ko-mander, Ko-mander!" They tried to make a difference between Ron and me, as if I were taking advantage of him because he was junior. Sometimes they would fasten me down, but they wouldn't tie Ron's legs, giving him a little break. This was supposed to indicate that I was the really bad one, and he wasn't so bad. Ron was made out to be the sucker following the orders of "the old one." They were always trying to split our loyalties, but they never came close to succeeding.

For a couple of days Ha was our turnkey. One night, he didn't tie my irons down. I thought I fell asleep, but Ron said I passed out. We had been sixteen days without sleep. I rolled off the boards, my legs went up and over with the irons, and I hit the floor head first. I was out cold, and Ron yelled "Bao Cao" for the guards. About an hour later, Dum Dum showed up and accused me of playacting. From then on, I was always tied down. Ha disappeared, and Ron said that he got the feeling that Ha kind of liked me, and that I had a strange effect on some of those people. I remembered that back in '65 Ha had told me with sign language that when the bombing stopped, he would take me downtown for drinks. He even went so far as to send the Green Hornet to get cigarettes for me! Although I didn't smoke, I faked it, just to get the cigarettes. Then I hid them in the bath areas for the guys who needed them.

It was our rotten luck to get Slug back as turnkey; he really loved to abuse us. Everytime the damned cell door opened we were beaten, sometimes by Slug, other times by five to fifteen guards, who took turns at us. That was when I learned that the old street expression "getting the piss slapped out of you" had real meaning. No matter how I tightened up before they started slapping me, or how I tried to keep my bladder empty when expecting a visit, when the beating started, the water ran out of me, and there was nothing I could do except pee all over myself.

The first chance we had gotten, early on, we had learned to punch holes between the bed boards with the leg-iron bar and rip our shorts and pajamas so we could manage to pee on the floor during long lockups. One night, Slug came around with a couple of guards and put Ron in the irons, but he didn't tie him down. Then he came over to me, and I tried to scrunch my legs up high on the boards, because I knew that later I could get some slack in the ropes if I could get away with the scrunch move. Slug screwed my hands together first, then yanked me way down on the boards, the edges of which were rotten, broken, and irregular, and felt like sawteeth eating into the backs of my heels. He put on the irons and tied them so my feet were off the ends, with the ten or twelve pound weights bearing on top of my lower shins. He was so proud of himself! Then he invited the guards to beat us. One of them did, but the other refused. Slug was annoyed with that, but the other guard was Nosepicker, and he pretended that his hands hurt him. The fact was that Nosepicker wanted nothing to do with any of us. If he saw us walk out to quiz he went the other way or turned his back, because he knew that if we failed to bow he would be forced to beat us, and he wanted none of it.

Soon after Slug and his cohorts left, my shoulder was paining me to the point where I couldn't hold back tears, and my hands were all blown up out of shape from the restriction of circulation. Ron gave me a couple of good tips. "Don't try to hold up your arms to save your wrists from being cut, let them hang and relax. Fall over as much on the right side as possible, and then try to put pressure on the painful area on the point of your shoulder." Sure enough, the pressure not only eased the pain, but it even numbed the shoulder area, providing me with some relief.

After a couple of hours, I felt like my mind was going to snap. The weight of the irons and the cutting edges of the boards had me in near panic. It was like the old Chinese water torture, one drop at a time on your head till you go nuts.

The overhead light had blown out, and we were in total darkness. Ron could tell I was at the very edge of sanity, and he said, "Wait, Larry, maybe I can do something." He got up, (he wasn't tied down) and slowly made his way the fifteen feet across the floor with his legs spread by the bar, the irons pinching his ankles. He groped for me and very laboriously squatted down at the front edge of the boards, feeling for the ropes. "I've got 'em, lemme see if I can work 'em loose." God, if the guards looked in right then, they'd have beaten him almost to death! But as Ron said, "What the hell can they do to us, torture us?" He worked and worked, and I felt the ropes loosening. I pulled myself back until I got my heels up on the board. Ron did that for me twice, because he knew if he didn't, I was out of my squash for good.

We had not seen one another in good light for a couple of weeks. One morning, the guards opened both doors, and I got a look at Ron's face. It was blue, a beautiful bright blue, from all the punching and beating he'd taken. He's staring at me, I'm staring at him. . . . We say nothing, each thinking that the other guy looks like absolute shit. A couple of old, beat-down, blue-gray-faced warhorses. We spared one another any comments at all.

About three horrible weeks passed, and still we sat in the dark, in irons—both physical wrecks.

"Okay, Ron," I whispered weakly, "let's go over it again. What have we got going for us?" A very long silence followed. Finally his faint reply came.

"I'll tell you what we've got going for us, nothing, that's what we've got—nothing, zero!"

Jesus Christ help us! That wasn't Ron talking, was it? He was supposed to be optimistic no matter what! What the hell was he doing? That was not what he was supposed to say! I was severely jolted by his role reversal; I never thought he'd turn around on me; I wasn't prepared for that. Long silence again . . .

Ron said, "When are we gonna confess? Let's confess something, anything."

"No."

"How long can we hold out?"

"Well, I'm gonna let 'em kill me."

"What? Why?"

"Because I'm the SRO, and they are not going to get a confession out of me! Screw them! But if you want to confess, go ahead. It's okay with me."

I had him in a bad spot. How is he gonna confess, if I won't confess? He hated it, and I didn't like it any better, but I wasn't giving in to Dum Dum, and my mind was made up. I cried, whimpered, suffered, and everything that goes with it, but I wasn't giving in to that little fink. I repeated my little chant over and over to myself, "Beat Dum Dum, beat Dum Dum."

"Your turn to pray, Larry."

"I can't pray; I'm all prayed out; I've prayed ten million prayers. We're not getting any help, and I don't think we'll *ever* get any help! He doesn't give a damn for you and me. He just worries about the real big things, like whether the world is gonna keep spinning, but he can't be worrying about us little guys. Anyway, Ron, you pray a lot better than I do, so you pray."

"I'm all prayed out, too."

So weary, so hopeless, nothing in sight. Dum Dum wants it all. No place to go from here.

Then came one of the strangest experiences ever . . . don't know whether it was a dream, a vision, or just a hallucination. I was alone in a curio shop where they sold fancy glassware and crockery—all was quiet except for a light tinkling of glass wind chimes in the background. I saw some fancy crystal cocktail glasses I admired, and, being impatient because no one was around to wait on me, I unzipped my flying jacket and slipped four or five glasses inside, then zipped up again. I continued to browse around the store. I saw a piece of Dresden, which I picked up to examine . . . suddenly I felt eyes on me, and turning around, I saw an old white-bearded man leaning across a counter, looking at me over the top of his spectacles . . . he wore a knowing smile.

"See something you like?" he inquired.

"Yes, this piece of Dresden, how much is it?"

"For you, nothing. Take it as a gift . . . why don't you just put it into your jacket?" I tried to do so very carefully, but there was a give-away sound. . . . He was enjoying it. Making my way toward the door, I began to experience great difficulty in breathing; the glasses under my flight jacket seemed to have expanded, and my jacket was very tight on me; the glasses began to crack against one another. He asked, "Don't you feel well?" I was now gasping and grabbing the counter edge for support. With concern, he said, "Perhaps you should get out for air."

"Yes, yes, I'm trying to. . . ."

Very weak now, I leaned toward the door, opened it, and fell to my knees in the street, still fighting for breath. Over the doorway to the store I saw it . . . a large golden bell. The old man said, "Hurry, Larry—hurry before it's too late—hit the gong, hit the gong!" Groping around with my hands, I picked up a large stone, and with the last of my strength, while I was on all fours, I threw the stone up across my shoulder at the gong and hit it. It went off with a very loud clang that triggered a blinding, golden light—then all of the light faded, and it became dead silent. The bell had disappeared, and hanging on the hook in its place was a set of rosary beads.

Then I was back in the cell, on the rack.

"Ron, are you here?"

"Of course I'm here."

"Can I tell you what just happened to me?"

I related the story to my buddy. He stiffened and said the hair on his head was standing straight up! The message had the effect of a ten-ton truck hitting us head-on. It was enough to kick us both out of the depths of despair, and back to the only solution there was for us in the whole universe. The solution was prayer and more prayer! It was the *only* thing there was for us. If we had had rosary beads, we would have snapped them until they wore out. Prayer, we found, *was* the secret weapon!

Finally, after a full month of beatings, irons, and cuffs, on the fifteenth of September, they moved Ron out and gave us a ten-day reprieve, during which we were supposed to write confessions. Then Dum Dum called me out and suggested that if I wanted to show a good attitude, I should write another letter to my wife. That seemed like another illogical follow-on, so I thought, "Well, he's giving up on the torture for a confession and moving into something else. Maybe the letter is his face-saver.''

Dum Dum dictated a letter, which I wrote in a way that Evelyn would immediately recognize was not my real handwriting. I wrote it in Dum Dum's English, exactly as he dictated it, which would be a dead giveaway. The letter was probably reviewed, censored, then thrown out by one of Dum Dum's superiors. It read, ''Dear Wife: I am feeling fine, and now you must answer certain questions. Number one: What is the extent of the antiwar movement in the U.S. of A.? Number two: What is the extent of the black movement, the black militant movement, in the U.S. of A.? Number three: How long do you think it will take the black movement to stop the bombing of North Vietnam?'' Evelyn never received this letter.

On the twenty-fifth of September, Ron was moved back into our cell. I was taken out to quiz and put on my knees all day, at bayonet point, for a confession. They did the same to Ron in another room. That night, I had a severe case of diarrhea. They put me only in leg irons, so I was able to sit on the can all night. The next afternoon, they took us both out to see the medic. He looked us over, tapped our knees, checked our blood pressure, then told us, through an interpreter, that we had brought it all on ourselves. It was the same medic who had accused me of communicating in the Library. When it was over, Ron looked at me and said, ''CFT, Larry,'' which meant ''cleared for torture.''

The next day we were taken out again, to separate rooms. This time, Dum Dum was wearing an automatic pistol in a side holster. The room had several open windows, and there were about twenty people, including women, looking in, watching the show. Dum Dum first sat at a desk, beside which was a heavy steel safe. The torturer was Chisel Chin, a little guy with a huge undershot jaw and big, ugly broken teeth. Chisel had just graduated from torture school. (He had been seen out in the yard, showing the other guards how proficient he had gotten in manipulating ropes and irons.)

Dum Dum already had me in the leg irons when Chisel put me through the rope torture. I didn't yell, and I'm sure that all the observers were very disappointed in my lackluster performance. In my weakened state, it didn't take much for me to pass out, so Dum Dum carefully watched an alarm clock on his desk. Every thirty minutes or so, they took off the ropes and irons, and he ordered me to stand, then walk to the far wall, probably to get some circulation going. When two guards hit me, my legs felt like jelly, and I fell forward on my head. There were noises from the crowd (in Vietnamese, of course), but I'm sure none of it was sympathy for me. They were probably saying, "Kill the bastard!"

They put me back in the ropes again, and as I felt myself passing out, I last remembered the steel safe coming at me. Again they took off the ropes by the clock, and as best I can recall, it was the fourth time around that Dum Dum pulled his pistol and slid a round in the chamber. Dum Dum wore a steel helmet and carried the gun during all air raids. "Now Ga, I give you one last chance to confess, and if you don't, I will kill you right now!" He put the gun to my lips, and I looked up and said in a quiet voice, "Please, do me a favor, will you?" Well, that really pissed him off, and he belted me a helluva blow with his gun hand, rolling me across the floor, and I heard the birdies again. My ears were ringing, and my equilibrium was crazy. Next thing I knew, Chisel was hitting me again. Then I found myself sitting in front of the desk. After giving me some time to clear my head, they roped me. Dum Dum lifted my head by my hair and said, "And now I give you an opportunity, you can speak, you can say anything you want, anything! Go ahead! I allow you to speak!"

Even beaten to a pulp, my mind seemed to be clicking out a message to me, like a damn trip-hammer. "Why does he want me to speak?" To me, the answer was clear. If I open my mouth, no matter what I say, I'll hand him a face-saver. Nobody else understands English. He'll tell everyone that, at last, I've admitted my crimes. Well fuck him, I'll keep my mouth shut. So I just looked down, and he must have hit me again, because when I woke up I was lying on the floor, with no ropes or irons.

On my way back to the Hut I fell several times, because I was so dizzy and rubber-legged. Slug beat me on the way back, because I did not bow to a Vietnamese standing there in the yard.

I was sitting in a stupor on the board limp as a wet rag, when Ron returned.

"Larry, what a time I've had! They put me through the ropes twice!"

"Jeez," I said, "you got a really good deal! I got 'em four times that I can remember." The two of us were in pain, exhausted, blubbering, as we embraced to comfort one another. Then we just sat there, tears running down our filthy, bruised, and bleeding faces, completely pounded to nothing, wondering when or if this nightmare would ever end.

The next day, about the twenty-sixth or twenty-seventh of September, they separated us again. I moved to Ron's sack, against the nailed-up doors, with the good peek holes, so I could get some view of the outside.

For the next two weeks there was just me, the boards, the leg irons, and the cuffs twenty-four hours a day. But I had the impression that the worst was behind me, and I laughed a lot. The door still opened at least four times a day, and I was beaten every time it opened, without fail. I bobbed around, even though I was securely tied, trying to make them miss, and they did miss plenty, but most of the time I was pretty goofy by the time they quit and left.

I had had duodenal ulcers since I was in China in 1944. In January of 1960, I had suffered a massive internal hemorrhage and was grounded. It took me a year to get the medics to do surgery. They removed most of my stomach and my vagus nerves, and in four months I was back on flying duty. The irony of it went through my mind as I sat, a bag of bruises and cuts, stretched out in the "rusties." If I had kept my big mouth shut, I'd be a fat little lieutenant colonel in the Pentagon, instead of being here in this miserable pigsty! How about that? . . . Nah, I decided, I'd rather be here in Hanoi than a guy out there without wings. (That kind of thinking proved the V made a total flake out of me!)

Dum Dum had a routine of stopping by every day at 3:30 in the afternoon with several guards to beat up on me. I naturally feared these visits, and by late morning a desperation, even a panic, started to overtake me, and then I would pull out the secret weapon. I prayed . . . and I prayed. I dedicated each daily Mass, the best way I could remember it, to someone's birthday—a relative, a friend, starting back from the very beginning of my memory. And the memory is amazing, because the names of almost every person I ever knew were recorded on my mind's tape, like a computer's memory bank. The kids in first grade, their names, where they sat in class. The same with my schoolteachers, every one of them! My high school football team, varsity right down to the subs, the numbers on their game jerseys, and yes, all the coaches and managers, too! It was all stored up there in my head, and I could recall it at will in my times of deep meditation. I prayed for everyone, and I know He heard me the same as in the days on the trip to Hanoi. He never left me, and He showed me how light the load could be. I dragged out my prayers for two, three hours or more. By the time that son of a bitch Dum Dum showed up, I didn't give a damn *what* they did to me!

A new procedure was added. Every day, before they started the beatings, the medic came in and yanked the shirt down off my left shoulder. Then he stuck a needle in me, probably something like dextrose to boost my energy or to keep me alive so they could continue the torture. Can you believe that? Later, Ron told me he was getting intravenous feedings while we were separated.

One day, Slug came in and gave me three delicious oranges. I couldn't believe my eyes. Then, an hour later, he threw me three more! I carefully saved the peels, because they would come in handy, since I had no toilet paper, no soap or toothpaste. These little deprivations only served to increase my anxiety. It's amazing how seriously little things affect you when you have nothing at all.

Then came the topper. At noon, in came Slug with a *meat* sandwich on a whole loaf of French bread! *Wow!* This was bigtime stuff! I counted the pieces of pig fat—there were fourteen. I multiplied that times maybe two hundred prisoners that were in the Zoo and the Annex, and guesstimated they used about twenty pounds. Twenty pounds of meat! They can't afford that—they don't *have* that much meat! What then? Simple. The war is over! This war is over! I got hysterical with laughter; I rolled from side to side even with the cuffs on. I yelled, "The war is over and I beat Dum Dum! The son of a bitch never broke me, and now he's trying to figure out how to take off the irons because he's embarrassed, and he knows I'll thumb my nose at him. Man, this is a howl!" Yeah. Sure.

On the tenth of October Dum Dum and Slug came in together. They made me kneel on the floor, still in leg irons, but without the cuffs. Dum Dum said, "And now, what did you do with the dagger?"

I didn't understand what he was saying. I answered that I did not know the man, thinking he was asking about a guy named Dagger. He repeated it several times until I realized that it was a phony excuse he had dreamed up for all the torture he had laid on me! He was accusing me of stealing a dagger from one of the guards! I never saw a dagger on a guard. Then he made me pull up a couple of cobblestones and dig in the soft black earth as if in a search for this nonexistent dagger. I went along with the bullshit, because I saw it was a game he wanted me to play. So I told him one of the guards had found the dagger and taken it back. He liked that! Then he told me to kneel and had Slug hit me four or five times across my face. "Now tell me your thoughts!" he said. Well, I didn't know what the hell he wanted now, so I gave it a shot. "I have been punished," I said using the past tense, hoping it was over. Then he jumped right in and said, "That is right! You have been punished, you are being punished, you will be punished!" Balls! "It ain't over yet," I thought wearily. Dum Dum left, and I got back on the boards, but Slug said, "Tsk, tsk, tsk," looking at the hand irons, then picked 'em up and threw them out the door. "Man, only in leg irons tied to the bench, a piece of cake, my hands are free." I stayed that way twenty-four hours a day until the twenty-third of November. Then from that day to the end of the following April 1968, I was only in leg irons at night. They stopped the daily beatings on the seventh of November.

Of all the cruel sessions that I went through up there, that stretch in 1967 gave me at least some satisfaction, because I felt that I had whipped my hated adversary, Dum Dum. He got a big fat zero from me, and I believed then, and still do, that besides the secret weapon, it was hatred, a total abhorrence of Dum Dum above all the others, with Slug a close second. But Dum Dum was in a class by himself in my book—the one man I truly hate! As for the others—Rabbit, Bug, Frenchy, Chisel Chin, and the Duck—I think they believed that the torture they inflicted on us was their job, and I don't feel any particular ill will for them now, but I hardly think that my opinion would be shared by my fellow POWs. I don't knock hatred. It's a necessary and useful emotion, and it can tip the scales in your favor when not much else will work.

Having suffered so much at Dum Dum's hands, and developing the special hatred I had for him, one of my favorite fantasies was sitting with him by the side of a swimming pool. I say, "Hey Dum, did you ever try on a set of these irons?"

"Hell no," he answers. "What for?"

"Why don't you try them on, just for kicks, so at least you can say you've done it?"

"Well, okay, but just for a little while." Then I help him into the irons and I say, "How does that feel?"

"Not too bad."

"Do you think you could swim with them on?"

"No Ga," he says, "I doubt it, I can't swim very well even without them."

Then I say, "Well at least *try*," and I shove him into the pool. He goes right to the bottom and he stands there, his hair is straight up, reaching for the top, with a lot of bubbles coming out of his mouth, and he is frantically pointing down at the irons. Then I say, "Well, *try* will you? Come on, flop your arms." Then I look at my wristwatch and I say, "Listen I've got a lunch date. See you later, Dum!" And I walk away.

My long encounter with Dum Dum in 1967 taught me that they did not, and would not, ever understand us. Their brains functioned on different frequencies from ours. If our brainwaves look like sine waves, theirs must look like inverted V's, and "ne'er the twain shall meet." So I gave up any thought of reasoning with them and declared them to be "just gooks." It was the first time I ever used that word. It was comforting to know it didn't offend the few South Vietnamese captives or Thai captives who were with us, because whenever they communicated with us they called our captors "the gooks," too.

The north winds were blowing again. There is something about weather cooling off in the fall that picks up a man's spirit. It was November, and I knew that the war wasn't over yet. I was still on a morale yo-yo. After months of starvation and torture, any slight improvement in treatment made my mind go wild.

Just getting a smidgen of decent food became a major "indicator." The first time they brought me a small saucer of steamed cauliflower with some lumpy tomatoes on it, I just knew (again) that the war had to be over! They wouldn't be giving me such delicious food if it wasn't! The cauliflower was cooked exactly the way Evy made it—a little garlic, black pepper, and a splash of tomato. To this day, whenever I peek into a pot on the kitchen stove and see cauliflower I say, "The war's over, Evy!"

Ever since being moved to the Hut, we dumped our *bo*s right out in the front yard. The women had planted rows of kohlrabies there, and the turnkey made me carefully pour the contents of the *bo* evenly across the rows. The plants responded well to the fertilizer. My daily pastime was to lean against the louvered window in the south room, look out, and count the plants. I also kept track of the leafy shoots coming out of the bulbous part of the kohlrabi. Occasionally, a woman would come by and trim the leafy parts away, and soon they would appear in the soup. They were bitter and tasted like rope. When the bulbs were ripe, they were cut, sliced up, and either cooked in soup or served as a second dish with some soy sauce and pig-fat grease.

It was nice leaning against the louvers in the quiet of the late afternoon. Such a comfort to be out of the irons! When the key said *"Lei va cuom"* at night, I really didn't mind the irons all that much.

I had been suffering badly from cold hands and feet—probably from injury from the irons and cuffs. Now nature came to my rescue. Every evening, I tried to walk some just before the key came to lock me in irons. I flexed my toes rapidly whenever I could. Then, one night, an amazing thing happened. I felt heat at the very tips of my toes, and slowly the intense heat moved through my feet and up my legs. I was never again bothered by cold feet! Guess it was some kind of a metamorphosis. To this day, my feet are so hot at bedtime I have to leave them uncovered! Sometimes the key wouldn't show up until noon to take the irons off, but I could hobble around with them by picking up the bar. In December it appeared that things had quieted down for the Christmas season, and the "good guy treatment" would start soon. One day, I heard the door opening. It was Dum Dum. He made a little speech about my bad behavior.

"Now we show you the good heart of the Vietnamese people again." He threw me another badly needed blanket. I was so glad to get it I would have kissed his ass if he suggested it.

"Sir, I think you have forgotten something. You know I'm still in irons."

"I know." He slammed the door in my face, proving once again that he was all heart.

I was continuously ravenous. Slug came in and told me I could have all the rice I wanted that day. He came back on the third trip with a couple of guards who didn't believe his story about how much rice I was forcing down. I ate a pile of rice eighteen inches high, then picked up every grain I dropped on the floor and ate that, too!

At that same time, there was a very good-looking young woman who replenished the drinking water daily. I watched her approach through the keyhole. She had great balance and precision as she carried a pole over one shoulder, with heavy water cans suspended by wires at each end of the stick. This type of labor is exceptional for developing the buttocks, and she sure was well developed in that department! She had a regular routine. As she neared the hut, she would set the cans down, tuck her shirt back into her black slacks, and then she'd adjust her boobs in her strange-looking bra. Finally, she'd come to the door, throw open the peep, and gruffly demand my water jug. Handing it over, my face at the peep, I'd watch her next moves. Keeping eye contact with me, she removed the jug top, held the jug at arm's length, and slowly poured out what water was left. With her other hand, she fondled or fluffed her long, shiny black hair. This girl was enjoying putting me on! I didn't need to be hit over the head to get the idea, and I thought, "Well, lady, maybe some other year, but not this one." Up to that point, my thoughts of sex had been very fleeting. Its place on the priority list of urgent needs was probably dead last.

Beginning Christmas Day, they let me sleep two nights in a row without irons. The food was excellent, and included a tiny piece of turkey! On Christmas night, they took me to the head-quarters building to a room that was set up with Christmas lights, decorated tables, and potted miniature tangerine trees. I sat on a chair in front of a long table covered with a green cloth. I was alone for a few minutes, so I downed a couple of glasses of orange liquor and stuffed some candy up my shirtsleeves. Then in walked Spot, smashed from the liquor, with three other junior gooks. He gave me warnings, as usual, about my "attitude and behavior," then poured me one inch of liquor and gave me three pieces of "socolat." After such a long year of mental and phys-ical torment, the arrival of Christmas was another terrible heart-breaker.

I figured out that, so far, I had spent thirteen years away from home, including eight Christmases. That equated to half my married life, and more than half the lives of each of my four sons! I had still not learned to cope by minimizing or eliminating thoughts of home and family, which brought self-pity and were debilitating to my mental well-being and ability to survive the situation I was in. If I had known we still had another six years to go, I probably would have wished Dum Dum had shot me. But that probability, thank God, never entered our minds—at least not then. We were sure our rescue was imminent—a matter of months, at best.

Chapter Twelve

RELEASES AND RESISTANCE

1968

Peeking through the keyhole daily, I could see the kitchen help carrying pots of soup and baskets of bread slung from their pogo sticks, heading toward the gate in the south wall. We had been hearing sounds of construction work going on over there since July '67, so it was just a matter of time before the Annex area of the Zoo would be filling up with new POWs. On several occasions I counted forty-eight loaves of bread, which meant that there were at least forty-eight prisoners over there.

The V had just started issuing bread again, having stopped it just before the Hanoi March. They put us on a rice diet because they knew we liked bread (bread, over the years, was the lifesaver). Then it turned out that cooking and carrying rice was too much like work, and it was a lot easier for the lazy bastards to have bread brought in from a source outside the camp. My Briar Patch group had a stretch of about two years of subsisting mainly on rice. Throughout our imprisonment, we ate fifty different grades and types of rice. I never knew how many growing seasons they had, or if any of it came from outside the country. Some of it was puny and small-grained, loaded with impurities like dirt and bits of gravel. Biting on the poorer grades of rice caused me to lose every filling I had in my teeth. Other grades tasted absolutely delicious to me, and I could never get enough. Even today, I can't get too much rice—I love the stuff! About Tet time, usually in February, the rice was always a very heavy, sticky type that needed something added to it to make it palatable. Every once in a while, I got the smell of what seemed like my back-home favorite, toasted pound cake, wafting through the Hut from over the fence. It was either the smell of the chow being carried to the Annex, or it was the guys in the Annex dumping their *bo*s. Everything smelled like food to me!

Whenever any of the guys passed by my cell, they would try to make brief remarks to encourage me, like, "Hang tough boss, you're doing a great job," but they only had seconds to do it, because the key or a watching guard was right on them with the fists.

One day, Slug decided to make my day more interesting. He opened the door, and in came a Thai prisoner named Sirion, pushing a wheelbarrow full of wet coal dust, which he dumped into a corner of the room. I talked to Sirion when we first moved into the Zoo. He asked me if I had taken off from Korat, and I told him that the Rabbit thought I had, but no, I took off from Da Nang. (It was possible that Rabbit had planted him, and I saw no reason to tell him the truth.)

Slug explained that I was supposed to compress the wet coal dust into balls about the size of a baseball. Then I was to lay them out on the floor until they dried out. The cooks would eventually have the coal balls picked up and brought around to the kitchen area, so they could burn them in the cookstoves. I was really excited about this project. I had something to do, I could produce something of value! I worked like a dog, squatting there in the corner squeezing coal balls. I did it very artistically, making the balls as round as I could, setting them down in very neat rows so they were easy to count. Now I could use numbers, work my brain in a new thought pattern, figure my production per fifteen minute period, by the hour, or by the day. I figured how to avoid lost motion and increase production. I was proud of what I was doing. At chow time, Slug came in with a guard to inspect my work. I had made 360 goddamn coal balls! He actually showed surprise and approval. They called in a few other guards to check out my pile of work.

My hands, arms, and feet were solid black, so I held up my hands and said, "Wash?" He shook his head. "No!" So I took the top off the *bo* like I was going to wash off my hands in piss, and that really freaked him out, but it did the trick. He took me to a wash area and waited while I washed up a little. When I wasn't working the coal balls, I still liked to check on the kohl-rabies. Some of the kitchen help showed up with the turnkey, and they criticized my coal balls. I was crushed! He said I had to make them twice as big. That threw off my entire work schedule. I had to refigure everything, and it made my production numbers seem puny. I was furious. Incredible how important those production numbers were to me then. But a project, any project, any activity, kept me sane.

There were lots of geckos in my cell, and also another type of lizard, very scaly and much heavier—about ten inches in length. They were not nearly as agile as the geckos, and neither could they hang onto the walls as well as their little brothers. When they were directly over me I really sweated, fearing they would fall on me. They never did, but they managed to dump on me regularly. One day, when I was near the well, one crawled into my freshly washed pajamas. As I carried the wash back to the cell I noticed the key staring at me. He took a swipe at my shoulder, knocking the wash (and the lizard) to the ground. Then he threw his heavy ring of keys at it and scored a bull's-eye, killing it. He looked at me, threw his hands up, and rolled his eyes back, meaning, "One bite from that beauty and you'd have had the schnitzel." That type of poisonous lizard has a very small mouth, and although it is a docile creature, it will bite to defend itself. The effect of its bite is about the same as that of the coral snake—the poison attacks the nervous system and very quickly kills.

A hot story came across on the Box that night about a U.S. Navy spy ship that had been caught by North Korea off its west coast. It went on to say that the U.S. ship was captured without a fight and towed to a port in North Korea. God, that made me think of the mission we had had out of Okinawa to protect ships operating in international waters off the west coast of Korea. I guessed that this time our friendly planes never got there in time to protect the ship, and there was going to be plenty of hell to pay for *that* screwup!

On the morning of the seventeenth of January, the door popped open and I was treated to a welcome sight. There were Ron and Fred, carrying their gear, coming to join me again! The first thing Ron said was, "Boy, have *you* got a head of hair!" I hadn't had a haircut, or shave, in months. As the day progressed, they told me their stories of what had happened since we were separated.

My voice was raspy, and lower in tone, probably from talking to myself all the time. I think Ron and Fred noticed it and thought I had gotten pretty weird. The continual punishment, the solitary confinement, and the hopelessness of it all had definitely gotten to me by then.

When Dum Dum sent Cherry back to the Barn the previous August, they had put him in leg irons, and his arms were tied behind him, though not tightly. But even that was too much of a restriction for his crippled and infected left shoulder. For anyone else, it would have been a minimal punishment, but for Fred it was more than he could handle. After just a few days, they removed the ropes. Then they couldn't decide what to do—he was in them, then out of them. Finally the gooks told Fred that in this process, a bone chip had floated into one of his lungs. They warned him that any unusual movement could cause the bone chip to kill him. From that day forward he was ordered to restrict his head movements, and also he was excused from any bowing. We tried to help Fred minimize his movements. We asked for more soap so we could wash his clothes. We also helped any way he needed with washing his body, mostly his back and his head, which were hard for him to manage. I blamed Dum Dum for Fred's plight. More fuel for hating him. Thankfully, someone with better judgment had arrived and decided not to mess with Cherry at all.

We had a couple of heavy discussions with Fred about race relations between colored and whites. Ron and I explained to Fred, in response to his questions about it, that most white people referred to Negro people as "colored" because they thought "colored" was the most polite term to use. Cherry, who said he always put his country before his color (and he was most emphatic about that), told us that "colored" was wrong—the only accurate term was "Negro," because that is what his people were. (Of course we in the prison camp had no way of knowing that the negroes of America had by then adopted use of the word "black.") Fred said that southern whites used the word negro, altered to "nigra," and that, he said, was "close." However, that word then was corrupted into "nigger," which became a derogatory term, so the people switched to "colored," to avoid any misinterpretation of their meaning. He told us about his family's origin in the West Indies, and his childhood on a farm near Suffolk, Virginia.

Fred had had no word at all from his wife, kids, or parents since his capture, and naturally he was very worried about what was happening to them. One night, as we sat quietly, I ventured a question.

"Hey Fred, do you like to sing the old spirituals, you know the old Stephen Foster stuff?"

"I sure do," he replied. "I love those old songs."

"Well, okay then, how about let's rip off a few bars?"

Then, softly, to avoid rousing the guards, we sang together,

"My Old Kentucky Home," "Suwannee River," "Old Folks at Home," and my own favorite spiritual, "Old Black Joe."

"I'm comin', I'm comin' . . . and my head is bendin' low, I hear those gentle voices calling, Old Black Joe." It was nice singing those beautiful old tunes together. It's sad that today there is a backlash against them because of what is presumed by some to be a put-down of the blacks. I believe, and so did Fred, that these folk songs are not only beautiful, but an accurate reflection of history.

The Chinese Lunar New Year celebration, Tet was approaching and the gooks weren't treating us too badly. At mealtimes Fred was getting some extra nourishment. Ron told me that when I was getting those pig-fat sandwiches for lunch, there were only four people in camp getting the extra food. He said the V must have thought I was going to cash out on them, and they better feed me to keep me around a while longer. "Yeah," I said, "Dum Dum needs me." We laughed, but hollowly.

The day before Tet, they brought us each a *Ban Chung*, a kind of holiday treat. This is an eight-inch-square, two-and-a-half-inch-thick chunk of the seasonal sticky rice. It came heavily wrapped in green banana leaves. *Ban Chung*, a highly spiced goody, has a large pocket in it, stuffed with a thick slice of bologna, some chopped nuts, and bits of candied fruit, and must have weighed four pounds! The meat was okay, and I don't think the stuff was spoilable, but its density made it tough for us to eat very much of it in one sitting, even though we were always hungry.

On the holiday itself, they played all their patriotic music and made an important official announcement: "On the occasion of Tet [1968] the forces of the National Front for Liberation have struck the biggest blows of the war to ARVN and U.S. troops all over the length and breadth of South Vietnam!" While the usual political bullshit filler went on, I predicted their victory claims would be astronomical. "Listen to this, guys! This is gonna be fantastic, I bet they'll claim over 150 airplanes destroyed and God knows what else."

Ron said, "Nah, they'll never have the guts to do that."

"Well, you'll see."

True to my expectations, the Box told us that the North Vietnamese government's claims, after the first day's action, were fifteen hundred aircraft "destroyed," twelve thousand Americans "killed outright," forty-five thousand ARVN "killed outright," and two hundred twenty thousand ARVN "disintegrated," whatever the hell that meant. If we added up all of the "killed outrights," the "disintegrated," the "hundreds of thousands of wounded and captured," the numbers were in the millions! By the end of the Tet action (we didn't know what the exact date was) they announced "aircraft destroyed" were over six thousand! We naturally "exxed out" the whole thing as pure horsecrap. I later learned they actually accomplished more than we prisoners gave them credit for. Although Tet was not a big victory for them, and it cost them dearly, they counted on the western press to make it look like a huge victory. True to form, the western press did.

North Vietnam very effectively issued a barrage of propaganda designed to convince the world that they had won the war. Applying our usual thin logic, we POWs figured that if the North was satisfied with that, then they would earnestly have to seek a cease-fire agreement, which would be followed by a POW swap or release. Hah.

Slug finally sent a guy to cut our hair. He shaved it right down to the bone, and Ron, now back in form as the eternal optimist, said, "This is the way they want us to look if we get released, like real criminals." He reached pretty deep up his rear end for that one! Weeks passed, and with them our hopes of cease-fire dimmed once again.

Some time later, the Box announced that a black American, an antiwar activist named Martin Luther King, had been murdered. Fred knew that Reverend King was loved by black people all over the country, and that his primary interest was to gain civil rights for blacks. A day later, Fred was taken away, with all his gear, to go to a hospital for surgery. We wished him well on his way out, and he seemed in good spirits.

In early April, the Box revealed that three American prisoners had been released from Hanoi on the Sixteenth of February. This news had been withheld from the rest of us for over six weeks. It was announced that they were Captain John Black and Major Norris Overly of the air force and Ensign David Matheny of the navy. The Vietnamese then played taped comments of the three which applauded our captors for the good food and treatment they had received and also sternly advised us to obey the camp regulations—all of which was a good stroke of propaganda for the Vietnamese.

I remembered that while I was in the Hut by myself the previous October and November, the V frequently played a tape featuring a POW playing a guitar and singing a song that, according to them, he had written. The title of the song was "The End of the War Will Surely Come Our Way."

It was twenty years before I found out that the POW had stuck his own words into an already written song to suit the occasion. The real name of the song is "Love Like Yours Will Surely Come My Way." The altered version of the song had no bad effect on me; in fact it was rather a hopeful tune, and I enjoyed it many times in my darkest days in irons. Reportedly one of the released men had written the words and sung the song.

We didn't know from which camp the three prisoners had been released, but we guessed correctly that they were "purees"—meaning they were pure, having little if any information on other POWs to pass to people outside. Everyone outside of North Vietnam was hungry for information, any information. There were many POWs whose names had never been released as captives. The Rabbit said, "We do not tell your side who we have up here. We keep them guessing. That is our tactics."

None of the statements of that group of released prisoners was damaging to me personally, although their praise of the supposed good treatment was patently ridiculous. The very idea of anyone being released gave some of us the faint hope that this could be a start for a complete exchange. More wild dreams!

On the twenty-eighth of April, Slug came over and told us to roll up our gear—we were leaving. He threw the leg irons outside in the dirt, and I took that as a sign that the punishment was over. We were moved into a back cell of the Pool Hall building where we had been at Christmas of '65. It was obvious that there was a major in-camp move going on. People were being moved every which way.

That night, the building was rocking; the communications going on between the walls was unbelievable. . . . Everyone was talking at once, either by tapping or through the cup. They wanted to know where I'd been and what happened to me. We discovered that since the summer of '67 there had been a hard push by the gooks to stop all communications between prisoners. It was quite successful, because for the remainder of the year not much communicating was done by the POWs, and consequently hardly any information had been moving.

Normally, when the gooks dislodged people from their cells a lot of apprehension went along with it, but not this time. This was a joyful reunion for everyone, and Ron and I were happy to be back in the mainstream of communications.

The next morning there was another shake-up, and Ron and

I were moved to the front, east end of the Pool Hall, room five. There were ten rooms, and twenty men, in the building, mostly O-4s (majors or lieutenant commanders) but also four O-3s (air force captains).

In just a few days we had excellent in-building contact, and we knew exactly who was in all ten of the cells. Many of the cells had been modified again, so that the cells whose windows had previously been totally bricked up now were bricked up only to just above eye level, leaving the top eighteen inches or so open for light and air. They were, of course, still barred and had shutters, which the turnkeys had the option of closing at any time. The cells at the back of the Pool Hall, and similar cells that never had had windows, still had only small air ports high off the floor.

We couldn't imagine why the Vietnamese put me, still the camp senior officer, right back into circulation and in an excellent position to communicate policy, and, if necessary, to direct resistance against them. Could they have thought that the severe punishments of '67 had permanently suppressed all organized resistance? We didn't know what to think, but it was a good move for all of the POWs, and we made the most of it.

Dum Dum was nowhere in sight; we speculated, and I fervently hoped, that he was gone for good. The interrogators in charge of our building were a skinny little guy called Zoorat and another called the Elf. I don't know why the name Zoorat, but the Elf looked like a little elf, and at any moment you expected him to hop up into a high corner of the quiz room.

Ron had told me a story that he had picked up just before he rejoined me. In August of '67, two Cuban officers had joined the staff of Zoo interrogators. One of them was a handsome, very tall fellow, mean as a snake, called Fidel. The other was a shorter, older man named Pancho. They had been put in charge of a group of seventeen Americans, to make "useful citizens" of them should they ever be returned to the United States. Fidel was important, because he had a sedan, with an officer as driver, at his disposal. The regular gook camp commander rode a bicycle. I wondered what this portended, but put it out of my mind.

Within a few weeks, we had established very effective lines of communications, an accomplishment of great pride to every man at the Zoo. Through the walls, we either tapped, or used the preferred method of talking into our tin cups. Building-to-building comm was done by standing on a bed, the *bo* can, or,

COMMUNICATIONS LINES

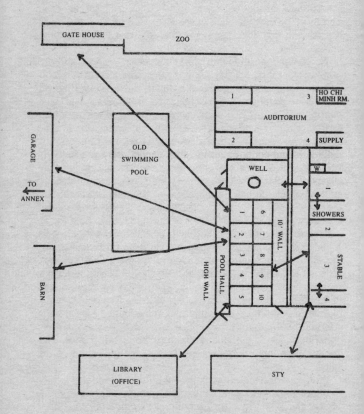

as Captains Ed Mechenbier and Kevin McManus did, by one man standing on the shoulders of the other, hand through the port, using one or two-handed flash-tap, whichever was easier. From building corners to guys out for exercise, it was done with a piece of paper or the handle of a toothbrush stuck barely out from under the door, using the flash-tap code. We coughed to get attention, and sometimes used a combination of cough, hack, and sneeze, in the tap code, to communicate. We dropped notes in designated areas, mostly near wells or the *bo* dump. Using the broom sweep for messages was very effective and could be heard over most of the camp at one time. Snapping our wet clothes in tap code for short messages also worked well. Communicating with each other worked wonders at keeping up our morale.

By accident, and fortunately for all of us, Mechenbier and McManus were assigned as dishwashers and *bo* dumpers for the Pool Hall building. As dishwashers, they sometimes had to wash the cook pots. When the soup was dished out, what meat there was, if any, settled to the bottom and was still there at pot-washing time. There were times when they could sneak some of this passed-over meat, and, considering the workload in their shoulder-stand communicating, they needed the extra food. In any case it would have been thrown out by the V, had our two-some not been there to get at it first. As *bo* dumpers, they looked for, and passed, the messages we concealed there.

Sometime in May, the Box said that the "two sides" had agreed to send representatives to Paris to initiate peace talks. At first, it was exciting news. Thereafter the Box gave us a weekly report. During the first few months, the sides argued about who was agressing whom, then who would sit at the table at the talks. As it dragged on, we knew it was little more than a forum for each side to make the other look bad on the world's stage, and nothing helpful to us would come of it.

It was during the last week in May that Ron and I were in the well area washing clothes when suddenly we heard a deep-voiced American boom out, "I know what you are doing, you're trying to steal my blood, you're trying to steal my brains, you're all spies!" We straightened up and stared at one another.

"Ron, I think someone's gone out of his squash."

"Sure sounds like it." Soon after, the key rushed us back to our cell, and we passed the word through the building via Spiker and Coniff in cell four. This was the main in-building comm route. Directly behind them in cell nine were Captains Mc-

Manus and Mechenbier. Any comm going to and from the Stable building had to go through them. For the next fourteen months, Mcmanus stood for hours every day, with Mechenbier perched atop his shoulders, flashing to the Stable.

It didn't take Kevin and Ed long to get the story. The SRO there was Major Jack Bomar, a navigator from an EB-66 electronic reconnaissance aircraft that had been downed in February of 1967. In the cell with Jack were eight men, but the number varied somewhat. One of them was air force captain Carl Corley. "Thrown in" is how Corley was put into Stable Three; he was literally tossed in, barely conscious, by Fidel, the brutal Cuban official, who was in complete charge of the Bomar group and other "selected" prisoners. One of the main sources of information about Corley was navy lieutenant J. J. Connell, who lived in the Gate House and was in position to see or hear much of the brutal treatment Corley got from the outset.

Captain Corley was shot down while in the backseat of an F-105F as a navigator, or systems operator. It was believed that before the Vietnam assignment, he had been a navigator in the Strategic Air Command. Corley's determination to resist giving any information whatsoever showed that he possessed a level of toughness equaled by few, if any, of the rest of us. Whatever his personal motivation, not only did he refuse to answer, but he hardly seemed to notice that he was being questioned, or tortured, and he wouldn't bow before them. This infuriated and embarrassed the Vietnamese, and they became determined to break him, or kill him in the process. It was reported that Corley was very suspicious of the several cell mates he had had in the first months of his captivity, so much so that he would barely answer any of their questions concerning his military background or his family.

J. J. Connell reported by voice to Ed Hubbard, now one of the Bomar group, that Corley's torture had originally been administered personally by the Lump. Lump's efforts were futile, so Corley was then turned over to Fidel. Fidel beat Corley relentlessly, both with fists and with three-foot-long rubber hoses, over a sustained three day and night period. This not only nearly killed Corley, it pushed his mind over the brink and out of the real world.

The entire story on Captain Corley took about a week to get to us, and it was passed throughout the camp. Fidel put Bomar and his group in charge of Corley. At the slightest provocation (or none at all), Fidel would beat Jack Bomar and some of the others with a fan belt for failing to produce positive results with Corley. Fidel kept insisting that Corley *had* to speak politely to him, answer all questions, and bow to him, and to all Vietnamese. Unhappily for everybody, Corley was out of his gourd and having none of it. He steadfastly refused the slightest cooperation with Fidel's demands. That brought on more furious beatings, in the presence of all of his cell mates. The most horrifying thing we were told was that when Corley was severely beaten in the face with rubber hoses, he didn't even blink! Jack and the others were getting frantic, because they were forced to watch these animal brutalities time and again. They feared for Corley's life, and their own.

Early on, several of Corley's cell mates were not sure whether he was insane or putting on a show of insanity—impossible under those nearly killing conditions. It took a few weeks for all of the men in Stable Three to conclude beyond a doubt that Corley's mind was indeed gone, and that no ordinary, sane human could possibly survive that kind of punishment.

It was terribly demoralizing to everyone. We'd witnessed, and endured, many instances of extreme cruelty, but this case topped it all. I sent out a message, which I hoped would help in some small way. "Keep this in mind, one of these days we'll be leaving this hole. . . . But these people will all have to stay here!"

Finally Bomar decided they'd have to force Corley to bow. He had his people hold Corley's arms and push his head forward in some semblance of the act. The Vietnamese finally accepted that and eased up a bit on Corley afterward.

Stable Three had a movie screen on the west wall, probably to test run films in the old days, when it was used as a film repository. To a person in Corley's condition, it could have given the impression of a special "setup," because he continued to accuse his mates of spying, stealing his brains, replacing him on earth with a space alien, and God knows what else.

Jack and his group, seeing that Corley was not eating at all, and afraid he would starve to death, tried force-feeding him. It was a mess. Several of them had to hold him down, stick a metal spoon sideways in his mouth, and pour soup down his throat. He'd spit most of it back at them, and all over the cell, but it was partly successful. After a couple of weeks of this, the Vietnamese must have disagreed with Fidel's opinion that Corley was faking, because they became slightly more cooperative in helping the group with Corley by providing a few things that Bomar asked for.

The V medic informed Jack that they were sending Corley to the hospital for electric-shock treatments. After about four treatments, Corley seemed to improve. He ate limited amounts of food without force-feeding, but when the gooks tried to force him to bow again or pick up his own food, he resisted, and again they beat the hell out of him. He slipped back into his shell of insanity. His condition then became the source of violent arguments among his cell mates. Corley eventually was seen leaving the camp again in an ambulance and was gone for several weeks.

You'd think that the extreme horror of the Corley situation would have drawn the group together, but it didn't. In addition to that problem, Bomar was having some conflict with Dave Duarte. Dave was a fighter jock who maintained that even though Bomar outranked him he, Duarte, should be in charge because navigators, such as Bomar was, were never given command authority. In short, Duarte didn't want to take orders from a navigator. They did not ask me for any decision in the matter, since Duarte finally gave in grudgingly to Bomar's authority. Had they asked me, I would have upheld Bomar's date of rank, and therefore his authority.

At that time, and indeed since its earliest days, it was a pilot's air force. Everyone else was deemed to be a second-class citizen, and that included everyone who wore a set of wings designating a crew position other than pilot. That meant that navigators, bombardiers, systems operators, gunners, and all nonrated (no aviation badges) personnel were in the same situation—no command jobs were made available to them.

From April to July of 1968, the Vietnamese informed us via the Box that a great battle was underway at a place called Khe Sanh. It was a victory for our side, but to hear the North Vietnamese tell it, you would have thought that the day-to-day battles were overwhelming tragedies for the U.S. Marine Corps. Having no other news source for comparison, we had no way of knowing the truth. We had no new shoot-downs coming in, and, with Johnson's order halting bombing north of the twentieth parallel, we knew we probably wouldn't be getting any more new guys for a while, if ever.

As North Vietnam told it, the U.S. Marine Corps and all supporting units were ''completely wiped out'' by June 1968. The real truth was that the NVA was totally neutralized. (The battle stories are among the most inspiring in marine corps history. Our guys really kicked some ass at Khe Sanh!)

Intermittently, some of the experiences of Major Jim Kasler

had gotten limited circulation throughout the Zoo. Ron and I, out of touch in the Hut, had heard none of them. Now we began to get much more information.

I had met Kasler while he was going through Command and Staff School at Maxwell in 1960. Jim was over six feet tall, and besides being one of the top fighter pilots of the U.S. Air Force, he was also a flat-bellied, low-handicap golfer, and was in many other ways a keen competitor. He had what could be called a Hollywood twin, for that reason I called Jim "the poor man's Gary Cooper." He commanded respect easily with his soft-spoken, easy-going demeanor. Like Risner, he was a Korean war ace. Major Kasler was coleader of the Hanoi oil tank farm strikes in June of '66, which were devastating to North Vietnam. Naturally the strikes got huge publicity in the papers and also in *Time* magazine. The V had their own copies of *Time*, and they were anxious to someday get their hands on Kasler. On the eighth of August 1966, Kasler was out in his F-105 on a search for his downed wingman, Fred Flom, when he himself was hit. His hydraulic-powered flight controls froze up, with the stick locking full back, right-hand corner. As Jim triggered the explosive seat-firing mechanism and went out in a high-speed ejection, the locked stick broke his upper leg in two places. Captured by hill people, Jim was taken to Hanoi. Even though he was in extreme pain from the shattered leg bone, which had been jammed up through the groin and into his stomach, he was interrogated by the V and tortured to give a confession. His X rays were shown to him, and they were so frightening that Jim was certain his leg would be amputated. The Vietnamese operated on his leg, inserted a steel bar, and wired the broken femur bones to it to hold them in place.

Dum Dum was appointed as Kasler's interrogator. Jim suffered equally from his shattered leg, and Dum Dum's torture for confessions and for him to send letters and tapes to U.S. senators imploring them to end the war. It was October before Jim was finally left alone for a while, to mend as best he could without further medical attention.

By January, the leg was so bad that Kasler felt he was dying for sure. Again he was tortured to do propaganda work, but still he refused. Finally, more surgery was done on him to try to stem the stinking infection that had set in. Afterward, he was taken back to his cell in the Pigsty, and had Captain John Brodak as his cell mate. The leg would lay wide open with green, sickeningly smelly pus steadily oozing out of it. It was Brodak's job to fan the flies away from the open wound. A short time later, Jim was moved into the Pool Hall, where he was soon accused of communicating, and again was tortured for acting as SRO and "forming resistance against the camp authorities."

Kasler got a little rest now and then, but even though the V were well aware of how bad off he was, they viewed him as a prize—a prize to be broken and used. In September, Chisel Chin put him through the rope torture, and although Jim had heard about how painful an ordeal it was, this was his first opportunity to find out for himself. Each time they did it to him, Kasler would yell that he capitulated, and the gooks thought they had him at last, but by the time they released him and got around to making him write or tape something, he'd tell 'em "Go to hell!" He was one incredibly tough man!

Kasler remembered me very well, and when I took over as SRO in '68, he sent me some warm messages of support.

President L. B. Johnson, or "Libby Gion-Son" as the V put it, had limited the bombing to the twentieth parallel, so the north was relatively peaceful. Also "Gion-Son" had announced that he would not seek reelection. Over the Box, Van Tuong said that "Gion-Son always spoke the truth, except if his lips were moving, then he was lying." In the case of President Johnson, I'm afraid I was practically un-American, because I thought the moving lip remark was kinda funny. By that time I was convinced Johnson was an uninspiring, indecisive person who would probably leave us up there to suffer forever and die as prisoners.

We got the terrible news that Robert Kennedy had been assassinated. That, along with the murder of Dr. King, made us wonder what the hell was going on back there in the States. We didn't know who would be running for the presidency, but we felt that whoever it was had to be better than "Gion-Son."

We were getting more taped American music, brought into Hanoi by the antiwar activists. One of the people the gooks bragged about was a guitar-playing folksinger named Pete Seeger. He wrote special tunes to fit the situation, usually mocking the administration and praising the clever ways of the Viet Cong. They played a tape of a black person singing antiwar songs, beginning with, "Ain't Gonna Study War No More." Joan Baez came across very often. Featured on her guitar, she sang, "All Those Lonely People," "Daddy is on my Mind," and others. I thought she had a nice voice, but she was, like most of the antiwar supporters of Hanoi, very confused on her personal values and stance.

Americans were, and are, free to be against the Vietnam War, or any war, free to think it, and to say so, but those who traveled to the capital of the adversary country, thereby giving aid and comfort to the people actively involved in fighting and killing our own Americans, were *way off base*. The very young draftees, who were required to serve, went because they believed it was their duty. They really had no choice, and neither did any of us career military officers and men. The choice to wage war is made by politicians, not soldiers, and it was wrong of those activists to victimize our fighting men, holding them personally accountable for the war and the conduct of the war. Those men believed in fulfillment of their honorable and legal obligation as citizens to serve their country—and that is a world apart from the "rights" or "wrongs" of war. So Joan Baez, beautiful voice notwithstanding, was, and still is, along with others of her ilk, considered a rotten and traitorous bitch by most of us.

In one of our rare lighter moments in the Pool Hall, we took a vote on the most popular tune. It was no contest. Far and away it was "Downtown" by Petula Clark.

We found out that my close friend, Major David Everson from the 80th Squadron at Itazuke, had been just a few feet away in the Library building for over a year without our knowing about it! Now David was in the end cell of the Pigsty, and we could see him and his cell mate Joe Luna by peeking out through a door crack. David had been flying a "Wild Weasel" aircraft, an F-105F two-seater, with Joe Luna in the backseat. The Weasel birds were set up to detect surface-to-air missile radar as soon as it was turned on. Once in range, they could fire a homing missile that would impact on the van or building housing the SAM radar, surprising a lot of Russian technicians. The SAM crews then figured a way to know when they were being stalked by a Weasel bird, and they would shut down the radar. In effect, the Weasel had done its job, because once the SAM radar was shut down it no longer posed a serious threat to any strike birds in the area.

The first time we ever heard about Weasels was in December of '65 when John Pitchford came to the Zoo, shot down while flying the Weasel version of the F-100F. That aircraft and its equipment and tactics were developed back at Eglin Field, Florida under Major Garry Willard. After bailing out of his aircraft, Pitchford, surrounded by enemy soldiers, was shot through the elbows while his arms were raised in surrender.

His wounds were only halfheartedly treated, and it was a long time between treatments. His arms drained from infection all the seven years of his incarceration, and even today, more than twenty-two years later, he is not much better off.

There was an occasional chuckle that relieved the misery of our existence. One day, we got the word from Cole Black's foursome in Stable One, that the Vietnamese women were making frequent trips to a small storage room at the back of the Auditorium building. From this little room, the women could look out at the POWs whenever they bathed, in a small secluded area at the west end of the Stable. The women must have heard about how Americans were hung compared to their own men, and they wanted to see this for themselves. They pressed their noses against the wooden louvers and enjoyed "peter peeking," while the Yanks washed off.

Fidel made the prisoners start a number of work projects. Some of the guys spent a long time building an outside oven for the production of bread—it never worked for even one loaf. Other guys behind the Pigsty dug trenches and filled them with water, to raise fish for food. They had tiny minnows in the ditches, on which Fidel pinned great hopes for a fish harvest. Norlan Daughtrey presented himself as knowledgeable about raising fish. One day, when all the minnows happened to be facing the same direction, Norlan told Fidel that fish do that just before laying their eggs! Other prisoners were put to work making wooden shoes, but nothing worked out well enough for Fidel to take any big credit.

Early in August the Box announced that three more American prisoners had taken an early release. They were all air force officers, Captain Joe Carpenter and Majors Fred Thompson and Jim Low. All three were recent shoot-downs and had been kept over in the Plantation jail, from which the first releases had also been made.

None of us knew the first two, but many of us knew of Major Jim Low, another Korean War ace. Low was famous for being a nonconforming individual. In Korea, he was noted for breaking flight integrity to go off on his own in search of a MiG kill. He was a very capable man, but his lack of flight discipline very nearly got him court-martialed. It was decided that it was in the best interest of the air force to drop the case against him since he had recently downed his fifth MiG-15, making him an "ace."

We did not know the conditions of their release, only that it was against the Code of Conduct, unless they had been directed by their senior ranking officer to accept release, which was most unlikely. We heard their taped messages when they departed Hanoi with one of those so-called "Peace Delegations." Low said, "We expected fish heads and rice, and instead we got French bread." They all made the usual statements that everyone knew were hogwash.

There were mixed emotions when those three went home. Many of us pictured how it might be to go home, and entertained ourselves with the thought "maybe soon," but the war in the south was still raging, so we knew that realistically there was little chance for us.

During the summer, Fidel turned on Kasler again, trying to get him to meet a delegation "on the occasion of shooting down the three thousandth U.S. plane." Kasler refused to see anyone and threatened that even if he should agree to it under torture, then they'd be sorry they brought him before any delegation, because he'd never say anything they wanted him to say.

Fidel then began what turned into weeks of nightmarish, inhuman torture. He went at Kasler with fan-belt beatings, ropes, irons, and fists. Jim was knocked cold innumerable times; he had a busted eardrum, a broken rib, loosened teeth, and the skin was flayed clean off his buttocks. He also bled profusely all over his body, including his already-split leg! God only knows how any man in his right mind (and Jim was in his right mind) could take on and survive that sustained a level of animal cruelty. It was beyond our ability to comprehend. But, somehow, Jim withstood it, and survived with his sanity intact.

The last time Kasler saw Fidel, he was told that the V were going to take care of his leg. Then Fidel said to him, "You think you're pretty tough, don't you?" Jim didn't answer. Fidel produced a package of American Viceroy cigarettes and said, "Take a cigarette . . . just one . . . take some chewing gum. . . . " Kasler refused. Fidel said, "Kasler, you take 'em or I'll beat the shit out of you again." Kasler finally took them, just so he'd be sent back to his cell.

There were a lot of American heroes in Vietnam. Perhaps the experiences of the most heroic will never be known because they died alone, away from any friendly eyes. But for my money, of those men we know about, Jim Kasler is the greatest hero ever, and my hat will be off to him for all time. He should have gotten the Medal of Honor.

In August 1968, some of our guys noticed that the gooks were having some kind of celebration. It was a farewell party for Fidel! The gooks were thanking him for all his "good work," and that was the end of Fidel's two year tour in Hanoi! (In 1981, thirteen years later, the American syndicated columnist Jack Anderson wrote a column identifying our torturer "Fidel" as a major general in the Cuban army. He was a top favorite of Castro for his superspy work, and for his successful efforts in Central America.)

The Vietnamese are a very modest people, and in public men rarely showed affection toward women. Conversely, the men were openly very demonstrative and affectionate with each other. Also, as in many parts of the world, homosexuality is not that big a deal. In Vietnam, we saw frequent demonstrations of homosexuality. Watching the V from our peepholes, one day, I saw Rabbit embracing Spot, who had an unmistakable look of "purple passion" on his face. We assumed that a lot of the men were probably bisexual, but the women seemed to be very normal. It was also interesting to see how varied the POWs' opinions were on the subject of female beauty. I thought that Vietnamese women were pretty good looking, and I noticed that they did most of the real work, from menial kitchen tasks to soldiering and manning antiaircraft guns.

One morning, the peephole dropped open and there stood the water girl. Ron rushed over and picked up our two ceramic water jugs and passed them through the peep. We thought that she was very nice looking, with even, white teeth and a wide, well-shaped mouth. After she finished her rounds, Spiker tapped the wall to ask if we had seen her. We said yes. Spiker tapped, "Her name is Mugs."

"Why Mugs?"

"It stands for Miss Ugly Shit." Well, each man to his own opinion! Ron and I had probably been locked up too long—any woman looked pretty to us! One day, I was by myself in the bath area. As I stood there in the raw, the gate opened and a woman came in, pushing a big cook pot. I was supposed to wash it. She stared openly at my lower body, then gave me a big grin, showing red, betel-nut-stained teeth in a rough, red face. She had wide, flat feet, splayed toes, and even after three isolated years I had to admit I was wrong—there was at least *one* really ugly woman in North Vietnam!

It was mid-August, and the summer winds were whipping up into a severe tropical typhoon. It was the rainy season, and down it came. Through the closed and locked shutters we could hear the winds whistling through the trees in a sixty-mile-an-hour blow. On the second day of the storm we got only stale bread, with "sewer-greens" soup. After five days, the meal was the same, but the bread was moldy, and some of it had scores of dead red ants in it. Hanoi was at sea level and could easily have had the water supply contaminated because of flooding. Fortunately, they remained dutiful in boiling water and safeguarding the supply. We got a message through the wall that there was a veritable mountain of leg irons piled up alongside the Auditorium, just in case the camp had to be evacuated and all of us moved to higher ground, but it never got to that.

Things were not too bad over in Stable Three, now that Fidel was gone. Corley had responded somewhat to the second round of electric-shock treatments. He was not being force-fed; he was eating by himself—not much, but better than before. The guys with him were still jumpy and cross with each other. The one person who appeared to be the most compassionate where Corley was concerned, was navy lieutenant Larry Spencer. He and Ed Hubbard volunteered to move into a separate room with Corley to take care of him and to ease the pressure on the others, but the V refused.

The Stable guys sent me a message asking if it would be okay to try to get early release for Corley, since it was their considered opinion that he probably wouldn't survive without good medical care, which of course was nonexistent. I agreed with that, and came up with an internal policy on release for nine seriously wounded prisoners. I sent Norlan Daughtrey a direct order to volunteer to escort Corley home if the opportunity arose. Norlan, like Pitchford, had been shot through both elbows, and needed immediate care. He sent a message back that he didn't like it, but would obey my order should the opportunity ever present itself. I couldn't see any end to the war. Ron and I discussed it thoroughly and figured we had best try to get some of our people out if it was possible.

As the days stretched out into months and years, it seemed like we had been there forever. Our days began with the six A.M. gong. We rolled up our skeeter nets, folded up our blankets, and sat on them, fanning away the mosquitoes. The light was snapped off by a roving guard, and we sweated out the day, hoping something good would happen.

Mostly we stared out over the eye-level bricks, through the bars, at the daylight outside. When our cells were closed off altogether, we stared at the crack of light under the door. We were like bugs, always looking for light. When it looked like it might be a nice day outside, we would try to think of what our friends were doing back home.

"Bet Bill Craig is on a golf course somewhere enjoying himself. That's what I'd be doing on a day like this."

Ron replied, "On a beautiful day like this I'd take a ride with my family in my new station wagon. You know, I swapped cars about every two or three years. Cars kept me broke."

"Yeah, sometimes I wonder if anyone other than our wives ever thinks of us. Maybe they don't even know we're here."

Early one bright morning we heard the unmistakeable *flop-flop* of a helicopter's blades. There it was, coming right into our view, at very slow forward speed. It was a Russian chopper, and by far the biggest helicopter I had ever seen. Slung underneath, hanging by stout cables, was a MiG-17, the main fighter plane of the North Vietnamese Air Force. The MiG was being airlifted to a downtown maintenance dock for overhaul. An in-town depot would be nearly impossible for American aircraft to spot and destroy. Pretty clever!

After three years of confinement with little or nothing to fill the hours between interrogations, torture sessions, and propaganda blaring from the Box, any little distraction was welcome. Occasionally the Box would brag about some of the "People's Heroes" who had recently downed American aircraft. One of our guys was told by the Lump that even though their pilots were doing well against U.S. pilots, it was still very difficult for them to master the newer model MiG-21s. They were now accepting volunteer pilots from nations friendly to them. They had Russian, Polish, German, Cuban, and yes, even American volunteers, flying their planes. I didn't doubt that a bit. For the right price, mercenaries have always flown in wars. I'd like to think that the cause would also have to be right for an American to participate, but then again, you never know. Some guys have no scruples or conscience, and will do anything for the almighty buck.

Major Bud Day was the ranking man over in the Barn building, and, piece by piece, we got his interesting story.

Bud had been in command of the "Misty" detachment of F-100s at a small South Vietnam airstrip. These aircraft were two-seaters and the mission of the Misty unit was to act as airborne Forward Air Controllers (FAC). Their job was to detect enemy targets such as trucks, other supply vehicles, radar sites, enemy troops, and so on. Then the FAC could direct the strike aircraft in for the kill. When Bud was hit, he bailed out just north of the demilitarized zone (seventeenth parallel) breaking his right arm in three places, badly wrenching his left knee, and temporarily losing sight in his right eye. He was captured, and one of the V medics put a rough cast on his arm. That same night, he crept out of his bunker and managed to slip by a few inattentive guards into the woods. He managed to put a couple of miles between himself and his captors. Then, without warning, he found himself caught in the midst of a barrage of bombs from our own B-52s!

He woke up bleeding from his nose and ears, and vomiting. He managed to keep moving for several more days, but was weakening rapidly from hunger. He ate the few berries he found, and a couple of live frogs, until he came to the Ben Hai river at the DMZ. He was suffering terribly, as his wounds had become infected by then, but he kept moving and felt encouraged when he saw an American spotter plane, then a U.S. helicopter. He decided to slow down and rest, because being so close to freedom, he didn't want to make any foolish moves. His luck had run out. . . . He was spotted by two well-armed soldiers. He dived for thick foilage, but they got him—less than a mile from freedom!

On the way to Hanoi he was interrogated, then hung up by his arms when he resisted. Between his wounds and the torture, he was nearly driven crazy. When he finally had to agree to answer questions, he gave false information.

Bud was a rough and tough fighter pilot, and we were proud to have him in our company. He, too, sent me messages of support, which reflected his confidence in our POW organization and in me personally.

The Stable people's request for a release for Captain Corley opened up a Pandora's box of questions about the meaning of certain articles of the Code of Conduct. Exact meanings are difficult to nail down, because the Code is not written in very specific terms; there is some flexibility and room for interpretation in the application of the Code.

The Code of Conduct of the American Fighting Man came out as an executive order in 1955, signed by then-President Dwight Eisenhower. Because of the notoriety given to the brainwashing tactics of the Communists, and due to a small number of American defectors or turncoats during the Korean War, it was decided that more guidance was necessary to assure the correct conduct of Americans held by the enemy in time of war. The Code of Conduct for all members of the armed forces of the United States consists of six basic articles, as follows:

I

I AM AN AMERICAN FIGHTING MAN. I SERVE IN THE FORCES WHICH GUARD MY COUNTRY AND OUR WAY OF LIFE. I AM PREPARED TO GIVE MY LIFE IN THEIR DEFENSE.

II

I WILL NEVER SURRENDER OF MY OWN FREE WILL. IF IN COMMAND, I WILL NEVER SURRENDER MY MEN WHILE THEY STILL HAVE THE MEANS TO RESIST.

III

IF I AM CAPTURED I WILL CONTINUE TO RESIST BY ALL MEANS AVAILABLE. I WILL MAKE EVERY EFFORT TO ESCAPE AND AID OTHERS TO ESCAPE. I WILL ACCEPT NEITHER PAROLE NOR SPECIAL FAVORS FROM THE ENEMY.

IV

IF I BECOME A PRISONER OF WAR, I WILL KEEP FAITH WITH MY FELLOW PRISONERS. I WILL GIVE NO INFORMATION OR TAKE PART IN ANY ACTION WHICH MIGHT BE HARMFUL TO MY COMRADES. IF I AM SENIOR, I WILL TAKE COMMAND. IF NOT, I WILL OBEY THE LAWFUL ORDERS OF THOSE APPOINTED OVER ME AND WILL BACK THEM UP IN EVERY WAY.

V

WHEN QUESTIONED, SHOULD I BECOME A PRISONER OF WAR, I AM BOUND TO GIVE ONLY NAME, RANK, SERVICE NUMBER, AND DATE OF BIRTH. I WILL EVADE ANSWERING FURTHER QUESTIONS TO THE UTMOST OF MY ABILITY. I WILL MAKE NO ORAL OR WRITTEN STATEMENTS DISLOYAL TO MY COUNTRY AND ITS ALLIES OR HARMFUL TO THEIR CAUSE.

VI

I WILL NEVER FORGET THAT I AM AN AMERICAN FIGHTING MAN, RESPONSIBLE FOR MY ACTIONS, AND DEDICATED TO THE PRINCIPLES WHICH MADE MY

COUNTRY FREE. I WILL TRUST IN MY GOD AND IN THE
UNITED STATES OF AMERICA.

In the long form printout of the Code, after each of the articles
is a short paragraph that restates and clarifies the basic article.
The Code has always gotten wide dissemination in the military,
especially among those exposed to the real risks of war, including capture. We could therefore assume that each and every
aircrewman had read or studied the Code, and had a reasonable
understanding of the *intent* of the articles. Because of frequent
shuffling of prisoners around the various prison areas, the iso-
lation, and changes of the senior ranking American officers during the first couple of years, only sporadic guidance was given,
mostly only when requested.

There was no question that each man was capable of making
his own decisions as to how much punishment he could or should
be taking, depending upon the value of the material that the V
were after. Back in '65 Robbie Risner and Jerry Denton had put
out the word to back off when in danger of losing life or sanity.

Our long-time imprisonment was getting people down. We
kept looking between the lines of propaganda for something
positive, something to hang our hopes on, but nothing was there.
When we could get in touch with new shoot-downs, we asked
what was happening out in the world. The answer was always,
"Nothing, no changes, just bigger."

So there we were, dealing with an enemy who did not care
about Geneva agreements on the treatment of war prisoners, an
enemy who denied the International Red Cross entry into their
country. After years passed, we realized that we were, and would
probably always be, imprisoned in an environment of continuous physical and mental torture.

Everyone understood the intent of the Code, which, under
classroom conditions, seemed quite clear. The question put to
me back at the Briar Patch in '66 by Airmen Art Black and Billy
Robinson probably illustrates best what most of us were thinking.
"*Must* we take torture every time we go out for interrogation?"
Implicit in that thought was, is it the intent of the Code that we
all die, or lose our minds from years of unremitting torture?

The Code says an American prisoner is "bound to give only
name, rank, service number, and date of birth." We resisted
every question put to us over and above that. We soon learned
that there were times the enemy did not persist, but if they
earnestly pursued an objective, they had ways to elicit response,

whether we gave them truth, part truth, or out-and-out falsehoods. They *did* get answers!

A POW who is being tortured and senses that he is in deep trouble with a hard-driving interrogator will tend to fall back to a secondary line of defense. He knows what is required of him, but how much torture can he take and still hope to survive and avoid permanent physical or mental harm?

There are wide differences in people. A very few men, like Jim Kasler, have the stamina and courage to stick to a hard line during severe punishment and continue to hold out. Most men, although they want to do a good job, will gamely resist the cruelties, but not for very long. Oftentimes, the interrogator will be satisfied with some minor contribution, orally or in writing. Each prisoner has to exercise his own judgment and choose to do battle on those issues he feels are worth the resultant pain of torture.

Sometimes, hanging in there too long can be as disastrous as giving in sooner. The torturers smash the victim down so completely they get more than they originally hoped for—a "free ride," so to speak. The Rabbit once said to me, "Now I warn you, if you continue to resist, we will break you down so far that you will have nothing left. Do you know what I mean?" I thought I knew what he meant. Later, I was to see it happen.

Experience taught that some of us invited trouble by being extra antagonistic toward the interrogators when we should have kept our mouths shut. We did that because we thought it was the right thing to do, it was "resistance," it was "refusing to cooperate in any way." But what that did was force them into a corner, and they reacted predictably to show us who was boss.

Years later, when we were invited to dinner at the White House by President Nixon, I chatted with another guest at my table— movie idol John Wayne. "Duke," I said, "I tried to think about how *you* might have handled the interrogators." He listened intently. "So when they asked questions I told 'em to go to hell, when they asked me to do something, I told 'em to stick it up their asses. . . . And do you know what, Duke? They beat the shit out of me!" The Duke shook with silent laughter, but there were tears in his eyes. He knew that the Hollywood solution never works for us mere mortals.

There is another kind of man—one who gives in before taking *any* physical punishment. Heavy threats and mental torment are, to him, as painful as physical torture to others, and he is simply not equipped to handle it. This was admitted to me in face-to-face situations by several regretful and guilt-ridden fellow prisoners. There weren't many of them, and allowances had to be made for them. They knew their shortcomings and felt badly about them. If the group ostracized them, it might have had the effect of driving them over to the enemy side. They needed constant encouragement, needed to be told that everyone stood behind them, that they could do better with a little more effort. The long range objective was not to lose them, but to get them home again with the rest of us.

All things considered, I believed that choosing a reasonable line of resistance would provide greater assurance that most men would be able to handle interrogation and do a better job over the long haul. When the Vietnamese backed off, we could inch forward. If they pressed hard, we could ease off, thereby "staying in contact" but giving the absolute minimum with which to get by.

The news of the second release of three prisoners upset most of the men in the Zoo, because no mention was made of any of them having critical physical disabilities. The opinion was that they themselves had negotiated their early release . . . contrary to the Code. We decided that in Corley's case, the air force and the government would concur with our decision to get him out, along with the other seriously wounded.

When I agreed to put out a release policy, a list of wounded was compiled by the ranking officers of each building. The Geneva accords provide for exchange of prisoners, but our situation here was unique, and the Vietnamese were not about to go along with anything of the kind. Eventually our list reached fourteen. I knew that I had the flexibility and authority to make decisions that were consistent with the intent of the Code and in the best interest of all.

In addition to getting men out who were insane, or in danger of losing limbs, or going blind, we felt that an important side benefit would be the passing of huge amounts of intelligence information regarding prisoner identities, treatment, torture, and locations.

However, deep down inside, we believed there wasn't a prayer in hell that anyone would ever be released from the Zoo, because we were a torture camp. The two releases so far had been of "purees" from the Plantation camp. The Vietnamese were not going to risk getting bad publicity because of their treatment of us. They were supersensitive about outside opinion, including that of the American antiwar segment, on whom they placed a good deal of hope for bringing American opinion around to favor the North Vietnamese position.

My specific order to Norlan Daughtrey (while Fidel was still there) was, "You can tell Fidel that if he will let Carl Corley go home, you would go with him, and you may sign an amnesty request for both of you."

The release policy went out as follows: "If asked by the Vietnamese, the following named men [list of fourteen] may accept early release and sign a statement of amnesty, but go no further. Do not sell your soul for early release."

The next question concerned written statements.

Question: What is your policy on writing?

Policy: In all good conscience, depending on how long it has been since last tortured, and your mental and physical state, do one of the following:

a. Refuse to write altogether.
b. Use delaying tactics.
c. Write things the gooks can't possibly use.
d. Write outright lies.

That sequence was pretty much what everyone was doing, anyway. What we hoped to accomplish with the policy message was to take some of the pressure off the individual by coming out with an official interpretation of the Code, which gave the POWs some personal peace of mind and some flexibility in dealing with the QZRs.

I heard from several sources that one or two of the Zoo prisoners were very critical of the way some of their fellow prisoners conducted themselves at quiz. They could now say, "I did it in accord with policy" and that was okay by me.

Question: What is your policy on making Christmas tapes?

Policy: If you honestly feel that it will help your family to hear your voice and you would feel good about it, then do it.

Without an SRO commitment on this one, the POWs would have criticized each other without mercy. Not all were given the opportunity to tape, but in some cases men who had never received a letter were able to get a taped message out. Better some, than none at all.

Question: How about going to church for Christmas?

Policy: If you feel that you need it and may get a spiritual boost from it, go.

This is the best example of the trade-off situation. Yes, the V

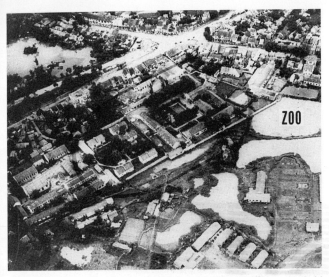

The Zoo, a prisoner of war camp where the North Vietnamese held American POWs captive. *Department of Defense*

Hoa Lo, the Hanoi City Jail. The most famous of the POW camps, it came to be known as the "Hanoi Hilton." *Department of Defense*

Larry Guarino stands in front of a Spitfire Mark VIII near Napoli, Italy, November 1943. *Larry Guarino*

Pilots just before takeoff on a mission over French Indochina near Hanoi. Guarino is second from right. Poh-sei, China, March 1945. *Larry Guarino*

Larry Guarino (left) with fellow pilot Jack Childers at Osan Air Base, Korea. January 1954. *Larry Guarino*

Four F-86-Fs and pilots on two-minute alert at Osan Air Base, Korea, March 1954. Guarino is at left. *Larry Guarino*

Larry Guarino returns from a mission with Captain Bill Elander, who was captured by the North Vietnamese seven years later. Korat, Thailand, May 1965. *Larry Guarino*

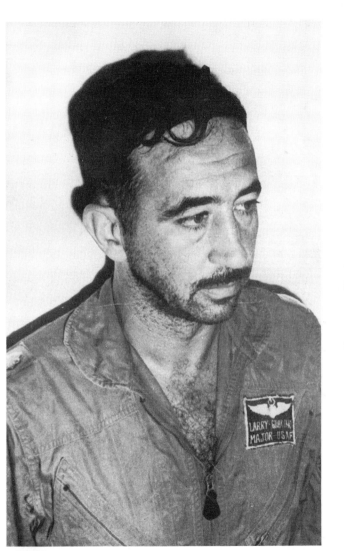

Major Guarino just after arrival at Hoa Lo, June 1965. *Vietnamese propaganda photograph*

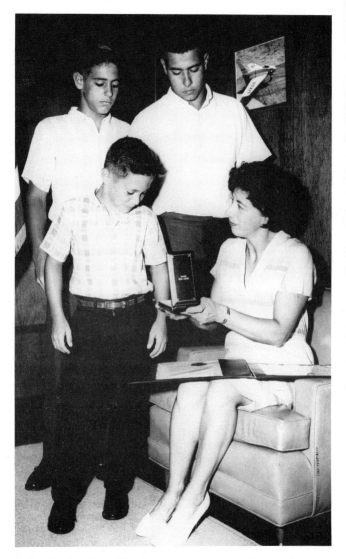

Evelyn Guarino shows Silver Star to sons Ray (12), Jeff (9), and Tom (18). June 1963. *Larry Guarino*

Christmas services, 1965. From left: Byrne, Cormier, Guarino, Father Ho Than Bien. *Vietnamese propaganda photograph*

American POWs march through Hanoi, July 1966. Front row: Keirn, Berg, "Groucho." Second row: Shumaker, Harris. Third row: Byrne, Guarino, "Spot." *UPI*

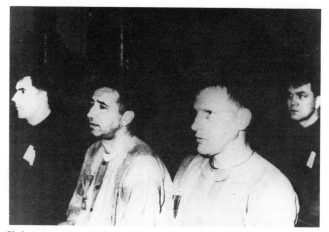

Christmas services in downtown Hanoi, 1969. From left: Byrne, Guarino, Dutton, Sima. *Vietnamese propaganda photograph*

NGÀY VIẾT (Dated) 4 JAN 1972

EVY DARLING, I AM WAITING FOR PICTURES OF YOU WITH YOUR SUMMER VISITORS AND FAMILY NEWS. AS I HAVE SAID BEFORE, ENJOY YOUR LIFE BECAUSE EVEN THOUGH IT HAS BEEN 7 YEARS, IT MAY BE 7 MORE OR LONGER, SO DONT WAIT FOR ME, I KNOW YOU CARE, HOPE, WISH AND PRAY, BUT THAT IS NOT GOING TO DO IT SO DONT WASTE YOUR TIME. I DON'T NEED ANYTHING BUT TO GET OUT OF HERE, I DONT WANT YOU TO BE LONELY FOREVER, IF YOU WANT TO REMARRY, GO AHEAD, IF ITS POSSIBLE, TO HELL WITH WHAT PEOPLE SAY. LARRY,

Letter from Guarino to his wife Evelyn on official form. January 1972.

NGÀY VIẾT (Dated) 4 February 1972

Jerry- Now bear this- don't appreciate you writing about not writing, remarrying, etc. Sorry to tell you you'll have a job shaking me. Think you will like this area better than So. Fla. House has 2300 sq. ft. living space- plenty of room for all family to visit, fireplace, on canal, wall-to-wall carpeting throughout. You will love it. Little more patience please! Want you to like all. Your Evy

GHI CHÚ (N.B.):

1. Phải viết rõ và chỉ được viết trên những dòng kẻ sẵn (*Write legibly and only on the lines*).

2. Gia đình gửi đến cũng phải theo đúng mẫu, khuôn khổ và quy định này (*Notes from families should also conform to this proforma*).

Reply from Evelyn Guarino on official letter form. February 1972.

Everett Alvarez, Jr. Lieutenant Junior Grade, U.S. Navy.
Shot down 5 August 1964
Released 12 February 1973

A G R E E M E N T
ON
ENDING THE WAR AND RESTORING PEACE
IN VIET NAM

The Government of the Democratic Republic of Viet Nam,
with the concurrence of the Provisional Revolutionary Government
of the Republic of South Viet Nam,

The Government of the United States of America, with
the concurrence of the Government of the Republic of Viet Nam,

With a view to ending the war and restoring peace in Viet
Nam on the basis of respect for the Vietnamese people's funda-
mental national rights and the South Vietnamese people's right
to self-determination, and to contributing to the consolidation
of peace in Asia and the world,

Have agreed on the following provisons and undertake to
respect and to implement them.

Robbie Risner
Harvey S. Stockman
Swede Larson
Vern Ligon
Earl Crumpler
Bud Day
John S. Finlay III
Thomas Hall
Jerry Guarino
Fred Crow

Byron Fuller
Chuck Gillespie
Bill Franke
Ken Coskey
Jim Mehl
Hal Moore
Leo T. Profilet
Bill Lawrence
Verlyne Daniels
Charlie James
Al Brady

First page of Peace Agreement between the Democratic Republic of Vietnam and the US, signed by American POWs.

Arriving at Clark Air Base in the Philippines, February 1973. *Clark Air Force Base*

Brigadier General Jim Ahmann pins on medals the year after Guarino's return. May 1974. *Patrick Air Force Base*

Four ex-POWs get together, January 1989. From left: Ligon, Guarino, Keirn, Finlay. *Larry Guarino*

are going to get something in return, if only propaganda, but the POW gets out of his cell and into pleasant circumstances for a couple of hours. Perhaps he will even get a chance to communicate with people from other camps and get some new information into the system.

Question: How about taking special food?

Policy: If the medics say you need the extra food, take it! And take anything you can get from the V without paying a price. . . . That includes letters, socks, clothing, extra blankets for the sick, etc.

Question: How about the guys who were tricked into sending for money and now refuse to accept extras?

Policy: Take the goodies and hide them where other guys can pick them up for the sick and wounded and starving. Spread the stuff around.

I had already answered this question before, but a formal statement was needed.

We had other policies circulating via our now-excellent communications system. We adopted an organizational slogan and passed it to Spiker and Coniff for dissemination; it was, "Home with honor." Spiker came back and recommended that we add, "or not at all." I said, "Hell no, somebody might get himself killed trying to live up to it. That's not what we want." I was later told that Spiker had added his words despite my instructions to him. It was the second time he disappointed me. I had already heard, from several reliable sources, that the year before Spiker had sent a personal message to a man just coming back from a fierce round of torture. The message was, "Your standards of resistance disgust me." I could not imagine any more cruel remark to a tortured man trying to get himself back together.

We had a lot to be proud of in our communications system, because it was a weapon that enabled us to keep abreast of what the gooks wanted from us. By keeping ourselves fully informed about their programs, we could get the jump on them by being prepared with a course of action.

One of the key men in our comm system over in the Gate House was Lieutenant J. J. Connell. Soon after his arrival in Hanoi, J. J. was severely tortured with ropes but managed to hold out for an extended period. J. J. lost control of his arms and all feelings to his fingers. As the gooks backed off, J. J. decided not to show any improvement in his physical condition, but instead continued with a ruse, feigning loss of feeling and incoherence of speech. Faking this physical condition, he stayed in continuous touch, informing us of gate traffic, flow of prisoners to and from interrogations, and a lot of other information. He was able to pull it off so well that the Vietnamese even sent him to the downtown hospital with Corley for electric-shock treatments. He did a remarkable job up until June of 1969. I called him my "worldwide connection."

Eventually I became fearful that the V would find out his disabilities were an act. I sent a message to J. J. telling him that I was worried, and suggested that he should begin to "improve" following the electric-shock sessions. His message back was, "Don't worry about me; I know what I'm doing."

From time to time we would lift back the frame of the door-peep so we could see farther to the left of the yard in front of the Pigsty building. Once we heard the rattling of irons, ran to our peep, and saw that the gooks were working Jack Van Loan over with irons and beatings. That lasted several weeks. We could also see that some of the guys were getting outside a bit to exercise. I saw two strange, very skinny guys and called Ron over to see if he could identify them. "Holy cow, the tall guy is Pop Keirn!" I looked again, and since I had last seen him in '65, Pop had lost at least a hundred pounds! The other guy had bad arm wounds. . . . It was John Pitchford. I'd only had one brief peek at him in December of '65, and at that time he was heavily bandaged and had quite a lot of weight on him.

Early one September afternoon we heard trucks rumbling about the perimeter road. Soon we were blindfolded, and a large number of us, maybe the whole camp, were loaded aboard. Our hearts pounded . . . where are we going, maybe home? Nah! We always guessed we were going home, even when we were on the way to torture. Wishful thinking never stopped.

Half an hour later we were off-loaded, and the blinds were removed. We were somewhere at the edge of Hanoi at another war museum. We saw POWs all over the place, but there were so many guards, officers, and quizzers around, it was hard to say more than "Hi." The townspeople crowded against the high hurricane fence, waving and smiling at us, not at all unfriendly, and we waved back.

The main attraction was a huge junkpile of U.S. aircraft of all types. Choppers, A-4s, F-105s . . . at least one of everything that flew over the north.

Fish was there, and he came over and grabbed me like an old

friend. "Ah, Ga-reeno, how are you? I heard you were caught leading a communications net."

I answered quickly, "Oh no, they only said that to punish me, but I was innocent."

We were led into a large theaterlike building with many small rooms. Our commentator was Dum Dum. The walls were covered with photographs of the French occupation. One was a shot of a bunch of French soldiers standing around in their long johns, rifles in hand, all having a great time laughing and yakking with a cute bunch of young Indochinese girls. Another huge photo showed a number of armed soldiers in a punishment yard. An Indochinese man, in the tribal garb of the early century, was shown grinning as he leaned on a huge, wide-bladed executioner's sword. On one side, a few bodies were piled up, and at the executioner's feet, set straight up in the sand, staring right at the camera, were three or four severed heads. Dum Dum said, "See, the French imperialists make our own people bury their friends in the sand." He didn't realize that the heads had been severed! No wonder he was called Dum Dum!

In another room were sets of leg irons and a bunk with the heavy stocks just like in New Guy and Heartbreak. "See," Dum Dum said, "how cruel and inhuman the French were in using these implements?"

"What do you mean?" I said. "You're still using that stuff on us!"

"Shut up!" he screamed.

We were then taken to view the famous bronze drums. During a raid early in the war, American bombs made some pretty big craters. The V investigated the holes and found two huge, fully intact bronze drums that were supposed to be two thousand years old. They pointed out that the failures of the kings and princes were because, in their revelry, they were only interested "in that little thing," that is, the luxuries which came with rule. They said that royalty was entertained by an orchestra perched on the back of a huge tortoise, which swam about in a lake in the center of Hanoi. Occasionally, the tortoise would dive out of sight. They mixed reality with fiction as though it were all true. It was very difficult for us to separate the real bullshit from the imaginary bullshit.

Then we were taken into the main theater. It was an accurate, to-scale model of Dien Bien Phu. It clearly depicted the height of the hills surrounding the airfield, and all of the French defensive positions in the valley. It showed the Viet Minh Army la-

boring to lift heavy cannon up the sides of the hills to fire down
at the French. The positions of both sides were shown with
raised battle flags, the French with the tricolor and the Viet Minh
with the lone red star on the white field. (Somewhere along the
line they changed the white background to gold.) A tape of
stirring military music, with the sounds of guns and cannon,
played in the background. Then, as each French position was
taken, the tricolor would fall, instantly replaced with the red
star, amid the blaring of bugles, until in the finale, the whole
panorama was covered with the red-starred flags. It was an impressive show.

Their propaganda efforts never ceased. A couple of days later,
at the Zoo, they set up the auditorium to show us a film. Using
ropes and blankets, they managed to make numerous little
alcoves on the inclined theater floor so we could be seated
relatively isolated from each other, thereby reducing communications.

I found the flick interesting. It was actual film coverage of the
French evacuation of Hanoi right after the Dien Bien Phu shel-
lacking. One scene showed the inside of a home, where several
Vietnamese women were clutching at French soldiers about to
leave them. Little children were hanging onto the soldiers' legs
and had to be pulled away. Everyone was crying, which showed
that deep ties and love existed between the French and the Vietnamese people, and that the parting caused anguish. The Rabbit
was the narrator during the silent film. *His* version was, "See
how the women cry? They are so happy the French are finally
being thrown out!" The more of that kind of bullshit we witnessed, the more difficult it was for us to believe that any of our
fellow Americans could ever be seriously impressed by anything
the Communists might say.

Bud Day told us (through the walls, of course) that he was in
a cell at the Plantation with Norris Overly when they brought in
Lieutenant Commander John S. McCain. John had bailed out
of an A-4 Skyhawk right over Hanoi and had landed in the
middle of the West Lake. He broke his leg and both arms on
bailout. Unable to pop the air cylinders of his life preserver, he
went to the bottom, then kicked himself back to the surface to
breathe, time and again. Luckily, the water was only five or six
feet deep. He was running out of steam when he was finally
rescued by a couple of young men who swam out to save him.
Once they got him in a prison cell, even though he was badly
wounded, the Bug worked him over for information.

Then a foreign dignitary called Hanoi to inquire about the condition of "the admiral's son." The gooks got really excited when they learned that they had captured none other than the son of Admiral John McCain II, who would soon take over as U.S. CINCPAC (Commander in Chief, Pacific). Young McCain's physical condition was appalling, so they moved him in with Bud and Norris. Since Bud was also crippled, a heavy nursing load fell on Overly.

McCain had all kinds of visitors to his cell, and later at the hospital during his brief stay there. His visitors included the minister of defense, General Vo Nguyen Giap, and many of the highest-level party people. The V were wetting their pants with joy at all levels, but McCain wouldn't lend himself to any of the propaganda the V so desperately wanted. They told Bud Day gleefully, "*You* are nothing! We have captured the prince!"

Bud told us that the gooks commented that Overly had a "good attitude," and then one day, after a quiz, Overly announced that he'd been selected for release. He was moved out soon afterward and left North Vietnam as one of the first three men to accept an early release in February, 1968.

McCain was offered early release a number of times, but he did not accept favors. Although in bad physical shape, he believed it would have been wrong to take an easy out. His dad's position must have had some effect on his thinking. He insisted that he be treated the same as the other prisoners. So they obliged him. They often beat on him unmercifully, as they did on the rest of us, for no reason at all, or for trumped up reasons.

In the fall of '68, another movie was shown to us that really upset a lot of us. This was another interview of an F-105 pilot, Major Clay Kirsten, by Wilfred Burchett. Kirsten was sitting straight in his chair, almost like an aviation cadet in the presence of a high-ranking officer. To every question that Burchett put forth, Kirsten gave a quick reply, beginning with the emphatic word "Sir!" Kirsten described the simultaneous missile hits taken by his aircraft and his wingman's. "Both our aircraft were eliminated." At one point Kirsten clasped his hands, and, to our amazement, he was still in possession of his wedding ring! Major Kirsten looked to be in good physical condition, and spoke very smoothly, but looks don't mean much, we knew that.

Soon after we were returned to our cells, Spiker asked if we noticed the ring, and wondered how come Kirsten still had it. We had no answer, because we knew that the first thing the V did was strip you of all personal possessions and valuables. A couple of hours later, Spiker messaged that he had taken a poll through the building. The question was, "Do you think Kirsten was tortured before the Burchett interview?" Spiker said that not one man in the building thought that Kirsten had taken any punishment. The idea that Spiker had initiated such a poll infuriated me. Had he told me he was thinking of doing so, I would not have allowed it. To my mind, there is no place for polls in a military organization. Polls are for popular opinions. "Popular" is the last reason any commander should use as a basis for decision-making. Seeing the wedding ring on Kirsten had certainly affected the morale of the people who participated in the poll. Most of them were resentful at having had their own wedding rings stripped from them. A key point is that a wedding ring, or any highly sentimental piece of jewelry, should not be worn on a combat mission in the first place. It only gives the enemy more leverage against the captive, and they've got enough of that without helping them to more.

I told Spiker that he shouldn't have taken the damn poll, but inasmuch as he had, Ron and I strongly disagreed with the consensus on Kirsten. We said we believed that Kirsten *did* take torture before the interview. We made no mention of the ring.

Over the years, boredom and frustration exacted a price. Ron and I became argumentative and ridiculously competitive. The gooks had recently given us a paper chess set, which pleased me, since I liked to play chess, although I didn't consider myself an ace at it. Ron knew very little of the game, so I taught him whatever I knew—basic opening moves and how to get the opponent into checkmate. He learned fast, so fast that soon I could seldom beat him. The times I managed to squeak out a win, he'd refuse to play for a week, just to punish me. He hated to lose!

Cramped into our tiny cell together for endless hours, days, and weeks, we became hypercritical of everything the other one did: how he ate, sat, folded his blankets, or tapped the wall. We gave one another a huge pain in the ass. Among our few possessions, Ron still had the beads the priest had given him, and I wore the tiny gold medal on a string around my neck. One day Ron was praying, and I said, "What are you doing?"

He said, "I'm saying my daily Mass."

"Is it necessary to say a Mass every day?"

"I can't stop, I feel guilty."

"You've been snapping those beads since Christmas '65, and what the hell have we got to show for it?"

"What do you expect, a miracle?"

"You bet your ass I expect a miracle, that's the business He's in, isn't it? Now are you quite through with those beads?"

"Yeah."

"Hand 'em over and let me show you something. Now . . . what time you wanna get out of here?"

If looks could kill, I would have been belly up!

Throwing myself on the floor, I started a series of push-ups. On the downstroke, my medal would tick the floor, making a tiny click.

"Are you damaging that medal?"

"Maybe, and if I do I'll take it to a body shop and get it straightened out, you son of a bitch."

"Larry, would you feel better if you threw a few punches at me?"

We flew at one another in rage and frustration. We bear-hugged and wrestled like we wanted to kill one another, but did not throw a single punch. We didn't really want to fight or hurt one another, just blow off steam. Then we sat on our bunks, seething. I realized there was no one in the world I thought more of as a close buddy than Ron Byrne. Within a couple of hours, we forgot all about it and were friends again.

We continued to organize. Ken Spiker asked to be camp athletic officer, since he was an exercise nut, and he felt he could get everyone going in a morale-lifting exercise program. He did come up with a good program, and everyone who could participate did so.

I appointed each building's senior officer as historical officer and expected him to commit all notable events to memory. These programs were all morale builders—something pleasant on which to focus our minds. I promised the enlisted men at least one promotion for every two years as a POW. (They got better than that.) We figured we could get reserve officers a regular commission if they wanted it. (That was done.) I knew that Evelyn had moved to Cocoa Beach, which was right next to Patrick Air Force Base, Florida, so I told the guys I would see to it that everyone got their deserved awards and decorations after we got home, and that we would do it at Patrick Air Force Base. (Which is how it actually happened.)

These "programs" caused quite a bit of excitement. Guys started playing with numbers in their heads, trying to figure out what they had coming, or what their wives had saved for them. A question came through: "Do you think we'll get any extra bonus for being here?" I remembered asking Ron out in the Hut the year before how much he'd want for enduring that round of torture. Ron said, "I wouldn't do it for a thousand a day." I agreed that a thousand a day was dirt cheap!

Manipulating a few numbers, I tried to figure my leave pay due, daily subsistence, and compensation for injury or wounds, and came up with, "twenty a day plus sick and torture pay." It was really just something we did to keep the imagination going along healthy lines—we would have a future, we would get home, and collect our back pay.

Talking through our back wall to Gary Anderson and Joe Milligan was an enjoyable experience. They were both F-4 "back-seaters"; Joe was air force, and Gary, navy.

Milligan had come down near the target his squadron had under attack. Wounded, he was carried to the shade of a tree, where he continued to watch the bombing. A young girl brought him two bottles of beer. As he was being put into a small vehicle, he was assaulted by a soldier, but the fellow who captured Joe was very protective of him.

Gary was badly tortured when he was first captured, and he had some deep dark ankle scars to show for it. He loved boats, and so did I. He gave me tips on purchasing boats and told me about some of his adventures when he hired out as a mate on luxury cruisers traveling the inland waterway south to Miami.

We were getting daily reports from Stable Three on Corley's progress. It wasn't good. He wasn't eating much, but Jack Bomar was still trying to hold off force-feeding him again.

Back in the States, it was getting close to election time. We knew that Richard Nixon was the Republican choice and that Hubert Humphrey hoped to succeed Johnson. One of the guys saw Lump at quiz, and Lump made a prediction. "Something very big will happen soon . . . Gion-Son is going to pull an election extravaganza!" We shot that around the camp in a hurry!

I guess the North Vietnamese knew President Johnson better than we did, because sure enough, a couple of days before the presidential election, Johnson announced an unconditional halt in the bombing of North Vietnam. Alvarez sent a message that he was so happy hearing the news, it made him cry for the first time since '64, and he kissed his cell mate. He was sure the war was over. The poor guy had already been there four and a half years.

Most of us were jubilant to some degree. When asked my opinion, I said, "Well if he really has stopped the bombing, he couldn't have done it on his own. He must have a deal going with these people. I think within a month the wounded guys are gonna have to be out of here, because Johnson wouldn't stop the bombing without an agreement on a swap of wounded prisoners, at the very least."

Over in the Barn, Bud Day was positive the V were wrong about the bombing halt being a strictly political, unilateral American move. Bud thought that *no* American president would ever play politics with the war at that stage. When the announcement came, Bud was stunned. There *had* to be mutually agreed upon preconditions, and he bitterly resented anyone in the Barn even hinting otherwise. Like me, he believed that the sick and wounded would be going home soon. Nobody wanted to think it could be any other way.

We waited . . . and we waited, for good news. We didn't want to believe that Johnson would pull a slimy stunt like that, just to get his own man elected. It wasn't until late 1970 when I chanced to speak to Red Bedinger (brought into Hanoi from Laos after being downed in late 1969) that I got the straight truth. Bedinger said the bombing halt was Johnson's own idea, and the Vietnamese weren't in on it at all! So it was finally confirmed that the bombing halt was just a rotten vote-getting trick, and it hurt like hell. That was Johnson's second stab into our guts. (The other was the "guns and butter" speech.)

Even as we waited, our morale was good, and most of us were optimistic because the V were being comparatively decent to us. The medic was coming around almost daily, and the regular chicken-shit guards had been replaced by some real soldiers. Naturally, we thought it was all tied into a deal for an exchange of prisoners.

Soon after Richard Nixon was elected president, Averell Harriman was replaced by Henry Cabot Lodge at the Paris peace talks. Both sides still argued about the shape of the conference table and who would sit where. They finally decided that, in addition to the U.S. and North Vietnam, that both the Viet Cong and the government of the south would also be represented. The main negotiator for North Vietnam was a man whose name I couldn't spell, but it was pronounced Swan Tree. Earlier, one of the first conditions stipulated by Swan Tree was that all bombing of the north would have to be stopped. But even after Johnson had come through with a large piece of that proviso, it didn't appear that the Vietnamese threw anything in the pot.

The Vietnamese camp personnel also seemed to be in pretty good spirits. They had good reason to wish for the end to the war, perhaps even more than we did. They decided to put on a show to entertain themselves.

There was singing going on all over the place by both male and female personnel. They practiced endlessly to put on their version of an amateur show. It was another of their troop-morale programs for the coming Tet holiday of 1969. Some of the girls had nice soprano voices, and many of the men sounded just like them.

The Vietnamese kept some very cute little chow dogs around the camp. I knew they ate dogs, because I'd seen skulls in the soup, and so had Kasler. One of our men reported that the V played and fussed around with the little dogs, which we thought were pets. He was horrified to see the gooks break the legs of the little dogs, then watch them flopping about the ground whimpering. They believed that the dogs' suffering made the meat tastier! We were in the hands of true sadists!

A few nights before Christmas, they played a taped message from a captured American pilot to his family back home. The tape has the usual good treatment mush, but the main point was the pilot's expression of his deep concern for the welfare of his children, and even more so for his wife, who was confined to a wheelchair. Hearing that tape was a sad blow to me personally, because the pilot was one of my people from the 44th Squadron at Okinawa. He had told me that he had a couple of children and a completely disabled wife. She would be needing constant assistance for an indefinite period. He expressed an urgent desire to get in as much combat flying as he could, because we were at war, and that was what he was trained for. He added that he'd been drawing a regular paycheck as a combat-ready pilot, and he felt a strong obligation to serve in that capacity. He impressed me as a typical fighter pilot, eager to do battle. I told him I'd think it over and try to give him a proper job assignment.

In the following several weeks, he flew five combat missions, and he did well. Meanwhile, I had made a couple of phone calls, and had touched base with Colonel Grant Smith, the wing director of operations.

Once again I spoke to the pilot. "Listen old sport, I've been talking to Colonel Smith and we've got a great job lined up for you. With your experience in the 105, you should be a big help to every pilot in the wing. I consider this job to be a very prestigious one. The job title is fighter wing weapons officer.'' He seemed very pleased to hear that, because it was a good assignment. ''Just one other thing . . . the fact is, your family needs you close to home a lot more than the air force needs you here. I wouldn't want to think about what would happen to them if you were lost in combat. . . . Well?''

Three years had passed, and the next thing I know he's making a tape from Hanoi! I was upset that he went back to combat, and that anyone at Kadena would allow it to happen. Now he was entirely dependent upon the ''good-heartedness'' of the gooks for news of his family, and that wasn't a good position to be in. His wife died while he was still a POW in Hanoi, and we all felt very bad about it.

It wasn't good for guards to be seen being nice to the *"Mỹ."* That word is written with a dash over the *y*, which gives the word the pronounciation of *meee*. It means ''American'' or ''Yankee.'' Even so, we had two guards who talked to us in the evenings.

Ron and I would stand in front of the open peep as though we were watching TV. We let our pajamas way down to cover our toes (the skeeters were fierce), and we listened. The first guy had a wide, flattish face, so we named him Buddha. He wore a perpetual smile and never ratted on us. Buddha was there purely for the fun of it. The first thing he asked about was our families.

''Wifa?'' We both nodded ''yes.''

''Childin? Boy?'' When he said boy, he crooked his index finger and held it near his fly. Ron answered ''*Bon* boy,'' meaning four sons, and I repeated the same. Buddha then asked if we had girl children by first putting his hands to his breasts, then bunching the fingers of one hand, grabbing at the back of his hair and pulling down as if stroking a braid. ''No girl,'' we replied. We then went through the respective ages of both families, and he got a big kick out of it.

We pointed to the stars on his collar, and that started him off on a long discussion. He began with one plain star and went up all through the enlisted ranks and the pay scales. He gave the rank titles in his own language. The private, depending on grade level, got from two to six bucks a month, the same as a working peasant. Each soldier had to give a little back for his subsistence. The more senior sergeants made fifteen bucks per month. He pulled out his wallet and showed us his "dongs." It was freshly printed, pink-colored paper money with Uncle Ho's picture on the face of the bills. A dong was then worth about thirty cents U.S.

He pressed on with the officer ranks, starting at the plain horizontal bar, which was like a warrant officer. Spot, Rat, Zoorat, and other juniors wore the bar. Next was one star over the bar. That's all the rank Rabbit had, maybe that's why he was always so damn mean. The camp commanders, with their three stars over a bar, made fifty bucks a month (which was more than they were worth) plus all they could steal. Commanders Cochise and Buzzard were often seen loading up their bikes with food and goodies and sneaking out the front gate. Buddha carried the rank structure all the way to Ho Chi Minh, and we understood that the word for president was *chu tich*, like in "chew tick."

The other guard was a real actor. We asked what he did in the army simply by looking quizzical, and he told us: *"Do-Doo . . . Do-Do-Doooo,"* etc., tapping out the international Morse code. He was a communications technician. He kind of crouched over, looking secretive while sending code, then he suddenly went "Boom! Boom! Boom!" and then, throwing himself backward, yelled, "Ahhhh!" Evidently his bunker was hit by bombs from one of our birds. Then he got quiet to indicate he had been knocked out. He straightened himself, then looked up, index finger of right hand moving in a circle. *"Plop, plop, plop."* Helicopters for sure! *"Bap-bap, bap, bap,"* like he was shooting his AK-47. Then proudly he held up a hand with four fingers. He had credit for shooting down four choppers!

Dit-Dah (as we named him) then stood at strict attention and said, *"Ha-noi, chu tich!"* followed by a long *"oh ohhhh!"* (I think it meant everybody to attention.) Then he pressed his right thumb hard to his left breast four times. He got four medals for bravery from Ho Chi Minh.

The next night, Dit Dah went on a different tack. He said, "Me, two wifa." Vietnamese were allowed more than one wife. Arms out like grabbing handlebars of a bike, he mimicked the sound of an engine: *"hudn hudn."* Then he showed us his wristwatch, and topped it all off by acting like he was holding a portable radio to his ear. It must have been payday, because he had a wallet full of dong. Man, this guy was as high on the hog as any Vietnamese could get. Two wives, a motorbike, wristwatch, radio, and a pocketful of money! He showed us pictures of his wives. The twenty-eight-year-old was rather ordinary, but the eighteen-year-old was a beauty. He didn't say whether the wives got on well together or not.

Somewhere in his conversation, he took time to tell us something not actually connected to the discussion. He pointed down toward our crotches, then held his hands a foot apart, frowning in disapproval. He then put his forefingers two inches apart, smiling approval. He pointed to himself, saying, "Vietnam okay." He was telling us that the little Vietnamese peters made a lot more sense. The Frenchmen must have had a hell of a ball with the Indochinese women! Another very good reason the gooks were glad to see them go, I'm sure! His big finale was to impress us with his education as he drew imaginary triangles and parallelograms and recited a number of geometric theorems. Each of his little shows lasted an hour and a half, and we were pretty well pooped out from swatting mosquitoes. But it certainly was an entertaining change for us.

That year, Ron and I were not asked if we wanted to go to church or to see a priest for Christmas, but many others were. We looked forward to the holiday, mostly hoping we'd get letters from home and some good food. We talked it over, and this time we were determined to approach the holiday season in a different frame of mind.

If we were told to go out to rooms they set up and decorated for the holidays, we would go, and would take anything they offered in food or drink. We would steal anything we could lay our hands on when their backs were turned. Whatever food they gave us, we were going to *pig out*, and to hell with everything else!

We also decided that this year we would allow ourselves *no* thoughts of home, our wives, or our sons, because that kind of sentimentality only helped to break us down and make us feel even worse, and who needed that? No more of that "feeling sorry" crap! It was our *fourth* Christmas in a North Vietnamese prison, and we were just starting to learn how to deal with it.

Quincy Collins had arranged for a small group of guys to sing at a church service. It turned out to be a brazen communications session between our men from different camps. That really torqued the gooks, but they couldn't do much about it, because they had crowds of reporters and photographers in the place to film and report the "humane treatment" occasion. Soft-Soap Fairy, the sweet-talking QZR from Plantation who was in charge of grooming early releasees, tried to stop the comm, but without success. However, Soft-Soap managed to keep a smile pasted on for the cameras. The next day I saw the Rabbit, and he sternly informed me, "Ga—your fellows, they have committed an outrage on your holy day!"

Christmas week was quiet, and on New Year's Eve we wished each other and everyone in the building a happier 1969. Well . . . '68 had been slightly better than '67 in the Hut, '66 at the Patch, and '65 in the little cement room! "Should old acquaintance be forgot, and never brought to mind"—screw that song, too, that's no good for us either!

Chapter Thirteen

1969—PURGE

In January 1969 Stable Three reported that Corley had been eating little or nothing, and Bomar was about to start force-feeding him again. The good news was that our very first packages from home were being given out. (Families had been sending packages for years, but we never got any until 1969. The Vietnamese kept any that came until then.) Three men in Stable Three had already gotten theirs, including Corley, whose package contained pictures of his wife and children. Corley never showed any sign of recognition of his family, and he threw the package and photos across the room.

The man who usually saw the packages come in was J. J. Connell, in the Gate House. He said they arrived by pushcart, in mailbags marked *"Muskova."* A new problem arose. The gooks printed an inventory form of the contents of each package, then asked the recipient to sign a receipt, which had the usual "due to the humane policy of the DRV, I received this package from home," etc. This upset the guys, because even signing a receipt seemed wrong, and getting goodies through the Vietnamese made them feel guilty. It wasn't known if everyone was going to get a package, so some felt it could be considered taking "special favors" from the V. A lot of harsh words about what to do flew back and forth. Some guys were put on their knees for refusing to cooperate. It was getting bad—"ridiculous" is a better word.

The POW reaction to the receipt thing probably perplexed the Vietnamese, because inventories and signatures for anything and everything were, to them, the normal way of doing business. Lump told one guy, "You would complain if we shot you with a golden bullet!" What could you answer to a screwy statement like this?

Something had to be done, and while we were still thinking it over, the question came: "What is your policy on packages from home?"

Policy: "Our families and our government have gone through a lot of trouble and expense to get packages to us. They want us to have them. Take the packages, sign the receipt, and quit bitching and quibbling about it. Share what you can with the guys who didn't get packages." This defused the package situation, and thereafter the only sore point was the pilferage by the gooks.

A lot of excitement among the V attended the arrival of packages. Those poor people had never seen anything like the things we got from home: scented soap, toothpaste, quality underthings, thick and fluffy terry washcloths and towels, candy, and dried fruit. There were pretty aluminum-foil packages containing wondrous dried things that required only the addition of hot water to grow into a delicious breakfast or lunch. Ron and I often thought about how they must have wondered about the luxuries of our world, ten thousand miles away.

There was no doubt that early in this package program, they took a little from each. We saw them running around with vacuum bottles of hot water. Rabbit suddenly gained weight. We POWs bitched among ourselves continuously about theft, but I think that by 1970, the V had finally quit stealing stuff from them. (Years later, I found out that Evy kept a checklist of everything she ever sent, and after studying her lists, I realized that, after 1969, I got all of the items she sent.)

My first package came before Ron's, and I split everything with him. One pair of boxer shorts and an undershirt each, plus this new miracle toothpaste with something in it called "fluoride," which was actually supposed to prevent cavities—how about that! It tasted so good we had to resist the temptation to eat it. The one thing Evy stuck in the package that I wondered about was a dozen packages of chewing gum. I had never chewed gum, and neither had Ron. Zoorat came to the peep and said, "So you received a package from home." He was twitching and giggling as usual. I looked at Ron and winked. "Yes, would you like to have this package of chewing gum? We have plenty." We were setting him up. He took it; then we immediately inquired about Fred Cherry. He told us that Fred had surgery and that "it was very successful." We asked, "Who is taking care of him?" He answered, "The Vietnamese people are taking good care of Cherry." We already knew. Fred was alone in the Library building. I handed Zoorat six packs of gum and said,

"Would you please see that Cherry gets these, because we know he does not get letters." Zoorat took the gum, and a couple of days later we heard Fred had gotten it, which surprised us.

In about a week, we had used a bar of Dial soap down to a tiny piece. One of the cute little water-jug girls came to the peep. I offered the sliver of soap to her. She looked around to make sure no one was looking, took the soap, smelled it, and tucked it into her blouse. I also had a very small white washcloth with pink flowers printed on it, and I offered it to her. She took it, felt it, and smelled it—such a temptation! But I could see she was afraid of being caught accepting a "special favor" from one of the *Mỹ*, and she knew she would be severely punished for it. Reluctantly, she handed it back.

One of the few things the Vietnamese always took from our packages, and never let us have was American cigarettes. They understood the power of the American cigarette; it was like cold cash—you could buy almost anything with it. Americans were still being given three cigarettes a day of the locally produced unfiltered Truong Son brand, so the V kept all cigarettes that came in the packages.

Things were fairly quiet in the beginning of 1969. The V decided to demand that the POWs read the news over the system, so it would be better understood, or maybe they hoped that the "news" would sound more believable if it was announced by one of our own. So, after taking some minor punishment, a POW would agree to read, then he would fracture pronunciation or in some deliberate way make the news report sound even dumber than it was.

The Tet holiday came again, and we got the usual *Ban Chung* rice squares, along with a decent meal. While things were quiet, I sent a query around the building: "What action should we take if the gooks launch another round of torture?" That went over like the proverbial lead balloon! Nobody wanted to think about it. Some replied that they were sure it was all behind us. No suggestions on specific action came in.

Again I messaged that it was possible, and that we should all stick together and try to stop it. I suggested, "How about if we all go to the windows and scream in unison, *'Stop the torture! Stop the torture! Stop the torture!'* " A lot of silence greeted that suggestion. One day, on the way to the well, while we had to wait for the guard in front of cell one, Ray Merritt came to the window and saw me. He whispered, "I don't like your idea." Well, I knew it wasn't that good, but everyone was bankrupt of suggestions at that point. So nothing was resolved on the question of torture.

We went out to see another movie. This one was the answer to our own Bob Hope–type USO shows. It showed a traveling Vietnamese entertainment unit, which was composed of about ten people. The setting was supposedly in the jungles of South Vietnam, and it showed the entertainers walking to the outposts to help troop morale. The cameras followed them all through their jungle trek. It showed how enthusiastically they were greeted by their "fighters." There were six young and beautiful girls dressed in short skirts. They looked very professional in their singing, dancing, and entertaining. The soldiers obviously enjoyed their little break from the battle, and then the troupe moved on to another jungle encampment.

The North Vietnamese regular soldiers made do mostly by themselves in the field. They received very little support from the home front by way of food, medical supplies, and weapons. I wondered what it took to get an R & R (rest and recuperation).

We have often heard it said that "human life is cheap in Asia." That is an oversimplification of a sad fact. I know from personal observation that Chinese mothers, Korean mothers, Japanese and Filipino mothers scream just as loudly as American mothers do when their children are killed. Nobody wants to die. Everyone bleeds the same color of warm blood, and I think that it all comes down to this: In a battle, if Americans learn that two marines or GIs are pinned down in a foxhole, we'll send out two fighter squadrons in multimillion-dollar planes full of expensive fuel to help them, or do anything that it takes to rescue them, because the cost of it is not as important as the people are. The most expendable thing we have is money.

Americans are willing to spend whatever is needed to provide the best of medical care, food, weapons, and entertainment for our troops. It shows the American military that the folks back home are concerned about the personal well-being of the people who protect them.

On the other hand, when the Asian fights, he doesn't have the luxury of unlimited support. The Chinese who fought the U.S. Marines in Korea sometimes suffered losses of ninety to one hundred percent. They didn't have enough weapons to equip all their troops, so as the first line of armed Chinese went down, others stepped forward, picked up the weapons, and tried to continue the advance. What Asians have the most of is *people*, so they send them before the guns. Humans are *their* most expendable item! They don't like it, but it's a fact. They do sacrifice huge numbers of people to gain an objective.

Over in the Stable, Bomar finally had to start force-feeding Corley again. It was either that or watch him die. After three or four weeks, his condition worsened, and Jack maneuvered the gooks into thinking it was their own idea to hospitalize Corley. They took him away, and he was gone for three or four months.

Morale improved all around the Zoo, as packages and a few letters continued coming in. One day we got reports that during attitude checks the QZRs were asking a lot of questions about fish. That was unusual—what the hell is that all about, we wondered? Some of the stuff sounded mighty familiar to me. I kept turning it over in my head, and finally I hit on it. "Ron! I know why they're asking so many questions about fish! One of my favorite books is *The Book of Florida Fish*, and it has dozens of color photos of every fish in Florida waters. I'll bet Evy sent me that book in a package, and they kept it and are entertaining themselves with it, the sleazy little bastards!" (It was exactly as I had surmised, but they never did give me the book.)

Then Zoorat went on another kick to "check attitudes." This time, instead of calling the POWs out to quiz, he had the guards let them out in front of the cells, where he chatted with them. When he came to see Ron and me, we sat on the edge of the walk while he asked a lot of nothing questions. That day, he was interested in American nightlife. He wanted to know about the drinking, partying, and how brazenly the show girls dressed. While on the porch, we walked up and down and stared at each of the door peeps. We knew that everyone in the front cells of the Pool Hall had peek holes. It was always good to get a head-on view of a buddy for a more positive identification. After talking to a man through walls for years, you felt very close to him. But your only sighting of him might be looking up at him through a crack, or a fleeting side glance as he passed. Then when you finally met him face to face, he looked totally different from what you had pictured in your mind—you might not even recognize him.

Spiker reported that everyone in camp (including the crippled and injured guys) was actively and enthusiastically doing calisthenics—that is, everyone except Jim Clements, who preferred sitting on the boards, thinking. I told him to get off his duff and join in, but it would be a cool day in hell before Jim would be interested in exercise. People were setting individual goals, like fifty push-ups and one hundred sit-ups per day, or running in place for several thousand steps. The younger guys, who were still in good shape, were even doing hundreds of handstand push-ups! It was amazing what some of our people could accomplish, once they decided to go ahead with it and set some firm goals for themselves. Communicating encouraged competition and helped us stick to achieving our goals.

The camp quizzers launched into another program to get us all back into writing. It wasn't too serious a push, so we handled it easylike, and only wrote if they absolutely insisted. Some ridiculous writing was done, but the gooks didn't care what you wrote or how short the story was, as long as you didn't refuse to write. One of the prisoners wrote a short story on "How to Surf," another on "How to Sail." Zoorat leaned on me until I wrote two paragraphs on "How to Catch the Wily Lemonfish."

One afternoon, the two of us sat in our cell discussing popular songs, and Ron asked me what my all-time favorites were. I replied that I had five on my list: "Poinciana," "Black Magic," "Brazil," "I'll be Seeing You," and "I've Heard That Song Before." (No doubt about which generation was mine!) Then our talk moved to Hollywood stars. I asked Ron if he remembered one of my old-time heroes who starred in *The Crusades*. His name was Wilcoxon. Ron didn't remember him. About a half hour later, the peep opened. It was Zoorat. "Ga, here is something for you." He threw a letter in on the floor, and I snatched it up. As I dumped out the contents, a couple of snapshots hit the floor. I already knew from Evy in late 1967 that our eldest son Allan, who was then at the University of Florida, had a steady girl. But I wasn't prepared for the news this letter contained. There was a picture of Tom, our second son, standing at an altar with a cute little red-haired girl! That was a shock— a totally unexpected wedding announcement! The letter also said that Allan (now an air force lieutenant) would marry in a month. It was tough to accept that two of my boys, kids when I last saw them, were now married men, and to realize life was certainly going on without me. The letter was already ten months old! The other news that struck us, in light of the conversation we had just had, was that the family had moved into base quarters at Patrick AFB, the new address was 15A *Poinciana* Drive, and Tom's new wife's maiden name was *Wilcox*! Ron could only shake his head. Is that some form of ESP, or what?

In April I was called out to a quiz with the Elf. He sat there on a large, straight-back chair with a younger gook-in-training on each side of him. Three men on one chair! Of course the chair wasn't wide enough to accommodate them, and the quiz-kids on each side had just enough room for one cheek. They each stuck out one foot, off to the side, to keep balanced. Elf had his rubber slippers off as he sat cross-legged in the center of the chair. Between us there was only a small wooden field desk. As usual I sat on the little stool. Elf was busily paring down his toenails with his fingers. It was an interesting, if revolting, sight.

"And so, Ga, how do you feel?"

"Okay."

"And how is the treatment, according to you?"

"Not bad." I had learned it was useless to complain.

"So what will you do after the war?"

"I'll be very old by then, so I will retire and go fishing. What will *you* do?"

"I will go back to my old job as a schoolteacher." He threw a couple of toenails away and started working on the big toe.

"Will you go back to your village with your wife and your parents?" I persisted. (Now I was interrogating *him*!)

"Oh no. That is not our custom. My wife will go back to *her* village to live and will take care of her mother and father."

"Where will *you* go?"

"I will go wherever the government sends me to teach."

"But not with your family? You like that?"

"You do not understand. I told you the government will send me. After all, who knows better than my government where I should go?" At that point he took control of the quiz again and recrossed his legs, switching working feet.

"So, Ga, what does your wife do?"

"She is a housewife and mother."

"And what does she *do*?"

"She takes care of her home, she cooks, and she cleans. She takes care of our four sons, makes their meals, drives the younger ones to school. If she has time, she joins the ladies in a game of bridge, or plays a round of golf."

"See, see! Your wife is a prisoner of your society!" What a jubilant discovery for him. I thought of Evy, driving around in the Florida sunshine in her Chrysler New Yorker—God, what a prisoner, what a punishment!

"You see Ga, *our* women are truly free, truly! See for yourself." I looked out the door and saw two old women carrying pogo sticks, one with a double load of bricks and the other with two "honey buckets." This is *freedom*? I wondered.

"And your wife, Ga, tell me, does she ever demonstrate?"

"Yes, once a month, but nobody even notices." Wasted Yankee humor. It was clear that our ways of life were too far apart to bridge with any understanding.

In camp communications, there was sometimes a misunderstanding in the use of "camp commander." Whose commander—theirs or ours? So I came up with the idea (not too bright an idea) that in all comm we would use "GKB" to mean the gook boss, and "YKB" to mean Yankee boss. I also hoped that, should another purge get underway, the coded designator might offer me, as SRO, some protection against discovery. That was foolish, for several reasons. For one, if the V had a memory problem and forgot that I was senior (hardly possible), they could have gone into their notes to refresh themselves. The other reason is that when a number of men are tortured and the gooks run a cross-check for information, there is no way on God's green earth that the truth won't come out. It would be nice if everyone could protect the information, but it's only a dream—it will never happen that way. You can invent all kinds of code words, letters, or whatever, but the result is that the senior guy will eventually be fingered as the leader. One of the responsibilities and realities of leadership, as Truman so aptly stated, is "the buck stops here."

The second-ranking officer in the Zoo was Lowell Groves. He told us the newest program was to have our guys fill out a formal biography. Well, I didn't think it was that serious, because they had started that back in April of '66, and we all wrote a bunch of fairy tales then. Lowell replied that this one was different—a twenty or thirty-page form. There were questions with lined spaces for answers. Bound between bright blue covers, it was referred to as the "Blue Biog." Lowell suggested that we put out a resistance order, to slow down production of these Blue Biogs.

Some of our people thought it was possible that copies of the finished product might be furnished to China, Russia, Cuba, and North Korea. But if the V had ever chosen to do that, they would have looked even more foolish. Anyone with an appreciation of Yankee humor would have recognized the Blue Biogs for what they actually were—a collection of fantasies. But I concurred with the recommendation and put out a message that said, "Take significant punishment before agreeing to do the Biog."

Zoorat called me out and told me I had to do two things for

him: "First you will make a tape of the news Ga, and then you will fill out this form." With that, he threw the famous Blue Biog on the table.

I told him, "Nah, I'm not going to do that. I don't read well, and furthermore, I've already given you all that personal information two or three times."

Then he tried to get gruff, and said, "Get down on your knees!" I was very slow about it, and he stepped out of the quiz room. I sat down on the floor. He came back and yelled, "What are you doing?"

I said, "I don't want to kneel down, my knees hurt—see?" and I pulled up my pajama leg and showed him a big scar from having cartilage removed years before.

He said, "Well okay, then sit on the floor and ponder." He left me there. Late in the day he returned.

"Are you going to write?"

"No."

He sent for my gear and had it put into Auditorium Two, which was the right front cell of the Auditorium building. It was about seven feet wide by twenty-five feet long. It was actually a hallway, closed off at the ends—that's why it was such a long room. There were two bricked-up windows at the side and louvered double French doors in front, with a hasp and padlock. Everyday, Rat came in and ordered me to my knees. As soon as he left, I got up. He caught me again and made me stand against the wall and reach for the ceiling. For the next few days I was either kneeling or reaching, but I stopped as soon as they left, with the exception of a few rough three-hour stretches when Rat left a guard on continuous watch. It wasn't that bad, and I figured I could last a long time that way, because Zoorat simply wasn't hungry enough to really nail me.

On the third day of May, Zoorat came in and was noticeably friendlier, so I decided to try to charm him out of his project. I kept saying, "Really sir, I don't want to do it." Although I would have bet my last buck on his homosexuality, I wasn't quite prepared for his next declaration.

"But, Ga, *you* of all the prisoners here, I love you very much."

"Holy shit," I thought, "this guy is not only a fairy, but a crazy one at that!"

"Yes, *you*, above all the others," he repeated.

"Well, I don't want to do it."

"You must, you cannot refuse." He insisted.

Assuming that he was still talking about the Blue Biog, I thought ahead. "Well, I'll play this guy's silly game, and if he commits himself in some embarrassing way, I'll put the son of a bitch in such a spot he'll never be able to pester me again. I'll have him off my back for good, and he won't be able to force anything on me. I'll just threaten to tell the gook commander, and it'll be his ass for propositioning one of the $M\bar{y}$."

So I sat on the boards and asked him to sit and chat, "because I am very lonely." I fluffed up my blanket, and he sat down next to me, all the while giggling like a little girl. We named him wrong—it should have been "Giggles."

"Gosh, you are a fine-featured little fellow. Are you bigger than the others, or smaller."

"Oh, I am much smaller." Z. R. replied.

"Really?" And with that I gently touched his wrist with my thumb and forefinger to measure across the bones to compare with mine. He was so pleased he was practically jumping through his own rear end. Then he got real nervous, maybe needed to collect himself, so he stood up and said, "Now I must go! And you, Ga, please fill out the book!" This droll story was so good I foolishly decided to share it with my buddies in the Pool Hall, just to pick up their spirits on that Sunday morning.

Still having the blue notebook and the pencil, I composed a note: "Hey guys. I think Z. R. is queer as hell. I'm going to sucker him into making a move, and when he does I'll chop his pork off and threaten to tell the GKB. He'll never press me for anything again! He wants blue book and tapes, and I won't give. Don't sweat me, I'm fine. YKB."

I rolled up the paper as tiny as I could and tied it with a string I pulled out of my blanket. I dropped the note into the *bo* can so it was above water, then tied the other end of the string to the base of the handle and closed the lid. At six A.M., the guard opened the door and I set the *bo* outside, in the shade. The sun was just hitting the front of the building. Then I sweated it out.

Ed Mechenbier came to pick up the *bo*s, and he moved mine right out into the bright sunlight! Damn! I could easily see the string, even through the dusty louvers. I moved away from the door. Suddenly, I heard the guards yelling my name, "Ga! Ga! Ga!" I knew the note had been found. Shortly Groucho, the old hard-assed key, threw both doors open, wearing a wide victory smile. Then Zoorat, the happy gook, joined him, standing there in his blue shorts wiping the early morning sand and glue out of his eyes. Holding the note high he exclaimed, "Jackass! Jackass! We caught you! So the old jackass wants to carry a heavy load, so we *give* you a heavy load!''

He and Groucho were so happy they were slapping one another on the back, because they knew they'd come out of this with a ''well done''! Again slapping his thigh, he said, ''We caught you in the act! Now here, Jackass, you read it to us!''

Never expecting Zoorat to goof up like that, I grabbed the note and backed slowly down the long hallway, talking easylike. ''Oh no, sir, you don't want me to read this, it would be so embarrassing.'' What I was sweating out most was that now I'd have to explain what a ''queer'' was. Oh, they knew all about that all right, but not in English. They were still congratulating one another as I popped the note into my mouth and started chewing. Suddenly, they both realized what was happening. They did double takes. Groucho yelled the equivalent of, ''You stupid SOB, why did you give him the note?'' Zoorat was petrified, but only for a moment. By that time I had retreated all the way to the back of the long cell. Then they were both on me, beating my head and face, trying to make me spit out the note. I fell, still chewing and swallowing. The note tasted shitty, but what the hell, no choice there. They left for a minute, still arguing. I had swallowed half the note, so I quickly spit out the rest, tore it into tiny pieces, and randomly jammed the pieces back into holes in the rough brickwork.

When they came back, Zoorat was shaking like a dog passing peach pits. By then I had calmed down, and pleaded very gently, ''Please sir, don't be upset, you didn't want to hear what I wrote.'' Groucho was still giving him hell for giving me a chance to hide the pieces. They searched the room, but came up empty.

''On your knees!'' Zoorat shouted.

''Yes sir, I always do what I'm told.'' I answered meekly. They left again. In a few minutes, Zoorat came back, still trembling, and handed me a couple of sheets of blank paper.

''Now, here is paper, you write the note word for word! We know what the note said, so if you don't write it exactly, you are going to be severely punished!''

I got up off my knees and said, ''Listen sir, don't make me write it, I tell you, you will not like it. It will be an embarrassment. You will know why I didn't want to write.''

''Write, or be severely punished!''

''Okay, if you insist, I'll write the note.'' He went out, and Groucho locked the doors. I wrote the second note, and it came out this way:

"Hello out there. You don't know who I am and don't try to find out. It's not important. It's just that today I am so happy that I want everyone out there to know that at last I have found a little Vietnamese that I really like. I call him General Lee, cause he is such a stately little fellow. I'm happy because I have found out that an American and a Vietnamese can truly be friends. Don't worry about me, I'm okay, and please don't try to communicate with me.

Signed\
A Yank in Uncle Ho's Court

When he came back for the note, I handed it over, saying very softly, "Here sir, now you can see why I didn't want you to have it, because you must show it to the camp commander, and he will know that you and I are friends, and it's going to look very bad for you." He took it and stomped off. He returned later. "You had better do the blue book, Ga!" Well, I figured I had pushed Zoorat to his limit, and since he let me off comparatively easy, I had better fill up the blue book with the usual horseshit. Between the wrong signatures, the poor printing, and the backhand slant writing, I ruined three books before he finally accepted one. That bothered him plenty, because they didn't like wasting paper; in some ways they were very frugal. On the whole, I was satisfied that I had delayed the process and gotten away with murder.

Zoorat came to collect the Blue Biog, and he had his tape recorder and a copy of the *Courier* with him. I refused to tape, so he had me escorted to the Carriage House, which was at the entrance into the Zoo and just across the road from J. J.'s building, the Gate House. I didn't see J. J., but a couple of the Thai prisoners sat in the doorways (they had a rather free run of the camp) watching everything that was going on. Once there, I had to kneel in four-hour stretches, reaching for the sky. Zoorat was getting exasperated, so he called Slug to help. I wouldn't kneel anymore, so Slug attacked me and beat my head so hard my ears were ringing, and I thought he had burst my eardrums. Finally, I agreed to make a tape. It was a rather insignificant news report, but I messed it up anyway. He did let me off the hook on a few articles that I felt listeners might have thought were statements written by me. The tape was never used, because something far more important would shortly get their focus. I went back and joined Ron in Pool Hall Five on Friday night. I had been out for about ten days, and told Ron all my adventures. He thought the story about me eating the note was incredible.

At five in the morning, on the eleventh of May 1969, we were awakened by the Duck, the tall sergeant who was the official torturer up at the Briar Patch in 1966. I got the impression that he personally wanted to see if I was where I was supposed to be. Several others were with him, and since the peep was still open we peered out. We could see that some of the guards were excitedly pointing to the south wall, toward the Barn or Garage cell blocks.

We had no idea what was going on. We only knew that the daily routines were way off schedule. Sunday was usually a stand-down day. No baths or clothes washing went on, because many of the guards were off duty until Monday.

About twelve-thirty or one o'clock in the afternoon we received a shocking message through the wall: Two POWs had escaped from the Annex during the night or early Sunday morning! Spiker was elated and said he wished we were with them, but it came like a kick in the stomach to me. My response to Ron, Spiker, and Coniff was that the two were probably already dead. I reflected on the fact that the Duck had come to check on me, even before anyone was interrogated. This proved that the V knew very well that I was the camp SRO.

The senior ranking officer over in the Annex was Conrad Trautman. We knew that, for security reasons, nothing concerning escape plans had ever come over the fence from him.

A few minutes later a second message came by hand-flash, from the garage across the swimming pool to Moon Mullen in our cell number one. The message said that two men had just been brought into our compound, blindfolded and in handcuffs. It was believed that they were the two escapees, Captains Dave Atherton and Anthony Scorpio. We didn't know the exact time of their departure, or the time of their recapture, but we figured they were outside the walls from ten to fifteen hours.

I believed that any escape attempt was gallant, but, all things considered, also foolhardy. Risner and Denton's initial guidance on escape told us not to try it "without outside help." My interpretation of "outside help" was an agent or agents outside the prison walls, or a helicopter rescue, by our own troops, at an isolated camp. The possibilities of an escape of an obvious westerner, out of the city of Hanoi, toward the west into Laos, in our physical condition, with the lack of available clothing and footgear, made the chance of success a big fat zero. Nor could

I visualize heading east toward the Gulf of Tonkin. Caucasians would stick out like sore thumbs among hundreds of thousands of Asians.

However, we couldn't rule out *all* escape efforts, because some very unusual opportunities might have presented themselves. The very fact that Atherton and Scorpio even got outside the walls proved that there was some merit and logical thinking to their plan.

Then we heard that American prisoners had been put in all four of the corner Auditorium cells and also out in the Gook House, which was the headquarters building. We thought there might be someone in the Carriage House, and in the Chicken Coop. We never could nail down exactly how many men were brought in from the Annex initially, but our first report said seven. A few hours later, we heard screams and the lashing of whips from those directions. It went on most of the day and continued throughout the week. It was awful to hear and worse to know we were unable to do anything.

I knew we were all in serious trouble. The gooks wouldn't let up until they felt repaid for the insult. I didn't know any message then, nor have I been able to come up with anything in the years since, that I might have sent out to everyone to help them prepare for the upcoming ordeal.

Spiker said that he and Coniff had been discussing it with the others in the building, and they all felt I was making too big a thing out of it, that it would all blow over in ten days. That floored me, and as I sat down on the bed I said to Ron, "Could our people actually *believe* the gooks are going to let us off the *hook* on this? They've got the goods on us, and the leverage! They won't stop until our skulls are crushed in. It's going to be maximum torture for everyone!" Either everyone in the Pool Hall was trying to kid themselves, or it was Spiker's own idea that it would "blow over." Fat chance!

The guards began by harrassing us with thirty or forty look-ins a day. A "look-in" meant that every time a guard came to the peep you had to get up and bow. They would look at you menacingly—point at you, talk to the other guards, point again, and repeat the process. It was all very ominous and intimidating, which was exactly what they set out to accomplish.

People were getting caught communicating all over the camp. Each time they were caught, some junior English-speaker would tell them that although they made a mistake, he would "forgive them their crime." This encouraged some of our people to think things weren't too bad. I thought they were nitwits to read any-thing good into that. It was just that the torture facilities were overloaded because of the escape attempt, so the V couldn't be bothered by minor rule infractions at that time. They probably had a wall chart to plot all of the communications incidents, which would help them figure out where the main comm points were throughout the camp. That possibility seemed a hell of a lot more logical to me than shoving our heads in the sand think-ing we were actually getting away with something because the gooks were getting lenient with us.

They took me out to quiz, and I was asked to make a tape, according to what they said was "an agreement" I made at the time Slug was punching my ears in. I refused, and they put me on my knees, and I still refused. Then the Rabbit came in. "We know what you have been doing, but don't rush it; don't give my guard a hard time; go ahead and make the tape and you can go back to your room and tell the others that you were punished to make a tape." We already knew that Rabbit asked a lot of our people why they were so obstinate about making tapes, and some of them went so far as to say, "I can't do it unless I am punished." He made a joke out of it by telling me to "go back and tell the others you were punished." I didn't go along with his suggestion, but after a while I gave in and made a tape, and I made a very poor job of it. The Rabbit also said, ominously, "Don't rush the program. I will be seeing you in a couple of weeks. We will be all set for you then, and I will be your OIC." That meant "officer in charge." Rabbit loved to learn our ex-pressions and abbreviations, so he could talk like he knew ev-erything about us and could also converse colloquially. Answering a simple question of mine one day, he held his hands palms up and answered, "God only knows." He was an atheist, so we must have taught him that one, too!

When he said "OIC," I looked him dead in the eye. I knew what he was talking about, and he knew I knew. He was saying, "You just sit where you are, and when I'm ready to pluck you, I will pluck you."

The tape I made was a short report of a battle in South Viet-nam, the usual trash, that they destroyed 450 trucks and killed nine million Americans. It was a token thing, to make me, the SRO, bite the dust and also to intimidate me, because I had to make the tape right up there where I could hear the screams of our people being tortured. A couple of days later, the twenty-fifth of May, they called me out again. This time they took me

to the front room of the Auditorium, room number one. I sat
down with a young English-speaker, who tried to get me to
make another tape, and I gave him a hard time. The Lump came
into the room and talked to me for a few minutes about why I
refused to make the tape. Then he went out and came back in
with a very senior gook. He was referred to in other camps as
Major Bi, alias "the Cat." He looked to be a very sharp individual. He was friendly with me, patted me on the shoulder,
playing cat and mouse. Then he looked at me and said, "We
think you know many things."

I was plenty nervous, my stomach was churning, and I hadn't
eaten anything that day. I knew my breath was pretty stale, so I
let him have it right in the face.

"Sir," I exhaled, "I don't know what you mean."

He caught it square and jumped back. He almost threw up.
Pointing to my tin cup, he commanded, "Drink water, drink
water!"

"No, it's okay, I don't need water."

Major Bi backed up, and Lump repeated, "Ga, we think you
know all about the camp."

"What I know wouldn't amount to a fly-speck on a horse's
ass. Do you know what I mean?"

"Of course!" Lump said. Then, flapping his arms like a bird
he said, "You mean you fly."

"What's the use," I thought, "you can't make any sense."

"We know you are the SRO," Lump added.

"Oh, I am still the SRO? Don't you have any colonels in this
camp yet?"

"No, you are still SRO. Everybody does what you tell them
to do." He laughed and kept dragging it under my nose. Then
he said, "Have patience."

Cat got in his two cents. "In a few more weeks I will see you
personally again, have patience," he repeated. We both laughed,
but I knew they'd have the last laugh.

Lump told me that he would not force me to make the tape,
because he noticed that my voice was hoarse. "We will even
give you special food, because we want you in *very good condition*," he said, giving me a knowing look. Back at the cell,
we got continuous look-ins by officers and guards who were
anxious to see the SRO, the one they were told was responsible
for all of their problems. They wanted to believe that. They
needed a scapegoat as an alibi for their security shortcomings,
and it looked like I was going to be it. There was no way they

would ever believe the truth—that I had no knowledge whatever of the escape. Ron guessed that Cochise had already been fired from his job as commander, and probably many gook heads would roll over this one.

The number of Vietnamese camp personnel and guards was up considerably because of the large number of prisoners being tortured. They may have been anticipating a riot. My earlier suggestion of banging on the bars yelling "stop the torture" didn't seem so ridiculous now. But it's a tough deal to try to give guys living in semisolitary conditions the feeling that they are working together on an issue that's bound to result in horrible punishment. Each man, in his own mind, hopes that the enemy won't pick on him. People all over the world are still wondering why the Jews going into the gas chambers went quietly. I believe that each of them hoped that a last minute miracle, or change of heart, would come about just in time to save his life. Some POWs had the same kind of futile hope about the retribution over the escape attempt.

Ron climbed up on the *bo* to peek through the louvers, which were now closed most of the time. He looked right into the eyes of Fatass, one of the meaner quiz kids. Fatass then opened the peep. "Ha, I have caught you looking out, but today I forgive you." Bullshit! I put out the word to curtail all bull sessions and to try to hold down the number of people getting caught. But the guys must have felt the need to talk to each other more than ever before, so comm continued at a hot pace. I could understand that need, but I also knew we were putting ourselves in more danger. We knew nothing about the escapees' fate.

From time to time, the whipping sounds, and the screaming, would increase in intensity. Then, after a few days, it would be almost nothing. Then a new cycle would begin. We took that to indicate that a fresh batch of POWs was being put through the torture mill. Slug would often come to the well while we were there. He carried a stiff switch, which he slashed through the air as he looked at us. We knew it was all part of the big scare operation. It was working well!

My appetite dropped off because of my nervous anticipation, and also because they were now putting whole potatoes into the soup. I must have developed an allergy to potatoes. My throat swelled up so much it was impossible for me to eat them.

For the first couple of days of the torture sessions, we were not allowed into the bath area at the end of the Pool Hall building, because of its proximity to the Auditorium, where they had some of our people. Later, when we resumed taking baths there, we realized they no longer had our people in the Pool Hall, but were using the Coop building exclusively for torture.

On the night of the twelfth of June, at about nine P.M., the peep opened, and a dark-skinned guard, Jose, looked in. He opened the door and told me to dress. He walked outside the room and waited. Ron came over, shook my hand, and said, "Good luck to you, Lar." I said, "God, here we go again—my turn in the barrel." Ron had a real sad look—he knew very well what was happening. I felt that it was going to be just as bad on Ron, being alone and worried back in the room, because he suffered a hell of a lot when we were apart. Well, I figured, what the hell, it was no surprise, we knew they were going to come for me one day. I had never missed a year without getting tortured, so it was a matter of it being my time again.

When I stepped outside, Jose grabbed one arm and pulled it behind me, then shoved it up high, to hurt or scare me a little. He walked me that way down the street, directly to the Ho Chi Minh room, room number three—in back of the old Auditorium. He took my slippers away from me and shoved me into the room and onto the floor. He put a very heavy set of leg irons on me, then closed the door. The room was dimly lit, as usual, with a very small light bulb.

Big festoons of cobwebs hung down to shoulder height, and huge gray spiders crawled on the floor. They were at least four or five inches across. But those furry-looking things didn't bother me a bit. Dozens of daddy longlegs spiders were hanging on the cobwebs, and the floor was covered with ants. The cell swarmed with mosquitoes. Parts of the ceiling had fallen down. There was bamboo lath up there, and you could hear the rats scurrying around the rafters. Alongside the wall were stanchions a foot high, which would normally have held a bed board. There was no bed board, and my seat was the famous little wooden stool. Every five minutes or so, a guard came in to peak and make me get up and bow. They did not let me sleep at all, but kept interrupting until I just laid on the floor and put my head back. They had to yell at me to get me up, harrassing me all night long. The next day I got a cup of water in my own little cup, which they had gotten from Ron. All the next day I had to sit there in the cell, and guards harrassed me every few minutes. A little English-speaker, a young man from the Briar Patch with whom I had some rapport, came and said, "Ga-reeno, now your time has come for all you have done against the camp authority—

now you must account for it all. Now it is your time!" He
seemed to be particularly offended by the idea of my being im-
plicated in this escape, as if I had personally stabbed him in the
back. He was also trying to tell me, "I am for my side and not
for you." That day, I got the normal food ration and water.

That night, they harrassed me again and wouldn't let me sleep.
I lay down a couple of times, and they'd yell at me and get me
up again and again. When I did fall down, exhausted, I found
myself eyeballing a huge furry spider just a couple of inches
from my eyes. He eyeballed me right back, but never moved
one inch closer. It was a standoff.

Saturday morning, the fourteenth of June, was the fourth anniversary of my shoot-down. And I was a lot worse off than I
had been in earlier years. The guards came and motioned me to
get up and move out. I stooped over to lift the crossbar of my
leg irons, then hobbled down the steps and across the yard to
the Chicken Coop, room five, where most of the torture had
been going on.

They made me kneel down and reach my arms up high. In a
few minutes the Rabbit came in, and he was *so* smug! "Are you
ready to confess your crimes?"

"I don't know what you mean."

"I told you—you know very well what I am talking about. I
am going to be your OIC." He continued to play with me,
grinning at times, then quickly changing moods and giving me
that black, ominous look that Rabbit often used to strike terror
into your heart. While he was talking, I could hear whipping
noises and men screaming horribly in the same building, but
the Rabbit didn't bat an eye. I could never tell who the men
were.

"Well, I will come back when you are ready to confess," he
said. The thought crossed my mind several times: four years,
nothing changed—still on my knees, still in torture, and the war
didn't look any better, even though there were negotiations going on in Paris. Last November we thought we'd be going home
in a month. Now, I was looking desperately for something, anything, to cling to. It was so hot that my sweat formed a puddle
where I knelt. Occasionally they gave me water. They knew I
had to have that to survive.

I continued to kneel from seven that morning until just before
noon, when a goon squad came in. One of them pulled my pants
down, then kicked me over on my belly. They spread-eagled me
and tied my arms and legs with ropes. A couple of people stood

on my hands, and someone beat me with a fan belt. Not much, only a half-dozen strokes. Just enough to let me know what was coming, and that it was going to be excruciating. At chow time they let me sit on the floor for fifteen minutes to have some soup, with half a loaf of bred. Then back on my knees I went. I tried to rest by falling down now and then, but the guard would force me back up at bayonet point.

Lump came around. They added a blindfold. That made it difficult to keep my balance without falling over. Lump said, "How is YKB today?"

"I don't know." I gave no sign of recognition of my call sign.

"And how is YKB?" the Lump repeated. "Your fellows over in the next camp, in the Annex, they sent you a nice message. They say that on the occasion of your forty-seventh birthday, they surprise you by each man completing fifty push-ups and one hundred sit-ups." I didn't bat an eye to that either. (I did send a message out later on the bottom of a bowl with an aluminum spoon: "TY NO ABT YKB," meaning, "they know about YKB.")

"*You* have led the camp resistance to authority, and *you* have caused us a great deal of trouble. You hear your fellows, how they scream and suffer now!" Then he left me alone. Shortly, a new game began. Everytime an officer (Lump, Spot, or Rabbit) was through interrogating me, the goon squad returned and repeated the fan-belt beating, each time increasing the number of strokes. Between the interrogations and the beatings, I had to stay on my knees, until about six in the evening. Then they sat me on the wooden stool and harrassed me all night long, refusing to let me shut my eyes. My legs and feet started to swell due to restriction of circulation from the irons.

Three mornings later, I was getting nutsy because I had been awake seventy-two hours. Spot came in while somebody down the hallway was being whipped. With the victim's screams and the yelling of the guards providing background, Spot teased me about being the "ko-mander." I tried to think of an out, a way to get it all over with for all of us. There didn't appear to be any gain in continuing to deny knowledge of the escape. Maybe I could reason with the gooks, show a willingness to take it all upon myself. . . . Would they stop torturing people? I might as well give it a shot. "If I say, 'Yes, I do lead the resistance, I am the SRO,' what else can they do to me?" I thought. "They're going to torture me anyway, no matter what I do or say." Later that afternoon, after being on my knees all day long, Lump returned to ask, "Now are you ready to admit your crimes?"

"Yes," I replied.

"Good, then tell me." I told him I knew about what had happened.

"You are willing to admit that you know it?"

"Yes, I'm telling you I know about it, and it is all over with. You caught the men again, and I don't see any point in you continuing to torture people. So ask me anything you want to know, and I will tell you and you can stop."

"So you are willing to admit?"

"Sure." I was still on my knees and blindfolded at the time.

"Ga-reeno, for all you have done against us, we are going to make you pay! You know the camp commander has already lost his job, and I am in very great danger of losing my own."

"Let's try not to make this a personal thing between you and me," I reasoned. "I am the SRO of the prisoners and you are the camp commander. I have my job to do, because I am senior, and you have your job to do. If you lose your job, this camp is not that good a deal. You can get yourself a better position somewhere else in Hanoi." I don't think the Lump got the point of the jab, but even as miserable as I was, I couldn't resist throwing it in there.

"No, no, Ga-reeno, for what you have done, you must suffer, you must pay a price!" Then he asked how long it took to get the messages, and I told him I thought it was just a few minutes. Then the Lump paid us a backhanded but honest compliment. "I am very impressed by what you have accomplished. I am very impressed by the efficiency of your communication system. But now you must pay!" So they weren't going to let me, or any of us, off the hook. So much for that!

From the fourteenth on, they kept me in room five twenty-four hours a day. I was on my knees from six A.M. until six P.M. Sometimes I was reaching for the sky, other times it was hands tied, or thumbs wired behind me. Most of the time I was blind-folded, and always in the leg irons. There were two fifteen-minute interruptions for food. I don't ever remember having to go to the toilet at all. My tin cup was always with me, and they replenished it readily since they knew I couldn't last without water. I sweated profusely. All night long they kept me awake, sitting up on the little stool.

On the fifteenth, the Rabbit came in from time to time to ask me questions about why I resisted and why I caused trouble by making the men resist? I would always go back to the Code of Conduct: "Because it was the proper thing to do."

In the afternoon, Spot wanted to know what I had gotten in the first message, and I told the truth, that the message was that two men had escaped that morning from the Annex. He asked about the second message. I told him the truth again, that two men were caught and returned in irons and blindfolded. Then he wanted to know what my return message was. As I recalled, I didn't send back any message. He insisted that I did, and I insisted that I did not. He accused me of ordering the escape, that it was my fault. He kept it up for hours, and I kept denying it.

The goon squad came and beat me again. This was my fourth or fifth beating with the fan belts. The first few times I was hit I cried out, because the sensation was so unusual and so horribly painful. There is a severe burning feeling when you are hit, and it feels like your buttocks have been set on fire. I tried not to scream, but involuntary noises came out after seven or eight whacks, no matter how hard I tried to hold back. Oddly enough, the more torture a man takes, however, the more he *can* take. The best thing is to try to learn how to screw them out of all their fun, because for them to get real kicks, the victim must be screaming. This excites the crazies even more, and then they really lay it to you. Not yelling or screaming is easier said than done. I tried hard as I could to cheat them out of any pleasure they got from beating me.

There is another side to this kind of torture—the perverted side. Sometimes they pulled my shorts all the way down, and some of the weirder bastards played with my buttocks with their bare toes. This naturally makes you tighten up in anticipation and fight it, which gives them even more kicks. Spot put the bottom rung of the stool across my neck and pinned me down, while the others stretched me out with the ropes. The way Spot screamed in ecstasy, I am sure he got complete sexual satisfaction from torture. No surprise. Anyone who can torture another human being the way they did has to be sick or perverted.

During the next couple of interrogations by the Lump and Spot, the subject moved to policies. I told them that my policies were in accord with the Code of Conduct.

"What do you tell them about making Christmas tapes?" I told them that my policy said that it was okay to do it. Spot turned to me with a sheet of paper in his hand, and damned if he didn't read my policy back to me word for word! Then he asked me about the "package policy" and why was it that I told them to sign the inventory statement? I explained it by saying, "Signing a receipt is not a statement; there is nothing wrong with that." Well hell, I thought, there's nothing wrong with our policies anyway.

"You tell them to lie when they write, don't you!" Spot said.

"No."

"You tell them to lie! I know you tell them to lie! What do you tell them?"

"Well, I tell them to try to delay, and so on, like that." He then read my writing policy to me, word for word. He had a bunch of sheets of paper in his hand, and I knew he had them all. They showed great interest in our policies, and sure enough, they eventually read them *all* back to me! Again I asked them to stop torturing the others, but of course they would hear none of that. The gook had been embarrassed, and now he would have his pound of flesh. They were having one hell of a good time extracting it from us.

The other poor fellows took some long volleys with the fan belts. I heard some pretty heavy numbers of strokes. Some told me later that I got the same whippings, but I didn't think so because I never remembered any more than ten to fifteen strokes before I passed out. Once, when I regained consciousness, it was very quiet, and no one was in the room. I lay there alone in a puddle of urine. I raised my head very weakly and looked toward the doorway, just as a very young sentry came into view. He stared at me briefly, wide-eyed in horror, and slowly backed away. Then he turned and ran. I must have been an awful sight.

It's impossible to say with any accuracy whether it was on the same day or another day that I was on my knees, trying to invent some way to stop them, and I came up with an extreme idea, a last resort, desperation idea, which was as stupid as it was desperate! However, in the condition I was in at that point, it's hard to think smart and brave.

"If I try to kill myself," I thought, "I can get the attention of higher headquarters. These people will have to report it, and if some of the senior people come in, they'll see that the camp commander has completely lost his head in taking revenge on the prisoners and will stop it." I was *hoping* that would happen, but I also knew that it was possible that higher headquarters had *directed* the torture in the first place.

I saw that one of the torturers had left a stretch rope under the desk. If I could just manage to wrap it around my neck, then climb up on the wooden stool and reach the metal brackets that the windows were hung on, I might be able to get the other end of the rope looped over, then fall off the stool and hang myself. Then I saw that the brackets were held only by wood screws that might pull out. The hemp rope also looked frazzled and could snap immediately from my weight. I didn't want to botch the job that badly. No, I decided, hanging wasn't a good choice.

I didn't really want to die, I just wanted to do something drastic enough to attract attention, so they might think more carefully about what they were doing. Another idea hit me. The Coop was the only building in the compound that had glass windows. I decided I'd slash my wrists. I hoped that somehow I'd luck out and live through it. Most of the time I was blind-folded and tied, but this day, because of the laziness of the guards, I wasn't tied or blindfolded. I was only on my knees in the irons. One of several things could happen. I'd bleed to death . . . or they'd catch me and punish me more . . . or they'd have to stop the torture to take care of my wounds. They could find me on the floor bleeding and sew me up, and I'd end up with a crippled arm, provided they could get some blood back into me to keep me alive. If the medics were around, I'd have a chance to live. I decided that that was the best course of action, and the more I thought about it, the more reasonable it seemed.

An American in the next room started screaming. He was yelling, "You're killing me, you're killing me, stop, you're kill-ing me." Then another poor fellow across the way in the Gook House started. Hearing a bunch of gooks yelling, I turned to the window and saw them running toward the center room of my building. I caught a flash of white uniforms—the medics! That triggered me. It was now or never! I got up off my knees, grabbed the iron bar, and hobbled to the windows. I punched one of them through with my left hand, throwing glass all over the yard. Pressing my left arm down against the edge of the glass, I turned it as hard as I could. Nothing. I looked at that damned glass. It had broken in rounded edges! Panicked, I reached up for two long shards hanging down from the top of the pane like icicles. With my right hand, I grabbed one and broke it off. As I did, I cut the hell out of my right palm. I slashed the piece of glass across my left wrist twice, as hard as I could. All I got was a couple of bruises! I was astounded! Wasn't Jesus Christ *ever* going to let me go? Why wouldn't He let go of me? At that point, I screamed. The gooks had heard the windows break. Duck came on the run and was on me. He checked my wrists, then banged me all over the floor. By that time the medics were there—everybody was jabbering at once. Duck blindfolded me, and I felt several of them pick me up and throw me. The voices became soft and very far away. Sometimes I heard irons clanging, sometimes it was quiet, then I was awake, as I drifted in and out of consciousness. I was on my belly. Here came the fan belts burning me. I don't know how many times I was hit, but everything in my bladder and bowels came out on the floor.

I was being forced to sit up, and a voice came through. Hard to hear at first, I was so dizzy, and my ears were ringing. It was Lump talking.

"So you want to die, hey, Ga? Okay, we allow you to die! Not fast, like you want to die! We are going to make you die, but nice and slow. Okay? So you don't want to go back and see your wife and children anymore? You think we care about that? We don't care! I can sign a piece of paper saying Ga-reeno died in the prison camp. It's very simple. I can do that."

I was sure they had already done just that with others, in their hysterical whipping sessions. Then Rabbit came.

"So you want to die, huh? We don't care! We can deny ever knowing you. We can say we never heard of Ga-reeno."

With great effort, I whispered hoarsely, "You can't do that—I've already written letters home—my people know I'm here."

"What do we care? We can deny it! What can they do about it?" He was right, and I knew it.

Johnson had stopped the bombing in '68, and now for sure they could tell us all to get screwed, and that's what they *were* saying. We had removed our own fangs. He repeated the line to make sure it sunk in:

"We can deny we ever heard of you Ga-reeno."

That night, from my stool perch, I saw that all of the windows had been taken out of the Coop and were leaning against the side of the Gook House. They were also careful not to leave any ropes around. They weren't about to let me or anyone else cheat them out of their fun.

My suicide idea was destined to failure from the outset. A small plus was that it took their attention away from the other poor guys, if only for an hour or so. They dropped them like hot potatoes, to concentrate on beating the living shit out of me!

(In later years, I related that experience to members of the Air Force Chaplains' School. It choked them up because they believed, as I always have, that it was a kind of miracle.)

I had seen the gooks in action so many times that I knew that, without some supervision, in their hysteria they *would* kill. The next day, I remember only that they roped me by the neck and pulled up all my weight so the noose closed up. Just before I passed out, I dimly heard a voice calling *"Veet, veet, veet!"* I think it means "stop." Otherwise, I would have been just another of the returned remains, as Lump promised.

Conrad Trautman had already been put through a horrible torture ordeal. Later he told me that while they were putting him through the mill, he chanced to look out in the yard and saw the gooks lead me up the steps of a scaffold and hang me by the neck. Connie was positive he was actually watching them kill me. How he came to be so sure it was me was just a trick his mind played on him, because he had never seen me, had no idea what I looked like.

The next mark in time I knew for sure was the third of July. So sometime between the nineteenth of June and the third of July, while I was on my knees again, Fatass came in to get his jollies. I hated him with a passion. He demanded that I take a rigid position of attention, balanced on my knees and toenails. It was not possible for me to maintain that position for more than a minute at a time. I kept falling down. Furious because I couldn't comply, he grabbed my leg irons and started twisting them and flipping me around on the floor. I was not blindfolded, nor were my hands tied. Weak as I was, that was my snapping point, and I flew into a wild rage. I wrenched the irons away from him and jumped to my feet. I picked up the iron bar so I could hobble better. I saw real fear cross his face as I screamed, "You miserable sadistic son of a bitch, I'm gonna kill you!" I went after him, and he backed off and ran around the desk. Then he ran toward the door—there was a sentry standing there, with his pistol drawn. He said something to Fatass in Vietnamese, maybe, "Stop, don't show you are afraid." Fatass kept his eye on me, very much afraid as he danced around, trying to stay away from me, because I was definitely going for his throat. He made it through the door, saying something to the guard like, "To hell with that, this guy is crazy!" As I tried to follow Fatass out the door, the sentry walloped me on my right ear with the gun, knocking me senseless.

Hours later, when I was conscious and could see again, I found that my right shoulder had been badly skinned from being flipped and dragged, and all the hair on the right side of the top of my head had been ripped out by the roots. My knees were puffed up like two rotten jelly doughnuts, and felt like they were stuffed with broken razor blades. I was still in room five, when Spot returned to question me as I knelt there.

"What message did you send to the other room?" (He meant back to the Annex after we learned of the escape attempt.)

"I told you. I didn't send any message."

"Yes, you sent a message. You said, 'Congratulations, our entire country will be very proud of you.' "

"I didn't say that."

"Oh yes, you did. And now we punish you some more." They sat me on the floor and wrapped me up in ropes as tightly as they could. This time I was determined not to make a single sound, and I didn't. A gook stepped behind me and grabbed my cuffed hands and pulled up, lifting my weight off my seat, putting the strain on my shoulder joints. He bounced me up and down on my battered rear, and the pain in my shoulders was excruciating.

In the course of that rope "exercise," I could feel my bones bend, and my skin stretch. I realized that the body can take a lot more punishment than the mind wants it to. More than ever before, I felt like I could stay quietly in control. Spot was wondering whether I was awake or passed out.

"Ga! Ga! Are you faking?"

He reached over and lifted up the blindfold. I looked him in the eye and said, "I'm still here." I seemed not to mind what they were doing to me. Could he have been impressed by that? When it became too much I said, "Okay I'll confess."

"Good. What was the message you sent?"

"Congratulations, our whole country will be proud of you."

"You lie!"

"Okay, here's another confession. I ordered them to escape."

"You lie!" I realized that neither Spot nor any of the rest of them gave a damn what I said—they just wanted to pound my brains in. It didn't make any difference whether I spoke or didn't speak, it was a fun time for everyone. Spot stopped questioning and left.

While I was sitting, the torturers bent me over so far that I ended up with my head pushed under the bar that was across my ankles. I don't know how the hell they got me in that position, but there I was. I remember thinking, "Good Lord, I didn't know I could do tricks like this!" They rolled me back and forth on my tailbone, and up on my back. I couldn't feel my hands, so I don't know whether I was on my hands or off to my side or what. They rolled me around like I was an exercise dumbbell, not a living human being. Soon they became bored with that and chatted among themselves for a while. They must have agreed on a new game to play. They pulled my head back out from under the cross bar, and with a man sitting on each side, they beat me with bamboo rods, from above my knees down to my toenails, and especially across my shins. It hurt like bloody hell, but I found somehow I could keep my mouth shut and didn't have to make a sound.

They rubbed their dirty sandals on all of my open sores, which were soon infected. Several days later the bamboo beating had turned my legs a pretty blue color, with big shin bumps that would be a lifelong souvenir. It seemed quiet for a long time. I was in and out of it. They must have loosened the ropes, because the next thing I realized, I was sitting on the floor, and Spot came charging back, hollering, "Ga-reeno, Ga-reeno! Now today we test your endurance! Who do you want to talk to today? Do you want to talk to your mother? Your father? Your wife? Your sons? You want to talk to them? Very well, I allow you to speak to them! You will call out for them all now." They rolled me over on my stomach and stretched me out with the ropes, and Spot pinned my head again with the stool. He put his face close to my ear and yelled, "Call your mother! Call your father! Holler for your father, holler for your children!" Another gook pulled my shorts down, spread my legs apart in the crossbar, and then a two-man whipping team went to work on me. I did pretty good in not yelling, although during a long volley some involuntary sounds did slip out. Whatever I had in me again came out on the floor.

I have no idea how long they continued beating me, because I had escaped into the clouds. When I awoke, lying there, the room was quiet. I felt something dripping on my buttocks, which I thought was blood running off me, but later I realized that a medic was dropping some kind of solution on my open wounds.

Slug came in, removed my blinds, and tossed me a cigarette, which I ignored. I thought they were going to beat me again. What the hell . . . ? I didn't care anymore. He shook his head "no, no"—he meant for me to get up and go out to wash! Two of the Thai prisoners came in with buckets to swab off the floor, which must have been a real mess. Dragging my long pants behind me, I stumbled into the road, tripped and fell several times. My eyes! I was seeing double, and was so dizzy and nauseated I couldn't navigate. A few gooks sitting on the steps of the headquarters building laughed uproariously at the sight of me flopping around, falling and staggering, trying to make it to the well.

I fainted on the ground near the well. Slug came and kicked me to get up. I tried to haul up water but couldn't. There was water already there in a big pan. I tried to wash my pajamas but couldn't—I just took them with my left hand, which was a little more usable than my right, and threw them at a clothesline. Then I flopped down on the ground again. As I was lying there, several guards came by and pointed at my rear, chattering loudly. They seemed stunned at its condition. Lifting my head a little, I looked back and saw it was swelled up bigger than a basketball, and ripped open in numerous places, and running with blood and fluids. One of the guards picked up another pair of pajamas from my cell and told me to put them on. They didn't want to have to see the result of their handiwork.

Back in Chicken Coop Five that night, I sat painfully on my swollen and bloody rear in plain sight of people on the outside. They were having a meeting for camp personnel, right down to the kitchen help. They had a power generator going and spotlights on their briefing team. They were using a huge blackboard and telling their people about the escape. They had a light focused on me, too, and frequently mentioned my name. "Ga" this and "Ga" that, using a stick to point in my direction, saying, "There's the cause of all of our problems!"

Slug now walked slowly, ceremoniously, from the briefing officer through the yard and through the open door. He stood by me, giving me a long look, kind of like he was in a movie. Then he reached in his pocket very dramatically, took out a pack of cigarettes, put one in my mouth, and lit it for me, as if to say, "Even though you are a rotten S.O.B. and the source of all our problems, we give you better treatment than you deserve."

My legs were all puffed up, and my feet and toes, Lord, were puffed up like little balloons, all soft and watery. An English-speaking gook medic came in while everyone was still watching. He shook his head and said, "Oh, that's no problem." Maybe *he* thought it was "no problem," but I thought it was a *hell* of a problem! When the meeting was over, Slug came back, and I told him I needed to lie down and sleep. He said, "No!"

A little English-speaker we called Boris came in as I sat on the stool. He spoke quietly, and in a kindly manner.

"You see, you have caused the camp commander much problem, much problem. That's why he punishes you. Now we don't want to punish you. You can go back to your room and live there quietly. But you must not cause trouble.''

"Can I sleep?"

"Of course, you can sleep." I slid off the stool to the floor and instantly fell asleep. Only minutes later, Slug came yelling and kicked me back up to the stool. Boris returned: "The guard says it is not time for you to sleep yet."

Early the next morning Spot was again asking, "Why did you order an escape?" I told him I had already offered to confess, but he refused to accept it.

I lost track of everything, except when I knew I had been about two hundred hours without real sleep. My brain was asleep many times. That night I told Slug, "I've gotta sleep, I've gotta sleep." He said, "Sleep okay." Son of a gun, I couldn't believe my ears! I flopped down on the hard, filthy floor, which now looked like a beautiful king-size mattress, and conked. The mosquitoes were all over me, but that was nothing after what I'd been through!

They say that the Nazis played classical music at the death camps of World War II to keep the Jews calmed down as they marched them into the gas chambers. Many times, as I lay on the floor recovering from those beatings, the V piped in ballads sung softly by Eddie Fisher. Sadly, I'll always think of his songs as "Music To Be Tortured By."

The morning after my first real sleep, a young man came in to say, "We have seen that you still have a very bad attitude!"

"Whatta you talkin' about? I don't have a bad attitude."

"Oh yes! You attempted to kill one of our fellows the other day!" So that was being talked about in the camp! That was good. I had not seen Fatass since. He had lost face, but it showed them I was still clinging to my "old, aggressive ways." I was perversely pleased that they took notice of the incident.

Darned if Fatass didn't come in by himself to see me! He must have figured that I was totally subdued now and no longer a menace to him. He got on the "bad attitude" kick—then asked me to surrender my T-shirt. I refused, and he didn't persist, but in a day or two somebody did get it off me. It was just another torment—to help the mosquitoes get to me even better.

I was moved to the room at the far end of the Coop. Duck came in and took the irons off long enough to make me remove my pants, leaving me there in only my undershorts. They still had me kneeling through the daytime, but the guards had become bored with it and were not totally vigilant. I was able to spend a good part of the day down on all fours. Everyday I was beaten with the fan belt, but now only a few blows.

Spot brought a pencil and paper and told me to write to ask Uncle Ho for amnesty. I knew then they were determined to make me do everything they knew we had put out a policy against. They had told me, "In the eyes of your fellows we are going to humiliate you, for all that you have done against the camp authority!"

After that, whenever Spot came in, it was for information on committees. They had a lever on me. The questions skirted around a very sensitive and unmentionable subject that scared me silly. I ran from it, denying any knowledge of it with all my strength. I think they knew they'd have to kill me for it, but it worked for them anyway, because I was glad to give them something else as long as they moved away from that one.

The things I did give them as a trade-off were in answer to four questions put to me by Spot:

"Who is the 'historical committee'?"

"All of the building senior officers." I answered, giving the least harmful answer I could think of.

"Confess to your athletic committee."

"Now confess your communications committee!"

That one scared me, too, because they could have made a major issue of it if they chose to do so. He pressed me.

"Who is the committee, what do they do?" I told him that once again, all building leaders were on the committee, and their job was to think up and inform me of new ways to communicate. Spot surprised me when he accepted that simplistic answer. Once again, it illustrated that sometimes we worried more than the situation demanded, because in many ways the Vietnamese were a very simple people, and we sometimes made things more complicated for them, and ourselves as well.

A couple of more days went by, and I was still on my knees, in the irons, when Spot came in with a big one.

"Now, I want you to confess all about your escape committee!" I denied having any such committee, and I stuck to my guns. Somehow Spot sensed that he wasn't going to make any nickels on that line of questioning, and he gave it up a lot easier than I ever imagined he would.

"Committees" were a real big thing, and they continued to interrogate me about them all through July and August. Eventually, I learned that other poor guys in torture had volunteered as many as sixteen "committees," inventing them as they went along! In their words, they "would have done anything to make them stop the incredible torture." I know how they felt. They already had my policies word for word, and the satisfaction of having kicked in our skulls. Now they wanted to carry it just one step farther with me . . . to total humiliation. But I was past worrying about something so minor as humiliation.

I was also at the end of my ability to tolerate the endless hours of kneeling. The next time I fell, the guards tried to force me up, and I called *"Bao Cao"* for the first time. Lump came. I told him, "I don't give a damn if you kill me, I'm not gonna kneel anymore." The goon squad came and beat my ass again till I passed out. But after that, except for just a couple of brief moments so they could make a point, they didn't force me to kneel any more.

Spot told me I had to "write a Fourth of July message." My brains were pretty scrambled by then, but I think I wrote the same old crap about the four thousand-year-old history of the Vietnamese people, and, if you can imagine, compared George Washington to Ho Chi Minh! They loved that—Washington was one of Ho's favorite people, because he led a revolution.

By then, the torture session had gone on for about three weeks, during which they had tossed me in and out of every room in the Coop. I started hallucinating, and once thought an elephant was trying to crush me. I was almost over the edge of sanity. One day they made me pick up the irons and hobble to see Rabbit.

I sat on the bench and looked at him, and there were two of him. I had double vision. I sat there glaring. He knew I was out of it and said, "So now do you repent your crimes?"

"Sure."

"Do you admit your crimes?"

"Yes."

"Now do you want a way out?"

"Yes."

"I give you a way out. You agree, and I will give you a way out. I want you to write a series of articles. I want eight articles from you for the camp magazine." Up to this time I had never seen a camp magazine. I had only heard them talk about it back in '67.

"Okay," I responded wearily. "What kind of articles?"

"You know our appetite."

"Yeah, I know what you like." (The worst, filthiest trash I could generate, I vowed.)

"You must first write me an outline."

"Okay."

"It is agreed?"

"Agreed."

"Okay, you can go back and sleep." So I hobbled back to the room, and when I got there I found my mosquito net. I put it up, tying it to the barred window and a nail in the wall. As soon as I got on the floor, under the net, they had a power failure that lasted a week!

One night, I heard them beating some poor American only about fifteen feet away from me. Finally, he agreed to make a confession, which Rabbit taped. The POW confessed that he had "committed crimes." I could hear everything. In the future, he promised to obey the camp regulations and squeal on his "fellows" whenever there were communications going on.

A little later, still listening intently, I heard a bunch of gooks outside, and one was the Rabbit's voice. Then it quieted down. I heard a broom scraping the ground, and I thought it might be a signal from an American out there. I promptly responded with a couple of coughs. Just two quick ones, meaning, "I hear you" or "Roger." As soon as I coughed, all the gooks broke into loud laughter, as if they knew there was going to be an answer. I had the feeling that the Rabbit was saying, "See, what did I tell you about that perfidious Mỹ. No matter how you pound his brains in, he still tries to communicate!" Would you believe the broom scraped once more . . . and I answered again! They must have loved that!

They had to take me out every day for a couple of hours, into more light, to write the articles for Rabbit. I sat on the floor, using the little stool as my desk. My hands were nowhere near recovered from all the times they had put me through the ropes, so the handwriting was atrocious. My pants stuck to my bloody ass and to my knees, and I had to squint through my goo-goo eyes, still seeing double. But there I sat, "writing" for the camp newspaper!

I wrote an outline and said I planned to write a coloring book story, then a song to the tune of "Wabash Cannon Ball." I don't remember what other garbage I proposed, but Rabbit accepted the outline.

I laughed a lot as I wrote. By then, I was really a fruitcake. My first story was called, "A Coloring Book." It began with, "I am the commander's aide. I run all his errands and take care of his dog. Paint my nose brown." Then, "I am the commander's intelligence officer. I am always good to him, because I know that many nice things come from the commander. I write him up for decorations and plant many ideas into his head. Paint my fingers green." Then, "I am the wing statistical officer. I always claim that we drop more bombs than we really do because we have to beat the navy. Color my head red." The sad one was about kids: "I like kids, you like kids, everybody likes kids. So how come we kill so many of them in the wars?"

For "Wabash Cannon Ball," I mixed together two fighter-pilot songs. I started with some changes to the words of "Itazuke Tower," a song famous in the air force during the Korean War. Instead of using Itazuke, I substituted Cam Ranh so Rabbit would think I wrote it especially for him. In the other song, "Halle-lujah," I changed the Yalu River to Red River. The mixed words went something like:

"Hello Cam Ranh Tower, this is Air Force 505, just got back from North Vietnam in a bird that's barely alive. . . . "

Rabbit paused in his reading. "Why do you use 505?"

He thought it might be a secret message I wanted to send out. I answered "Five-oh-five rhymes with *alive*."

"Why can't you use 947?"

"Nine forty-seven and a bird that's *alive*? It doesn't go together. You like that better?"

"Yes," he answered.

"Okay, 947 then. Let me know what else you don't like as we go along." I didn't give a damn! That it rhymed, or sounded right in English, didn't mean a thing, since our sounds were foreign to him.

It all went way over Rabbit's head, but he was pleased that I was producing something. I was producing something all right . . . time. It was trade-off time. Time to get off the hook, re-habilitate, get some guts back to survive and bounce back again, if I could.

My brain slowly healed, but it took a lot longer for the body. I was pushing fifty, and I didn't bounce back as high, or as fast, as I used to. The double vision receded after a month or so, and that was a big relief.

I managed to dawdle about two weeks on the writing exercise, and Rabbit was getting pissed. He said I was "dragging out the job." My stumble-fingered journalistic masterpiece was eighty-eight pages of bullshit. When I handed it to him, he went into a rage and tore it to pieces.

After that exercise, my hands started working again, and now Rabbit unveiled the real thing.

He handed me three formal-looking documents, which he said were written by other Americans. I looked them over. Rabbit said he only wanted me to make one copy of each, but I wouldn't have to sign any of them. I couldn't figure why he was asking me to copy them. Maybe he had already told the real authors that their papers were useless, and he didn't want them to know that he was going to use them. The first article was signed by a U.S. naval officer. It was intelligently and cleverly written. The title was, "Who Are The Betrayers?" The crux of the message was that Truman, and all of the presidents up to Nixon, had continually betrayed the American people.

The second article addressed the Uniform Code of Military Justice. The UCMJ is "the Bible" for military conduct, discipline, and punishment in the U.S. military services. This code was adopted following WW II, replacing the Articles of War. The piece was well written, and it was signed by an officer of the United States Marine Corps. The gist of it was an advisory to all that it was not necessary to obey "illegal orders." According to the author, an "illegal order" was any order given in an "undeclared war." It advised that these orders should have been disobeyed, then contested and beaten in a military court.

The third article was entitled "The Code of Conduct." It applauded the Code as a magnificent and idealistic piece of work, which a military man might suffer torture and even death to uphold. However, the paper went on to declare that "the Code is not at all applicable in Vietnam, because it is an undeclared and illegal war."

I believed, because of the proficient use of English, as well as the thought processes reflected, that the first two articles were actually written by American military officers. The writers were either writing under extreme duress and force, or they were having serious personal problems in sticking to the values and principles deeply ingrained in American military officers.

The third article had too many propaganda expressions and too much convoluted Communist logic to be genuine. I had to believe it was penned by a Vietnamese, possibly the Rabbit himself.

Around the third week of July, I was taken before four or five Vietnamese officers. I bowed and sat on a chair before them. The Buzzard (a much older man, in his late fifties or sixties) was now camp commander. He was skinny as a stick, severely buck-toothed, and his eyes were a watery, faded blue. He had very thin, gray hair. He pretended he couldn't speak English and used an interpreter. I knew, however, that he spoke very well, because I had heard him before. His eyes drifted a lot, and I thought, "This guy hits the water pipe." Lump was there, along with Rabbit and Cochise, the former camp commander, who got booted in May after the escape attempt.

They recognized I had a vision problem, or perhaps Rabbit had already mentioned it to them. With my clothes on, you couldn't tell what terrible condition my body was in. The only indicators were my ankles and feet, which were stained brownish red from being in rusty leg irons so long.

The interpreter advised me I had been "carefully selected to see a visiting delegation" in a few days. They gave me a half-dozen minor questions to answer, as a test. The first few were the usual personal ones. Name, family, type aircraft, when and where shot down. Then, "What do you think U.S. forces are doing in Japan? Do you think they are there to protect the Japanese people?"

Answering the questions involved no disloyalty to the United States. I took my time and wrote true answers. They said my answers were satisfactory and ordered me to memorize them. The final question on the list was, "How are you feeling?" The Rabbit, with a big smile, told me what to answer to that one. "You will smile, Ga, and say, 'Oh, I am fine, look at me!' " he ordered with a menacing look. They said that I would be meeting a Japanese delegation.

On the way out, Rabbit said, "And now we get your head cleared up, with vitamin pills." He did send the medic around. I took twenty pills at a time for the next couple of days, and they seemed to improve my sight and my general physical condition.

On the night of the twenty-fifth of July, they brought me someone else's pajamas, with number 156 stenciled on the back of the shirt. I "suited up" to meet the delegation, with socks on to hide the telltale iron marks. They hauled me off in a truck, blindfolded and in irons. I was taken to a waiting room in a building I had not seen before. I was given a bottle of beer and some cookies, and told I could have all I wanted. I was immediately sick from eating and drinking such rich and unaccustomed food, and they had to rush me to a broken-down toilet. After that they kept moving me from room to room, probably so I wouldn't see any other Yanks. They made me face the wall a few times, and I could hear Yanks shuffle by, one by one, in their clogs. I learned later that Vohden, Kasler, Groves, and one or two others were there that same night.

My time arrived, and by then I was shivering like a leaf, weakened by diarrhea, heart pounding from even this small exertion. Since the answers I would give were not harmful to my country, I was hoping it would go okay and might get them off my back for a while. I went in and was directed to a chair in front of bright lights and cameras. It was hot as hell from the lights. Sitting just under the cameras was the Rabbit. There was an adjoining room with a wide open archway, very much like an open living room. Major Bi and the Lump sat there, watching. There was also a strikingly beautiful girl looking on, whom I initially took to be Japanese. I looked around for more Japanese and saw none. It finally dawned on me that there weren't any Japanese there. The whole "Japanese" bit was a sham! The girl, who was a Vietnamese, was from the movie detachment of the army, and so were all of the other technicians.

They made me practice the answers twice while the Rabbit sat across from me, calmly eating peanuts. Then they shot the scene, with Rabbit asking and me answering, just as I had practiced it, right up to the last line, "Fine, look at me!" Then I had to dash away to relieve my cramps.

A year later, as part of a movie show, we saw a cut of a Japanese delegation visiting Hanoi. It was done very simply and believably. The scene showed an American captive sitting there, apparently in good health. He seemed at ease as he answered questions. The camera panned across the room where there was a long table with ten very fine-looking Japanese gentlemen using words and gestures as if questioning the captive. Of course the film was cut and spliced as if it were a live show. The viewer would see smiles, gestures, and moving lips, but all the words were from a narrator—presumably using the language of the country in which it was being shown. A neat and believable fraud, simple and inexpensive to put together, to send out to audiences who wanted to believe.

The next day the Rabbit, very pleased with himself, said, "All right, Ga! For you the road is over. For others just the beginning." I figured he meant I had "paid for my crimes" and was off the hook. Wrong again.

Toward the end of July, I decided to start a project to keep the ants from coming in under the walls. Of course they could still come in through the huge holes in the ceiling, under the door, and around the window. However, I needed something to do to use up the daylight hours. So I caulked the cracks all around the base of the room where the walls joined the floor. I tore up old rotten pajamas into small pieces and jammed the pieces into the cracks. Then I smoothed it off with my yellow soap. I worked very hard at caulking, like a driven man. It made me feel better, because I had a goal. I had to do something, anything, or I would go nuts.

Since Ron and I had had our spat a few months before, I had backed way off from prayer. Whenever I knew torture was imminent, I would say, "Looks like I'm going to need You again." But then when it actually got underway it was, "I'm going to be busy now, see You later." I found it impossible to pray while being tortured, because even though I was on the receiving end and could do nothing about it, I needed to concentrate on what was happening. It was as though I could only handle one thing at a time. This may not make any sense, but that's how it was with me. It shows how different we all are from one another. I heard that some of the guys were actually able to quote Scripture during torture! That, to me, is incredible.

Zoorat had started coming around to see me in the Ho Chi Minh room, because he wanted to know more about "committees." Even though I remembered admitting to a few committees, I denied it to him. He got mad and ordered me to get on my knees, which were still soft, pus-filled balloons. I resisted, but he was insistent, so I helped myself a little by getting into a four-point kneeling position. I was wearing only shorts. As soon as I put the tiniest bit of weight on the knees, both bubbles burst, and yellow stuff and blood squirted out all over the floor. Zoorat turned away, sickened at the sight. "Oooh! oooh!" he squealed, "get up!" The pain was terrible. I rolled over and the yellow cores on both knees stuck to the floor. He ran out, retching, ordering me to "clean up that mess."

Around the tenth of August he came back and said happily, "Now today, I do you a favor." He unlocked the irons and removed one stirrup, from my right leg, which was a really good deal, because I could walk around pretty well dragging the iron bar by one stirrup.

"You know much about these committees." He was giving me hints again. It was his favorite game, like charades. He wanted to get credit for getting *something* from me.

"How about the car?" he'd question.

"The car?" I said, then snapped my fingers as if a light dawned, "I got it, the 'car-buying committee'?"

"Yes, that's right." He was *so* pleased that I got the hint!

"Oh yes, the car-buying committee."

"Write about the car-buying committee." So I took the piece of paper, figuring that anytime I'm writing something, at least I'm not getting tortured. So I wrote a bunch of horse crap about what a deal we were going to get buying cars when we got home. I wrote that there were two hundred people in the camp and each guy would buy a Cadillac. If each Cadillac cost about eleven thousand dollars the total cost would be two million, two hundred thousand dollars. I took my time multiplying this out in long form. Then I said, "We are going to get a thirty percent discount," so I calculated the discount amount and subtracted it. By the time I finished, I had two pages of figures! Zoorat pored over all these figures for three or four hours! I pointed out that, if there were four hundred Americans held in North Vietnam (they claimed thousands), we'd have to redo all our figures. So I wrote 'em all down again with new numbers, and the total "savings" was well over a million dollars.

"What are you going to do with these savings?" he asked.

"We are going to give the money to a charitable institution to care for the orphans of war."

"Are you going to send money to Vietnam?"

"It all depends on the others. It's like in your country—if the people want to do it, then we'll do it." From start to finish, the "car-buying committee" business killed three days.

After he digested all that, he returned to ask, "You know more about committees?"

"I don't remember," I said, cagily, waiting for his inevitable hint.

"Yes, you want to get together some time."

"Come on, give it to me again."

"You want to get together with the others after you go home."

"A 'reunion committee'!"

"That's it!" he said, so we continued to play the silly game. It was dumb, but a great time-killer.

"We are going to have a reunion-committee meeting some time after the war," I allowed.

"Who's the reunion committee?" Z. R. asked.

"Quincy Collins." I named Quincy right off the bat, because I knew damn well the gooks wouldn't hurt him—he put on the Christmas shows, and they needed the production.

Quincy Collins was a very talented man, and people of talent suffered in solitary more than the rest of us, because if they didn't have an outlet, it really drove them up the walls. The gooks may have thought Quincy was doing things for them to help their propaganda, but that was the farthest thought from Quincy's mind. He was doing it for *us*, for our morale, and it was a help for the people in the groups he assembled to work in the shows. A side benefit was the chance to exchange information between the prisoner participants, some of whom were from other camps. No, the gooks weren't about to hurt Quincy. They looked at him as the goose that laid the golden egg, but he wasn't their man—he was ours!

Zoorat asked where these reunions would take place, and I named some cities that I felt sure he'd heard of, so he could identify with the story. Miami, New York, Washington, New Orleans, Las Vegas, "Chee-Cago." He loved it and bought the whole bit. This took a lot more time and paper, which would prove to his superiors that he was producing! He could color in a few squares and take some credit.

This was such a good deal, the very idea that I could kill blocks of time with fables, that it encouraged me to volunteer more fairy tales.

"Hey, here's one I almost forgot about, the airman's promotion committee."

"What do they do?"

"Well, that falls on me, because I'm senior. I am the committee of one. You see, our airmen, or enlisted men as they are referred to, do not make very much money. It is my duty to see to it that they receive one increase in rank or pay for each two years that they spend up here." I think that hit him right in his sympathy spot. He liked it and agreed with it.

Then, wishing to continue along in this harmless vein, I dropped the "investments committee" on him.

"What does the investments committee do?"

"Well, I figure that with the total number of prisoners up here, we can get—say, ten to fifty thousand dollars from each as an initial investment, to use as working capital." Here I was, giving a Vietnamese peasant a lecture on investment firms, discounted money, interest rates, block share-purchases, fleet sales, charitable contributions, etc. Zoorat was enthralled, even mesmerized. It was like having a kid on your lap, telling him about the Big Peppermint Stick and the Sugar Plum Fairy.

I said that raising ten million dollars would be a snap. Then I remembered that the V don't use the word "million." To them, a million is stated "a thousand thousand." I clarified the number by restating it in his terms, "ten thousand thousand." He looked stunned. "Then we'll go to one of the larger investment firms like uhh, lemme see, oh yeah, like Merrill Lynch, Pierce, Fenner and Smith [as it was known then]. When they see us roll in there with ten million, excuse me, ten thousand thousand dollars, they'll be anxious to grab our business. As an incentive, instead of taking the usual five percent commission fee, they'll probably only take a fourth of a percent." I wrote more figures. "Christ, that's a savings of over $450,000 in one shot! Do you realize what we'll be able to do with that kind of money?"

"No. What will you do with the money?"

"I've already told you! We can give it to charity, or to the poor negroes in America, or to clean up our rat-infested slums." I wrote down all of the figures on numbers of POWs, contributions, interest computation, and so forth, and made sure that the bottom lines added up correctly.

When he left, he was holding up the papers, studying the figures, mumbling to himself as the guard closed the door behind him. Some people might not concur with some of the things I did to keep the V away from more sensitive subjects. But it really didn't matter what anyone else thought—I needed to do whatever I could to delay any further reprisals for the aborted escape.

In addition to caulking the cracks, I had now added some exercise to my day. Using the extra ankle iron as a dumbell, I started arm lifts, and during the night I walked, dragging the bar. I had to be careful of my knees, but no matter how careful I was, it was easy to knock off the scabs, and then the blood really ran. Because of the poor light, it was several days before I realized that I had left footprints in blood all over the Ho Chi Minh room.

I also had two new "think projects." The first one involved my old boyhood friend, Larry Tobia. We had palled around together in his 1931 Chevy convertible. I decided that since we both had the same first name, when I got back we'd open an Italian restaurant and call it Lorenzo's. The idea of a restaurant must have been hatched by my constant hunger and thoughts of food. Never in my right mind would I have thought of a restaurant as a business venture, because they are such hard work and usually fraught with management problems. And my friend Larry wasn't the type for restaurants either—in general, he shunned physical labor and entrepreneurial endeavor, having had plenty of experience with both. Nevertheless, I pressed on with my daydream. I chose a location, drew up the floor plan, drafted the kitchen floor so water would run off and it would be easy to keep clean. I put indirect lighting, soft, music, and rustic atmosphere in the main dining room. Dinner would be by reservation only, and would feature the very finest Italian cuisine (what else?). One of two polished maître d's would always be on duty to greet our high-class clientele. Handsome, well-dressed men, beautiful women, great food—a first-class place, nothing less.

I got so deep into this fantasy that when Rabbit called me out to quiz, I was annoyed. He was actually causing a major interruption to my project! Getting back to the cell, I'd lie down on the floor again and say, "Okay Lar, where were we?" And off I'd go into my own little world with my buddy Lorenzo.

I also liked reminiscing about my flying days in Sicily and Italy during WWII. Recalling all the names of the pilots of the 308th Fighter Squadron was a mental feat in itself. But I did it. Some of the pilots I flew with there were among the best and most fearless I've ever known. Others had marginal abilities and were genuinely afraid to fly, but more afraid to admit it.

From the invasion of Sicily to the linkup of Cassino and Anzio on the way to Rome, the combat missions were either very exciting or a complete bore. For every grim story in our air war in Italy, there was an equally funny one to balance it.

In the blackness of the Ho Chi Minh room, I focused my recall powers on one mission in particular. It was March of 1944, and we were supporting GIs who were fighting desperately to dislodge the Germans from a huge, centuries-old monastery at the foot of the valley leading to Rome. On that day, four young American fighter pilots flew air cover in British-built Mark VIIIC Supermarine Spitfires. The weather was really sour, with cloud cover down to fifteen hundred feet, in rain, smoke, and dust from the heavy bombing and shelling of the target, the Monte Cassino Abbey. We scooted around the floor of the valley at three hundred miles an hour, to discourage enemy fighters from intruding into the battle area. The visibility was so bad it was impossible to get a good look at the abbey, now the main objective of Allied ground forces.

The lead Spitfire was piloted by Richard Hurd. Dick was the most aggressive pilot in our squadron. The idea was to shoot down enemy planes, and if there were any of them around, Dick was the guy to be with. I flew as the lead of the second two aircraft. Because of the poor visibility, Dick did a lot of maneu-

vering to stay near the target, and I did my best to anticipate his
turns, so we'd end up in a "line abreast" formation for the best
coverage of our tails in case any Me.109s tried to sneak up on us.

Looking slightly to my left, I spotted four aircraft and called
in, "Helpful Red Lead, four bogies [unidentified] at eleven
o'clock, same level."

"Don't have 'em yet."

"Lead, we're closing fast."

"I've got 'em! Get the bastards, they're 109s!" Dick racked
his Spitfire up in a hard left turn, swinging in directly behind
the fourth enemy plane. The Germans were trying to out-turn
us and were strung out one behind the other. As we got close,
I saw that the Me.109s had a strut holding up the horizontal tail
planes and had nonretractable tail wheels. "My God, the Jerries
must be getting awfully hard up, those are old E models!" (By
that time most of the 109s in the war were the latest G-6 models.)
Dick already had the tail-end Jerry on fire, and several seconds
later, the number-three man was climbing out of the cockpit.
"Holy cow, Guarino," I scolded myself, "he's going to get all
four if you don't do something fast!" I cut in hard across the
circle after the German flight leader. He saw me coming and
rolled hard left and down to the tree tops. He was trying to get
back on a northerly heading, up the valley and away from our
Spits. The Jerries had an aversion to the later model Spitfires. I
stayed with him, but slid off to his right and down to the trees,
even lower than he was. I figured that when you're flying on the
deck, it's hard to spot an aircraft that is even lower. Also, fighter
pilots always look over their left shoulder to clear their tails, and
knowing that, I stayed out to his right side. Apparently he thought
he had some safe separation, and he made a bad mistake. I was
overtaking at a rapid rate because my Spit was a lot faster, but
then he pulled up to five or six hundred feet, and I ate him up.
Putting my electric sight reticle on his cockpit, I held fire until
I was only a hundred feet behind him. My gun selector switch
was set at "all guns," and as I touched the button, it was like
his airplane was hit by sledgehammers. It fell apart, and the
engine caught fire. Off came the canopy, quickly followed by
the departing pilot. Kicking off to the right to avoid collision
with the abandoned plane, I powered back to stay with it to
impact. The German plane rolled left, and I had to do a couple
of violent rolls to avoid crashing into the ground with the crippled Messerschmitt. It hit upside down on a dirt road and
bounced and rolled end over end for half a mile. Turning hard

left, I caught the pilot at five hundred feet. He was wearing a gray winter flying suit and still had his helmet and goggles on. As I headed for him, he drew up his legs, expecting me to gun him down in his 'chute. I laughed and pulled into a tight circle, thumbing my nose at him as he prepared to touch down. Just then, all the Jerry ground gunners in the valley opened up on me. I hauled ass and managed to get the hell out of there with my skin whole!

It took us only about two minutes to get all four Messerschmitts. Three of the four German pilots had safely bailed out; the number four man went in with his burning aircraft. I loved to picture the three pilots showing up at their airstrip, each with his parachute under his arm. The stern Kraut commandant would ask, "What happened?"

"We ran into Spitfires, that's what happened!"

"I'm going to *hate* to report this! Marshall Goering vill be pissed."

"Screw Goering—tell him to get his fat ass into an airplane and cruise down the Cassino valley—let's see how *he* makes out!"

The fantasy about the Messerschmitt pilots standing there with their parachutes struck me as hilarious, and I rolled around the floor laughing aloud. I was wacky all right, but the laughter was therapeutic relief from pain and suffering, and the dreaming lifted me out of there and back to freedom, and flying, and white puffy clouds—far, far away from Hanoi.

Rabbit asked how many prisoners' names I had learned since my shoot-down. He wanted me to sketch a building layout of the camp and write down the names of people who were in the various buildings. I put a lot of question marks in different cell blocks. I finally admitted knowing eighty or ninety men. Rabbit then filled in the correct names in all of the buildings! I was shocked! He said he wanted us "to be conversational" about who was who, and where they were. Then he asked me to write a report. I asked, "What kind of report?" He answered, "According to their attitudes." He wouldn't give me a hint about what he really wanted, so I wrote a report placing forty men in three categories, which I quickly invented. The categories were: Pessimistic, Optimistic, and Noncommittal. I wrote such things as:

"Cherry, poor fellow, is very seriously wounded. Most of the time he is very pessimistic about his chances of going home. He needs medical treatment badly. . . . Vohden is about the same—pessimistic. . . . Groves is up and down; as an example, once he sent me a message saying, 'I think I see a light at the end of the tunnel, but it's a train coming the other way.' . . . Another man, Jim Bell, is a very quiet fellow and never commits himself in any direction; yes I would say he is noncommittal." Then I wrote about Byrne the optimist, myself the pessimist, and others in camp. It was just another pile of horse crap and told them nothing, but it killed more time.

A few days later, he brought my "report" back.

"I don't want that. I want you to grade them as to resistance. I want to know strong resistor, weak resistor, and average resistor."

"Okay." I put down all the guys who were badly wounded, and others whom I thought would have a very hard time in solitary confinement, as "weak resistors." If I put any of those people down as strong resistors, the Rabbit might try to crack them open by putting them in solitary. All told, there were eleven people I named as "weak resistors."

For "hard resistors," I put down Kasler and myself. Jim and I had already been pounded to pieces time and again, and they knew us as hard resistors, so no point in denying that. I put four others with us, because they were the youngest men in the camp and had not been harmed since their initial torture. They were Joe Milligan, Gary Anderson, Ed Mechenbier, and Kevin McManus. None of them, including Kasler, was ever touched as a result of my labeling them with me. I checked closely on that. I put down the twenty guys that were left as "average." The Rabbit knew I was bullshitting him, and protested and threatened, but I told him it was the best I could come up with. He finally accepted it.

Then he told me to write the answers to these questions:

1. Do you think that you are going to be court-martialed for what you have done, when you get home?

2. Do you think that your career would be very much affected by your long stay in the prison camp?

These questions gave me a boost. They showed that the gooks believed we were going home someday. At that time, in August of '69, I didn't know they had just made another prisoner release. The men were Hegdahl, Frishman, and Rumble. Then he asked me how I thought the lives of men who were released early would be affected, and I coughed up another load of skywriting.

He said, "I want statistics." So I made up a whole bunch of

statistics. I said thirty-five percent of all of the prisoners would get out of the service within a year after they got out of North Vietnam, either for old age or disability retirement; forty-five to fifty percent would be divorced because of long-time separation; fifteen percent of the younger pilots would ask for discharge because they wasted too much time in prison camp and would not have much of a career left. That satisfied him. Once again, I felt any time I could waste without getting tortured was time well wasted.

My buttocks drained slightly and were still well stripe-marked, but, physically at least, I was finally improving. The sores on my knees were closing up, but were still painful down to the bone. I no longer had double vision, but my eyesight had deteriorated badly. I came in with twenty-twenty vision, and now I found reading and writing increasingly difficult. For the next few years, with rare exception, I had moderate to severely painful headaches every day. According to later medical examination, they were due to concussion.

To take any kind of stand, let alone a hard stand of resistance, was physically impossible for me at that time. Rabbit called me out and told me to sit. He saw that I was still dizzy, unsteady, and visibly shaky.

"You did well at the Japanese delegation, Ga-reeno. Now we have your biggest task to perform! If you refuse, we start your 'treatment' all over again, right now, so give me your answer, yes or no! I show you I mean business!" There was no doubt in my mind he meant business, because with this SOB it was automatic torture.

I asked, "What is it?"

"We have a part for you to play in a movie."

"Tell me about it." (Jesus Christ, here we go again!)

"It is very simple and very short. I will give you your part."

"Okay," I said.

"Agreed," he said. I got up and went back to my cell. I was sick that I had agreed, but I had to buy more time. I needed to get my guts back.

Sitting on the floor, I heard the rats scurrying about overhead. They did that when they were chasing a live dinner. Several times gecko tails fell on the floor. They bounced around like baby eels, squirming even after being separated from the bodies. I heard more scurrying and looked up just in time to see a large gray rat falling down on me! I leaned to one side, and he landed on the floor and ran around wildly, trying to get his bearings.

He was more scared of me than I was of him. Finally he stopped and stood in a far corner. Picking up the spare leg iron, I threw it, and it ricochetted off the floor and nailed him. I picked him up by the tail and dumped him in the *bo* while he was still quivering. Why couldn't that be Rabbit?

When it was light the next morning, I forced open the frame of the peep. This gave me a partial view of the hallway and a piece of the yard out to the side. I saw a silver-haired Yank walk toward the Gook House with a couple of guards following him. Then there was a lot of yelling and screaming and lashing of the fan belt—about ten to twenty blows—and it became quiet again. I knew then I couldn't possibly live through a repeat of what I had just been through. I thought about my label, "strong resistor." Hah! Right now I didn't have the strength to be an "average resistor," and they damn well knew it, the bastards! I raged inwardly.

Later, the Rabbit handed me part of a script and told me to memorize it. My part would be "The Colonel," with three or four lines to speak. I went out to another quiz a day or so later and met the Cat, who brought me a bottle of beer. I drank the warm beer, promptly got sick, and dashed out to the *bo*. Soon after, Cat said, "So now, in a movie that we are going to do, you are going to be helped by your deputy commander."

"Who's that?"

"You know, your deputy . . . Groves."

"Oh, is that right?"

"Yes. Your deputy—oh, we have talked him into playing the part with you. He was very happy to hear that you have consented to play in the movie with him." I thought, "Sure he's happy. Misery loves company, don't we know!"

"How are you doing on the part?"

"Okay."

"Soon you meet with Groves, but first let me hear your lines." So I recited my "lines." Then he explained the play.

I don't remember the exact lines, but the setting of this one-act play was in headquarters in Saigon in 1957. There were two American army officers, a full colonel (me), and a lieutenant colonel (Groves). The full colonel was a clever and sinister guy who masterminded a plot to overthrow the Hanoi government by the infiltration of agents into North Vietnam and Hanoi itself. The agents would be, as the gooks put it, the "lackeys of the U.S." in the form of South Vietnamese officers. The colonel's assistant, the American lieutenant colonel, was an ambitious and crafty person. My character was to be the real "bad guy." My face would be marked with scars, making me ugly and easy to hate. The younger man would be handsome, with silver hair. Groves was made for the part. He would be smooth-tongued, but dangerous, because he was so ambitious. He would try to push the old colonel, but the colonel would not be pushed.

Sounded like a pretty dull plot to me.

The next day, walking into the Coop to meet the Rabbit again, I saw a handsome, silver-haired American face to face for the first time. "Hi Larry, how are you?" It was Lowell Groves, my second-ranking man at the Zoo. Looking me over, his eyes showed his shock and sadness at the mess he beheld. I was a sick, shaky wreck, and he picked up on that immediately. Looking down at my rust-stained legs and feet, he said, "Good Lord, are you still in irons?"

"Sure, aren't you?"

"No, they haven't touched me yet. I've been sitting over in Pool Hall One, waiting my turn." That was a surprise to me, because I thought the entire camp had been hit by then, and I'd certainly thought they'd go after my deputy and play us one against the other.

Rabbit questioned Groves about some of the younger guys in the camp. I acted dumb when Lowell asked me about a guy in the Library. I said, "I don't know him, Lowell, my memory just isn't that good that I can remember everyone." He took the hint and clammed up.

Lowell had his script in front of him. We read them through a couple of times. Rabbit stepped out for a moment. "Lowell," I said, "I think we're doing something bad doing this movie scene."

"Larry, I can't take torture like you and Jim Kasler, so we have to do what we have to do. We can't worry about that now."

The second of September was the Vietnamese Independence Day, and we were given an unusually good meal, including egg rolls and sliced potatoes. My stomach was unable to hold any good or rich food, or anything a notch above the regular sparse bill of fare. Holiday food always gave me stomach problems.

On September 4, we were informed that all "criminals" were to "dress in long sleeves and sit quietly, politely, and listen." There was a formal announcement of the death of Ho Chi Minh, the old assassin himself! There were speeches and plaudits about his deeds over the years, and fervent affirmations that his "struggles against imperialism" would be continued. I hoped that all of my fellow Americans would behave themselves during the solemn ceremonies, because the Vietnamese would be in no mood to tolerate any nonsense.

Would the switch in leaders have any effect on us? I think we all prayed for a major turnaround in their treatment of us. Judging from comments over the years by the Voice of Vietnam spokesmen, Ho had personal charge of the scoreboard of American planes shot down. Always trying to show how modest their claims were, the announcer would say, "And today the people of Ha Tinh province claimed eleven airplanes shot down. Our wise leader, Ho Chi Minh, chuckled and said, 'Then I give you six.' " They never said anything about substantiation by wrecks or captured pilots. If Ho said there were six shot down, then who could dispute that?

With Ho's death, we worried that treatment could get worse—they might conduct mass public executions and torture us more, or it could also go the other way, and we'd get better treatment. It was a dicey prospect. But nothing happens rapidly in Asia anyway, so we knew we'd just have to sweat it out.

The following night, I was taken downtown to a huge official building. I waited in a hallway a long time. Finally, I was shown into a room where there were eight or ten Vietnamese. Looking me over, one of them said, "So, you have agreed?" I guessed he was talking about the movie scene. Should I drop my drawers and show them my striped ass? Better not—these people are very modest; so instead I said, very softly, "I have no other choice." They served tea and spoke to each other calmly and leisurely, ignoring me. So much for that visit.

As Groves and I were about to get into a truck for another trip, Rabbit put us in the small handcuffs. Groves said, "Ooh," and "ouch" a couple of times, because the cuffs were so small they pinched his wrists. Rabbit said, "Does that hurt?" Lowell said it did, so Rabbit removed them and went for a set of double leg irons. When the truck was underway, I told Lowell he should not have complained.

"Why?"

"Well for Chrissakes, it's going to be just a short ride, and we're a lot better off in individual cuffs."

"Why?"

"Because the roads are wet, and the roadside ditches are deep and full of water! Their drivers are terrible. If we go into a skid and end up in a klong, we're definitely gonna drown with these irons on!''

When we arrived, they removed the irons, and we were taken into a large warehouse. It was the property of the army movie company and contained various "sets" just like Hollywood. All lighting equipment and cameras were from the Soviet Union. Our "set" looked like an office, with several desks and chairs and not much else. They had a couple of real actors dressed up in GI camouflage clothing, boots and all. Of course we didn't know what they were saying, but they sure looked like first-class actors. Both looked Caucasian.

At the front of the set were rows of seats. They were occupied by fifteen or twenty people—set assistants, light and camera crews, makeup artists, and so forth. They sat quietly and stared at us. They seemed nice and showed no overt hostility toward us.

I was still feeling punk, shaky and diarrhetic, so I frequently had to dash to the western-type toilet they had in the building. The Cat understood what was wrong with me and didn't press us at all. I did see something that night I'd never seen before in North Vietnam. There was a couple among the people seated there. The man had his arm around the woman's shoulder and held her close. They displayed a lot of open affection, and it was the only time I ever saw any tender feelings shown between a man and a woman in North Vietnam.

When Lowell and I got back from the movie set, he'd be taken back to the Pool Hall, and I'd return to the Ho Chi Minh room. I was always put back in the irons. On the twenty-second of September, after 110 days in irons, they finally took them away and brought in a bed board, which I mounted on the cement uprights.

Weeks went by, and we had not shot a single foot of film. Cat said, "Sometimes it takes many weeks of rehearsals just to make three or four minutes of film." It was a boondoggle, and everybody involved, including the Rabbit, was making the most of it. There was good food, including meat, drinks, candy, and French pastries. In Communist countries, people involved in the professions, arts, and sports are given a lot of latitude in their personal freedoms. They also receive special incentives such as expense accounts, clothing, and living quarters. If it wasn't such a rotten propaganda project, and I hadn't been so physically and mentally ill, it would have been a hell of a good deal for me.

Eventually, we were taken to the site where the film would actually be shot. Removing our blinds, we dismounted from the truck and found ourselves in the brick-faced parking lot of the Gia Lam Airport, the main airfield of North Vietnam.

I had last seen Gia Lam in November of 1944, when our B-24 and B-25 bombers were knocking down all the bridges in the Hanoi area. In our fast, sleek P-51 fighters, we circled the area, keeping a watchful eye on Gia Lam to make sure no Japanese fighters took off to intercept our bombers. That was twenty-five years before, and French Indochina/Vietnam certainly hadn't changed for the better. It showed age, and little or no progress. Buildings and facilities had deteriorated badly since the departure of the French. Everything seemed to be held together with wire, tape, rope, and string.

The lobby of the terminal building was set up with desks, carpets, lounge furniture, and "computers." The Vietnamese like to portray Americans as using unfeeling computers for all of the necessary day-to-day decision making. The computers were played by a row of mounted cathode-ray tubes from old Russian radar sets. We would shoot the one and only scene right there, and that was all there was going to be to it. The film wasn't going to be shown to sophisticated audiences anyway, so the set was adequate for their purposes.

The film crew arranged metal tracks on the floor so the assistants could push the wheeled camera platforms to and fro, depending on the desired closeness or angle of the shot. The technicians went about their business, and there was one bright spot. The young woman operating the main camera was an absolute knockout. She wore black silk slacks and a white floral print blouse. She was tall, slender, and had a nice, neat figure and long silky dark hair. I was mesmerized by her and could have stared at her for hours. Lowell was passive about her, and I realized that any sexual emotion on his part had been effectively eclipsed by the rigors of captivity. As I got to know him better, I realized his morale had also been badly affected, because he felt something was very wrong at home.

One of the scenes had the Cat walking in, carrying a briefcase and looking very important, while we (the "perfidious Americans") sat on a couch waiting for him. Maybe he was playing the part of a South Vietnamese lackey, but we never really knew what the hell was going on. Nobody seemed interested in what we said when our turns came anyway. Then we found out there was no sound track—it was a silent film. At a later time, the sound would be dubbed in, using the "lip-sync" method.

One shot had me coming down an open stairway, pausing, then looking out the window. Another time I was supposed to be smoking nervously and "looking very crafty and sinister." I slitted my eyes and flipped my cigarette, trying to look like a real bad-ass. Whenever it wasn't my turn to act, I kept an eyeball lock on the camera lady as she sat there, very straight in her chair, with her knees apart (presumably to keep her balance on the camera platform). She was a very sexy lady. I don't recall experiencing any physical response to seeing her, but at least my brain recalled that such a thing existed!

During lunch and siesta breaks, they took us up to rooms on the second floor. At first they kept Lowell and me separated, then, on the second trip there, they let us stay together. Rabbit warned me "not to get too curious." I don't know what he meant, but I was sure there was a bug planted near a pass-through opening in the wall into the next room. Every time Lowell started to tell me something secretive, I shushed him, because I was sure the place was bugged. He thought I was paranoid, and that I overestimated their capabilities, but even now I think I judged them correctly.

The Cat decided that he didn't like my trousers, and said that he would send someone to make me a new pair. I couldn't imagine why they'd even bother. They took me to another room on the second floor, brought in a woman, who looked about forty, with a pretty face and a nice figure. She had a teenage girl with her. She came close and went through all the motions of taking my measurements for trousers, touching me lightly everywhere and smiling at me. "What are these people doing *now*?" I wondered. "Are they trying to get me sexually aroused, so I'll defect, and marry this woman, and stay here forever? The way I feel right now, if I thought I'd never get tortured again, I'd do it!" Thinking the whole thing was a ploy, I was really surprised when she showed up in a few hours later, with a new pair of pants for me!

Looking out the second-floor window, we could see the main runway, probably eight to ten thousand feet long, and the far parking ramp. There were several Russian transports, one old Il-28 bomber, and a couple of small utility aircraft. All of them appeared to be broken down and in need of maintenance. No fighters were visible, and while we were there it was very quiet, with only one arrival. The hangars on either side of the main terminal had been destroyed sometime in the past. Compared to our airports, Gia Lam was like a small-town commuter airport.

On our second trip we got a fleeting glance of two Caucasians. The first was a tall young man of about twenty, dressed in combat fatigues. He was supposed to be one of the colonel's (i.e., my) personal guards. The other was a buxom lady of about twenty-five, in western dress, who played the colonel's secretary. Both were Cubans. It was impossible to get them into conversation; they seemed jumpy and anxious to please the Vietnamese. My part required me to walk over and throw a stack of papers on the secretary's desk. The young Cuban, playing the part of the guard, just stood there during this very short take. The movie's hero (and best actor) was a beautiful German Shepherd dog. The dog's trainer sat in front of the camera giving commands, but the viewers would think the dog reacted to my commands. He panted happily and almost seemed to be smiling— you had to like him. I pointed my finger toward the door and said, "Get him, Bonzo!" (As a kid I knew a seeing eye dog by that name who looked just like him.) The dog gave a hearty "woof-woof" and leaped forward toward the door. (Of course, at the precise moment, the dog's real master had given the command.)

The cameras were grinding and Cat came over and said something to me. I don't recall what it was, but I remember I became very exasperated about the whole business, and with my legs crossed, I flipped one of my clogs high into the air. That night Rabbit said, "Today you have made my senior officer very furious—he said you showed very bad attitude. You know, you don't have to do this if you don't want to."

"What?" I was incredulous. He had threatened to start the "treatment" immediately if I didn't agree to it! Something was happening that I couldn't get a handle on.

"Well anyway, it is over," he said. If he was trying to confuse me, he did a good job of it.

The Duck was waiting for me back at the Ho Chi Minh room and told me to roll up my gear. He led me to the back side of the Pool Hall building, room six. I went in and saw that it had been freshly whitewashed. It was one of the cells with the air vents high up the front wall. He closed the door. I realized there was no light bulb and damn near panicked, believing that my torture was going to begin again in that dark cell! A guard came by to check on me and noticed the light was out. He returned with a ladder and a light bulb, and I breathed a lot easier.

It was like a sanitized hospital room, compared to the Ho Chi Minh room. I lay there quietly, thinking over the "movie" experience. Cat had initially said that the object of the exercise was to humiliate me "in the eyes of your fellows." They must have had a change of heart, because the film was never used for anything much. It was never shown to anyone except the camp guards. They'd come around and give me a jab, saying, "Ga, . . . woof-woof!"

For a change, I had several quiet and peaceful days while Duck was my turnkey. He was very gentle and never gave me any difficulty. He was a real soldier. Over the years, when he was ordered to harass or torture, that's just what he did. He followed orders to the letter and didn't add any whimsical extras.

In mid-October, I was taken out to quiz and met an interrogator I had never seen before. He was called Stag, which stood for "Smarter Than the Average Gook." He was seen around the holidays, during "good guy" treatment, and we think he generally spoke the truth.

Stag was from Can Tho, in the delta area south of Saigon. He said the villages in his province made a good living by producing hot and spicy fish sauce. He was particularly proud of the quality of food and the skill of the cooks of his own village. He thought things were much better in the south than up north, where the living was very "harsh," as he put it. He admitted that the Vietnamese had taken some staggering losses in their battles against the Americans.

He asked casually if I knew a Colonel Edward Burdett. I said that I'd never heard of him, which was true. Then Stag held up a military identification card and said, "Yes, Colonel Burdett is very senior officer, are you sure you don't know him?" "Never heard of him." Stag dropped it there. A year later I learned that Burdett had been wing commander at Korat. Jack Flynn, the wing deputy commander, and Jim Bean, director of operations, were also captives in Hanoi!

Stag also told me that from now on things were going to be much better for us. I asked pointedly, "Are you going to continue to torture us to make us do things which we do not want to do?"

"What do you mean?"

"You know what I mean. Make statements against our government, against our country. . . . Well, tell me, so I'll know if we are ever going to have any peace in this camp."

He squirmed around a lot, then finally said, "At this time, it is no longer planned." Of all the Vietnamese I ever met, I thought he and the Dog were the sharpest ones.

I had a "pet" who lived in a hole in the rotted baseboard of the sleeping pallet. I'd lie down at night and be very still for ten minutes or so. When I looked toward my feet, this large white rat with a football-shaped head would stick his head out and look up to me. "Hi there, fella. You don't bother me, and I won't tell anyone you're here, okay?" We let it go at that. One morning, the peep opened before I was out of the sack. It was Rabbit, trying to pull a switcheroo by being a nice guy. He was handing out dishes of raw white sugar and bread. I told him no thanks, it would give me diarrhea. Later that day he gave me a package from Evelyn, and a letter that had some wonderful snapshots enclosed. First we looked over the goodies. I noticed that some of the pecan pralines, jelly candies, and dried apricots were missing. I asked about that, and Rabbit replied with a straight face, "We had to take just a little of everything to test, to make sure no one will poison you, and blame us for it!" What a crock!

Several pictures were of my sons, who had grown so much I didn't really know one from the other. Others were snaps of Evelyn standing on the porch of her home at Patrick Air Force Base. She looked terrific, very neat and well groomed as always. I swallowed the lump in my throat at seeing them. Rabbit decided he'd give me a couple of jabs.

"And how old is she?"

"Forty-five."

"She looks very strong. How is that? Why do you think she looks so well? Someone must make her happy! You know, in Vietnam we have a saying about women her age. It is 'woman come second time springtime, and then they can break your back.' " He laughed happily at his little joke. I had had enough of his shit, so I picked up my stuff and left. Boris, now the turnkey, let me back into my cell. I was amazed to find I *was* feeling pangs of jealousy!

Still pissed off about the Rabbit, I stuffed some dried apricots into my face and read Evy's letter. It was one of her usual wonderful letters, telling me everyone was fine and not to worry. She said that her refrigerator had broken down, and she had purchased a new one, one that made ice cubes automatically. I had never heard of that before in a home refrigerator. The big news was that she had just returned from Allan's graduation at Williams Air Force Base. Now she was telling me he had the silver wings of an air force pilot! The tears rolled down my cheeks as I read that. I was really proud of him, but from then on I worried that the gooks might try to force me to write him antiwar letters. And, deep down, I fretted about the awful possibility of his coming to fight the war in Vietnam and being shot down.

When Allan was fifteen or sixteen years old, he built and flew some beautiful gas-powered model airplanes, and was always pleased if I came out to watch him fly them. However, he had never told me he wanted to be an air force pilot, and I had no desire to push him in that direction.

During the terrible purge of 1969, everyone in camp had been shuffled into different cells. Spiker and Coniff were now in cell one, at my back wall. I had gotten in touch with them as soon as I moved back in. I tapped to them about the letter from Evy. Later, Spiker came back with, "Why do you think she needs an automatic ice-cube maker? She must be having a lot of parties!"

"Thanks a lot, Spiker," I thought, "with friends like you I don't need the gooks for enemies!"

Rabbit told me to prepare to go out with Groves to dub our voices onto the film strip. That night we were taken to a building that looked like a three-story cement tower, located beside a large lake. We went into the sound studio, which was entirely lined with acoustic tile.

You watched your part closely, trying to match the movement of your lips with the script words. It wasn't exactly scientific, but all you really had to do was start and stop talking at the same time as your screen image.

First, we watched some of the Vietnamese movie actors do theirs. I was surprised at their display of temper when they didn't jump on the line soon enough and had to do it over. They got pissed just the way we do! I still had stomach problems, and that was my loss, because the food and pastries looked great. No wonder Rabbit was getting fat as a pig! Lowell could drink six beers, but more than one made me sick and gave me the runs.

The second time out, Lowell tried to tell me something in secret, and again I shushed him. They put our film on, and we watched. The sound equipment was so sensitive that when they repeated the scene we'd been watching, you could hear my stomach rumble on the tape. Good thing I had shut Lowell up!

Rabbit came in with an attractive young woman. She had a short hairdo, and wore high heels and a tan sweater and black slacks. Rabbit seemed to have the hots for her, and we watched him turn on the charm while we ate during a break period. Then he put on a tape of Latin music. He asked, "And would you like to dance a bossa nova?" Lowell said, "No, I only dance with my wife." I forgot what excuse I gave, except it had something to do with my case of the trots. The setup was that Rabbit was going to get us to make some kind of move on the girl, then he would film and tape it. The girl was probably a high-class hooker, available to party members. I could just picture it—"American POWs have fun partying."

Rabbit was probably bisexual. He was interested in women, even though Spot was his obvious darling. During one of his tirades, he once told me that Americans "stunk" and that we "multiplied like rabbits." "Furthermore" he said, "when I go home at night I have a difficult time embracing my wife. She won't come near me because she says I stink from associating with Americans all the time. Do you know you people stink?"

A couple of days later, Rabbit threw a pencil and some paper through the peep. "And now, you request amnesty!"

"I've already done that."

"No you haven't."

"Yes I have."

"Do you want to be punished again?" He left. I went to the boards and slowly knelt down on the floor, to see how much my knees would take. The wounds had closed all right, but after a couple of minutes of kneeling it was excruciating; like my knee bones were crushed. I knew I couldn't handle it again. I tapped my situation through the wall. Mullen and Groves advised me to write a nothing statement, just to get by. They said they were very worried about me. I was worried about me, too. Spiker came back true to form: "Don't do it! Continue to resist, and we'll pray for you."

"I can't take any more punishment now. My knees are killing me."

"Don't do it! When we get home you'll get the Medal of Honor."

"Will you listen to that bullshit?" I thought. "He can shove the Medal of Honor!" I tapped back, "*You* go out for me, and I'll sit here and pray for *you*!" I finally wrote, giving the absolute minimum. Rabbit took it so he could fill in that square. They must have lost the one Spot got from me earlier.

On the twenty-second of October, 1969, the Box said something about the moon, or a moon voyage, which I couldn't make out. Boris let me out to dump the *bo*.

"Is there someone on the moon?"

"Yes."

"No kidding, who is it?"

"There is one man, an American. But he is now very weak and will die soon."

"How long has he been there?"

"A few days. You know the Russians could have done that easily. But they would not, because they are not stupid. They know there is nothing on the moon, so why should they go?"

Around the twenty-fifth of November they moved me to room eight. There was Fred Cherry waiting for me, and it was good to see him again. He told me about the surgery they did on him. He showed me the scar, which ran from his chest, over his shoulder, and down his back. It looked like it was four feet long! We spoke to Bud Day and Jack Fellowes through the wall. Jack was quite a character, a naval officer, who always gave the gooks a hard time. Often I had seen him through the keyhole of the Hut. The gooks were always whacking on him with switches.

I was with Fred only a couple of days. We heard a lot of sounds of building modifications. Sure enough, there was a camp project going on to knock down some of the walls to restore the cells to their original full size.

Boris moved me back to the cell I had shared with Ron (number five), which was now double-size and included the space once occupied by Milligan and Anderson. Kasler and Groves were there to greet me, and I was tickled to death to be joining them. I had been alone too long.

Kasler told me that he was also severely tortured during 1969. The first time was when he was accused of having one of the junior officers in his building, naval officer McSwain, act insane. Jim had had nothing to do with it, but he caught it anyway. The second time was after the escape, when Kasler was another one of those who was taken out and brutalized for three long weeks.

Lowell told me that since the purge, the guys who had been taking care of Carl Corley were scattered all over camp. Corley was now living by himself in cell two, at the front of the Auditorium. That was the cell I was in during the note-eating adventure. Going out to quiz one day, I saw Corley sitting there, cell door wide open and still not knowing or caring about his whereabouts or anything else. A few days later, Corley was moved from camp. I never saw him again, and later it was rumored that he was seen, in very bad shape, in Heartbreak. (We were saddened to learn that he died in captivity. His remains were finally shipped home in 1974.)

Jim and Lowell were interested in J. J. Connell and asked if the V had ever mentioned him. Yes, there was one day that Spot told me they had "broken Connell, the faker," and wanted to know if I "put him up to pretending insanity." The only comment I *ever* made about J. J. was that I heard there was a man with crippled hands living near the headquarters building. Spot dropped it at that.

Jim and Lowell asked if I had heard the "Bob and Ed" show. I didn't know what they were talking about. They explained that a tape was played over the Box, and supposedly the voices were those of two Americans, a marine and a naval officer. The tape was a shocking revelation of the antiwar convictions of both of them. They said it went on for an hour and the two were real characters. They didn't sound like they were forced; they both spoke freely and easily as if they were very pleased with themselves." The only thing I had heard on the Box since June was the announcement of the death of Ho, then much later, the announcement concerning the release of three more POWs.

Jim told me that before his Asia assignment he had spent a couple of years in Germany. Around 1965, he read a newspaper account about a welcoming-back of more than three hundred Germans who had been released from Russia. They had been held since their capture at Stalingrad in 1941 or 1942! Twenty-four years! We were talking about whether the Vietnamese would try to keep some of us there indefinitely, as they had often threatened to do. Jim's little story didn't cheer me up any.

Early in December they came for my two buddies and moved them out of the Zoo altogether. Within a couple of hours I got three new cell mates: Fred Cherry, Jack Bomar, and Clay Kirsten. The latter two had been together, but neither Fred nor I knew them personally, although I had met Kirsten years before.

I was particularly glad to be with Bomar so he could fill me in on Fidel and Corley. Jack was a very interesting person, who had accomplished a lot in his life. He had many talents, from artwork to musical instruments, voice, crafts, and athletics. Although he had a private pilot's license and had owned airplanes, he was a navigator, not an air force pilot.

Jack's recounting of his personal adventures was better then anything you could see on TV. He was an excellent golfer, model-builder, auto mechanic, and a driver of stock cars. He had his little problems and hang-ups, to be sure, but, all things considered, he was very impressive.

Cherry was finally feeling better. He was low key and generally agreeable to whatever we wanted in the issues that arose with the Vietnamese on a day-to-day basis. Cherry's big strength was getting along with people.

Clay Kirsten was a different story. The only other time I had seen Clay in camp was on a day that Ron and I went out to quiz together. The guard made us wait in the hallway near the Ho Chi Minh room while he cleared the way to the Gook House. As we stood there, I heard a sound come out of the room. I left my sandals near Ron, raced up the stairs, and threw the peep open. It was Kirsten—I said, "Hi Clay, hang tough and God Bless." It took him by surprise, and he remembered it and told me it was helpful and picked up his spirits.

But in the cell with us, before many days went by, he and I were at swords' points. His first declaration was, "Look Larry, we don't want to hear any of your bullshit torture stories—we've heard enough of those!" I don't think I ever got over that. A man who is fresh out of a long-term torture session needs the therapy of unburdening himself on what he has been through. The best time to get accurate details of what occurred is as soon after as it can be told. After Kirsten's comment, I gave parts of the story to Jack and Fred, when they asked, but never a complete picture.

Something was bothering Clay, but he never told us what it was. Bomar told us that Clay had been quite a combat pilot and had been put in for some very high awards. However, the only thing he was known for in Hanoi was the Burchett interview.

One day we were talking about checking out in various aircraft. I mentioned that in 1957 I had gone to George Air Force Base, California, to check in the F-100. Clay asked me, "Did you ever know a Bob Shimp?"

"Yes," I replied, "gave me my checkout in the C-model."

"What did you think of his squadron?"

"Nice bunch of people."

"Well, what was wrong with Shimp?"

"Wrong? I don't know what you mean. I don't think there was a damn thing wrong with Bob Shimp—I liked him a lot."

Clay started to laugh. Then he said, "Shimp is a very good personal friend of mine. I just wanted to see what you had to say about him." I realized that he had set me up, and I told him I thought his "test" was a pretty cheap trick to pull.

It was then that I felt the timing was right to tell Kirsten about the "poll" Spiker had taken about the Burchett interview. I let him know that the only two people who had stood up for him were Ron Byrne and myself. Kirsten said nothing. He gave no explanation about the conditions of the interview, or how he happened to keep his wedding ring. I did not press him or question him. I left it up to him to fill in the blanks, but he didn't respond.

The extended period of incarceration, and the close-in living conditions, led to many clashes between fellow Americans. Certainly every military man is entitled to his private opinions, but in the interest of good order, he is also expected to bridle his own frustrations and behave cooperatively and respectively toward his superiors. A few did take advantage of the situation, knowing disciplinary action would be difficult or impossible to administer while in Hanoi. Occasional insubordinate remarks, given our situation, were understandable; routine disrespectful behavior was inexcusable. For the seven months we were joined, our relationship did not improve. . . . It deteriorated further.

Christmas was just around the corner, and the V brought around pencils and encouraged us to make postcards, or write poetry or stories. There was a lot of discussion on the pros and cons of doing it. My view was that we had all been there for such a long time, if people wanted to do that, it was okay with me. I felt that was consistent with my position on what I considered to be relatively trivial problems.

I couldn't seem to get well. The severity of my headaches had increased, and my stomach went on the fritz. I had such bad cramps I was convinced that I was suffering from stomach ulcers again. My jangled nerves from continuing clashes with Kirsten aggravated it further. Sick and weak, I could no longer get up off the bunk. Jack and Fred were sympathetic and called the medics. That night, they brought me a pot of special food. It was vermicelli with a thin tomato sauce, as close to Italian spaghetti as you could hope for in North Vietnam. The vermicelli was cooked "al dente," and we all shared it and thought it was very tasty. However, my stomach continued to worsen. Finally, we summoned the duty officer, who arranged for me to be taken downtown to the hospital. It was a dark and dank place, and I spent a lot of time waiting in a blacked-out hallway. Ray Vohden was also there that night. I went into the X-ray room, and the doctor (or radiologist) did a gastrointestinal series. The Vietnamese never told me anything about the results of the tests.

They just let it pass, and eventually whatever it was healed by itself.

On Christmas Eve, services were available for any who wished to attend. Those of us who were Catholic were taken to town by bus to an old French cathedral. They spaced us three to a bench to cut down on communications, because they had had a bad experience the year before at the Protestant services. Father Ho Than Bien was still in charge. It was an ancient Gothic-style church with a very ornate vaulted ceiling. A Vietnamese choir sang "Adeste Fidelis [Oh Come All Ye Faithful]."

Suddenly, the sanctity of the Mass was interrupted as Soft-Soap Fairy, the quizzer from the Plantation, went to the pulpit. His bit was to remind us of the continuing perfidy of the U.S. ruling circles, and to decry the bombing of innocent women and children. We all went up to the altar for Holy Communion. After the Mass, Soft-Soap allowed us to go up to look at the nativity scene. There I saw Ron Byrne for the first time in six months. He looked about the same, and as we shook hands warmly he told me he was living in the old Pigsty building with a group of six men. We didn't have time to say more. I also shook hands with old friend Bob Purcell, who seemed like he was still full of pee and vinegar, and willing to give the gooks hell. We chatted briefly, when a very young-looking prisoner came over and asked my name. I gave it to him, and he got wide-eyed and whispered to the others crowded behind us, "Hey guys, this is the SRO!" His name was Mark Ruhling. He looked like he was about fifteen years old, but of course he had to be in his twenties. He was a little guy not over 120 pounds. All too soon, Rabbit came over, snarling as usual, and rushed us back out to the buses. It was a nice evening, and gave me the comfort of my faith and a feeling of fellowship with the other POWs there, and we all needed that.

Christmas Day, 1969. The Vietnamese had a table stacked with food on the front porch. The photographers were there to reap whatever propaganda they could from it. They took shots of us as we came out, cell by cell, to pick up our food. There were some gook VIPs in camp, making the rounds. They came into our cell and asked about our health. Then they told us we were no longer required to bow before them, a simple head nod would suffice. As was their custom, it was time for them to say something to cool down whatever holiday spirit we had built up, so they told us about a massacre, which they said had been committed in a village in South Vietnam call My Lai. They would never have known about that incident except for the notoriety it was given in the western press.

Later that day the Box squawked on, and we all heard the voice of Quincy Collins offering Christmas greetings from "C . . . B . . . S . . . ." The V thought it was a spoof of the well known broadcasting company, but we laughed because we knew very well that Quincy was saying, "Hello guys, this is the *C*amp *B*ullshit *S*ystem coming at you." His group had prepared some of our favorite songs; then, with the appropriate musical accompaniment, Quincy went into his Sergeant Joe Friday routine from "Dragnet." I had heard it at Itazuke a dozen times, but I didn't mind hearing it again, because it was hilarious.

"I needed some more clues, so I looked into the clues closet. Just then the door opened and in walks this beautiful blonde. She had a pair of 38s, and in each hand she held a gun." Most of us thoroughly enjoyed the show. There were always a few who were hypercritical of what Quincy was doing, but he had my blessing every time. We needed any morale builders we could get.

Chapter Fourteen

1970—TREATMENT IMPROVES

We had a deck of cards, which Jack had received in a package from home. He asked if Fred and I were bridge players. We said we weren't, but we would certainly like to learn. Jack and Clay both were very patient in giving us the ground rules. Fred and I were both elated when Jack dealt out the cards for our first hand and announced, "Gentlemen, we are playing bridge!" It was more fun than making coal balls.

Early in the new year we went into the Auditorium, which had been set up to show a "Super Gook" movie, the story of a young, patriotic soldier, who was willing to do his all for the gold flag with the red star. From beginning to end, he whistled and sang his national anthem, without letup. He single-handedly laid an ambush and wiped out a whole platoon of American GIs, all the while singing happily. Super Gook was then seen wending his way down the side of the mountain, singing and looking for more $M\bar{y}$ to kill. The music rose in stirring crescendo, and the film ended with a huge HET! (THE END) across the screen.

Boris called me out to quiz and gave me a package from home that had new photographs, a set of very welcome long johns, and a pair of warm, nylon-insulated slippers. It also contained a box of Evelyn's wonderful butter cookies, which she makes only on festive occasions. Boris said, "We see your pictures from home. We know this is your government's propaganda. They put in automobiles, swimming pools, and many other things."

"You mean you do not believe those things belong to us—you think they belong to the government?"

"Of course." I didn't bother to challenge his belief. It wouldn't have done any good.

Sometime in January, in one of my quizzes with Rabbit, he said that it wasn't so bad if we communicated. It all depended upon *what* we communicated. The Rabbit usually veiled what it was he was talking about. Then he added, "Of course if you are caught, you must be punished, because it is still against the camp regulations and our people know that."

A couple of weeks later, two of our seriously wounded men, Jim Bell and Ray Vohden, who were just two doors down from us, were caught dead to rights communicating. The guard let them know they had been caught, then he went to get the duty officer. They immediately asked me what I thought was the best course of action. I told them not to take punishment, but to admit that they communicated. I talked it over with my cell mates. We had to try to break their hold on us for communicating. If asked by the gooks, all of us should admit to communicating. What the hell could they do about it, torture us? On checking throughout the prison camp, we found out no one was being physically abused at that time. However, the scare tactics of mental harassment and threats continued, especially for communicating. We approached this issue very cautiously, because it had always been the main crime in the eyes of the Vietnamese.

This was the first (and last) time Kirsten ever agreed with me. He said he liked the idea of admission very much. Jack said he didn't like it, and Fred wouldn't commit. That annoyed me, because I wanted an answer from him, so I rattled his cage.

"Fred, you never commit yourself on a goddamn thing, do you? You're always playing it safe. A hell of a lot of good you do me. I want your opinion!"

"Okay, okay," Fred answered. "I don't want to admit comm. We know what we have, but we don't know what we're gonna get." So much for *that* staff consultation! I got on the wall and passed the word.

"From now on, every man who is asked about comm will admit without hesitation. We are not going to let Vohden and Bell take this one by themselves."

A day or two later Spiker went out to quiz, which was a rare occasion, because as long as I knew him he was never called out. When he returned, he sent through the wall that Rabbit had asked him if he communicated, and he denied it! I was furious that Spiker had the gall to disobey a direct order, and I asked him why. His answer was, "Your order didn't make any sense."

Later, he tried to excuse his noncompliance by saying he had misunderstood the order, but I knew better.

Bell and Vohden were not punished, which lent even greater credence to the belief that Rabbit knew very well that everyone communicated at every available opportunity. It did not serve his purpose, at that time, to make an issue of it.

The February winds were blowing out of the north, and the temperatures were down. The food was better than it had been and the bread was usually fresh, sometimes even hot out of the oven! On some mornings, we got cut pieces of stale bread, which had been reheated with sugar on them. It was burnt brown, and we regarded it as a treat.

Boris took me up to the Gook House, where the Buzzard and four others were sitting at a table, at a staff meeting. I went in and gave the newly approved slight head nod. They beckoned me to sit. Then they made a big to-do of inquiring about my health. Had I seen a doctor lately? Was I getting letters from home? They already knew the answers. One of them asked if I was cold, and I said, "Yes." (Actually I *was* chilly, maybe in anticipation of what they might want from me this time.)

"Would you like to get up and exercise?" "Well," I figured, "I've got to go along with the bullshit until they decide to get around to whatever it is they've got me out for." So I stood up and did a couple of feeble exercises and warm-ups.

They all smiled approvingly. After I sat down, Buzzard spoke up very clearly: "Do you speak any French?"

"Yes, I do."

"What can you say in French?"

"Well, uh . . . I can say, *non!* . . . *oui* . . . *pomme de terre* . . . *bifteck* . . . and *voulez-vous couchez avec moi, mademoiselle?*"

Darned if old Buzzard didn't have a sense of humor! He broke out into a big grin, almost losing his loose, broken false teeth. That was as close as I'd ever come to seeing a gook crack up and laugh.

Buzzard spoke again, choosing his words carefully.

"And now, we think it is necessary to explain to you once again the policy of treatment of the Democratic Republic of Vietnam, which has always been, as you know, humane and lenient." Here we had just gone through an incredible round of torture, and he's telling me this! He pressed on. "We know you don't understand it. So we try again to 'splain you. But our treatment policy is very complicated; in fact, it is so complicated that even the guards don't understand it. They know that the policy is humane and lenient, but they don't apply the treatment properly. That is why they mistreat you sometimes—they are not supposed to do that. That's why sometimes perhaps they beat you. They are not supposed to do that, because the policy is always humane and lenient. Soon you will see what we mean." This was turning out to be a most interesting session! We sat quietly, as they gave me time to mull over the Buzzard's comments. He continued.

"Now there are three ways to go." Well, my mind was running out way ahead in anticipation. What's coming off? Can this be good news? Rabbit told me that there was "clear sailing ahead," right after he got my watered-down pardon request (the "final humiliation," according to them).

"Yes, the first way, you can continue to oppose us and you will be severely punished as before. . . . The second way, you can cooperate and collaborate with us, for which you will be duly rewarded. . . . And the third way . . . *now*, you can withdraw. This means you can obey the regulations, and not threaten our camp security. We will allow you to live here until the end of the war. We will not force you to do those things you do not want to do."

In years past, there were only two choices: With 'em, or against them. But was this something that Buzzard and his friends at the Zoo had dreamed up, or did it come down from the higher policy level? This gave us the flexibility to avoid punishment by taking a "middle" stance. I don't mind admitting that my heart took a leap, because not only did *I* need a way out, but I felt that we *all* did, or we'd end up in a fruit basket. Our imprisonment looked like an indefinite stay . . . it could be five, ten, fifteen more years . . . or life. Who knew? All we could do was try to survive it and hope it would end before too many more years passed.

The Buzzard let me chew on that for a while, then popped the question.

"So what do you think of that?"

"That's great, I withdraw." I was thinking, "Hey, I never had such a good deal! Let me sign up for *this* one!" "Yeah, I withdraw," I repeated. Buzzard gave me a another crooked-toothed smile, and they all looked pleased with the results.

Back in the cell, I tapped out the message, telling the guys about the "three choices," and that the V had assured me we wouldn't be punished unless we "threatened the camp security." They could always, of course, trump up a charge and *claim* we threatened them, but they could always do that anyway,

right to the bloody end. The line that I liked most of all was
"We will not force you to do those things you do not want to
do."

The treatment *was* changing, but so slowly it was barely per-
ceptible. Boris explained it with some "old Vietnamese say-
ings." He gave them in Vietnamese, but the idea was, "We give
you a hand, you take an arm." He also liked "Step by step,
slowly slowly, step by step." The Vietnamese, imbued with
Asian patience, take a long time to make changes. From that
time on, only rarely did they resort to the brutalities that we
knew during the previous terrible years. Bomar, Kirsten, and I
packed up our gear and were moved down the hall into Pool
Hall cell one.

The Vietnamese wanted artwork from us, to show visiting
delegations that prisoners were being given artistic recreational
periods. It was supposed to back up the Vietnamese claim that
they had always been humane with us. Though we were no
longer being physically abused, they didn't stop pressuring and
browbeating us to produce something to make them look good
to the outside world. We would very likely have gone along with
it, except we discovered that not everyone in camp was given
the opportunity to do those things. The people who were left
out felt that the others were being extended "special favors." It
also came to light that some were getting out to exercise regularly, and even to bathe twice a day, while others got nothing.
The "special favor" complaint became a valid and serious issue.

Bud Day and Jack Fellowes put up a major beef about not
being included in activities or bath periods. Bud said if everyone
didn't get the same opportunity, then it was obviously "special
favors." I agreed with his point of view. I put out the word to
start phasing out artwork. If the gooks wanted it so badly, then
it couldn't possibly be in our best interests.

Spiker's group argued against what I thought was best for all
of us. Jack, Clay, and I had refused further participation in the
"artistic recreation" program long before things came to a head.
Then Boris, annoyed with the slowdown in art production,
taunted me by holding up a letter, a picture, and a greeting card
from Evelyn, saying he'd give them to me only if I'd draw a
picture. I told him to stuff 'em and never did get them.

I had a good excuse to quit, because the last time I drew
anything it was a tracing of a religious figure that Boris gave
me. I have to admit it was a frightful-looking creation, and

Rabbit said it was a "blasphemous defilement" of my God. Rabbit was very sensitive about that, for an atheist Communist son of a bitch. "Well see here," I said, "you guys are criticizing my work so forget it, I'm not drawing anything anymore!"

The Vietnamese set up the Auditorium to show a couple of movies. The first was a film of the Russian Air Force at work. It was an impressive showing of troop-carrier tactical airlift capabilities. Their planes were turboprop jobs and very much like our C-130 Hercules models.

The second, which was the last movie I ever saw at the Zoo, was put together by a Canadian producer named McLean. He did a marvelous job illustrating the total devastation of North Vietnam in the area above the demilitarized zone north of the seventeenth parallel. General Le May was supposed to have said, "We'll bomb them back to the stone age." We did exactly that near the DMZ, because the country, for many, many miles, looked every bit as bleak as the moon must have looked to our astronauts. Most of the film was a compilation of scenes of total annihilation. It was the old story, told ten thousand times over, of people whose unfortunate lot was to be in the path of war. When Americans last saw that for themselves, a hundred years ago, our country was not heavily populated. Now, we've lost touch with that sort of thing and don't understand what it's like to be civilians struggling to exist in a battle zone.

Boris remained consistent in his efforts to get some form of artwork from me. He knew I had no artistic talent, but he hoped that when the others realized the SRO was doing it, they'd all go along with it.

"But you don't like my work so forget it, I'm not gonna do any pictures."

One time he held up a picture of a car. "All you have to do is draw this picture."

"I told you I don't wanta draw a picture."

"I'll give you a benefit [Reward]."

"I told you I don't want to draw pictures."

"Kneel down!" A couple of months before, he had come to the cell block and told me to kneel down in front of Bomar, and I didn't pay any attention to him. After the summer of '69, I was through kneeling down.

"Kneel down!" he repeated.

"Listen, you better change that order, because you're gonna get yourself and me in a hell of a lot of trouble." I continued to glance around the room as if trying to forget what was happening.

"If you don't kneel down, I will go out and get the guard with the bayonet—he will force you!"

"I don't care." As he was leaving the room, I happened to turn around and saw the Rabbit crossing the street.

"Oh boy, I'm in big trouble now!" Boris went out and talked to the Rabbit, looking for advice. I had forced him, and he had to do something. Boris came back in with two guards and put one on either side of me with bayonets in place.

"And now, Ga-reeno, I give you the order for the last time—stand in the corner!"

"Oh yes sir, I always obey orders." I got up and went and stood in the corner. He had backed off, and that was encouraging because I had pushed him to the brink. In the recent past, he would have tortured me, but that day he didn't. I thought of what Buzzard had said, "We won't force you to do the things you don't want to do." What they were doing was trying to browbeat us into doing their bidding, but when it came down to the wire, they decided that my refusal to do artwork wasn't a threat to the camp security.

Cell number two, next to us, was still a divided room, with the front section occupied by navy crew Ned Shuman and Dale Doss. The back section still had Bud Day and Jack Fellowes. After telling them about the latest confrontation with Boris, and how he backed off, Ned said, "Boy, I like the way you handled that!" I told him I was very lucky it came off that way. Ned confided to me that he and Dale had never gotten along. I told him it was the severe frustration, and that my continuing hassle with Clay was probably worse than his with Dale.

In the spring of '70, regularly at the noon hour, we could hear a strange whistle from far away, or very high up. We wondered about it. Clay said it could be a high-altitude recce plane. Years later I met Bobby Campbell, one of my Itazuke fighter pilots who had some experience in the Mach 3 reconnaissance system, the SR-71 Blackbird.

"Bobby, did you ever fly over Hanoi?" I asked him.

"Yes," he replied, "every day, at noon."

The Box reported that President Nixon had secretly ordered the bombing of Cambodia, and a few members of Congress were so upset at his widening of the war they were talking of impeachment. As I listened, I stared up at the Box, tears streaming down my face. "That's the first thing we've ever done right in this war! Deny these people a sanctuary in Cambodia, and they want to impeach the president over it?'' What the hell is wrong with our country? They also quoted Hubert Humphrey, Johnson's vice president, as saying, ''Now that I'm no longer associated with the administration, the war looks very different to me.'' Here was a past vice president, who apparently approved of our direction while in office, now having second thoughts! The generals have come and gone, I thought bitterly, the secretary of defense who got us into this morass is long gone, and so is the president. The only ones left holding the proverbial bag are the Vietnamese . . . and us!

By May of 1970 the quality of food was down again. The main fare was very thin pumpkin soup and bread. Most of the time I gave Jack my soup—I hated the stuff. Jack had just as big a hate for kohlrabies, and I liked them, no matter how they were fixed, so he gave me his.

One morning, as we were lying there staring at the ceiling, immersed in our private thoughts, Clay suddenly jumped up and walked over to me. ''I'll bet when we get home you're going to tell everybody what a big hero you were up here!'' he said nastily. That left me speechless and almost wiped out anything I had left mentally. Shaking with fury inside, I paced the room. Then I called Bud Day to the wall to tell him what I was thinking. ''Bud, I'm so upset by this latest insult I don't think I can function any longer as SRO. I want to turn it over to you.'' Bud listened, then came back with, ''I'm sorry about the situation, Larry, and I know it has to be rough on you in your condition, but I think you should think it over for a while, sleep on it, before giving up and turning the SRO duties over to me. Hang tough! Don't let it get to you like that.'' I agreed to try to resolve the problem. Clay had replaced Rabbit and Dum Dum as my chief mental tormenter. The Vietnamese often said, ''We will let you kill each other!''

In my heart, I knew there was no way I could continue to tolerate his insults. Examining my conscience and all that had transpired since moving in with Kirsten, I could not recall a single instance where I aggravated him, intentionally or jokingly. Though I was his commander, I didn't insist on the details concerning his wedding ring . . . and I had a right to know. He may have been a pilot hero on the outside, but in Hanoi, he flunked the test. Possibly recognizing this inadequacy made him suffer the frustration all the more acutely, sharpening his need for a kicking post. I was determined that the next time I saw Boris, I'd go to the extreme.

Boris did call me out, and I told him I had to be moved away from Kirsten, and I did so very descriptively. He said, "Are you using bad words?"

"You bet your ass I'm using bad words! I don't give a damn who you move me in with, and I'll even welcome solitary confinement. But if you don't move me, my head is going to split wide open!"

The press for artwork continued, and my personal attitude toward Boris was so bad I was sure that I had the V on the verge of counteraction.

Late in the afternoon of the fifth of June, a Vietnamese official, known in other camps as Mighty Mouse, called me out. He denounced me roundly and soundly, telling me in no uncertain terms that once again I had "threatened the camp security," for which I would "be severely punished!" It was a long asschewing, and he succeeded in scaring the hell out of me. While I was there, he sent a bunch of gooks back to my cell to get my gear. It was night when they blindfolded me, slapped me in a set of leg and hand irons, and threw me in a truck. Well, I was getting my wish all right, but I had no way of knowing whether my tirade about Kirsten caused it, or if the V were tired of the slowdown in art production and had decided to fire me.

Twenty minutes later, they dropped me off, and I picked up the irons and walked laboriously into a building. They removed the leg irons, but left the cuffs and the blinds on. They brought me into a room in a place I'd never been before. There were a couple of gooks who denounced me again. Then they removed the cuffs so I could carry my stuff. They walked me around some more, until I was thoroughly disoriented. Then they shoved me into a narrow room, so narrow my arms bumped the walls. They snatched off the blinds and closed the door behind me. This dimly lit cell was half the size of the tiny cells I had had in the Stockyards and Heartbreak. I had to turn part sideways to walk its seven foot length. As I unrolled my gear, the peep opened and I saw the Bug looking in. Damn! "Shhhhh, shhhhh . . . don't make a sound . . . ! Don't make a sound . . . quiet . . . quiet!" he said threateningly.

"Well, Jesus, do you want me to put up my stuff or what?"

"Shhhhh . . . don't make a sound! Go to bed quickly. Quickly and quietly!" I put up the mosquito net and crawled under it. The stone cot was so narrow I could barely fit on it. The leg

irons in the place were all extra narrow. Of course I had no idea
where I was, except that it was peaceful and quiet, so I laid
down, said "Bullshit," and fell asleep. Though I didn't know
it at the time, this was in a part of the prison complex called Las
Vegas, in Hoa Lo, the Hanoi city jail. I had the very end cell of
the "Mint" building.

I woke as night faded to the early light of dawn, and got up
to survey my situation. Yeah, the cell was extra narrow all right.
But this corner had windows, double-barred windows, like my
very first cell in New Guy Village. By standing on the cot, I
could barely make out the twenty-foot outside wall of the prison,
topped with broken glass, horizontal electric wires, and barbed
wire. Over in the corner was a guard tower, with three armed
gooks looking down at me.

Half-jokingly, I said to myself, "Man they must think they've
got a really tough cookie here! Yep, I've got 'em scared silly,
right where I want 'em. They better hope they've got enough
iron and wire to hold me!" It was whistling in the dark, because
I knew they were going to land on me hard. They had laid the
magic words on me—I "threatened the camp security." An hour
later (surprise, surprise), an English-speaking gook came along
with a buddy of his. He said, "Are you all right?"

Am I hearing things? "What did you say?"

"Are you all right?"

"No, I have a headache." He said something to the other
one, who turned out to be a medic. He handed me a couple of
aspirin. The turnkey opened the door, and I saw that my cell
was one of several in a vestibule, with another door leading
outside. Listening closely, I realized that no other cells were
occupied. The key pointed to a table, and doggone if he didn't
have a plate of sugar and a piece of bread! Then he poured me
some hot tea! Well, that was a treat, even though I'm wondering
at the same time when the goon squad will arrive to pound the
hell out of me. The outside door was open, so I gave a quick
glance and saw what looked like a row of green drawers, in two
layers. I thought they were lay-down cells for torture—maybe
there are Yanks stuffed in them. My imagination was running
wild, but that happens when you're anticipating torture.

When the key took me out to wash, I saw that the green
"drawers" weren't drawers at all, but dutch doors that swung
out. Each door led to a separate little wash alcove. On the way,
I saw a nice-looking, brown-skinned man face-to-face and
guessed he was Thai. *"Sa-wah-dee,"* I said, giving the common

Thai greeting. He smiled at me in return. He was Chi-Charn-Harnnavee, a Thai, crew chief to civilian pilot Ernie Brace, who was shot down in an Air America helio-plane near Dien Bien Phu in 1965, one month before me. Chi-Charn was washing a pile of dishes, and I felt so sorry for him. What's he got to look forward to, poor fella! (Come to think of it, I didn't have a hell of a lot to look forward to either!)

At chow time, I went out for the pickup, and it pretty near floored me. There was a little plate of smashed potatoes, a couple of pieces of meat, and bread. "This whole thing's a big setup," I thought. "I'm goin' home! This is a goin'-home camp. They're not giving me goodies like this for nothing." Right off the bat, the war is over because I've got one smashed potato and four pieces of pig fat! But that was great, compared to what we were getting at the Zoo. Nothing much happened, and the days continued their relentless march.

About the third week I was called out to meet three Vietnamese interrogators. They began by chewing me out because of all the trouble I gave them at the Zoo. "Ga-reeno! Are you ready to obey the regulations again?" Then the most senior-looking guy said sternly, "And your wife, she has a very bad attitude also! If she does not stop speaking out against us, you will never hear from her again!" "How do they dream up all this crap?" I wondered. Then he said, "And your son, too, has a bad attitude, and he has come over to fight us! Soon we will have him here with you . . . soon!" My heart plummeted! I immediately thought Allan had been captured and was on the way to Hanoi. Damn! If they had him, they'd really play some dirty tricks with me.

I did not know what type assignment Allan had gotten after his graduation from flight training, but the war lasted so long anybody with a set of wings surely had to get in a combat tour. I was sick with worry. But nothing more happened, and I realized it was just more V scare tactics. Mental torture, instead of physical.

I didn't mind the cramped little cell in the Mint, because the food was decent by Hanoi standards, and it was peaceful. It was good to be alone and away from Clay Kirsten's antagonism. I could feel myself relaxing, though I still had violent spasms where I cussed out Kirsten soundly.

The peep opened, and there was the old Green Hornet from the Zoo! It had been three years since our last encounter—in the early days of the Hut, under Dum Dum. The Hornet beamed all

over. He was genuinely glad to see me! "Ga" this and "Ga,"
that. He was pretty excited, and I saw that he was describing
little children. Yes, he'd had two children since I'd seen him last;
he'd also gotten two stars on his collar. I made signs to show
my congratulations on his daughters and his promotions.

Passing my *fifth* shoot-down anniversary, the fourteenth of
June 1970, wasn't that big a deal, and nobody baked me a cake,
so I tried not to think about it. Toward the end of June, after
twenty-one days in the Mint, they moved me to the center cell
of the little "Riviera" building. It was a seven by ten foot room
with a barred window in back, which looked into the area where
women prepared food for cooking. Sometimes, by pushing
steadily and slowly, I could spring the shutters and get in some
excellent peeping time. Climbing up on the *bo* can, using my
toothbrush, I punched small holes in the matting that covered
the upper front door, until I had great peep-out capability to the
front also.

As soon as I got my bearings, I couldn't believe the strategic
position I was in. They had committed another royal screwup!
My Riviera cell was the best possible spot in the camp to ob-
serve everybody and everything. Within two weeks I had a positive identification of all fifty-six men in Las Vegas. On my very
first peek-out, I saw two Americans moving some portable mat
fencing into place. The matting was normally leaning up against
the side of a building. At bath and exercise time, the gooks had
a couple of our guys prop this fencing in place, to cut down on
visual sightings and communicating. I gave a slight cough signal, and in a few seconds there I am eyeball-to-eyeball with good
old Bob Shumaker! I whispered loudly, "Bob, Larry Guarino.
Where am I?" Bob whispered back, "You're in Vegas, your
building is the Riviera." Of course, I had heard of Vegas and
knew it to be part of Hoa Lo. Shu told me the fellow with him
was a navy buddy, Nels Tanner.

I had a good view of the front of the bath area and one exercise
yard, plus the little exercise yard between the end of the bath
building and my building. The guys were brought there from
the Nugget or from the left side of the Thunderbird. My days
standing on the *bo*, or looking through the keyhole, were very
exciting, a real adventure. Whenever night came, shutting down
my peek time, I'd pace my cool brick floor, thinking things over.
Though I tried not to think of him, Kirsten was in my thoughts
frequently. Soon I'd been in a mental argument with him and
find myself cussing him aloud, and the key would hear me mum-

LAS VEGAS AREA
HANOI HILTON

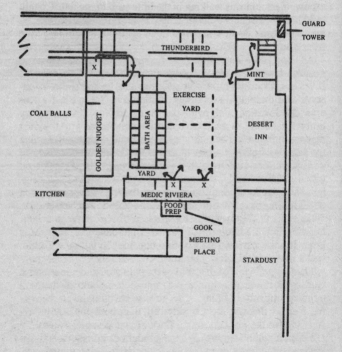

bling and ask, "What?" I'd say, "Just talking to a friend of mine."

The turnkey was about as decent as I ever had. His name was Hack, because he hacked and spit a lot. You could always hear him coming. It was like he was saying, "Hawwk-hawwk, I'm coming Ga, so stop peeping or communicating, I don't want to catch you!" He caught me lots of times, and the punishment was always the same. He made me stand outside while he dumped my gear all over the floor. "You see, if you insist on communicating, then I must continue to inspect you." He never touched me, and nothing ever came of his inspections. It was just a pain in the ass to pick up after him.

Norlan Daughtrey had just had surgery on one of his calcified elbow joints and was walking in the little yard to my left. Cough, cough, I signaled. Norlan looked up at the shutter and spotted my toothbrush, and I flashed him "Hi, L.G." He about pooped his pants in joy and told the other two, Gary Anderson and Curtis Meisner, also from the Zoo. They sent "R.U.O.K." I answered "R.R." (roger, roger).

My health wasn't all that good. I was still having severe headaches and dizzy spells. The spells started in '68 and got worse after I was bounced around the floors in '69. I also had an asthmatic cough, which weakened me considerably. At night I frequently called for the guard, thinking that if I could get some food, my dizziness might diminish. But Hack wasn't a guy to hang around, because once his chores were done, he cleared out of there on the run.

Well doggone, the next two guys in the little yard are Groves and Kasler! It was so good to see them! I gave Lowell the cough, and they both went nuts when I sent 'em "L.G." Lowell asked, "How's Evy, G.?" I said, "Oh she's right here, we're having a great time!" I often fantasized about how Evy would handle being in the cell with me. She wouldn't have liked it, especially when it came to mastering the technique of using the *bo*. For years, we suspended ourselves in midair, then finally we learned to invert our rubber shoes on the rim, so we could use a "thinking man's" position. After mastering that, being an active person, she would probably say, "What are we going to do now?" "Well, why don't we just sit and 'ponder our crimes' for five or six years?" She'd go nuts! I held a lot of imaginary conversations with my Evy during those years, but then I'd get really down from missing her, so I'd have to force my mind onto other things.

Two POWs came out, and after some light exercise they sat on a bench against the wall, shirts off in the sun. They looked like they must have had an awful time. They looked so very placid and monklike I wondered if they had been denutted. After my cough, one of them wiggled out a toe message. "Who U.?"

"L.G. fm Zoo."

"When U.S.D.?"

"June 65." The poor fellow visibly winced. I spelled out my full last name and they came back with theirs, Ligon and Stockman, both '67 shoot-downs. The next guy out was a sight. He was wearing his pajama bottoms and very heavy woolen socks. His body was a mess with two-inch-wide strap marks all over his torso and arms. It took my breath away. My God! I never heard of anyone living through torture that terrible! It was beyond imagination! He paced the yard, looking down, and when I coughed, he looked about furtively but avoided comm with me. Later, I found out that Lieutenant Colonel Jamey Hillary had not been tortured. The awful marks on his body were burn scars from a flaming crash, years before his capture. Things often are not what they seem to be, and you can't go jumping to conclusions like that, I reminded myself.

During the following weeks, I was in touch with almost everyone there. One fellow told me they were just settling down from a camp-wide fast that Jerry Denton had ordered. There were three men in solitary at the time, so Denton figured a fast would force the V into breaking up solitary. As a result, there were now eighteen men in solitary! Denton meant well, as always, but his "solutions" usually caused a lot of excitement and not much in the way of positive results. Then again, nothing we ever did got positive (meaning beneficial) results!

Jim Stockdale was somewhere in Vegas and so were Dave Winn, Norm Gaddis, Jim Bean, and Jack Flynn, all of whom outranked Denton, and since they all *did* outrank Denton, I wanted to know what the hell was going on in the camp. The people I asked told me that "Stockdale was hurt and 'gun-shy,' and a fellow he lived with tried to blow the whistle on him." I was told the other four colonels said "they felt out of touch." Maybe they were, but the guys felt "Denton is the only guy with the balls to take over."

There was never the slightest doubt in my mind that Denton was a great patriot and strong resister. It's just that with Jerry's high-level idealistic viewpoints, he was never able to think down at the same level where the gooks hummed along, and outguess them. I believe Jerry never understood them, and wouldn't if he stayed in Hanoi for another hundred years.

As I peeked through my keyhole, a skinny little gray-haired guy stared toward me and pointed to the end of the building. When everything quieted, I put my cup to the front wall and listened . . . I heard a tapping. Sure enough, the skinny guy had moved into the first room. We had one or two empty rooms between us, but using the cup as an amplifier we could hear one another's taps well enough. It was John McCain, the "Prince of Hanoi," (as Bud Day described him). John filled me in with a tremendous amount of information about all the people we could see out in the yards. I gave him what I could about the Zoo, but there were times I had to quit tapping and lie down to rest, because of coughing spells. When I went out to wash I "posed" for John, giving him a smiling head-on "shot" for a positive identification.

Eventually, we got around to personal stories of how we had been treated. I think they could have been bound into a book titled, *Stories You Won't Believe Anyway!* John told me about his wife, a beautiful career model, working for some big-time women's magazine. He also talked about his trials going through the Naval Academy and the pressures of being reared in a family with a line of generals and admirals back to Revolutionary War days. After a couple of weeks, I felt as close to McCain as I had to Jerry Denton back at New Guy in those first months.

There was a large board across my back window blocking my view of the rear. I think my constant pushing at it loosened it until it hung there dangerously, and finally someone removed it, leaning it against a far wall. I could see that the other side of it was a tally board of Mỹ soldiers killed and various other totals of equipment destroyed, including tanks, trucks, and planes. Nearly every day the numbers were changed.

I could watch the women prepare food. They weighed the vegetables on an ancient set of hand scales, whether it was swamp grass, squash, or pumpkin, then they washed the vegetables, cut them, and took them away to be cooked. They had two piles. One pile was much smaller than the other, and that pile of food was for the V camp personnel. The women always chose the best for their own people. The rest of it went into the Mỹ pile. The floor was their dining table. First they swept it, then, as the food was cooked, they set it there in dishes. Their people came in to eat in shifts, about six or seven at a time, carrying their own chopsticks, cups, and little enamel bowls. Watching them carefully I saw that no one ever overate or took more than one choice bit of meat. If they wanted more, they took a lesser piece of meat, fowl, or fish. They chatted amiably as they ate. Some preferred bread to rice. The portions were less than half of what it would take to satisfy one of us. They were very considerate of each other. Everyone got an equal share.

McCain called me to alert me about three POWs who were putting up the blinders in the exercise yards. He said they were people who had strained loyalties with the rest of us. They were tall, normal-looking guys. One of them was close to me. "Hi," I said. He asked who I was and I gave my name, then asked his. He shot right back, "Ed Miller, U.S. Marines." By God, it was Ed Miller of "Bob and Ed Show" fame! His partner Bob Forrester was helping him, and the third man who had been sucked into believing the Vietnamese propaganda was another naval officer, Gene Wilbur.

Three others came into view. I recognized George McKnight, but I'd never seen the other two before. They were George Coker, the GIB (guy in back) who came in with Jack Fellowes, and Anthony Scorpio (who had gone over the Annex wall with Atherton). I did not know at the time that McKnight and Coker had also attempted to escape and were successful for a few hours.

I met Ernie Brace, the civilian Air America pilot. His was a real horror story. When he attempted escape, the gooks buried him up to his neck in the earth. After a few weeks like that, he lost control of all body functions and was out of his mind. When he was taken out of the ground, he was fitted with a three-foot-wide wooden neck yoke that, I was told, he wore for three years! He and Chi-Charn were eventually brought to Hanoi. McCain said communicating with Ernie was very difficult, because for the first six months Ernie could only cry. This is another example of how far down they could smash a man's spirit. He seemed to be in relatively good frame of mind now, and every chance I got I pumped him up.

I usually greeted him with, "How are you doing today, Basil? You are a handsome devil—did anybody ever tell you that you're a dead ringer for Basil Rathbone?" He was always pleased and smiled pleasantly, and I wanted so much to make him feel good.

It was late afternoon when I chanced to look in on a meeting that I soon realized was a monthly political meeting. I had been told about these meetings years before, where, according to the dictum of Ho Chi Minh, each person would get his opportunity for "criticism and self-criticism." These monthly meetings served many purposes and were a general attitude check for everyone, as they gave the party member in charge a chance to see who was stepping out of line by encouraging each to tattle on the other.

Even though it was in their tongue, it was easy to figure out what was going on by the tone of voice, the inflections, the finger-pointing, and the shocked looks. Everyone was seated in the yard, so I shoved the shutters apart and knelt down to peer out. I had an excellent and undisturbed view of the proceedings. The meeting was called to order by the Bug, and once he did so, there was no horseplay. Bug made some opening remarks, in a soft voice and a gentle manner. He then seemed to be asking a question that went without response. He tried again, looking around. He seemed to be imploring them to respond. A young man stood up, but said nothing. Bug said something to encourage the man to go ahead with whatever it was he had on his mind. The guy finally started to speak, slowly at first, but then he picked up confidence and strength as he went along. He was describing something, some situation. Bug intervened, questioned, the young man hesitated, then pointed an accusing finger at the guy sitting next to him. The man who was singled out was taken by surprise, and pointing his fingers to his chest he jumped up—"Who, me?" Then the accuser got excited and argued back like, "Yes, you, just like I said!" Both parties got huffed up, and Bug had to step in and quiet them, making them both sit down. Bug spoke again, apparently to the accused, for a long time. The accused then spoke, giving his side of the story. He sat down, but I got the impression that he knew things had gone badly for him. Bug gave another spiel, again very softly, as though he was pointing out in a fatherly and understanding way the error or crime that had been committed. Whatever it was could have been as minor as the man taking too much food, taking something home that belonged to "the people," or not doing his job properly. Perhaps he was seen being too friendly with the $M\bar{y}$, or any number of other minor offenses.

When the Bug finished, it was very still. Then the accused rose very slowly and spoke, with his head down. He nodded toward his accuser and finished what seemed an apologetic statement. There was light applause. Bug closed by asking if there was any other criticism to be aired. No one responded; everyone had had enough for that meeting. It was the living example of how the commies keep people in line. A "self-purging system," used to assure that "each does his part, shows a good attitude, and is deserving of good treatment."

In September, Hack told me to suit up for a quiz. The quizzers asked the usual stuff about how I felt, and I told them "terrible," just to test them. They didn't even notice, because they were already tuned into the main purpose of the quiz.

"And tell us, how many different criminals have you lived with in the Democratic Republic of Vietnam?"

"Well, not too many. For many years I lived with Byrne, then Cherry, also Kasler and Bomar and, oh yes, there was Groves. I think that's all. Are they in this camp?" I asked innocently. The next day, Hack gave me the roll-up signal, so I got my gear together and he walked me out to the left and up a yard between the bath area and the Nugget and into the Thunderbird building, last room on the left. It was a great day for Groves and Kasler, and especially for me! We talked for hours, without let-up, about what had happened since last I had seen them in December of 1969.

Two or three times a day we heard an American yell "Horseshit!" I asked what that was all about. Lowell said it was Jamey Hillary, the guy with the bad burns who lived by himself in the Golden Nugget building right across from the bath stalls. "What's the story on Hillary?" Lowell said that Hillary had lived with Stockdale and they had not gotten along well. Hillary had several physical problems resulting from his severe burns. He had to ask the gooks permission to write home for certain prescription medicines that were critical to his continuous treatment. Hillary apparently felt guilty for having to ask for favors and reacted in some strange and unpredictable ways, both against the Vietnamese and us. His was another case of a pilot on combat duty with a physical problem, which, if captured, would immediately place him at the mercy of his captors. From the lessons we learned, I hoped that in the future people with serious disabilities would be barred from combat flying.

Just before I went to sleep every night, I signed off with "Bullshit!" It was my "cover-all" word. For example, "What do you think of our humane treatment?" Answer: "Bullshit!" "Senator Blabberface, what is being done to ease the plight of the American POW?" "Everything that can be done has already been done." "Bullshit!" For the typical news report: "Well, our side has made great gains on all fronts, but now that the rainy season is upon us, we will have to solidify our positions on high ground and get the VC again in the next dry season."

"Bullshit!" "Bullshit!" became my favorite response to drivel. (It still is!)

Next door to us were Daughtrey, Anderson, and Meisner. We communicated with them through the walls. The other cells near us were vacant. Limited communicating was done while we were in the bath area, but there was not much of that because of the vigilance of the guards.

One day, Lowell complained about not feeling well, and within twenty-four hours he had a very high fever. We *Bao Cao*ed the turnkey, who got a medic to come by. By that time Lowell was weak and listless. The turnkey brought two basins of cool water and a couple of cloths, telling us to keep placing cold compresses on Lowell's back to bring down his temperature. Lowell took off his clothes and laid down on his stomach. We folded a blanket under his feet so he could let them hang off the ends of the boards more comfortably. Then I went to work on him, changing cloths, wringing, changing, and so on. He loved the attention and said it was very helpful.

"You know Larry, my neck has been hurting near the base of my skull. Maybe it's a pinched nerve or something."

"Do you want me to try a little massage, or maybe a back rub?"

"Would you do that for me, Larry?"

"Sure, why not?" As I gave him a neck and back rub, I realized that humans are just like babies, they need the touch of another human from time to time or they become lost.

Jim was sitting on his bunk watching, and he noticed that Lowell was not only feeling better, but enjoying being fussed over. Kasler felt very left out. "You never fuss over me like that, and my back has been bothering me for a long time," he complained.

"No kidding, Jim—why didn't you tell me? I'll take care of you as soon as I get done with Lowell." Well, damned if Jim didn't flop over on his belly like a pooch waiting to be petted! He enjoyed his back rub, too, and that'll just "show to go you," even big tough ace fighter pilots need, and crave, the touch of the human hand.

Lowell cured up just fine in twenty-four hours.

Hack came by with paper and pencils, and let us all write letters. Then he gave all three of us packages from home! My package was exceptionally good, with homemade cookies and cans of Alaskan crab and chicken liver. Jim's was just as good, but old Lowell did not do well. His packages usually had hard

candy and "fizzies," which are sort of flavored Alka-Seltzers.
It looked like someone back home was giving him the bare
minimum treatment, and he was naturally sensitive about it. We
shared everything we had with him, trying to cheer him up, but
as Jim once confided to me in the bath area, "There's no way
that Lowell's wife is still out there waiting for him. Isn't this a
hell of a war to be caught up in? You'd think that some of our
people would decide to go ahead and win this damn war and get
us out of here!" I was surprised at the vehemence of his remark.

"No Jim, that's never going to happen. If we intended to win
this war we could have, and would have won it long ago. It's too
late for that now."

Hack threw a letter from Evy into the cell. The big announcement was that daughter-in-law Maureen had had a little girl,
Michelle Dawn, born July 22, 1970. Evelyn said Allan "would
be thrilled," which signaled me that Allan was not around when
his daughter was born. I knew that routine very well. On February 23, 1945, when Allan was born, I was in China, and the
telegram from my father, which I received fifteen days late, said,
"Son born. All is well, Dad." So now I was a grandfather! I
hoped and prayed that baby Michelle's dad was not in Vietnam,
too.

Then came another surprise. Our door opened, and in walked
our three buddies from next door! From that time on (early
October 1970), they came in twice a day to play cards or chess.
The food improved in quality and quantity, and the next new
wrinkle was eating outdoors, whenever weather permitted.
Sometimes we got smoked or cured fish. It was a bony, rough
fish, and the flesh was shot through with Y bones, so we had to
take great care to avoid choking on them. But the flavor was
good, and it was the healthful food we all needed, especially
the wounded guys. As we sat there eating one day, a rice mat
being used as a temporary blinder at the end of the yard fell
down, and there stood three guys who had been captured in
Laos. They were Walt Stischer, Steve Long, and Jim Bedinger.
They were lucky to have gotten out of Laos alive. (Most MIAs
from there have never been accounted for.)

Living conditions vastly improved, but even so, boredom
continued to plague us. I decided to grow back my moustache,
much against the wishes of Groves and Kasler, because they
knew the gooks never allowed such individuality. After a few
days, it got the V's attention, and they moved me into a solitary
cell across the hall, where they kept me for a week. Then they

moved me back, not into my former spot, but into the first cell, with Curtis Meisner. Daughtrey and Anderson were moved in with Kasler and Groves.

Meisner was a nice guy to be with, and very well versed in Shakespeare. In high school I was distracted from worthy literary accomplishments by things like football and girls. So Curt took it upon himself to fill this void. Each night as I listened Curt would recite Shakespeare. My very favorite was *Merchant of Venice*, and Curt obliged me with a number of repeats of that one.

One evening, in midstory, Curt stopped and said, "Larry, there's something I've been wanting to tell you for a long time."

"Well, what is it?"

"It happened back at the Zoo, when Fidel was still here and I was one of the group he was working over. I've been kind of worried about it and have been wanting to tell someone. By the way, did you know that in the time I lived with Kasler at the Zoo we became inimical to each other?"

"No, I certainly did not know that. 'Inimical'—you mean you actually were enemies?"

"Yes, that's right. You know how Jim is—big, tough resister, and all that. He thinks everybody should be that way, and we all can't. I'm not like that."

"I understand that we all do the best we can with what we've got, but go on with your story."

"Okay. Well, one day the turnkey came for me and told me to dress for quiz. Right away I started shaking inside, because I knew I was going out to see Fidel. When I got there, he was waiting. I bowed and sat down and he said, 'Okay, today Curtis, I wanna find out if you're a truthful guy. I'm gonna find out by asking you some questions about things that I already know, but I'm checking on you just to see if you tell the truth. Like I said, I already know the answers, so if you give the correct answers, no problem. If I see you're lying to me, I'm gonna beat the living shit out of you. Understand?' So I said yes, I understood, and I was really scared because he was testing me with stuff he already knew."

At that point, I interrupted Curt to ask, "What do you mean he already knew? How did you know he already knew?"

"I *know* he knew! Do you want to hear the rest of this story?"

"Sure, go on."

"Well, Fidel says, 'Curt, when the helicopter comes over to rescue you, how does he know it's you talking and not me?' So

I told him that the chopper pilot maintains a list of people recently shot down, along with their identifier code numbers. Fidel says, 'Where does he get the code numbers?' So I told him they are all kept in the intelligence section back at the base."

"Holy Christ, Curt!" I interrupted. "You mean you gave Fidel that kind of information? You know that's pretty sensitive stuff! Why would you do that?" Curt got upset and thoroughly exasperated with me.

"I told you! Because he already *knew* the answers!" Curt put me in shock because he had fallen for the oldest interrogator trick in the world, one of the first things a flier learns in the course of his survival training. I ventured one last remark.

"Curt, didn't it occur to you to just bullshit the guy? You know, just tell him an outright lie?" That must have touched a nerve, because he jumped off the cement cot with an incredulous look on his face, and standing almost rigidly he blurted, "Lie? Lie? An academy man tell a lie? Never!"

I backed off, because the damage had already been done, and there was no convincing Curt that he had done a wrong thing. In his mind, he believed that he must have the courage to resist, or he must fail. There was no alternative. His upbringing, his education, his survival training had not prepared him for that eventuality. He was unable to tell a lie! Curt was brought up in very well-to-do circumstances and attended private schools. He never had the rub of the street and didn't know anything about roughhouse, or playing tit-for-tat with his opposition. His genteel youth had made him idealistic to a fault. The military academy from which he graduated had a strict honor code, as they all do. But evidently they didn't accept or had never taught him that there would be situations in war that were contrary to the style of the "officer gentleman," situations where it was perfectly okay—no! even better—to lie, cheat, and steal. What better place than on the enemy's home turf, in a prison camp? Does an enemy interrogator deal in fact or truth? Hell no! Then we have to meet him on even terms and do whatever it takes to beat him, or at least to stalemate him. *Yes*, it's okay to lie, cheat, and steal! *Yes*, "all's fair in war!" Curt was certainly not a child, but his naïveté was childlike. As individuals, or as a country, we cannot afford to behave as though we are little white cooing doves trying to exist in a den of hawks, because if we do that (and occasionally we have done exactly that) the doves will most certainly be plucked bare.

When a man's fear carries him to a point where he rationalizes his position by assuming the interrogator "already knows," he has not only subconsciously set himself up to avoid harsh treatment, but he has also lost the battle without firing a shot! Interrogators always try to give the impression that they already know the answers and are "just rechecking." Most of the time they don't know a damn thing, and if they do, they are constantly striving to add to, or to confirm and reconfirm, details. All of us are obliged to give it our best shot. It isn't fair for one man to surrender too easily what another man has suffered intensely to protect.

In early December the Box came across with a garbled story. They quoted Congressman Mendel Rivers, a South Carolina Democrat, saying, "If we want to go right into downtown Hanoi, we'll go, and there's no power on earth that can stop us!" We stared at the speaker box, but the fragmentary report didn't give us the full story. We could only wonder about the context of the remark. Around mid-December, I was moved back in with Jim and Lowell, and Andy and Norlan Daughtrey rejoined Curt. Kasler and I received letters. There was one very big news item in my letter, which I had been sweating out since the gooks told me that my son "had also come over to fight." Evelyn said, "Allan is home safe, after the longest year!" What a relief that was! Even though I didn't want to think or talk about it, I had been half convinced that he had already been captured. Why did they let him come over in the first place? I suppose that if I were a young guy out there, full of piss and vinegar, and my dad was a POW, I'd want to go over and do whatever I could to get him out. The consequences of possible capture wouldn't have occurred to me either.

Christmas was upon us, and no one was asked to go to church services. A few days before, we had gotten a message from Jack Flynn, the most senior POW in North Vietnam, saying that he was taking over as SRO, and his code name would be Ace. Flynn was bagged in October 1967. I believe I heard his name in the system in '68 or '69, along with Jim Bean. But, due to injuries, or being out of touch, this was his first shot at acting as SRO.

All six of us ate our Christmas meal together. There was so much to eat, we saved some for later that evening, but when evening rolled around there were sounds of activity out in the yards. The turnkey came and told us to roll up our gear. He let us take only essentials, and nothing we had gotten in packages from home; not toothpaste, brushes, long johns, or socks. We even had to leave our Christmas leftovers behind, as we were marched out into the front yard. The sight meeting our eyes out there by the bath stalls was a jolt to us, however pleasing! There were dozens of Americans going through a very thorough body search. We had no idea what it was all about, but we enjoyed the thrill of talking to some old friends and men we knew through walls but had never seen before. The Vietnamese weren't too upset about all the talking. When they were satisfied that we were clean, they walked us through the Desert Inn area. We passed many frightened-looking Asian prisoners. They all wore striped pajamas, and there was no telling if they were common criminals or prisoners of war.

We were walked around various buildings and into an area with large cell blocks, capable of holding twenty to fifty prisoners each. Our group was moved into cell block seven. There were about twenty-two of us, all in the shoot-down rank of major or lieutenant commander or captain. There was a lot of handshaking and embracing between old and new friends. There were Bud Day and Jack Fellowes, Shumaker and Tanner, McKnight and Scorpio, McCain, Stratton, Howie Dunn, Ron Webb, Red McDaniel, and all the rest. I hoped I'd be seeing Ron Byrne again, but that wasn't to be.

Are they getting ready to release us? we wondered. They'd never move us in together if we weren't going to be released! There was all kinds of speculation, from the reasonable to the ridiculous, but any one guess was as good as the other. Lowell Groves looked around carefully and said, "Larry, looks like you're 'it' again, the senior man." We talked far into the night, and the next day was even more surprising.

The day after Christmas, the turnkey opened up, and in came a crowd of about twenty-two more O-5s, lieutenant colonels and commanders! There was so much hugging and handshaking going on, I had to sit down and patiently wait my turn. Here came my dear friend, Robbie Risner, then Jerry Denton, Jim Stockdale, Al Brady, Verlyn Daniels, Ligon and Stockman, Fuller and Lawrence, Jim Mulligan and Howie Rutledge! Our ranks swelled to about forty-five men as we set up on the cement sleeping pad.

Cell seven was fifty feet long and twenty-two feet wide. Except for a three-foot-wide perimeter walking space and fifteen feet of space on one end, the cell had a two-foot-high cement pad for all the prisoners to sleep on. The pad sloped down a couple of inches from the center to the sides so it could be washed down easily if prisoners in irons messed up the pad. At the front side of the building, at floor level, were numerous ports, about five by ten inches high, so the entire building could be flushed out when necessary. These cell blocks were constructed to accommodate large numbers of prisoners shackled in irons for extended periods. Irons were not used for any of us. This entire complex of buildings was named Camp Unity by the prisoners.

Bob Shumaker, a brilliant naval officer, cautioned, "Listen, guys, maybe we shouldn't get too excited about this. I think it's possible for them to keep us this way for another two years." We didn't want to hear that! We all wanted to think we'd be going home soon. Stockdale remarked, "Let's hope we can learn to live with prosperity."

As the new year came we felt sure that 1971 would be the big one, the year we'd finally be going home. Wrong again!

Chapter Fifteen

1971—JOINED IN CELL BLOCKS

We spent the first weeks together filling each other in on what had happened during all our years in North Vietnam. It was mostly an unloading of our personal horror stories on the sympathetic ears of fellow sufferers. The most irrepressible and talkative personality was John McCain, who got up before dawn to make the rounds, talking, joking, and entertaining. John couldn't be bothered folding his mosquito net or blankets, he just threw them in a pile. I tidied up his place for him, because he needed someone to look out for him. Often at night he'd ask me to sit under the net with him to rub his neck, just to calm his nerves and relax him. His gimp-legged sorties around the cell block had him wound up tight as a spring by bedtime. My part was to be a father (or big brother) figure to him.

Ben Pollard was another interesting guy, and I believed that Ben and Bob Shumaker had two of the best sets of brains in the camp. Ben had spent a long time in solitary and irons, and partly because of the irons he had developed huge, white, pigmentless blotches on his neck and back. It was Ben who enlightened me about something that had bothered me since September of 1965.

That was when I had heard the screams of women prisoners and assumed they were political prisoners being tortured. A couple of years later Ben occupied a Heartbreak cell, heard the same kind of screaming going on, and was able to peer out into the yards during these sessions to see what it was all about. Ben said the screaming came from pregnant female prisoners in labor, giving birth right there in the cells, probably with the help of other female inmates or, at best, by a midwife. Their subsistence and material care had to be provided by relatives or friends outside, because the state did not bear the burden of providing for them. In the absence of outside support, the barest living essentials were provided to inmates.

Ben had also seen a demonstration of how the Vietnamese taught children that "crime doesn't pay." Double lines of little children from five to twelve years old were shackled together in irons. They were made to hobble around the prison yards. Their reaction ranged from giggles and laughter to tears of terror and panic. The kids had been caught in very minor violations of civil law, most likely petty theft, from bananas to bicycles. This was the "object lesson," showing how it would be for those who chose to follow the life of crime. By our standards it was a cruel form of child abuse, but the Vietnamese believed it the most effective way to teach kids to toe the line.

As I learned more of the experiences of Bud Day, I was so impressed that I promised myself I would try to get him a well-deserved Medal of Honor. I mentioned it to no one, but filed it away in a corner of my mind for some future time. Bud filled me in on the happenings back at the Zoo since I left there in June '69. Not too long after my departure, he and Jack Fellowes were sent into solitary cells at Heartbreak. He discovered that several of our most senior officers had been in Heartbreak for *three years* and had never tried to communicate! "Can you believe that?" he asked. One was Commander Burl Flagler, in solitary for three years and in very bad physical condition. He had adopted an extremely rigid resistance posture, eating very little and refusing basic items of survival, including blankets in wintertime! In the earlier years, this would not have bothered the V at all. However, having moved away from cruel treatment, they now showed some concern for Flagler, evidenced by the fact that they had Bud visit with him a number of times to try to talk some sense into him. Flagler was distrustful. During these visits, Bud discovered that Flagler was throwing away most of his food, including bananas and special food given to him by the V to try to tempt him into eating. No matter how hard Bud tried to convince Flagler that he was way off base, Flagler remained unyielding.

A distrustful attitude can be a very normal, safe, and cautious approach to a new situation. I knew the feeling; I had my suspicions of the others early in the game. Bud Day did his very best to gain Burl's confidence and to convince him that he was somewhere out in left field by himself. But it was too late for that. Had Bud been there a year earlier, it might have been a different story.

Another person there was my main man from the Zoo, the dependable J. J. Connell. J. J. had been severely beaten when his sham was uncovered during the '69 purge. He wasn't eating, and his health was at rock bottom. He and Flagler were taken to the hospital in October of 1970, and neither was ever seen alive again.

Jerry Denton occupied the sack opposite mine, and he gave me his story, particularly his two years in the place called "Alcatraz." There were ten others with him, including Jim Stockdale, Mulligan, Shumaker, and Ron Storz. Jerry told me how badly the health of Jim Mulligan and Ron Storz had deteriorated. Storz had become obsessed with fasting, as if to spite the Vietnamese for his predicament. Mulligan pleaded with Storz to get him to start eating, and Jerry Denton finally gave him a direct order to eat. Ron replied that he had fasted so long, he no longer had any interest in food, nor could his shrunken stomach accept any. Most of them were moved to the Las Vegas section by 1970, into the era of better food and better treatment.

The story of Ron Storz is a tragic one of death brought on by extended voluntary starvation. Although he was alone in a small cell at Alcatraz, he was in continuous communication with ten others. No one ever figured out whether Ron had a goal in mind, or whether he was so mentally and physically crushed that he didn't want to go on living. He had no way of knowing that the worst of it was behind us, and that improved treatment ahead would give all of us the hope that maybe, maybe we had a chance. He was never seen again, and his date of death is marked officially as approximately April of 1970.

There is a sad but valuable lesson to be learned from the tragic loss of good men like Connell, Storz, and Flagler. Each of us had some latitude in establishing our own pattern of resistance within the guidelines of the Code of Conduct. It is incumbent upon all members of the military to resist giving classified information, and to resist participating in propaganda events, to the best of their ability. Adopting extreme measures to fool or thwart the interrogators may be understandable to a point, but when these measures amount to a suicidal degree of self-inflicted punishment, then it's time to move to a more sensible position that affords a better chance of survival . . . and survival is the name of the game! In the case of George McSwain, we had a man suffering from boredom and extreme frustration who decided to fake insanity. It attracted the attention of the V, and it was not approved by Charlie Plumb, McSwain's cell mate, or

Jim Kasler, the building senior. The gooks pounded the pee out of George for a month. Partway through that month, to George's great credit, he decided he was on a wrong tack and altered his course. That's the only reason he is alive today.

In the case of J. J. Connell, even though we suggested that he pretend the electric shock treatments were helping him to a slow recovery, he insisted he knew what he was doing. If J. J. had had a cell mate or two, it might have been a different ending. I doubt that he ever recovered from the beatings he endured when his scheme surfaced in the purge of '69. Insanity as a game is the most dangerous game of all.

The best advice is still to try to "run in the middle of the pack"—look to the left and to the right, and do what the group is doing. "If they're okay, then I must be okay." Don't attract any undue attention, and avoid extremes (except for very short periods), especially things like refusing food and other essentials of life.

Denton eventually got around to his view of the tactical value of group fasting as a means of forcing the Vietnamese to modify treatment in favor of the POWs. Denton maintained the position that in the long run, it was beneficial. I could never concur with his ideas on fasting. I still held to the belief that the lesson of survival school was correct—that we shouldn't punish ourselves. Jerry tried to convince me, and I told him he could talk until he was purple in the face, I'd never agree with it, but I would comply with an order from an SRO to fast.

In January and February 1971, the food was very good. We were getting canned fish from Russia and a canned meat similar to Spam or bologna. In a sandwich, it was so tasty I vowed never again to spoil the good taste of food by adding ketchup, mayonnaise, or mustard. Cabbage or pumpkin soup was still a daily standard.

Bart Hovick was down near his end of the sleep pad writing a list of names with a piece of broken roof slate. He had known of these men from the Plantation camp where Soft-Soap Fairy had been in charge of prepping the early releasees. Half a dozen of us watched as he wrote about thirty names there on the cement. When he finished, he went down the list systematically, grading each man with the comments, "He's okay, he's okay, this guy's a loser, he's okay, this guy's a fink." It amazed me that he had the brass to categorize each person, so I asked him why he said so-and-so was a "loser," or a "fink." He replied that he couldn't get into communications with this one, or that one was afraid, or that he had "heard" something or other about that one. I suggested that he was being hard on those he downgraded, that there might be extenuating circumstances he knew nothing about. He didn't like my comments, and his expression darkened noticeably. His face showed his feelings more than any man I'd ever met.

We had meetings among the senior people to decide what our new relationship with the Vietnamese should be. There were varying, and sometimes very opposite, opinions of what we should be doing. Many of us were spoiling for a fight, with years-long hatred pounding our insides. Others wanted to coast for a while and take a "wait and see" attitude. Rarely was there an overwhelming agreement on any one issue. The Vietnamese were not asking us, or pressing us, to do anything, only to live without "threatening the camp security."

Our Sunday church services gave them fits. Robbie Risner, George Coker, McKnight, Howie Rutledge, and several others conducted the services. The Bug came in to get a close look, and his eyes never left Risner. There was no dispelling the notion that Risner was a real continuous threat to them, and they worried about where Robbie might lead us. Actually, we wanted nothing except to be left alone for our Sunday religious services, but they could not believe that our plans stopped there.

George McKnight had the reputation of being a freewheeling bachelor who enjoyed fun and laughs and liked getting into more than his share of hot water. George was a damn good fighter pilot with the right attitude. I never knew, until the cell block days, that he and George Coker had been together before. They were the only Americans locked in a place called the Dirty Bird, near a Hanoi power plant. In October of '67, they escaped from there, made it to the Red River, and managed to get about fifteen miles downstream before they had to climb out to take a breather. They were spotted by peasants as they were dug into the mud, resting. They were recaptured and taken back. It was a good try from an insecure camp, and they almost made it. They also shared the Alcatraz experience with the Stockdale group of eleven.

Their most recent cell mate in Vegas was Anthony Scorpio, and for reasons then unknown to me, Scorpio and Coker seemed to be at odds. I took a liking to Scorpio, who had not been receiving any letters or packages. I offered to share a few articles of clothing, like shorts, undershirts, and a handkerchief.

Scorpio, Coker, and McKnight entertained us with their proficiency at doing handstands. Coker's and Scorpio's were very precise and beautiful. Scorpio said that it was an attention-getting gimmick he'd been doing since he was a kid at the beach. "All I had to do was a few handstands and I had a crowd around me." Tony was a phys ed major, very good and health conscious. He had kept himself in remarkable physical shape despite the conditions of imprisonment. He ate sitting straight up, never slouched, and sat just as straight on the *bo*! He was an excellent Spanish teacher and gave regular classes as part of the major education program we had started.

The most unusual "uniform" in the cell block was worn by John Finlay, whose wife Carolyn was friendly with Evelyn back in Satellite Beach, Florida. John wore his prison black pajama top over white long johns, white wool socks, his gook rubber thongs, and a muffler he had fashioned from scraps of old clothes. A pipe in his teeth completed the jaunty look. He was a sight! Vern Ligon's wife, Bebe, was also in the Patrick AFB area and friendly with Carolyn and Evy. That made the three of us practically related!

We organized ourselves into four work groups, ten men in each group, to handle housekeeping duties. The duty group helped to dish out food, collect and wash dishes, dump the toilet buckets, and keep the cell block swept out.

Allen Brady suggested that, within our work group, we each take time to give a brief bio of ourselves to the others. The first couple of guys took about twenty minutes each, then Allen took about fifteen minutes, and I did the same. When it was Denton's turn, Brady kept dozing off and falling over! I roused him and made him sit up time and again, reminding him this was *his* idea! Jerry looked down as he spoke and didn't notice Brady's faded blue eyes slipping up under his lids. Jerry's story was interesting even though it was quite long. After an hour or so, he was still talking about his great-great-grandmother who won a beauty contest back in 1888! He couldn't finish that day, so it was continued to the next session. We were all pretty stiff as we walked away, and Fred Crowe remarked in an aside to Brady, "Hey, Al—got any more good suggestions?"

We thought the V might have kept our personal gear and packages from us because they thought there were secret messages stashed in the gear. We were now getting welcome packages from home with really good stuff in them, including cans of ham and beef, fruitcakes, breakfast foods, and clothing. There were so many tiny rolls of microfilm in Byron Fuller's package of fruitcake, that, as the gooks sliced it up for him, the damn things were falling all over the ground! Fuller thought surely the gooks would spot them, but they didn't, not that day.

That night, when everything was still, Howie Rutledge held the microfilms up to the light one at a time and read them aloud, softly. It was an exciting event—the first uncensored news from home in *five years*! I don't know who the big brain was at home, but the first microfilm had year-old football scores, and the second one had last year's baseball scores! Finally Howie came up with a really hot item. It was about the Son Tay raid. It said that on the night of November 21, 1970, a force of helicopters, flown by air force people carrying Green Berets and Rangers, flew to the Son Tay POW camp twenty miles west of Hanoi, to attempt a rescue of POWs known to be there. It took the Vietnamese by complete surprise. There were no U.S. losses, and only one air force sergeant suffered a minor leg injury when a helicopter was destroyed in a hard landing in the Son Tay compound. Everything went off with precision, except for one small flaw—there were no POWs there! The camp had been vacated a few months earlier. The report went on to say that the overall commander and planner was air force Brigadier General Leroy Manor, whom I had known since 1951, and the on-scene commander in charge of the all-volunteer force was U.S. Army Colonel Arthur ''Bull'' Simons. We were impressed and heartened to learn that we were not forgotten, and that some of our people had the gumption to volunteer for such a dangerous mission, on Hanoi's very doorstep, to try to get us out!

There was a long silence after Howie finished. We were all thinking the same thing. How could anyone in his right mind allow a brave bunch of guys to go on a wild goose chase like that? Surely our intelligence system functioned better than that! We knew that we had superior reconnaissance capabilities and top-notch intelligence agencies. Could one agency have had information it didn't disseminate to the others? No, I couldn't believe that, and Roy Manor was much too sharp a guy to let one like that slip by him. What, then? We reviewed the details of the raid, looking for what there was for us on the positive side. For one thing, we were now reassured we were not ''forgotten men,'' and our people at home showed that they would go to extreme lengths to get us out. (That must have been the gist of that disjointed segment of news we had heard in Vegas, when we couldn't understand the southern senator saying something about ''downtown Hanoi, and there's no power on earth that can stop us!'') The second thing was that there was obviously still a lot of pride and comradeship across the services, and our officers and men still felt the strong obligation to ''take care of their own.'' Third, it had to have shaken the hell out of the hierarchy of North Vietnam to see the level of daring and courage of this close-in raid. Fourth, the raid probably scared the gooks enough that they shut down many of the small camps around the perimeter of Hanoi and joined us in cell blocks in the one main jail, a move that probably saved a number of lives. Bodies and minds would have continued to deteriorate in the brutal, solitary conditions of the previous five years. All in all, we concluded the Son Tay raid, though it didn't rescue anyone, produced some positive results. It was a giant boost to our morale.

The next morning, as we were folding up our blankets, Jerry Denton said, ''If our side has taken such desperate measures to get some of us out, they must think we are never going to be released.'' None of us had looked at it from that perspective. I could feel my heart sink to the floor, because I knew that Jerry was probably right.

Jim Stockdale and I had several conversations. We were talking about the treatment accorded us, when I said, ''Jim, it's the same thing they do to their own people! You remember their 'policy of humanitarianism'? I don't want to insult your intelligence by hashing that over.''

''No, please go ahead,'' he said. ''I don't remember that one.''

I repeated the policy word for word, because it had been hammered into my brain back in '67. As we talked, I got the impression that Jim had a speech problem, because he stammered a lot and spoke in halting tones. I was thinking, ''Boy his nerves are really shot! It's no wonder he's worried about whether we can learn to live with prosperity.''

That night, when it was quiet, Robbie Risner asked me to sit with him under his net; he had several things he wanted to discuss. Robbie had great trust in me and a strong regard for our friendship over the years. I felt the same about him.

''Larry, I'm concerned about what people may think of me on the outside.''

''I can't imagine what you mean.''

''Well, you know, in my long stretch of solitary and torture, they forced me to write a lot of phony statements, and they've got my signature on them.''

"So what? We've all had to do the same thing! There's nobody out there who will dare to sit in judgment, because they weren't here, they don't know, and they will never know how they would have handled it. We are going to write the book for them, and I'm not the least bit worried about it. We've all done our best, and if there's anyone out there who doesn't think so, he can kiss my ass! If we ever get out of here, and anyone gives you any bullshit, you call me collect, and I'll fly at my own expense to wherever you are. I'll explain it in terms that they can easily understand!"

Robbie gave me a big smile, and we shook hands warmly. Then he told me about some of his worst days, and how he was kept in a completely blacked-out cell. He woke at three A.M. and exercised and prayed all day, until he was thoroughly worn out. He repeated that process daily for almost a year. He was handled by a special interrogator whom he grew to fear. He said the guy knew everything he was thinking. "He actually crawled into my head and stepped all over my brains!"

Robbie may have gotten wind of the rumor that his promotion to full colonel had been delayed because of publicity about his "confessions." I never believed it. (Soon after release, Risner was promoted to brigadier, which proved the rumors were totally false.)

When Risner was finally removed from the "black room," it was another year and a half before he was joined with air force Lieutenant Colonel Gordon "Swede" Larson. Swede was also with us in Unity Seven, and he proved to be one of the finest men I'd ever met. He had a lot of physical problems, but he wasn't a complainer, he suffered in silence. He told me that Robbie was in a sorry mental state when they were joined together, and he doubted if Robbie could have lasted much longer by himself. As might be expected, Swede and Risner had become very close friends.

Swede told me that on the day he was shot down, he had completed his mission and was on the way home when he was called by a control center duty officer and told to return to North Vietnam to cover an attempted rescue of a downed pilot. Swede complied and was himself shot down and captured. The other pilot was James Hillary.

Swede knew enough about snook fishing to write a book, and according to him, the real "killer" lure was a 52-M Mirrolure, fished at neap tide. He tried to explain "neap" to me, but I never understood it. During the past couple of years, by tapping the walls and asking questions of everyone, Swede Larson had accumulated an amazing amount of information. He had become an expert on chicken raising, primarily for the production of eggs. "Golly Swede, do you really like chickens that much?"

"Hello, no! I hate the filthy creatures, but that's got nothing to do with making money from them."

"Is there a big profit involved?"

"You wouldn't believe how much, and there's very little manual labor involved, with automated processing. Here, grab a blanket and sit down, let me tell you how I'm gonna do this." For the next couple of days, every chance we got, we sat together, and I listened to Larson on the scientific way to raise chickens for profit!

For years, this had been Swede's mental therapy, and no one could believe the hours he spent working out the details, or the huge store of figures he had accumulated in his head! He knew the exact size buildings should be, the square footage allocated for cages, and how high the cages would be stacked. He knew how many square inches of cage floor space would be required for each chicken. He had worked out automatic systems for feeding, cleaning cages, and egg collection. Everything was done in an air-conditioned building, to keep the chickens contented and in a proper mood to lay six or seven eggs per week. Each chicken's production would be carefully monitored. If she failed to make the established minimum, a trip switch would be hit and the chicken would slide down the hatch, then off with her head and she'd end up in a grocery store freezer! All the chickens would be laboring like little fighter pilots under the slogan, "Put out, or get out!"

Swede pointed out that nothing would be wasted—everything, including the droppings, could be sold. I had a question. "Swede, is there a little hole in the front of each cage?"

"Why would we need a hole in the cage?"

"Well, I don't know—suppose the chicken turns out to be real nervous and maybe gets claustrophobic? She might want to stick out her head and yell, "*Bao Cao!* How do I get out of this chicken-shit outfit?" Swede and I laughed so hard the other guys wanted to know what was happening. Someone who knew about chickens told Swede that in fact each chicken only needed *half* the space he had allotted them! Swede went crazy, as he totally refigured egg production, doubling his profits! There was only one small glitch. Now that we could put two chickens in each cage, suppose one of them met the minimums and the other didn't? We couldn't figure out any way to identify which was which, so both of them would end up going down the hatch. Philosophically, I suppose, if you associate with a loser, you'll both end up the same way! (When Swede finally got home to Texas, the only chicken he ever looked at was one that was already barbecued.)

Rich Stratton told me about living with Doug Hegdahl, a young sailor who had fallen off a ship in the middle of the night. He was captured by Viet fishermen and brought to Hanoi. Rich said Hegdahl always played dumb with the Vietnamese, but he was actually a very intelligent guy with an amazing memory. The V looked at him from time to time with the thought of releasing him early, because they thought that at his low rank, and apparently low intelligence, he couldn't do anything on the outside that would bring discredit to them. Meanwhile, Hegdahl managed to commit over three hundred POW names to memory, many of whom had never been identified as having been captured. He was also given vital information about other camps and knew all about the torture methods of the Vietnamese and stories of the sufferings of some POWs. Stratton ordered Hegdahl to take early release if the opportunity arose. Doug objected, but Rich managed to convince him that the information that he would carry out with him would be a vital intelligence bonanza, and a boost in morale for all POW wives and families.

Then Hervie Stockman had become the senior office at Plantation, and he forbade early release, so Stratton backed off on Hegdahl. At that point I interrupted and told Stratton that, at the Zoo, I had a list of injured men who had my permission to accept early release. I added that I would also have included Hegdahl and was entirely in favor of his going home early, especially after realizing the amount and value of the information he would be taking with him. Stratton smiled and gave me a very Irish, "Bless you, my son."

The subject of early release had come up again back in May of 1970 when two new men came into the Zoo from the Las Vegas section of Hoa Lo. They sent word to me that a senior prisoner named Winn said that "no one would take an early release." This was almost a year after I had modified policy to allow the wounded to take the opportunity to go home if it was offered. I thought it over and decided that I should continue to run the Zoo as I had, dealing with the special problems that we had there. Winn had no idea of conditions at the Zoo. I did not feel that changing policy made any sense. The intention of the

Code was, and still is, to prevent people from release *without honor*, essentially "paying their way out" by volunteering to do propaganda stunts for the captors. There are many things to be taken into account by the senior captive, and the Code allows that person wide flexibility in decision making.

Our conversation was interrupted, and I never did get the full story about Doug Hegdahl. The main thing was that Doug *was* released, in August of 1969, and provided our representatives in Paris with some pretty heavy hammers about supposed "humane and lenient treatment." Although I later forwarded Stratton's recommendations for a medal for Hegdahl, I never learned whether or not Hegdahl ever received any kind of official thanks or appreciation or recognition for what he accomplished for our side. Many of us know it was considerable, and Doug had our deep gratitude.

Sitting with Tony Scorpio a number of times, I let him know I admired his courage. I also told him he was damn lucky to be alive; that I felt to attempt to escape from Hanoi was much too dangerous. I tried to be optimistic, saying that it didn't look like we'd be in Hanoi too much longer. I told him he had taken enough of a risk, and if anyone wanted to try it, he should let somebody else give it a shot. He seemed to agree with what I was saying. I was genuinely concerned for his safety.

We found an iron bar, which we used as a star drill, and took turns working on the wall between us and cell six next door. It took a week to punch through the bricks. Now we could voice talk to them. When my turn came, I asked for my old buddy Ron Byrne! We hadn't had a conversation since the night I left him at the height of the purge of '69. We exchanged a lot of family news, then Ron said, "Larry, I've learned a lot about the escape, and Connie Trautman is real anxious to talk to you." A few minutes later, Connie got on the wall. First, he told me about how he hallucinated about seeing me hanged from the scaffold. Then he went on to tell me about Atherton and Scorpio, and how difficult it was to deal with Scorpio. Trautman had directed a number of changes to be made in the escape plan before he would approve of it. Scorpio would not make the changes but continued along until the final night, when he and Trautman crawled up into the overhead of the cells (back at the Annex) and spoke by voice.

Connie said that it was tough to tell the two that they shouldn't be going, because he wasn't satisfied that they had improved the plan. We didn't go into details then, but the upshot was that

Conrad's final word was, "If you go tonight, you are going without my blessing." My return to Conrad was that I don't feel his parting word was decisive enough. He should have made it a clear okay, or *ordered* a "no go." I said if I were one of them, and eager to try, I wouldn't think that going without a "blessing" was any kind of violation of orders. We left it at that. Considering the terrible aftermath of the escape attempt, and the price everyone paid, Connie must have felt badly, especially losing Atherton, who didn't survive the aftermath of torture. I could also empathize with him as SRO. An outright "no" would have been tough to issue. Conrad said that Scorpio had sure as hell not endeared himself to any of the POWs at the Annex. That was the first hint I had that everything about the escape attempt wasn't generally approved at the annex.

Sunday the seventh of February 1971, we were setting up for church services. The Bug had anticipated it and showed up with a few armed guards. That day the church leaders were Risner, Rutledge, and George Coker. They had been warned that the authorities were not going to tolerate this kind of open solidarity. When the singing of the hymns started, Bug had his guards shove the three leaders out the door. When this happened the air became electrified, and Bud Day started, "Oh say can you see . . ." which was picked up by everyone, and as we sang our national anthem the volume rose. We felt a togetherness and strength that we had never felt in all of our years there.

The next song was "God Bless America," and, in a short lull between songs I started, "This is building number seven, number seven, number seven, this is building number seven, where the hell is six?" The chant was picked up right on cue by building six, then by each of the others in turn, becoming as loud as a stadium cheering section! Out in the yard, the Bug was beside himself, and his unruly left eyeball was doing corkscrews!

Armed soldiers, equipped with gas masks, came dashing into the yard, because to all appearances this was a prison riot. It wasn't a riot at all—we were just making a vocal protest to the authorities over the hassling of Risner and the others, because of the V's refusal to allow us to conduct our own religious services.

Naturally, the Vietnamese did not see it that way. As far as they were concerned, we were "threatening the camp security." So during the next two days the more senior of us were called out and verbally chastised. I went out to see the Rabbit, who told me that if we continued our unruly ways we would "go back to the old way of treatment—is that what you want?" He assured me in no uncertain terms, "We will punish you severely again, all of you, if you do not obey the regulations!"

"We do not want to return to the old way," I said. "You do not understand that we want only to have our weekly religious services, nothing else."

"No! You are just using that as an excuse to start a riot!" Rabbit replied.

When I got back, Denton suggested that we follow up the Sunday protest by fasting. There were plenty of us against fasting, but this was Jerry's favorite "shtick," and he convinced Stockdale and others that this was the thing to do. We were supposedly fasting to protest the removal of Risner, Rutledge, and Coker to Heartbreak, but I knew the gooks wouldn't understand what the fast was about either.

Whether we were in favor of it or not was beside the point. It was an order, so we went along with it, including the wounded. We all intended to do our very best, refusing to eat for a long period of time if necessary. Denton did not explain how we would extricate ourselves from the fasting situation if need be. No one was in shape to continue indefinitely on a fasting kick. By the second day, McCain and Norlan Daughtrey were pasty-faced. This just showed how we were foolishly punishing ourselves. In the case of the wounded, it created a serious situation. After the third day, we had to concede. We appointed someone to tell the turnkey we were ready to eat. The key ran to tell the officers, and from the way they reacted, they, too, were glad it was over. They showed up with a huge pot of rice gruel with chopped green onions on top. Anything heavier than that would probably have made us all sick, and the V seemed to know that. If anyone complained to Denton about the futility of fasting, I didn't hear about it. Neither did I say, "I told you so" to Jerry, but my feelings about it were strong. I felt we took an action that the V did not, and would not, ever understand, and that we could not really carry out because of our physical limitations. We didn't win, and we ended up having to kiss their asses for food.

Meanwhile, Jamey Hillary, our man with the burn scars, was writing some of the paragraphs of Geneva agreements that he remembered on a cell wall, using a piece of roof slate as chalk. Though he was not known as a "tough customer," he did this in full view of the V! Of course he was called out by the V to explain his brazen act. The next thing we heard was "Well, fuck

Ho Chi Minh!'' He was trying to show he had guts, but in doing so, he made the fatal error of insulting their late, beloved leader. The gooks took him to a corner of the yard, pulled his pants down, and proceeded to whip him! We heard him begging for them to stop. He had deliberately stormed into the proverbial kitchen, when he should have known he couldn't take the heat, so there wasn't a whole lot of sympathy for his plight.

Soon after the fast ended, more of the senior people were moved out, and for a while Bill Franke was senior in our cell block. One day I noticed Tony Scorpio, Coker, and McKnight in conference with Bill. When it was over, Tony told me that Franke had put him in charge of an "escape committee." He was supposed to get it organized and start it functioning.

"Are you kidding me?" I asked.

Tony said, "Well, he asked me to do it, and I couldn't refuse."

I walked around the pad to speak to Bill Franke. "I don't think it's wise to put Scorpio back in the escape business, Bill."

"The reason I did it is because he's the only one with the experience."

"Bill, I don't want to go through that bullshit again! You know it's impossible to escape from downtown Hanoi to freedom, so why do we have to go through the exercise?"

"I think it's something we have to do," he said stubbornly.

Scorpio came around and said, with Franke's concurrence, everyone had to contribute a piece of his rice mat to the escape committee for rope-making. He took a number of strands of rice straw out of each. There were about fifteen people twisting the strands together, like a little factory. I was amazed at how brazen we had become in such a short period. "Bill, if Bug opens the peep and looks in on us, don't you think he's going to notice that we are busy producing something?" I think Franke, whose judgment I had previously admired, was going along with it all, possibly thinking it was healthy "busy work." What bothered me was that neither Franke nor any of the other seniors seemed to have any feel for what could happen to us if we were discovered. Maybe the Geneva agreements forbade retribution for attempted escapes by POWs, but we knew the gooks paid no attention to Geneva. I felt that the predictable gook reaction, which we had already experienced, should be taken into consideration. But Tony, with Franke's approval, pressed on, and with each day he became more confident, and more arrogant, with his new responsibility. He had been content to go along peacefully, like the rest of us, until someone rattled his cage. Now I was looking at the other side of his personality, and I sure as hell didn't like what I saw.

Before many more days went by, there were no O-5s left with us, and I was again SRO in Seven. Building O, across the way, was loaded with Colonels and Commanders, including Flynn, Winn, Gaddis, and Bean. From then on, Jack Flynn was in command of the Fourth Allied POW Wing. We named it so because it was the fourth war of the century.

Inside our cell, at the bottom of the outside wall facing the yard, there were a few bricks missing. Someone found a hole in the ground outside, where some whitewash had been discarded and had hardened. Scorpio brought some of it into the cell, pounded it to pieces, and poured water on it, restoring it to whitewash again. He did an excellent job of sticking a cloth over the face of the hole in the wall. When it dried in place, he finished it off by painting it with the whitewash. It was a perfect place to hide things that could be used in an escape, such as the rope we fashioned from the rice straw, pieces of rubber tubing that could be used for snorkeling, and a few other items.

Ben Pollard and Bob Shumaker got together to set up classes in aero- and thermodynamics, which Ben had taught at the Air Force Academy, and the two of them could write wall-to-wall equations. Bud Day once observed, "Ben is your typical All-American boy, with an unshakable faith in Christ and Sears Roebuck." You could ask Ben the price of anything (1967 prices) from refrigerators to lawn mowers, and he would spit out the numbers under the headings of "good," "better," and "best," right out of the catalog!

The Bug and the other quizzers were being exceptionally dutiful about getting the maximum number of prisoners to write letters home each month. McCain got the idea that if the gooks were so hot after letters, maybe we should protest the removal of the senior officers by not writing home. We asked the cooperation of all, and got one hundred percent of them to go along with the idea. (We didn't feel it would be fair to make it an order.) Some had just gotten the chance to write home for the first time in four or more years!

Bud Day was his usual feisty self out in the wash area, not missing many opportunities. He imitated the V's talk with remarks like, "I critisigh you." We had all heard this so many times, we laughed it up thinking that Bud was pretty funny—

until he started to curse Ho Chi Minh, using some pretty rough language. I thought his judgment had slipped, or maybe he was feeling more secure in a crowd than he should have. But I wasn't too worried, because I figured he was a pretty crusty old bird with a lot of miles and lumps on him, and he could take care of himself. McCain was another story. We did worry about him when he followed Bud's lead by cussing out Ho Chi Minh.

Back in the building, I approached McCain to warn him. "Sooner or later, the English-speaking gooks are gonna figure out the meaning of your remarks, and you're gonna get your ass kicked good! Cursing Ho is like cursing their one and only God. If the tables were reversed and they cursed our God, we'd probably make it a memorable occasion for them too!" I don't know if John appreciated my warning, but I didn't think he should risk severe punishment just because he had the impulse to give 'em the needle.

During the day we had plenty of outside time, and we used it to walk around the yard or do mild exercises. When we were locked inside, we had a team constantly communicating with Risner's cell block and the others. The people who weren't involved playing chess, bridge, or studied languages or other subjects.

Our living together in cell blocks was a trying experience for the turnkeys in charge. At first, they were strongly influenced by the Bug and anticipated the worst. Then, with the passing of time, they eased off and appeared to be taking the new conditions in stride. They were carefully selected people who were comparatively decent to us and very dutiful when it came to delivery of food, water, and most necessities. Even when we gave them excuses to come down hard on us, they showed a surprising degree of self-control and avoided making mountains out of molehills. We were enjoying the lengthy outdoor periods of sun and exercise, and no one wanted to be responsible for the V cutting off outside time.

The gooks put up a bulletin board with the usual propaganda news items. One day they posted pages out of a book called the *Pentagon Papers*. This was reported to be classified material lifted from the Pentagon by a Professor Ellsberg, who was a consultant there. It was given to, and published by, the *New York Times*. Several of our guys were looking it over when I walked up to check it out. I recognized the material was once classified "secret," but I thought in the ten years that had passed, everybody at home should have known the contents. It told about our government's dealings with the government of South Vietnam, and disclosed some of the cover stories that were used for various projects at the time. I'd seen the material many times in '61 and '62 when I was on the operations staff at Thirteenth Air Force headquarters at Clark AFB. Some of the guys didn't believe the pages that were posted there. We had trained ourselves not to believe anything the gooks said. It was definitely authentic, but I didn't fuss over it, because somebody was bound to say I was "un-American" if I believed the gooks on this one.

We were getting more people in our cell block, replacing the senior guys. John Pitchford, Jim Clements, Lou Makowski, Ken Simonet, and A. J. Myers moved in. It was always good to get some new guys and hear their stories; it "freshened up" the atmosphere.

A. J. Myers was an intellectual whose hobby was collecting and defining new words. He made his list available to anyone who wished to expand his vocabulary. (In later years, while A. J. was at the War College, we exchanged letters several times. He sent me results of some polls he had taken among the former POWs. He was gratified to see that most POWs agreed with the departures from the Code that we had established in our policies. It was also evident that in highly controversial issues, where there was disagreement with the SRO, the disagreeing parties could not agree with each other, either. This proves the wisdom of Bud Day's remark, "The SRO is the only guy around here with a vote that counts.")

One night, late in the month of March, the V opened our doors, pointed to Bud Day, Jack Fellowes, and John McCain, and ordered them to roll up their gear in their rice mats. Day and Fellowes took it well, knowing that they had drawn attention to themselves by harassing the V. John McCain, however, was very upset and immediately hobbled down the walkway to see me. Sensing his alarm, I put my arm around him to calm him.

"Easy, John, they aren't going to harm you, they just want to throw a scare into you."

"Larry, these people just aren't going to take *any* shit from us, I'm telling you!" He amazed me.

"John, what have I been trying to tell you? You're right, they aren't going to take any shit. But be cool, they won't hurt you, they're going to separate you guys for a spell, but I guarantee you, you'll all be back here in a little while." I continued calming him down while others packed his gear, because there was nothing else we could do for him. Later, we discovered that the

Vietnamese had decided once again to employ "scare tactics," and they randomly selected thirty-six men from all of the cell blocks and moved them out to a "punishment camp." They were given the code name Hell's Angels. We had no idea where they'd be taken, and all of our guesses proved wrong.

Lowell Groves and Sam Johnson told me that all was not going well with the escape committee, and they recommended that we put Kasler in charge. I didn't think that Jim's bad leg and general physical condition allowed any strenuous physical effort, but Jim was anxious to get on the team. Nobody wanted Scorpio in charge, and Jim's calm nature might cool Tony's intensity. Coker said he wanted out of the escape group, because Scorpio would not tolerate anyone questioning his ideas. Coker's words were, "Scorpio refuses to use *any* problem-solving techniques!" So I let him off, and the team was then composed of Kasler, Scorpio, McKnight, and Spiker.

A group was talking about the false confessions and papers they had been forced to write over the years. Tony volunteered that he had never written anything. Coker stood there with his mouth open, then said, "Tony, you are full of bullshit!"

"What do you mean?"

"You know damn well what I mean! The gooks came to your cell and threw in one of those Blue Biography booklets. You didn't give them any static, you just filled it out."

"Yeah but *I* did it for a reason. I needed to get a roommate, and it was all bullshit anyway."

"Sure, sure, but you said you *didn't write*. Now you say, 'It was all bullshit!' It's okay for *you* to do that—in other words *you* wrote bullshit, but *we* wrote something good for them! It was okay for *you* . . . but not for *us*! I can't believe your twisted logic!" George stalked off, shaking his head in disbelief. In all fairness to Scorpio, I think many of us forgive ourselves for doing things that we don't forgive in others.

For several months, the V tried, unsuccessfully, to get us to write letters home. By that time, some of our people were beginning to question the wisdom of refusing to write home, because we had not noticed any beneficial changes. Bug called me out time and again and asked me why we were not writing. We guessed that the camp QZRs were getting top-level pressure put on them, because the cessation of letter-writing would be immediately obvious to our families, and they probably put up a beef in Paris. Bug asked me half a dozen times when we would write again. I didn't know, but I finally said, "Perhaps they will decide soon.'' Bug shot straight up off the seat, thinking he was getting some hot poop. I gave him that answer just to get him off my butt. He left the room at a trot, and I looked around. There was nothing to steal, so I went into the adjoining room. There was a half-pint bottle of ink lying in a corner. I picked it up and stuck it under my armpit under my shirt top; I put the pen in the waist of my pajama bottom. I was pulling off some long strings I saw tied to the wall, when Bug came back and caught me.

''Thief, you are a *thief*, you steal!''

''For the love of Pete, I need a piece of string, my mosquito net is falling down.''

''Drop it!''

''Okay, okay!'' I dropped the string, but got back to the block with the pen and ink!

We gathered to talk about the quiz, and I produced the things I swiped, giving them to Ben Pollard and Norlan Daughtrey. To this day, Norlan thinks the gooks were *giving* me things! Every time I swiped a pencil, I couldn't convince Norlan that it wasn't a ''gift'' from the gooks. My ''grand theft'' career eventually got us eleven pencils, the pen, the bottle of ink, and a new shaving mirror!

After the microfilm trick, the V had taken to pulverizing our packages as part of inspecting them. During the outdoors time, you could tell them what you wanted, then watch the guards chop the foodstuffs into little pieces. I almost went out of my tree when I saw them reduce Evy's beautiful butter cookies to crumbs, but Rob Doremus held me back, saying, ''Remember, no matter what they do to them, Evy's cookies are still delicious, right?''

''Right!''

Bob Craner and I became close friends, and Bob wasn't easy to get close to. He was a loner. Craner was tall and very athletic, and as I peeked out at him during my Riviera stint, I thought he looked exactly like the movie actor Robert Culp. He was a navigator before he went through pilot training, and while he was on duty at Goose Bay, Labrador, he met and married Audrey Adams, an English girl who was employed as a secretary at the base there.

Craner was a very intelligent person, who did not like to deal in trivia and strictly avoided association with anyone whom he judged to be a BS artist. He had a gift—an unusual ability to grasp foreign languages. He and Audrey and their two children

spoke French at home. Bob was also conversant in Spanish and
German, and picked up as much Russian as possible from the
people who knew any of it. Marine Larry Friese was one of very
few Russian-speakers. Jerry Marvel and Friese, his GIB, had
recently joined us, along with Barry Bridger, and AF Academy
grads Tom McNish and Leroy Stutz.

Craner told an amazing story about his trip by truck to Hanoi
with another American captive who was in frightful physical
condition. Captain Lance Sijan had bailed out of an F-4 on
November 9, 1967. His wounds included multiple fractures of
the left leg, a badly mangled right hand, severe lacerations, and
a brain concussion. Sijan had crawled around in the jungle,
without food, until Christmas Day, when he was captured. He
managed to knock out the escorting guard who was watching
over him, and crawled back into the jungle, though he didn't get
far before he was recaptured. Even in his horrible condition
(shock, injury, and extreme pain), he was tortured for information, but resisted as long as he could. When he reached Hanoi, Guy Gruters (Craner's GIB) was joined with them and did
everything humanly possible to aid and comfort Sijan, but Lance
contracted pneumonia and was strangling on fluids in his air
passages. Bug had him moved out, and later told Bob and Guy
that he died on the twenty-first of January 1968.

(After we returned home, I wrote a recommendation for Si-
jan, using information assembled from Bob Craner and Guy
Gruters. Captain Sijan was posthumously awarded the Medal of
Honor.)

Jim Kasler and I got together at my end of the cement sleeping
pad for a private discussion about the escape plan. The plan
provided for the team to punch a hole through the ceiling, which
was plaster over bamboo lath. They would then remove the clay
roof tiles for access to the rooftop. Once outside, they planned
to hop across the rooftops to a corner of the prison where they
hoped to be able to leap across to the top of the outside wall,
then down to the street. The plan became sketchy at that point,
which was understandable.

Even so, I was adamantly opposed to the initial phase, because I thought the breakout point in the ceiling would bring
them into plain view from the main courtyard of the jail. I told
Jim, ''Scorpio's half-assed plan is *not* going to get us all caught
in another torture exercise like the one we went through at the
Zoo! He is *not* going out through the ceiling!'' As I said it, I
emphasized the point by punching my right index finger into the

cement so hard I broke the top joint! Jim asked me just to go along with the plan for the time being, but I was in no mood for that. From that time on, Scorpio's back was up, and so was mine, and we had a problem that didn't ease off.

Bob Shumaker was one of the men whom I held in the highest esteem. I considered him practically infallible and deserving of the utmost trust and respect. Bob's wife had just had their first child when he shoved off on his last cruise. He got letters from home as regularly as most of us did, and occasionally they contained snapshots of his wife and son. The most recent photos of them were taken at Disneyland in California. The boy was now about seven and an absolute replica of Bob—like he was punched out with a Shumaker cookie press. Bob's wife stood there on the bridge leading into the park wearing a very short skirt, which was very much in style, but we, locked away from the world for seven years, were not aware of that. The first day, showing the pictures around, Bob was okay, but then the impact of the passage of time set in. The fact that he barely knew his wife and son, and was missing so much in their lives, really hit him. For several days after that, he would throw a blanket over himself, not wanting to speak to anyone, hardly moving, even to eat his meals.

Bob and others were heavily involved in confidential projects. Some people were assigned a list of names to commit to memory, others had to memorize historical events of the incarceration, still others had to memorize, word for word, the policies that came across from Risner or Flynn. Shumaker's morale appeared to be seriously down; perhaps it wasn't all that good an idea to have him saddled with so much responsibility. I believed that Bob should be relieved of as much worry as possible, to be able to relax and just think about something enjoyable, like the lesson plans he and Ben were putting together for the education program.

Lowell Groves, Johnson, and I discussed it, and agreed that the best man to fill in for Shumaker would be Lowell. I sent my decision across to the seniors and awaited the concurrence of Jack Flynn. Unfortunately, Shumaker did not understand my intentions, and his feelings were hurt. Stockdale, too, was extremely protective of Shu, and seemed to think I was out to screw Shumaker out of a job. But the only conscience that I had to satisfy was my own, and I wasn't concerned about misconceptions across the way because it was far too difficult to try to explain it by hand signals. Flynn bought the idea, and in a few days Shumaker seemed to forget about the hurt and even remarked he was glad to dump some of the many projects in which he had been involved.

A Vietnamese worker came into our cell block and put up a high stepladder. After a while another worker came in with a thirty-inch ceiling fan, and the electrician installed it. He mounted the control box outside the door, so the turnkey would have control. You wouldn't think that such a small fan in a fifty-foot long room would do much, but it gave us a surprising amount of relief in the long hot evenings of summer. The wounded men had priority to set up under the fan, if they chose.

Soon after the rains set in, the Heartbreak cells next to us were loaded with four or five men in each. It was Bud Day and the Hell's Angels. They were brought back to Hanoi from a camp in the suburbs called Skid Row because of the danger of flooding. They told us there were irons being used up there, some slapping around, and other minor abuses. They felt the move back to Heartbreak was only temporary. We passed them the latest poop, and the new policies of the Fourth Wing. One of our restated policies was that there was to be absolutely no writing of any kind, no letters home, no confessions, no propaganda, no signatures on anything. The policy was clear and emphatic. Five or six weeks later, the Hell's Angels were all taken back to Skid Row.

Daily headaches were still with me, sometimes so severe I was unable to think or do anything. One of our cell mates, Laird Guttersen, was an amateur hypnotist, and he suggested we give it a try. Laird said he could feel lumps that had formed at the left side of the base of my skull, so the first thing he did was to work at filling my mind with pleasant thoughts. "Okay, let's think about all the good things I know you like. You're out there on the deep blue ocean in your thirty-one-foot Bertram Sport Fisherman. The skies are blue, the waves lapping gently against the hull, as you troll along trying to get a sailfish to come up to your bait. No worries . . . nobody to bother you . . . just you and Evy G. . . . cruising along. . . ." He rubbed my neck and the base of my skull gently, speaking softly. I can't say for certain that I was ever hypnotized, maybe just mesmerized, but it sure did help. I think someone fussing over me, filling my head with happy thoughts, was a big part of "Dr." Guttersen's success, and I was able to relax and felt better. Norlan thought it was "just nerves." I thought it was a combination of nerves, having my head banged around so much, and Lord knows what all else! But it was minor compared to what the others suffered.

One of the more grievously wounded men now with us was navy pilot Dale Osborne. A cannon shell had slammed into the cockpit of his A-4. The fragments ripped some of the muscles of his left leg from ankle to thigh—he was loaded with steel splinters, and his right forearm was destroyed. In the several weeks it took to get to Hanoi, Dale was nearly buried a couple of times by Vietnamese who thought he was dead. He woke up in the nick of time each time and begged the people to stop burying him. He suffered inhuman neglect and unspeakable pain. In Hanoi, doctors cut off four inches of his right forearm and sewed the hand and lower wrist back on to the higher part of the forearm. Navy Commander Brian Woods was joined with him, and Dale could not have survived without Brian in constant attendance.

Then another guy took over to assist Dale in a type of rehabilitation and physical therapy, such as it was, right there in our cell block. This young fellow was Ralph Gaither, one of the lowest ranking naval officers. Ralph was in the front seat of an F-4 Phantom, and his GIB was Lieutenant J. G. Rod Knutson when they were shot down in October of '65. Gaither had been in the cell next to us up at the Briar Patch. He had the fastest knuckles in camp, about two hundred words per minute. I couldn't read him.

Not a day went by that Gaither did not work with Osborne, massaging his torn muscles and helping him to move his fingers. After a few months of steady treatment, Dale's morale improved considerably, because he had regained good movement of the fingers of his right hand. Then he really popped everyone's eyeballs by starting to do push-ups! We couldn't even imagine doing push-ups in that condition! He had to lean pretty hard on the left side, and it took a lot of guts, but Dale had plenty of that, or he wouldn't have come close to surviving for that long. His recovery was a point of great pride for Ensign Gaither, and well it should have been. Ralph truly lived the Golden Rule.

Occasionally, after breakfast, one of the guys would announce that, sometime after dark, he would "tell a movie." During the day he would pace the floor in deep thought, trying to recall all the details. Gaither announced that he was going to tell *My Fair Lady*, and that he would do his best without assistance from either Rex Harrison or Audrey Hepburn. That evening, we all got up close to Ralph and munched on pieces of dried bread, just like it was popcorn or some other goody, and we were sitting in front of our TV sets at home! Ralph sat down on the cover of one of the *bo* cans and started the "movie." He told it so beautifully that there was absolute silence in the cell block, and I doubt that anyone, for that hour, realized we were still in Hanoi. Nobody could have done it better, and when he got to the main song of the show, he spoke, and then sang, the lines. If you could just try to imagine the scene . . . and how he came across:

> I've grown accustomed to her face,
> She almost makes the day begin.
> I've grown accustomed to the tune,
> She whistles night and noon.
> Her smiles, her frowns, her ups, and downs
> Are second nature to me now,
> Like breathing out and breathing in.
> I was serenely independent and content before we met;
> Surely I could always be that way again and yet,
> I've grown accustomed to her looks,
> Accustomed to her voice, accustomed to her face.

I couldn't speak for the others, but when it was over, everyone shuffled back to his own spot on the pad in silence. I had a big lump in my throat, maybe everyone did. I walked around to Ralph and shook his hand and looked into his eyes. "Ralph, I want to thank you for what you've done tonight."

All of a sudden, we were hit with an epidemic of conjunctivitis, commonly known as pinkeye. The guards also got it, and disappeared for weeks at a time. The gooks started giving us shots, and by the time it passed, almost all of us had had it, the cases varying from mild to serious. My own case was so bad I had to feel my way along the walls to get around. Finally, they decided to give me shots to help me along. I had it for a month, but it took six to eight months for my bloodshot eyes to clear up. The Vietnamese said the whole country was suffering from it. They blamed it on the defoliation spraying in South Vietnam by the U.S. Air Force.

A turnkey from another cell block came into our yard with tin basins containing shaving gear and mirrors. Our turnkey had his own supply, and by watching carefully I knew there was going to be a screwup in accounting for the razors and mirrors. When the time was right, and no one was looking, I grabbed a mirror and slid it into one of the vents at the bottom of the cell wall, which was accessible from the inside. When the V picked up all the shaving gear and left the compound, they suspected nothing. After dark, several hours after supper, I told Kasler I had a nice surprise for him. Reaching down to the vent I pulled out a brand new chrome-framed mirror and handed it to him! He gave me a big smile and thanked me. "Jim, I'm not against escape anymore than anyone else, but I'm against stupid plans and clumsy methods of acquiring things." Scorpio came over and looked at the mirror. "Well, what do you think, Tony?" His answer was so typical. "Well, it's a consideration." I guessed that he meant it would be a minor consideration in my favor when he pressed charges against me for failing to support his nitwit ideas, but I wasn't at all surprised at his attitude.

With help from several others, Tony made a tiny American flag and stuck it to the wall so we could all recite the Pledge of Allegiance at night. He wanted to leave it up there, but I thought that a surprise entry into the cell block might be made at any time, so I didn't allow it. If it were found out, the gooks would be forced to land on us, and I saw no point in borrowing trouble. After a few days, I noticed that some of the guys were slouching during the Pledge. I asked Norlan what he thought. He replied, "Larry, I don't like anything that is ritualized." And that is exactly what it was.

All of us who flew over North Vietnam were volunteers, and most of us were patriotic hard-line regular military. We went to Southeast Asia eager to get into the fight to stop the Communists because we *were* patriotic—that was the driving motivation. When we were captured we resisted the enemy's every effort, sometimes taking fearful punishment for it, again because we saw it as our patriotic duty as America's fighting men. Now that we were in cell blocks together, and the Vietnamese were no longer pressing us or punishing us, why was it necessary to prove that one was patriotic or loved his country? It was because there were one or two who had to feed their egos by a constant effort, to show that they were braver, tougher, and better Americans than the rest of us. That behavior showed nothing of the kind. At best they were no better than the majority of us, and they caused us a lot more grief than they were worth.

Ninety-nine percent of the POWs, beginning with Alvarez, did an exemplary job of resistance during the first five harsh years. The high standards of behavior established by the Code were met by each man demonstrating his personal level of courage and resiliency while in solitary, or at best semisolitary, living. We were now living together in a kind of barracks situation, and the treatment had improved considerably. It was a far cry from Geneva standards, but it was a helluva lot better than we had known for years. Our biggest problem, as Jim Stockdale surmised, was getting along with each other, to function effectively as an organized military unit, because that is what we were. To assure our survival, and our honorable return, individual courage, bravado, and even personal opinions had to give way to the more important characteristics of loyalty and obedience. That did not prove to be an easy task.

Tony was egged on in his escape plans by only a couple of people. One of them was a badly wounded man who would have been one hell of a resister if his physical condition had permitted. But he knew that he couldn't stick his neck out and risk getting himself punished. He was so full of seething hatred of the V, his frustrations were choking him, so he chose Scorpio as his outlet against them. He said some pretty rough things to me, but I never held it against him because I knew what he was going through. When the buck stops with you, you have to expect to take a little guff now and then, and I know I took my share! Mostly it was a one-time affair, something they had to blow out of their systems. They couldn't do it to the gooks, so they'd take a pop at me, but usually they realized afterward they had behaved badly, and that was the end of it.

Tony's obsession with the escape plan permeated the atmosphere of the cell block and kept me and everyone else on edge, as if we were heading for a calamitous conclusion. I felt that his unyielding attitude threatened my ability to command, and if he was allowed to continue unchecked, he would be a serious threat to the well-being of the rest of us in the cell block, and perhaps the whole camp. Tony felt that I was the main stumbling block to his progress with a plan to escape from Hanoi.

One day, while in the bath area, Scorpio made some minor infraction of the rules and the turnkey ordered him to return to the cell immediately. Tony continued to bathe, in defiance of the turnkey, grinning all the while, as if telling the key to go screw himself. Surprisingly, the key kept his cool and waited for Scorpio to finish, then locked him in. Tony started either yelling or singing from inside, and it so angered Sam Johnson that he went to the door and hollered to Tony to shut his goddamn mouth. Several people came to me and told me that they didn't want to be shut off from outdoor time, just so Tony could "show his ass" (show off).

After we all went inside, I was still pretty bent out of shape, and I told Tony that he made the gook look damn good, while he looked like a snot-nosed kid trying to put one over. He was feeling his oats and believed that his position of influence over the others would allow him to get away with just about anything. He thought he had the support of the majority, but that wasn't even close to the truth, because they knew better. Every once in a while Tony would make an insubordinate remark, loudly enough to be heard by everyone. One of these "jewels" so shocked Rich Stratton that he bounced up off the pad and called him down, saying, "Captain Scorpio! Have you forgotten that you are an officer of the United States Air Force?" On another of his walk-bys, Scorpio glared at me and said, "The Code of Conduct tells me what I have to do!" He might as well have added, "and I don't give a damn what the SRO says!"

The last straw came when Tony shuffled by me, talking to himself. He stopped to talk to Leroy Stutz, pointed to me, and said, "He makes a mockery of the Code of Conduct." That about ripped it, and I decided to take some action, which, no matter how I chose to do it, would be very difficult. I met with Johnson and Groves, and we decided against any kind of legal action, because it couldn't possibly be done correctly under the circumstances. We thought that a formalized "ass-chewing" might do some good. Scorpio was told to put on his long-sleeved shirt and come over to my place on the pad. The three of us stood over him as he sat there. We told him he was behaving "in an insubordinate and mutinous manner," and that he had best shape up. He said nothing, but wore his usual sneer. Then, we called Jim Kasler over and lit into him. That was one of the most painful things I had ever had to do in my life, because of my high respect and affection for him. Jim was in charge of one of our four or five work groups, and Tony was one of his people. I therefore took the position that Jim had failed to exert the kind of supervision that was required to keep Tony under control. My remarks were a stinging blow to Jim, who never in his life had had to resort to anything but a "soft" type of leadership. Jim was followed and obeyed because he, and his military reputation, were so admirable that people wanted his approval. In Tony's case, Kasler was dealing with a person who was clearly taking advantage of a situation and using his own interpretation of the Code of Conduct as an excuse for insubordinate behavior.

The others in the cell block saw that Scorpio was responsible for the highly respected Kasler getting a verbal reprimand. That in itself served to cool Tony's fire. In the eyes of the others, Scorpio had gone too far. Not even he wanted the open scorn of his fellow officers. It was impossible to tell what it was that drove Scorpio, or why he chose particularly to emphasize Article III of the Code, which reads in part, "I will make every effort to escape and aid others to escape." Read with Scorpio's tunnel vision, this line told him that he was obliged to try to escape, regardless of the futility of it or the level of reprisals that would very likely be taken against him and all the others left behind. This narrow view, shared by a very few, convinced Scorpio that it superseded all higher authority, and therefore no SRO could order him to desist.

It remains a mystery to me why Scorpio, so big on the Code, did not read one article further. Article IV says, "If I become a POW, I will *keep faith with my fellow prisoners*. I will give no information or *take part in any action* which might be *harmful to my comrades*. If I am senior, I will take command. If not, *I will obey the lawful orders of those appointed over me*, and *will back them up* in every way."

Scorpio's military experience was considerable, and he was certainly intelligent. The essence of Article IV should have come through to him clearly enough to dictate that his strongest obligation under the Code was to follow the orders of those in command, who were obliged to act for the welfare of all.

Jack Flynn was camp senior, and the ultimate decision to approve or disapprove an escape plan would be his. However, as the *building* senior, one of my prerogatives would be to make recommendations, and I would have recommended against any escape plan using the ceiling as exit. In general, I opposed a breakout attempt from the city jail in Hanoi, because I believed it had no chance of success without outside help. Our own tragic experience at the Zoo had taught me that repercussions had to be considered, weighed against the gains, with the remote possibility of success factored in as well. In my opinion, the intelligence information Scorpio might have gotten out through escape was not substantially more, or different, from what had been achieved by the Hegdahl release. In short, the gain was not worth the risk.

Everything cooled down after the semiformal chewing out, but I think the real cooler was a message from Jack Flynn a month or so later. He informed us that for an escape attempt to be approved, it had to have a determinable chance of success. The success possibility had to be either ten or twenty percent.

Actually, the figures made no difference, because there were no criteria available by which we could assign realistic percentages. That requirement in itself was unreasonable, and I think the escape team also may have realized that the whole exercise was just another form of "mental masturbation," as the expression went.

The success proviso, as established by Jack Flynn and his staff of senior officers, was a wise one. It broke the tension in the camp. Whether or not it was specifically intended to do that, it had the same effect. The escape program was not as beneficial to morale as it might have been. Instead, it became the greatest threat ever to the command structure and the POW organization itself.

There was one other detail that improved the atmosphere of our cell bock and had a very positive effect on me personally. From that time forward, escape teams could send and receive messages on that subject by going directly to Flynn, meaning that I was bypassed and no longer involved. It was a great relief to me not to have to deal with any part of that controversial subject.

Rob Doremus, who was Bill Franke's GIB, had volunteered early on to act as medic for our cell block. Rob spoke clearly and deliberately, always making a considered effort to be understood, because he had been dealing with the gooks for so long. I remembered taking a peek at his bio while I was at a quiz back in April of '66. Rob had been freshly tortured for the story he wrote, and it was a humorous fairy tale. I thought at the time that here was a guy doing the job right by first refusing, then taking torture, then giving the appearance that he surrendered, before producing his "fairy tale."

He was a helluva guy, who took his job as medic very seriously. Lucky for us, the gooks did not see him as a threat. They knew he wasn't senior, and this enabled him to establish rapport to an extent that nobody else could. Every morning, he dutifully walked around the cell block to see who was ailing and what medical aid was needed. He let me know about the serious cases, then he went to work on the Vietnamese to obtain the necessary help.

He asked me if I knew about the declining health of Ray Saxton, and why it was happening. I didn't know much about Saxton, except that he was a lot thinner-looking than average. Marine Howie Dunn came over and filled me in on Ray, who had been the SRO up at Son Tay. Howie said Saxton did an outstanding job up there, but had gotten extremely picky about what he would eat. Though I was now aware of it, I still couldn't believe that Saxton carried his selective eating so far that he placed his health in jeopardy. I got better acquainted with him and mentioned that his friends were very concerned about his weight loss. Ray replied that he thought he was in good condition. Slim, yes, but not *too* thin, and he liked to keep himself that way. We let it go at that, but from then on Saxton had everyone watching him, because he had developed some unusual eating habits that were real attention-getters.

A week later Howie Dunn came over to say that he believed something had to be done in a hurry about Saxton's health. He would not eat any pig fat, bananas, beans, or even the sweet bean soup, which was usually served on Sundays. The V were even giving him extra food and all the bread he wanted.

Saxton never ate the white part of the bread, but would spend hours patiently peeling the thin brown outside crust and making a large pile of the peelings. The others said he was "skinning the bread." Howie suggested that the only solution was to give Saxton a direct order to eat his food. I didn't think that would work, because if Ray refused to eat, or even if he didn't refuse, but didn't eat anyway, there was nothing I could do about it. But Howie thought I should, and I didn't see that it would do any harm, so I decided to give it a try. None of us had ever heard of anorexia—I think in Saxton we were seeing a classic case, we just didn't know it.

Speaking to Saxton again, I pointed out that he was giving us a major problem, that he had become the main topic of conversation. Ray had a heavy Georgia accent and spoke with his teeth gritted together when he was questioned about anything. "Ray, I see you don't eat pig fat like the rest of us. I know it's not that tasty, but there *is* some meat to it. Tell me, what kind of food did you eat at home?"

"We ate nothing but dried meat." (He pronounced it *mee-at*.)

"You know, even the gooks are worried about you, that's why you're getting extra rations. Why don't you eat bananas?"

"Do you know what happens to bananas inside your mouth?"

"No, what?"

"They turn to sugar, and sugar can rot your teeth."

"Gosh, Ray, I didn't know you had teeth problems."

"Well I don't have, but I'd rather die than have rotten teeth."

"How about the beans—why can't you eat them?"

"Beans? Do you think I want to smell like Howie Dunn?"

"Jesus Ray, Howie doesn't smell any differently from anyone else! It's all between your ears! You are leaving me no choice, so I am hereby giving you a direct order to eat all your food. We want to see a marked improvement in your health." Saxton didn't like that order one bit! He said there was nothing wrong with him, and he wished everyone would mind his own business. He did say he would try to obey my order and eat more. The results over the ensuing months were about the same, Saxton just improved his techniques in faking it.

Rich Stratton and Laird Guttersen had been long-time members of the Toastmasters Association, and they discussed the idea of having Toastmasters meetings to practice public speaking once a week. The idea appealed to about half of our people, and the program got off to a good start. During the Bug's peep-ins, he again got a misimpression of what was going on. He singled out Collie Haines, Howie Dunn, and Bart Hovick and called them out to question them, but of course he was unable to comprehend the program. His mind was spring-loaded to the "black scheme" position and simply wouldn't move off it. He did nothing then, but bided his time. As the weeks passed, people started to drop out of the meetings. I was one. It was becoming obvious that Scorpio was using Toastmasters as his personal forum. My wipeout was the night Tony began by calling for a definition of "Americanism," for which he was well prepared. No sooner had that come out of his mouth than I moved away, because I knew that what would follow would be the usual "show" to prove he was a better American than the rest of us.

While Craner and I were exercising together he suddenly stopped his deep knee bends and said, "Larry, I have to say that I like Tony very much and have a lot of respect for him, but there is something about him that bothers me."

"What's that?"

"He's ashamed to admit to his Italian background. Have you noticed?"

"Of course I've noticed—I even asked him why he didn't change his name. Maybe his background bugs him so badly that he feels he has to continually prove he's American. Too bad for him. I'm damn proud of my Italian heritage!"

Besides Toastmasters, Stratton volunteered to give educational lectures. Most of his talks were in his college major— political science. It was always well done, almost as if he had memorized what he read. One of Stratton's main points was,

"Don't ever believe anything a candidate proposes in a political platform, because if elected, that is the first thing he wants to forget!"

Navy pilot Nels Tanner gave some informative talks on aircraft maintenance and the basics of auto mechanics. Nels was one of our unsung heroes in North Vietnam and so was his GIB, Ross Terry. They were the duo who had made international fools of the Vietnamese because of the wide publicity given to their forced interviews with foreign journalists. The Vietnamese had tortured them to admit, among other things, that there were aircrews aboard their ship who were too cowardly to fly against North Vietnam. Two of those named were Lieutenant Commander Ben Casey and Lieutenant Clark Kent. The subsequent article in *Time* magazine was followed by the editorial comment, "Can it be that there is something about Americans that the Vietnamese will never understand?" It did not reveal that the two were imaginary comic strip and television characters. But the Vietnamese eventually found out that the joke was on them, and there were some bad times for Nels and Ross. Nels's punishment round wound up with him playing a small part in a movie, much as I had to do.

Tanner was a best buddy of Shumaker, and as a permanent captain of our communications team he spent many long hours receiving and transmitting the orders and policies of Robbie Risner, and later Jack Flynn, who had been out of touch for a while in another area. Nels was put into some tough spots, where the loyalties of a lesser man would have been severely tested, but Tanner managed to do the job very objectively and kept his loyalties intact, and I admired him for that.

Half a dozen peasant workers were brought into our compound to repair the fence, but we were not told to leave the yard, so we watched them work. They had a couple of hammers and some crude knives. Watching closely, I saw they weren't very careful about where they threw their tools. One guy dropped a heavy knife on the ground, and soon after that they all left the yard for a little while. I don't know if they had such things as "coffee breaks," but the yard was quiet and the duty guard was not very attentive, either. Pretending I was walking up and down in a quick-pace exercise, I took the first opportunity to push the knife against a tree trunk. On the next pass by, I covered it by kicking dirt on it.

It would be a good weapon for Kasler's escape team to stash in the wall, but first I had to be sure it wouldn't be missed. After marking the spot well, we all went back into the cell. None of the other POWs noticed what I had done. I peeked out the front door to see if all was quiet, which would tell me that the gooks didn't know anything was amiss.

The turnkey came to our door, and I was right there to meet him. He was noticeably shaken. "There is something of the workers missing. I must tell my superior, and he will make us have thorough inspection."

"Wait just a minute." It was time to bail out, because an inspection was dangerous for us and to be avoided if possible. The gooks can always find something to take away from you, and we had the escape stuff stashed.

"I was watching your workers and I saw one who was very careless," I said. "If you come with me I may be able to help you find your tool." I led him out into the yard and shuffled around.

"I think it's around here, near this tree, help me look here." He started to look, and so did two other guards. I tried to head him in the right direction, but he kept missing it, so finally I "accidentally" kicked it.

"Ah, here it is, I knew it was around here some place." The little turnkey was so relieved to get the knife back, he didn't give me any hell about it. A few of the guys were looking out wondering what was going on. I told Kasler about it after the door was locked for the night.

Sometime in June of '71, we got the word that Risner, over in building O, had gotten in touch with Miller and Forrester of "Bob and Ed Show" fame, along with Gene Wilbur and four others in Building Eight. The four younger men knew they had been identified by the rest of us as "antiwar," with the other more senior three, and they wanted desperately to get back on track and join the Fourth Wing with the loyal Americans. Miller and Wilbur continued to procrastinate, and Risner tried everything he could think of to get them to adhere to the Code of Conduct and rejoin us. He told them that nothing would be held against them, and we would all forgive them and be glad to get them back. Messages went back and forth from Risner to Miller for a month, with a final demand from Robbie for a clear "yes" or "no." Miller and Wilbur said they would follow all legal orders, but they "would continue to work for an end to the war." They were still pumping out antiwar propaganda letters to congressmen back home. Risner then stripped them both of all military authority, and Forrester was placed in command.

Miller's group of seven disappeared from Building Eight, and unbeknown to us, the seven men of his group had been taken to the Zoo. The Vietnamese were aware that Risner's communications with them had split the group apart. We never knew if Miller or Wilbur reported it or complained about it to the Vietnamese. While at the Zoo, those two were the only ones who continued what they had been doing all along. The others stood fast in their loyalty to the Code and to the rest of us.

You could have knocked all of us over with the well-used feather, when one night in early November, Bob Forrester was brought into cell block seven! Every man was wary of him, but civil to him, because in accord with the Wing policy, we were supposed to welcome back, without prejudice, anyone who tried to turn himself around. The V had decided that, since Forrester was no longer cooperating with them, he was a deterrent to their progress in obtaining propaganda materials from the others. So he was moved out of the Zoo and brought to Unity. Bob said the new senior man at the Zoo was Roger Ingvalson.

Forrester's shoot-down rank was higher than mine, so he immediately became building SRO. I didn't think that the command should have been given over to him right away, but I didn't fuss openly. The rank problem had become a thorn in the side of many of us, because there was no way officially to update a man's rank while in prison, even though there was reason to believe that each man was promoted on schedule. In this case, I knew that my actual rank was about two years senior to Bob's, but we were using date of rank at shoot-down. I sent a message to Jack, telling him that if we were in Hanoi long enough, there could be new guys coming in with a higher shoot-down rank than most of us, and it was possible that they might not even have been in the service at the time we got into the war! That made sense to Jack, but no one was able to come up with a new system to resolve the rank problem equitably across the board, so it stayed that way. In the meantime the seniors said they would "work on it." (They did. The new system went into effect during the summer of '72, and we changed it to conform to fair promotion dates.) Forrester was an unusual person, mixing right in with the group as though nothing he had ever done was out of line. He was politely accepted by everyone, in the proper spirit of the Wing.

He hadn't been with us more than a couple of days, when he offered to fill in on one of our nightly talks. His session was well attended, but no one heard what he was saying. They wanted to study the man as he spoke, to try to figure out what made him tick. He was an excellent speaker and talked for over an hour. When he was finished, Jim Kasler came and sat quietly next to me on my pad. "Larry, I can't figure him out. He seems like such a good fellow, very likable, a good speaker and all. He's got a fine mind, too. What the hell *is* it that gets into a guy and gets him so far off base? Why couldn't he just have hung tough like the rest of us?"

Jim had brought up a question not often discussed, if ever. It had been in my thoughts since I was first captured, when I had reason soon after to question my own level of courage and my determination to resist the enemy. But for the Grace of God, there could have been many more of us in the prisons who flunked the test. We all knew men whose abilities, both physical and mental, in holding the line against the Vietnamese were disappointing. the majority of us were able to endure to a point where the Vietnamese backed off long enough for us to recover our faculties, and then we managed to bounce back against them. But some of us could not endure, and I think people must withhold judgment of men who have undergone such strenuous tests, because he who has not weathered the storm can never know the true nature of the cataclysm and the harm it works.

Another November highlight was when Bud Day and his Hell's Angels were again brought back to Camp Unity from Skid Row, after nearly eight months. We exchanged information, and Bud was very cool to escape plans since, like me, he had a vivid memory of the events of 1969.

Many of the interrogations at Skid Row were about the moratorium on letters home, which we had imposed on ourselves in March. The V wanted to know the whys and wherefores of it. In August, Bud had advised his people to start writing again, and he admitted there was some outspoken opposition to his instructions. My last letter to Evy had gone out in February, just before we stopped writing. My next letter wasn't until October 1971. For most of the others in cell block seven, it was about the same.

By November of '71, like many others, I was at low ebb, and particularly victimized by my own frustration over the length of our captivity, with no end in sight. I wrote a letter to Evelyn, and in it included a short, hidden, "jump-out" message. I did this by raising the key words above the line. We had no prior arrangement on this sort of thing, but I felt sure she would easily pick it out if she studied the letter carefully. There was nothing it could have accomplished (except to cause her more worry), and after I sent it I was sorry that I had done such a stupid thing. But it shows how one's morale is affected over time, and how frustrated I was that nothing was being done to get us out of there.

20 November 1971

Evy Dearest,

Can we afford a home somewhere between there and Miami Beach, that thought is most in my mind. We *must* have a home with a dormitory upstairs so my sons can spend lots of time with us and *we* can enjoy our grandchildren. Time has flown by. Hope no more relatives *die* while I am *here*. Of course it is inevitable but still I hope for no changes. Look forward to letters and more pictures of you in mail. I love you very much my dearest. Love to parents, sons, new daughters.

Always,
your Larry

At that time (1971), we were given the opportunity to help in the preparation of our own food. Our task was usually to clean and wash the vegetables—various types of squash, potatoes, and tubers. None of us thought there was anything wrong in doing work that contributed toward our own subsistence, and doing the general upkeep or cleaning of our living quarters. It gave us something to think about and something to do.

Early in December, Lowell and Sam Johnson said we were cleaning more than our share of veggies, therefore we should refuse to do it anymore. This happened twice in succession. Two weeks later, on the eighteenth of December, Shumaker's group had the work detail. Some of us stayed inside, chatting or doing personal things, when Shu came in and told Forrester that the gooks had brought in a couple of pails of whitewash so we could paint the inside walls. Should we do this? As far as I was concerned, this came under the heading of work that we *should* be doing for ourselves. I was surprised that Sam Johnson violently opposed it. Lowell Groves concurred with Sam, and so did a few others. I told Bob that I saw nothing whatever wrong in doing the work. Forrester's answer was, "Well, this time-Larry, why don't we go along with the dissenting group and tell the Vietnamese we don't want to do it?" Shu and Tanner carried the buckets back to the turnkey's little open hut in the corner of the yard and told him it was no go.

On December twenty-first, the gooks came in and put the finger on six of us—Collie Haines, Bart Hovick, Howie Dunn, Groves, Forrester, and myself. As we were rolling up our gear, Jim Kasler came over, and by his look was obviously very worried. "Larry, be careful, and take care of yourself." I was touched by his concern.

"I will, Jim. There *is* one thing I'd like to clear up. The day I had to give you the ass-chewing, I guarantee you it was a lot more painful for me than it was for you. I hated doing it, but I felt we had to do something to get Scorp in check."

"I know why you did it; don't give it a thought."

"Are we still buddies?"

"You bet we are!" We shook hands and gave one another a hug.

We were carted out by truck to a place answering the description of Skid Row. The next morning, we got our bearings. The building all of us, except for Forrester, were in had at least twelve cells on the front side, where we were. The cells had barred, shuttered windows, but the shutters were left open at all times. A mat fencing in front of us separated us from the quiz rooms and other buildings in the camp. In the center of the yard was a deep well for drawing water and a holding tank in a bathing area. At the far end, there was a separate walled-in building, where they had put Bob Forrester by himself.

I expected to be manhandled, but the open windows dispelled that early notion. After a couple of hours, a nicely dressed English-speaking turnkey came around with food. He gave me a loaf of bread and a can of Russian fish. Later I went out to bathe, directly in front of Howie's cell. "What do you think, Howie?" He just shrugged. He hadn't figured it out yet, either. I had the same feeling that I got when I first moved into the Mint, from the Zoo. Hell, this is no punishment camp, or they would already have beaten the crap out of us. Open windows, baths, bread, and fish! They aren't going to do a goddamn thing to us! I was convinced.

The next day, Groves passed by my cell, which was at the far end of the building, away from Forrester's compound. Lowell was out taking a little exercise walk. I asked him what was going on, and he told me he had already been out to quiz. He was very pensive as he continued his walk up and down out front. "So what happened at quiz?"

"Well, I wrote that I promised to obey the camp regulations."

"Jesus, Lowell, are we supposed to be doing that anymore?

I mean, how about the policy against writing?'' He just shrugged his shoulders. I think he was telling me he thought it best to comply with their demands. Later I saw Howie, who looked rather upset. "So how about it, Howie, don't we have a policy that forbids writing of any kind?'' Howie spit out the policy word for word.

The turnkey told me to sweep off the walk, and he didn't seem at all concerned with my speaking to Howie or Collie. I swept on down to the compound where Forrester was. I called him. "Bob, Bob can you hear me?'' He answered back in the affirmative, in sort of a hoarse whisper.

"Listen, Bob, hold a line, these people won't harm you, it's all bullshit, they aren't going to do anything. Do you hear me, Bob?''

"Larry, you don't know these people! They *will* hurt you, they're mean as hell!''

"No, Bob. I'm telling you, stick it out, they won't touch you!''

"It's no use, Larry. I've already written a confession, it's all over.'' He was really frightened, and I felt sorry for him. He couldn't do any better, and he must have been sick at heart because of it. He was no longer the happy, smiling guy that I was getting to know and like back in Seven. Both he and Lowell left our area either on Christmas Eve or Christmas Day.

A couple of days later, the turnkey told me to suit up for quiz, and I got all set for it. He took me out through the gate into a building that was set up as a typical quiz room. I sat there by myself for a while, then the turnkey came back and sat across the desk to talk to me. "You know, the camp commander here is very strict. He knows you have broken many regulations. . . . Now you must admit your wrongdoing so that you can go back to your fellows. . . .'' He used a lot of pregnant pauses, then he shoved some writing paper and a pen toward me.

"Here . . . you must write that you will obey the camp regulations.''

"Oh no, I'm not going to write anything.''

"But you must, or you will be punished!''

"No, I don't have to do that anymore because you know, your policy is 'humane and lenient,' and we have been told that we will no longer be forced to do those things we do not want to do.'' Without taking my eyes off him, I gently shoved the pen and paper back to him.

"But my commander will be very angry!''

"I think I can explain it.'' He sat there staring for five minutes, then walked out. At no time did he look very serious to me, and by then I could tell serious when I saw it. I didn't even know who the camp commander was, if there *was* a commander. Ten minutes went by, and I heard someone enter the room. I got up and turned around to see who it was. For the love of Pete! It was old Frenchy, from Briar Patch days in '66. He was the guy that Ron Byrne said liked me, because I was an old guy with whom Frenchy could identify.

"Well, Camp Commander, it's been a very long time!" I gave him my biggest smile, and the son of a gun gave me one right back as he sat down.

"Ah, Ga-reeno—and how have you been?"

"Not too bad, for the many years we have been here."

"Yes, you have been here for a long time. I have been told that you have broken many regulations. Why is that?"

"Don't believe that, Camp Commander. We live very quietly, it's just that the Vietnamese in the other camp do not understand us. But tell me, I remember the last time I saw you, your wife and children were still in the South. Have you heard from them?"

"Now it has been almost twenty years, and I hear just a few words of news now and then, but we must wait more years."

"Well, I can sympathize with you because I know exactly how you feel."

Well, doggone if Frenchy doesn't ask me how long I think the war will last, and we had a long bull session about that. Then he walked out, and the turnkey returned. We played the game of pushing the pen and paper to and fro. His final words were, "I tell you, my commander is getting very angry!" In came Frenchy again wearing a big smile, and talk about surprises—he handed me a very recent letter from Evelyn!

We discussed Evelyn's letter, which said she was building a beautiful home on a saltwater canal, where I could look out to watch the mullet jumping. I explained it all to him, and we had a few laughs. Old Buzzard came close, but Frenchy was the first one I ever actually saw laugh. Finally I went back and told Howie I didn't write a damn thing, and on top of that I got a letter from Evy! We heard a commotion, and then a window breaking—it was Bart Hovick. He, too, had written a confession, and realized that he had done a foolish thing, so he was raising hell to make up for it. That was useless after the fact—all it got him was a set of leg irons. Howie and Collie Haines had been quizzed about the Toastmasters. Maintaining their innocence and denying that it was a "black scheme," they were both sitting in leg irons. Neither were asked to write anything. No other abuses were piled on, the shutters remained open, and the food continued to be good.

At dark on New Year's Eve, the key told me to roll up to move. I was blindfolded, but no ropes or irons. On the ride back, I slipped the blinds, and sitting there grinning at me was my old turnkey, Hack, from the Riviera. He was all smiles, and all in all, I felt pretty good about my experience at Skid Row!

As I walked back into cell block seven, the guys crowded around, and Kasler, smiling, spoke up. "We've got some big news for you, Larry."

"What?"

"Your son Ray has twin boys."

"Impossible! How do you know that?" I felt like I had been punched in the stomach. It was such a shock.

"We got it through the walls! Jim Young's mother is a friend of Evelyn's. She said Ray has the cutest red-headed twins."

"I don't believe it! He's only about eighteen years old, no way!"

"We knew you'd say that buddy, but it's true, you're a grandfather for the third time now!" I was in a daze after *that* staggering news! Little Ray, the father of twins. How could that be? It didn't sink in.

The guys pressed on, wanting to know what had happened to me at Skid Row, and had I written anything? Lowell and Bob Forrester were standing there, and I had no wish to cause either of them any more embarrassment than I suspected they already had suffered. But though I played it down, I had to tell everyone that I didn't write anything. They had to know that they could refuse and not get hurt, in case they were taken out next. I told them about my talk with Frenchy, and about the letter from Evelyn. I also told them what I knew about the other three men, who were in irons, and that one of the three had written an apology. The next day those three were also brought back from Skid Row and put into Heartbreak.

As soon as the men had had all their questions answered about Skid Row, I sat down on my pad to reflect in private on the stunning news about my son Ray. I had left Ray first in 1953, when he was only a year old. Returning a year later from Korea, I saw that it was difficult for him, at age two, to readjust to me. In the following years, I was away from home on temporary duty so much, it was difficult for me to get close to him. He was a quiet kid, extremely bright, and an outstanding athlete. Once,

I watched him pitch a three-hitter in a Little League game. Afterward, I said, "Nice game, Ray. But you weren't burning the ball in." He said simply, "I didn't need to, Dad." Well, I guess the kid knew what he was doing and didn't need another coach. In '68, a letter from Evy had told me Ray was an outstanding running back, and his team had lost the state championship by a one-point margin. I could only think of Ray as a quiet ninety-pounder. Could he really be a married man? With twins?

And how about Jeff—God, he must be growing up, too! He was only nine when I left, and had earned the title of "World's Most Faithful Waterboy." He was very outgoing and had lots of pizzazz. We wondered why he was so respectfully treated by some of the bigger kids. Then we found out that Jeff had told them all to watch it—or he'd get his three big brothers after them! Nobody wanted Jeff's brothers, especially Tom, after him—Tom was really a big guy, over two-hundred pounds, and won the honors as "All-Island Linebacker" at Kadena High School. Evy's letters had some humorous notes about Jeff. Returning from ball games, he always carried a purple snow cone. We all knew life was going on, but we were going to be in for some major shocks if we ever got home.

Chapter Sixteen

1972, 1973—HERE COME THE BUFFs

After a few days, Bob Forrester returned to his usual happy, outgoing self. If he felt remorseful about having broken an important policy, he never showed it, and I finally decided that he was incapable of thinking that anything he did was really that bad. It was impossible not to like him. As we sat there together, he talked about Pennsylvania and his family. I knew he had chosen the wrong profession. He would have been a much better entertainer or actor. When he told the movie *Zulu*, he played all the parts and recited the lines, British accent and all, doing a wonderful job. I had never met anyone quite like Bob, who seemed to know every movie ever made, and every actor and actress. He must have stayed up nights since he was a kid, watching all the "oldies." You could ask him any obscure question about Hollywood, the movies, or the players, and he was never stumped. He even knew the old supporting actor from the '20s and early '30s by the name of J. Purnell Pratt!

After the Skid Row adventure, he was more inclined to listen to my advice, and he referred to me as his "father," saying that I kept him straight. (A few months after we were repatriated, I received a two-foot-wide pair of silver command-pilot's wings mounted on a wooden plaque. Behind it was the short message, "Thanks a lot Dad, for all your help." At first I thought it was from my son Allan, then I realized it was from Forrester! Shortly after that, to my great sorrow, Bob was killed in an automobile accident in California. That news was a real blow to me and to Jim Kasler, too—Kasler liked Forrester just as much as I did.)

Lowell Groves was different from Forrester. He wasn't an outgoing type, but a very reserved person who did an excellent job and worked hard on all of his responsibilities. Taking punishment was not his long suit, and he was the first to admit it. A leader can't expect everyone to be tops in every phase of the profession, but must try to utilize people according to their talents. In a prison situation, most of the time you don't control your people, the enemy does.

Collie Haines and Bart Hovick were returned to our cell block from Heartbreak a few weeks later, and we were happy to get them back. Why the Vietnamese continued to keep Howie Dunn in Heartbreak while bringing back Haines and Hovick was impossible to figure. They were all accused of the same thing, "scheming" during the Toastmasters meetings. Collie had continued to maintain his innocence.

Bart Hovick told the story of his interrogation with Frenchy, who, according to Hovick, was also known as Mr. Ed. He had the reputation of being a very mean guy. Perhaps at the other prison camps he was, but as far as I knew, Frenchy was pretty mild. Hovick was embarrassed that he had written an apology, but he readily admitted it. He asked me how I had handled Frenchy, so I told him about our pleasant conversation and my letter from Evy. I also explained how I was able to lead Frenchy away from the writing request by being a nice guy and throwing in a couple of funnies. Bart's face clouded up, and he pounded the cement pad with his fist. "You're the only guy up here who can get away with that bullshit!" I told Bart that everyone was entitled to use whatever methods he chose as long as, in the end, the result was a zero for the gooks.

Bart would not have been such a disappointment to me if he hadn't been so critical of others while at the Plantation. I can understand a man who falters now and then because he isn't that tough. But any man who has the reputation of being a "tough guy" shouldn't flunk his first minor test. I never said another word about it during the time we were together, but it was never the same between us.

The Toastmaster meetings fizzled out. People just lost interest. The longest lasting educational programs were the Spanish lessons and Ben Pollard's classes in aerodynamics.

The Vietnamese were anxious to get us to write as many letters home as possible. They were still smarting from the long dry spell. In January, I wrote another letter to Evy, which showed that my hopes for ever returning home were practically nonexistent.

4 Jan 1972

Evy Darling,

I am waiting for pictures of you with your summer visitors and family news. As I have said before, enjoy your life because even though it has been 7 years, it may be 7 more or longer, so don't wait for me. I know you care, hope, wish, and pray, but that is not going to do it so don't waste your time. I don't need anything but to get out of here. I don't want you to be lonely forever, if you want to remarry, go ahead if it's possible, to hell with what people say.

Larry

One morning, Jim Kasler was running vigorously in place, trying to improve his wind. Suddenly he stopped, falling to the pad and writhing in great pain. After checking him out, we decided that he must have done some damage to a tendon, and while his ankle didn't seem to be broken, he couldn't walk on it. I went over to talk to him as soon as he had settled down. "So! Our big tough guy, Jim Kasler, who's getting ready to excape from Hanoi, breaks his frigging leg stepping on his own toe! Aren't you a sorry example of a great hero?" Jim laughed. "So now what are you going to do, Baron?" (He loved to be called "Red Baron," like the German war ace Richthofen of WW I fame.)

"What the hell *can* I do? I'm grounded!"

"Yeah, okay, tell you what we can do." I posed in front of his pad and motioned him to get up on my back, piggyback style. Jim was a lot bigger than me; I was about the shortest guy in the cell block. He mounted up, and I carried him into the yard, where he could sit in the sun during the time we were allowed out. I also brought him his food and made a fuss over him. Jim liked that. It took a couple of weeks for his ankle to get back to normal, but then he was fine, and that was a big relief to all of us.

The young English-speaking turnkey was gleefully picking up our March letters as though handling a treasure. "This is very good, very good. Most important for you, too. Many, many people in the world want to know about all of you up here and our treatment. Oh yes! I know very much, very much about that!" The gooks were so relieved when our seven-month letter moratorium of 1971 was over. We could only hope that it had been of some use as a weapon against the Vietnamese in Paris.

One of the messages from Jack Flynn regarding policies

(which were now referred to as "plums") instructed us to try to give the impression that policies had "grass roots" origin. I couldn't blame Jack for trying, but it made about as much sense as the reference YKB I was trying to use at the Zoo. I sent Jack a message saying essentially, "If the gooks start torture again, you may as well proudly admit to your policies and your stand of resistance against them. Our experience in 1969 proved that when numbers of people are tortured, the facts will out, regardless of the exercise you go through to prevent it."

April 16, 1972 was a quiet afternoon. Some of us played bridge or chess, while others dozed. Suddenly we heard air-raid sirens. We had not heard much of that since 1968. The sound of jet engines, growing louder, told us that this was a big air strike, very close to Hanoi. We all wore great big smiles, and Kasler yelled, "Larry, happy fiftieth birthday!"

"All right! Isn't it nice of them to remember the old stroker!" We could hear the sounds of bombing now, and the antiaircraft artillery fire. One of the guys yelled, "Hear those whooshing sounds? Those are SAMs (surface to air missiles) being launched!" Well, well, so what did Tricky Dick Nixon have in mind? *This* was certainly a welcome departure from the "humane war" bullshit that had gone on since '68! We were so happy to hear bombs falling again, we were jumping up and down.

In late April, the Vietnamese set up for movies twice, just a few days apart. The first was a beautiful color film of a Russian circus. It was as free from propaganda as one could hope for in a Communist country. It was a top-notch movie. The cameras frequently panned around the circus audience, and their delight showed in their expressions. I know it must have in ours, too! It was such a pleasure for us to see pure entertainment, instead of the usual bullshit propaganda!

The second movie was an entertaining dance film from the People's Republic of China, which showed folk dances from some of the provinces. This film, too, was in color, and featured a dance troupe of six very beautiful young Chinese women. We thoroughly enjoyed both films, but tried to figure out why the gooks were showing them.

Then the Vietnamese informed us that China had been admitted to the United Nations General Assembly! *That* news was earthshaking enough, but they added that President Nixon had recently visited Peking, and had met with Chairman Mao and Premier Chou En-lai! Some of us were very disturbed at those revelations, because our view was that our president was meeting with one of the parties who was exerting a major effort to keep North Vietnam in the war. However, our trust in President Nixon was immense, and there was very little discussion about the new relationship between the U.S. and China. We knew that our view of the outside world was very limited at best, so we had to trust in our president.

From the sixteenth of April on, our planes came North regularly. In early May, the Box put up a helluva squawk about the U.S. Navy mining the harbor at Haiphong. We were elated to hear that. *Now* we were getting somewhere! We were finally putting some *real* pressure on North Vietnam again.

Shortly afterward, the gooks suddenly moved over two hundred POWs out of Unity to another camp (or camps) unknown to the rest of us. A couple of the junior people from our cell block were sent with them. The rest of us packed up our gear and were moved across to cell block one. Risner's group of eighteen men, which had been living in Building O, next to One, was moved one more building away, so they wouldn't be directly next door. Their building was called "Rawhide." Flynn's group was still in cell eight, at the corner of the Unity yard. Each cell block was still walled off from the others by flimsy matting. Communicating with the other cell blocks wasn't difficult, and we quickly drilled a hole through to cell two for voice comm.

There was one guard who had an especially rotten attitude. He would perch up on a ladder during air-raid alerts so he could peer at us, keeping the muzzle of his automatic weapon pointed inside our cell. That ticked us off, and we let him know about it, but it took a couple of weeks before he changed his ways.

Bud Day, Jack Fellowes, Bomar, Kirsten, and twenty-five others were over in cell two. Our comm guy called me over because Kirsten wanted to talk to me. I wondered what he could possibly want of me, since it had been two years since we were separated—and it could just as well have been twenty-two years, for all I gave a damn.

Kirsten told me that he hoped I didn't hold anything against him because of our conflict back at the Zoo. To get the conversation over with in a hurry, I told him I had forgotten about our differences. (But I hadn't, and for the rest of my life I never would forgive him.) When I got off the wall, Kasler said, "What was that all about?"

"I'm not sure, I think he was apologizing, in a way, for the crap he gave me at the Zoo."

"Looks like he's trying to repair a few fences as insurance, in case he needs you when we get out."

"I don't know what the hell he has in mind." I didn't care, because knowing him, I couldn't believe he was sincere anyway.

We were encouraged by the apparent change of American policy signaled by the renewed bombing. In our cell block, things rocked along fairly smoothly, with bridge playing and Spanish lessons as high points of the day. Our major concern, once again, was Ray Saxton's health. The V were giving us about a fourth of a cup of canned sweet milk several times a week. Saxton was getting a full cup, but he wasn't drinking it. He would walk around the sleeping pad with his cup of milk in hand, and when he thought no one was watching, he'd toss it into a *bo* or into the corner of a walled alcove where we had set up the "official" toilet area. He was still skinning bread and eating practically nothing, and the guys guessed his weight at just over one hundred pounds. He was over six feet three inches tall.

We no longer had Gaither with us to help Dale Osborne, but Dale was doing okay by himself. He had many bad nights, with nightmares, when he cried out and suffered. We all lived through it with him. Everyone was very sympathetic, and the nightmares were never mentioned to him.

As usual, the gooks loved to pass on bad news whenever they could, like the deaths of Jim Stockdale's mother, Roger Ingvalson's wife, and others. The latest downer was that Ev Alvarez's wife had left him to marry someone else. Alvy had been a prisoner for eight years, and even though he couldn't blame Tangee for wanting to get on with her life, it was a crushing blow to him. Ray Vohden also learned that his wife was trying to get a divorce, but Ray reacted differently from Alvarez. He was angry rather than disappointed. This was good evidence that a number of wives were weakening in the long-time separation. Well, it was bound to happen. So far Evelyn hadn't shown any tendency to look around. The last letter I wrote, I gave her a shot at freedom if she wanted to go for it. But her answer came in a letter that was written soon after she got mine, although I didn't receive it for several months. She told he how she felt about it, in no uncertain terms. She always used "now hear this" whenever she had a forceful, no-argument declaration to make to me. Seeing it at the beginning of her letter made me smile to recollect her ways.

CAMP UNITY
AREA

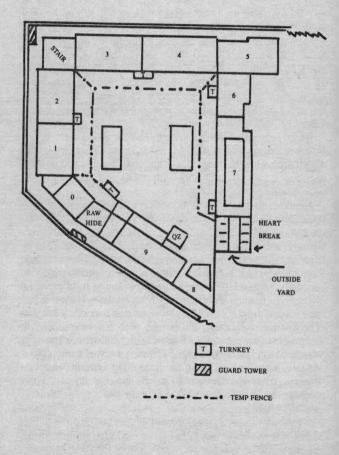

Feb. 4, 1972

Larry—

Now hear this! Don't appreciate you writing about not waiting, remarrying etc. Sorry to tell you—you'll have a job shaking me! Think you will like this area better than So. Fla. House has 2300 sq. ft. living space—plenty of room for all family to visit, fireplace, on canal, wall-to-wall carpeting throughout! You will love it. Little more patience please!

Your Evy

Several months later, the V removed the fence between us and building number one. We could now associate freely with them during our periods outside. My main man there was Bud Day, and we never seemed to run out of things to talk about. One day, another guy from One, Ramon Horinek, asked me if I had ever known an air force captain by the name of Wayne Ensminger. I sure did! Wayne was one of my best up-and-coming flight leaders at Itazuke. The last I heard, he had resigned his air force commission in May of '65 to go to work for the CIA airline in Laos.

Ramon confirmed that, and said he chanced to meet Ensminger when he himself was doing some classified work in Laos. He gave me the sad news of Ensminger's death. Ramon was an eyewitness to the last flight that Wayne ever made. He was flying a single-engine Helio aircraft, excellent for short-field, heavy-load operations out of secluded airfields in the contested parts of Laos. His Helio was loaded with grenades and other explosives, plus five passengers. Wayne took off and barely cleared the trees that were just off the end of the jungle strip. After the plane climbed a hundred feet or so, the engine started misfiring. Ensminger kicked it into a hard turn, trying to land in the opposite direction, but he clipped the trees on the way in. The little bird hit very hard and was badly smashed as it skidded to a stop. The passengers poured out on the run, but Ensminger was trapped because the airframe was damaged around his seat. He struggled to get out, but a cloud of gas vapor was rising. Wayne was still struggling to get out when the thing went up in a violent fireball. What an awful way to go! By the time this war would end, as with the other wars, the toll of my friends "Gone West" would be high.

In the fall of 1972, the Box hailed the arrival of a famous American movie actress who had "come to Hanoi to demonstrate her friendship with the Vietnamese people and her opposition to the illegal, immoral, and unjust war." The Box also told us that "their friend Jane Fonda" had met with some American prisoners, to talk about the war and their treatment. We guessed that the Americans had to be the same two who had refused to join us, figuring the gooks wouldn't have taken a chance with anyone else. The Vietnamese played a tape, which they said had been made by Fonda and a group of young American women, demonstrating against the war outside the main gate of the U.S. Army base at Fort Dix, New Jersey. We were all sitting on the pad listening to the women singing, in lusty voices, a song entitled, "Fuck the Army!" Actually, they didn't sing it, they screamed it, at the top of their lungs. We sat there in shock, trying to adjust to the harsh realization that these were our own American women! We couldn't believe that they would involve themselves in such filth to show their dissension and encourage our soldiers to desert! Fonda, like Baez and others who visited Hanoi to comfort the enemy, saw what the Vietnamese wanted her to see, and believed what she had already decided to believe before she traveled to Hanoi.

(After we were released, she called us "liars and hypocrites." Fonda's comments are on record, addressing students at Michigan State, November 22, 1969. She said, "If you understood what communism was, you would hope, you would pray on your knees, that we would someday become Communists." And again at Duke University, December 11, 1970, she said, "I am a socialist, therefore I think we should strive toward a socialistic society all the way to communism." Tom Hayden, (today Ms. Fonda's most recent ex-husband), came to Hanoi to make POWs, including my cell mate Ron Byrne, sweat while he badgered them, and to get other POWs to turn their backs on their fellow prisoners and on their country.)

Right after Fonda's visit, Hanoi had another American visitor, the former attorney general of the United States, Ramsey Clark! This one really threw us for a loop—our own former attorney general! "What the hell is going on back there?" we wondered! "It's okay to be against the war, but why are they letting people come all the way to Hanoi to say so?" They played part of Clark's taped interview with our antiwar guys over the Box. "If you are really acting in accord with your conscience . . ." It was as if he was saying, give me a call and I'll represent you.

We couldn't help but wonder why our government failed to prosecute those visitor-traitors! In any other country in the world, they would surely have been hung by their scrawny necks!

Late in the summer of '72, the V put up a volleyball net and a couple of Ping-Pong tables. We played whenever we were outside, and when we were inside, we watched the Vietnamese play. They were excellent in both these minor sports. They applied themselves well to these two activities, which were among the few that the government could afford to support. One day, they let us sit by the volleyball court to watch two Vietnamese teams play, and they were really good. There was one young guard who made a lot of exceptional plays. A few of us applauded his efforts, and he smiled back. I doubted he had a mean bone in him.

One day we got some satisfaction. Looking out, we saw some gook soldiers issued black clothing, like the Viet Cong. They were finally being sent to "dash forward against the $M\bar{y}$" in South Vietnam, as Ho Chi Minh was fond of saying. One was our old Zoo turnkey-torturer Slug, alias the Frog! So he was finally about to get his comeuppence! He didn't look thrilled over it, either! He'd much rather "dash forward against the $M\bar{y}$" in Hanoi, where he'd be guaranteed of the outcome!

Risner's group got a new man, a South Vietnamese fighter pilot. When I met Nguyen Quoc Dat, "Max," in the yard, he immediately asked if I knew Major Bill Hail. I said, "Yes, Bill is a dear friend of mine." Max then told me the sad story of how Bill had bailed out of an A-1 while out on a local test hop, and was captured and murdered by the VC. Max was a big help to us, since he could translate the Vietnamese radio broadcasts.

New shoot-downs were coming into the Unity compound, and with the exception of Bedinger's news about the '68 bombing halt being Johnson's idea, we were getting our first news from the outside since 1968. We got a look at some new Navy shoot-downs . . . they had very long hair! "What is it with you guys, don't you pay attention to dress and appearance regs anymore?" They told us that the navy had a new chief of naval operations, named Zumwalt, who was very liberal. Now it was okay to wear long hair and beards. He even did away with the traditional uniforms with the bell-bottom trousers! The sailors now all dressed like navy chiefs. We were dumbfounded! They said Admiral Zumwalt sent a lot of personalized messages all over the navy. They called them "Z-grams." We didn't approve of these wild departures from tradition.

We learned that the survival school was now saying that if you were captured, to go ahead and willingly participate in minor propaganda stunts, if you thought your pictures would be taken and your presence made known to the outside world. The services had also softened the interpretation of the Code to reduce the chance of torture. We were sure that was because of what Hegdahl had told them, which made us feel good about his release. Even so, we were also perversely disappointed to hear that, because we had suffered so much and resisted so hard up to now. Now, the new POWs could give it away for nothing! It was hard for us tough old war-horses to accept this new, more lenient position.

As far as we could learn, the V had not roughed up any of the new guys at all. They were finally being "very humane" because they smelled a possible end to the war, and probably because they had taken a lot of flack in Paris after Hegdahl's release.

The gooks made one exception to the no-torture position they were maintaining. Air force Lieutenant Colonel Joe Kittinger was captured on the eleventh of May, 1972, after bailing out of an F-4. I always said that a man has to be thirty-five percent crazy to fly a jet fighter. But feisty Joe Kittinger had at least ten percent more than the minimum requirement! I figured he had to have, since he was famous for bailing out of balloons from over 110,000 feet above the earth. Joe gave the gooks a very hard time. They almost couldn't get out of his way, because he was always on the offensive—charging them. Finally, in exasperation, they waived the new rules. They tortured the shit out of him, just to quiet him down! When it was over, and we knew he was okay, we were pleased and proud to have Joe with us.

Kevin Chaney was captured on July '72, and he sent me lots of news about my family. Kevin was Allan's roommate and fraternity brother at the University of Florida. He said that when Allan was the fraternity kitchen manager, the meals were the best in fraternity history. (I was not surprised to hear that, because our four boys were all spoiled by Evelyn's fantastic cooking. Allan was a big eater and would not tolerate second-class chow.) Kevin also told me all about Allan's in-laws, who he said were strict Catholics and wonderful people. One of their sons, Patrick, had been MIA since 1966. I was sorry to hear that.

One morning Bud Day and I were exercising in the yard when we heard the sound of a jet. We looked up, and not five hundred feet directly above us was one of our small, pilotless reconnaissance drones, just cruising along at about four hundred MPH! It was apparently undetected by the Air Defense System, and not a shot had been fired at it! The drone flew straight on for a mile or two, then made a programmed ninety-degree turn right, then a two-seventy left, putting it on a reverse track. Somebody yelled, "Smile everybody, we're gonna get our pictures taken!" It passed directly over the camp again, then continued toward the sea. Bud said, "Can you imagine a country with that kind of technology? Able to put a drone dead center on target?" He was very proud, as were we all. Too bad that the country with the great technology couldn't figure out how to get us the hell out of there! But that wasn't technical, it was political.

There was a rumor that some POWs would soon be released. George McKnight went out to a quiz in September and learned that his mother had taken a hard-line antiwar position and wanted permission to come to Hanoi to take him home! Jack Flynn got in touch with George to tell him it might be a good idea for him to go and carry out a load of intelligence information. Our commander was using the flexibility of the Code for our purposes, exactly as I had for our wounded men back in '69, and as Stratton wanted with Hegdahl. It was the right idea, but McKnight felt that freedom for all of us was close, so early release wouldn't be of any real value. Jack Flynn backed off. I told Bob Forrester that if there was a release, Gartley, whom Bob knew from the Miller group, was sure to go home. Bob said, "No Larry, Gartley is a good kid, he won't go home early."

"He may be a good kid, Bob, but get set for a disappointment, because if *his* mother shows up, Gartley will go home."

On the twenty-fifth of September, Jack Flynn and five other seniors in his cell block were taken out, supposedly to interrogation. There was no interrogation, it was a trick to get them to the war museum. The senior POWs made it very difficult for the V, and it took two dozen of them to get the six guys aboard the bus! They also had to be forced out of the bus at the museum, and they raised so much hell, the Vietnamese had to beat them all to control them. Flynn was bound and determined not to give the gooks any free propaganda that would make the outside world think that American POWs were enjoying the sights at the war museum like a bunch of tourists. Once the V realized that they would have to force it, the POWs were returned to Unity. It was the last time the V ever tried anything like that.

Jack Flynn changed the rank system based on probable promotion dates of the long-time captives, which made me building SRO again. Jack then directed me to send him a fitness report on Forrester for the time period that I knew him. I complied immediately.

A couple of days later, Gartley went out to quiz, raising our feelings that a release was imminent. Sure enough, Minne Gartley was there to claim her son, in the company of the antiwar activists Cora Weiss, Dave Dellinger, and a few others, including the wife of the navy man Norris Charles. The V played a tape of the comments she made on arrival. We couldn't believe her asinine remarks, which were, in part, "I do hope the North Vietnamese will give us a suite in a hotel." We thought it was bad enough that she came to Hanoi in the first place. The way we read those remarks, she was telling the world that she was so horny that she couldn't wait to get her husband home before jumping his bones. Charles Gartley, and an air force Major Elias were released. We were especially upset with those three, believing that they should have hung in there with the rest of us to the bitter end. Norris Charles had gotten to Hanoi so recently he was still passing stateside water! Well, as Frederic March said in the movie *The Bridges at Toko-Ri*, "Where do we get such men?" (And women?)

Shu was spending a lot of time in the yard with the new guys, catching up on news from back home, particularly with a young Philadelphian, Ralph Galati. Ralph had been active with the POW/MIA issue while in high school and college. He knew many of the wives, having met them at various functions. He told us about the POW bracelet program. Anyone wishing to support the POWs could purchase a bracelet with the name of a POW (or MIA) stamped on it. The wearer was supposed to keep it on until the day the man was repatriated. That surprised us and gave us a warm feeling. Our people back home hadn't forgotten or given up on us!

Out in the yard, with one of the new guys, Shu listened to, and practiced, a new movie to tell us. The movie was *Play Misty for Me*, and Shu did a fantastic job with it. It was particularly exciting to us, because we knew it was one of the latest hits from home, and we'd be more "up to date" after hearing it.

In mid-October one of our comm team called me to say, "Big news for you, Larry. You want it in private, or can everybody hear it?"

"What, private? Everybody here knows everything about everybody, so shoot."

"Okay Lar, your big buddy Bill Elander is here! He says he saw Evy and your boys in July. You have a beautiful home on the water right next door to his best friend. Everyone in your family is doing fantastic, waiting for you, and they believe it won't be long now!''

"How did Elander luck out to get here?" I asked.

"He was flying the latest Phantom, the new one with the Gatling gun; he had every piece of electronic equipment you could stuff into an airplane, and *still* he got shot down!''

Everyone in the cell block enjoyed listening to Elander's message, and one commented, "Larry, you've gotten more family news than any man in this prison camp! How do you manage it?"

"It's easy," I shot back. "All you have to do is arrange for all your best friends to get shot down, one after another!" Everybody laughed. I sent: "Bill, I'm happy to get all the news, and glad you're okay. Sorry you had to get shot down, but I compliment you on your sense of timing, you old SOB, you saved yourself about seven years of this bullshit!"

Everyone's morale was high, even though we had been dropped on our heads numerous times before by thinking the end was near. The Box said that our negotiator, Kissinger, had said something in Paris about "peace is at hand." The gooks seemed very excited, and as the saying went, "The gook balloon is up." (So was ours.) We all prayed that Kissinger's comment was true.

By that time, there were almost no fences separating cell blocks. We could wander pretty much where we wanted to, except that we were expected to return to our own cells if the alert sounded. I walked to the far side, cell block six, which was locked, but full of new guys. I had quite a head of hair and had grown my moustache back. I stood in front of their door and introduced myself. They crowded the door, shook my hand, and stared at me. "How long have you been here?"

"Lemme see . . . ummmh, seven years and five months." They just stared in silence, but some of their Adam's apples were bouncing pretty good. They were looking in disbelief at a Methuselah. They asked what us old guys thought of the gooks after all that time. I answered quietly, "We hate the commie bastards.''

"Even after all those years?"

"You bet your ass! *Especially* after all those years! For all they did to us, we'll *never* forgive them!" They could not believe that we old-timers still held such a hard line against the Communists. I thanked them all and shook their hands for coming up to North Vietnam and giving their all to try to help put an end to it and get us out. I realized they were different from us. The world outside had changed, and we were relics of another era who had been held in a time capsule.

Things began looking good, and I think everyone lost interest in trying to escape. Ray Saxton was a continuing worry. He didn't realize how far down he had gone, or how bad he looked. He was under a hundred pounds for sure, more like eighty-five. His back was straight and flat, and he had no buttocks at all. His ribs stuck out all around. His anus, which would normally have been neatly tucked under his buttocks (where we all keep them), was pinned to his lower back like a target bull's-eye—it was ghastly! His testicles, hanging between his skinny femurs, were bigger than tennis balls. We believed that we were watching a man die by his own choice, and the only thing that could save him was a sudden, miraculous end to the war. Doremus pointed out that Saxton could be separated from us at any moment, and we would never see him again.

The Box was still complaining daily about the mining of Haiphong harbor, the bombing by tactical fighters, and the BUFFs. That was a new word to us; we only knew the heavies as B-52s, but now they were called BUFFs—*B*ig *U*gly *F*at *F*ellas. The North Vietnamese had plenty of sympathizers all over the world, including our own country, but "war is hell," and the more of a hell you make it for the opposition, the better your chances of winning it quickly.

We didn't know how our man Kissinger was doing in Paris, or what had happened to "peace is at hand," but on the night of the eighteenth of December 1972, Hanoi and all of its inhabitants, including all us POWs in the "city jail," came to know the power of the BUFFs, and the Strategic Air Command.

Just after dark, the air-raid sirens went off, and we thought we were in for another air strike or reconnaissance flight by tactical aircraft. But no! We didn't know we were about to witness the start of the greatest show on earth! The antiaircraft fire and the SAM launches were deafening! Then came the bombs, and by the long volley of explosives, we knew immediately the birds were B-52s! Our side meant business, and the gooks were really going to catch it! In comparison to a B-52 raid, a major raid by twenty or thirty tactical fighters is piddling. Each of the BUFFs could carry about a hundred 500 or 750 pound bombs! Can you imagine every flight of three aircraft dropping *three hundred* bombs? You can't think—you can't talk—about B-52 strikes without using all superlatives! The sky lit up, and we all jumped up onto the pad to look out. The night wasn't black anymore, because of the continuous flashes of the flak guns, the rocket trails of the SAMs (missiles), and the fires caused by the bombs. The BUFFs came in several times that night, and when the bombs impacted nearby, we hugged the walls in case the jail was hit. This time there were no gooks peering in at us the way they did during fighter strikes! They were all hiding in shelters, or in holes in the ground covered by old doors or sleeping pallets. They didn't give a damn about us anymore, they were concerned about saving their own asses!

God, we were excited! . . . laughing, crying, yelling, "Hit the bastards, Dick! Give 'em hell!"

No doubt Nixon was taking maximum shit back in the States for deciding on the bombing, but he was definitely letting it all hang out! He knew, as our generals and admirals knew, that you can't win by licking everybody's face while they piss in your boots. You've got to bang 'em over the head, make them cry, make them beg for you to stop.

"Way to go Dick!" we screamed, "kick the shit out of them!"

We had a president with big brass balls, and we loved it! Not some pussy like McGovern, about whom the gooks said, "He will come to Hanoi on his knees to beg for your release." We don't want our presidents on their knees to anyone! We want 'em standing tall and telling the enemy what we are going to do, then doing it to them!

The next day the V brought in extra bed boards. They told us to lean them against the walls so we could shelter behind them if the bombers came again. Sure enough, they came soon after dark, and the bombs rained down. It went on every night for eleven nights. During the day, the tactical fighters hit them all over the northern countryside! We were in hog heaven! *This* was the country we knew and loved, kicking some serious ass! We knew this was one battle we would win!

When the bombs flashed, we'd count aloud the seconds until the sound of the explosion, like this: Flash—one thousand and one, one thousand and two, one thousand and three, etc. That's an old trick, and since we know that sound travels a thousand feet per second, we could figure that no bombs landed any closer to us than a half mile! Great credit is due those BUFF bomber crews for the high level of professionalism they showed in carrying out those bombing missions, over the hottest and most heavily defended target areas in the history of aerial warfare. The BUFFs had to plow through MiG fighters, heavy antiaircraft artillery, and a dense concentration of the latest Russian-made surface-to-air missiles.

Every night we were shrieking in excitement as the bombs landed, wishing and hoping that every bomb would hurt them badly. Once we heard what we thought was one of our fighters coming in very close in a screaming dive. Maybe he was launching a Shrike missile against a SAM site—whatever it was, he was supersonic as he pulled up, rattling everything in the building with a rolling shock wave. We cheered like crazy.

The night of the twentieth of December the bombers came again, and the shooting started right on cue. The V were launching SAMs as if they were thirty-five-cent fourth of July sky rockets! The SAMs lit up the entire neighborhood of the launching sites. There were occasional fires high in the sky, which seemed to last for a long time. We didn't know if the fires were falling B-52s, but if they were, it was a long way down, assuming their bombing altitude was over thirty thousand feet! The bombs that impacted close shook the building, and dust particles, along with bits and pieces of roof tile, fell on us. After one very close impact of a string of bombs, one of our guys, in near panic, yelled, "The next one is gonna kill us . . . gonna kill us!" Another voice yelled, "Shut up and die like a man, goddamn you!" My feelings were that I would love to get hit right on top of the head with a load of thousand-pounders, just to screw the gooks out of their bargaining chips. But I was torn, because I heard myself yelling, amidst all the excitement, "This frigging war is finally over! There's nobody on the face of the earth that's gonna take a pounding like this! We're going home! We're getting *out* of here! In one month we'll all be home!" (I was wrong. It took almost two months.) We later learned that the third night of bombing cost us six B-52s, and a total of fifteen B-52s were lost over North Vietnam in the "eleven-day war.")

The following morning, the gooks opened up the cell blocks to give us food and water. Someone said, "Larry, the new guys are outside, and Elander is asking for you." I leapt outside in my best dress, which was a pair of light purple nylon undershorts that Norlan had given me a year before. The gooks were trying to get everyone back inside, fearing a total loss of control should the air-raid alert sound. I was halfway down the yard when I spotted Bill. He waved wildly, smiling. "Hey Larry, you look great!"

Cochise, the former Zoo camp commander, came up to me, yelling in my face. I knew he wanted me to retreat to my cell block, but I kept looking over his head, waving at Elander. Finally, Cochise shoved me, and kept shoving me hard until I decided it was best to go back in.

Once we were all locked inside, it didn't take any time for the turnkey to come around to tell me to roll up my gear, I was moving. Damned if Cochise didn't get me fired, because of the yard incident! I didn't care, a change was welcome. The key walked me across the yard and stuck me into one of the cells in Heartbreak, but he didn't lock the door! I set up my mosquito net and arranged my few possessions on the far bunk, all of two feet away. Then I went back into the hall and looked around. I checked out each of the cells, since all the doors were open. Meandering back to my cell, to sweat out chow time, I heard someone out in the hall. Standing in front of my door was the nice young man, the volleyball player, grinning at me. He gave a couple of furtive glances in both directions to make sure nobody was around, and then he came into my cell and stuck out his hand. Holy cow, that was the first time a Vietnamese ever made an overt move to be friendly! (Other than Zoorat, and he had something else in mind.) I figured, what the hell, kid, you want to be my friend, why not? So I stuck out my hand, and he grabbed it and shook it hard. Of course they could soon teach him to be "one of the boys." But on the other hand, I had already taught him that, contrary to what he might hear, the $M\bar{y}$ had some pretty nice people among them! Then he ducked out quickly, not wanting to get caught being friendly to the $M\bar{y}$. Soon the key came back and told me I was moving yet again!

As we walked across the Unity courtyard toward my left, I saw Bud Day coming in my direction carrying his gear, too! He had also been "fired" from his job in cell two. The key threw open the courtyard gate of Rawhide, and there stood Robbie Risner, with our eighteen new cell mates! They were very happy to have us among them. They had been expecting us and had two spots set aside for us on the sleeping pad.

That night, our friends asked for a synopsis of what was happening on our side of Unity. They knew most of it through the comm team, but they wanted to hear it live. First Bud spoke, then I added my side of it, and when we were finished, John Finlay said, "We are really glad to have you both with us, it's like a breath of fresh air." We understood very well what John meant; people in restricted circumstances are bound to get on each other's nerves sooner or later. Even a few days of solitary, away from the bickering in a crowded cell, could be a welcome respite, provided it wasn't for too long and there was no torture involved. Of course, such perfect accommodations were rarely provided!

We talked about the bombing, and most of the guys agreed that it was almost over, but others were steeling themselves against more disappointment and avoided committing themselves. Bud and I both felt that the severe and continued punishment of Hanoi would bring about our release.

President Nixon sent the bombers again and again. As we sat there through it all, our thoughts and prayers were for the courageous B-52 crews of the Strategic Air Command. If there was anyone among us who was concerned about the Vietnamese people, it was neither expressed nor evident in any way.

Before the strikes on Haiphong and Hanoi, the B-52s were used mostly in South Vietnam. Any strikes into North Vietnam up to now had been close to the DMZ, so the heavy bombers had not seen action where there was a serious threat from enemy fighters or antiaircraft artillery. The last time SAC faced that kind of danger was when the B-29s bombed North Korea in the early '50s. We could not imagine the extent of modifications necessary to convert the SAC bomber force to carry conventional bombs. Before Vietnam, our armada of B-52s had been totally committed to nuclear operations.

It was a special treat to be in the company of this group of guys, who were all commanders or lieutenant colonels when shot down. They were noticeably more mature, lower key, and easy for Colonel Risner to control. Robbie required that each of us sit or stand for muster, without giving the turnkey a hard time.

Tom Kirk and Bill Franke worked hard on language study, mostly French. The V had also given the Rawhide group an American-printed Spanish-language textbook entitled *El Camino Real*, which made their teaching task a lot easier.

Chuck Gillespie acted as the room chaplain, and he handled Sunday services. Robbie Risner remained a very religious person. Sometimes we ate together, but there were times when I declined his invitation, because his prayers lasted so long the food got cold! I believed in the Lord, too, but I also believed that God wanted me to eat!

Al Brady told me the seniors had all heard about the effectiveness report on Forrester, which I provided to Jack Flynn, at Flynn's request. Al had known Forrester for years and served on the same carrier with him. "I think you rated him much higher than he deserved, Larry; he was pretty spastic and undependable aboard ship."

"Al, I don't know anything about that. I rated him only for the time I knew him, and it was as fair a report as I could possibly put together on the man."

Brady and Fred Crowe were especially good company. They had been together so long, they even sounded alike! Fred was air force and Allen navy, but they found that they had a lot in common, which they cultivated. They were both Scotch drinkers, and I promised that when we got back and they came to visit me in Florida, I would break out an unopened bottle of Haig and Haig Pinch and serve it up in our best glasses on a silver tray. Al said, "Sure, sure, you say that now, but that'll be the first thing you'll forget." (On the way home, I bought a case of Pinch. Within three months, they both visited us, with their wives and kids. As soon as they sat down, I told Evy that I'd take care of drinks. I brought in the unopened Pinch on the silver tray and went through the whole ritual! They never mentioned our "deal" and neither did I, but they both gave me a big smile and I knew they remembered. I wonder if they would have mentioned it if I had forgotten.)

The B-52s didn't come on Christmas Day, but they came storming in again on the night of the twenty-sixth, hitting both the Haiphong and Hanoi areas in the heaviest raids of the war. A few bombs landed close by, and among their usual lies, the Vietnamese claimed the jail containing POWs had been hit, but of course it wasn't.

(Two aircraft were downed on the twenty-seventh, when 120 B-52s dropped more than twelve thousand bombs. We had no aircraft losses during the last two days of the most impressive and record-setting bombing effort in military air history. The V claimed our targets were all civilian residential areas, hospitals, and schools, but the targets actually hit were SAM sites, tank truck conversion facilities, major storage areas, rail centers, and rail overhaul facilities.)

The nightly raids ended the twenty-ninth of December, when all became quiet again over North Vietnam.

Our morale was very high during the first weeks in January. Our Rawhide group was not allowed to mingle with the others in the main courtyard, nor was Jack Flynn's group down in cell block eight. On the twenty-ninth of January, the Vietnamese led everyone in Rawhide and cell block eight into a big room, where we were all together for the first time. When they finally got us calmed down, an interpreter got up and said, "And for you, the war is now over! Soon you go home." It didn't come as a surprise, but those words were good to hear, after so many long, awful years. The real meaning of it didn't hit home for me, and I doubt if it did for many of the others. The interpreter passed each of us a copy of the agreements, which were signed in Paris by the involved parties. As soon as we got back to Rawhide, we made sure that the face of each copy was signed by every man in Rawhide. I saved the top line of my copy for the signature of our first POW, Everett Alvarez.

About a week later the V came in and read a list of names of people to be moved to another cell block, in preparation for leaving Hanoi. The list was in order of date of shoot-down, beginning with Alvarez. I was number ten. I should have been number eleven, but Storz, who was captured before me, was dead.

In the new cell, we were with Shu, Harris, Scotty Morgan, Lockhart, Vohden, and other old-timers, for a total of about thirty. We were told that the first group to leave would also include the very seriously wounded, some of whom were recently captured BUFF crews. We were all excited, but still not sure that the end was actually in sight. They were saying we were going, but we had to wait and see, because for many years "home" was only a dream—Hanoi was real!

Out in the courtyard, I met Bernie Talley, who was on the same mission with Allan's brother-in-law, Patrick Wynne, back in '66. Bernie said Patrick had no chance—he saw his F-4 go into the trees down near the DMZ. He was convinced Patrick was KIA, not MIA.

Two people came to me and spoke to me separately, and privately, to apologize for not being able to hold a tighter line during the '69 purge. They said they regretted that they had named me as SRO and had confessed to all of my policies. I assured them that no apologies were necessary. I understood very well how those torturers could make a man say almost anything, if they so chose. I told them I knew they had done their very best, and I harbored no ill feelings toward them, or anyone who had been forced to make a confession. The V were determined to have a scapegoat for the escape attempt, and if not me, it would have been someone else.

My buddy and old cell mate, Ron Byrne, was one of the two hundred men who had been moved to a prison somewhere near the China border in May of '72. Now they were back with us in

Hanoi. He told me it was a quiet and pretty countryside area, but the facilities were primitive, similar to the Briar Patch. The living wasn't bad, and the food was better than they had been getting. We lost one man up there, marine Warrant Officer John Frederick, who died of malaria. Freddy was Howie Dunn's GIB. He had been badly burned during his bailout in '65. Despite his injuries, he did a whale of a job and took plenty of punishment while resisting.

There was a lot of greeting and handshaking going on in the yard the last few days. I don't know what the others were feeling—I was in shock. If the others were like me, then we were often lost in our own private thoughts.

On February 10, Robbie Risner said that Denton was writing a speech that we could use if we found ourselves spokesmen for a group of returning POWs. Robbie had glanced at it and didn't like what he saw. He asked me to check it out and discuss it with Jerry. Jerry was totally immersed in his writing when I walked up. "Hi, Jerry. Mind if I look at your work? Colonel Risner suggested I help out, because two heads might be better than one." Jerry was very gracious about it; in fact, I think he welcomed the help. Reading it over, I spotted some statements that were almost apologetic, something like, "We don't know if we have done a good job," and "History will have to judge us."

"Jerry, I realize that this is your first cut at this thing and I know you're going to change it . . . but it has the sound of a public apology, that you are prostrating yourself to public criticism. I don't think you mean to do that. Jerry, you did your absolute best up here, didn't you?"

"Of course I did, Larry!"

"Well then, that's the right attitude! We all did the very best we could, let's let it go at that." Nothing he wrote that day was ever uttered by anyone anywhere, and the wonderful, heartfelt remarks he made on the ramp at Clark AFB in the Philippines he wrote on the airplane, enroute home. Dr. Shields looked it over before we landed at Clark and was thrilled with it. He offered Jerry no criticism or help, not even the slightest hint of what he thought he should be saying. Later, some of the media suggested that Jerry's thanks to his president, and to the country, were dictated to him. That was completely untrue. The talk Jerry made came from the heart, and he did a beautiful job of it, as the world will remember.

On the night of the eleventh of February we went out, by the numbers, to a supply room to pick up our "going-home ward-robe." Each of us was issued a pair of black shoes and socks, underwear, shirt, and trousers.

We went back to our cell, but we didn't sleep much that night. We knew now that February 12 would be the *BIG* day! I would probably not make it home by the fourteenth, Valentine's Day, our thirtieth wedding anniversary, but it would be close. What a great anniversary gift for Evy and me! I was starting to believe it was possible.

The next morning we filed out in two lines into the Heartbreak courtyard and stood there under an arbor to wait. It was a foggy morning, so we suspected there would be some delay. "There's a young fellow back there who wants to see you for a minute, Larry," Bud Day said. I stepped out of line and walked back to a very handsome young fellow with either a broken leg or busted hip. He said, "Hi, Colonel, I'm Bill Arcuri, I've known about you for a long time. I'm from Satellite Beach, too." Bill was copilot of a BUFF that was knocked down on the twentieth of December. We didn't get a chance to say any more, as one of the V came up and suggested that I get back to my place, be-cause we were ready to board buses. We walked out and saw that the buses were parked on the opposite side of the street. There were plenty of civil police out there to restrain the crowds, but they weren't needed because the crowd was orderly and silent as we boarded.

As we drove around the edge of the city, we made frequent turns to skirt areas heavily damaged by the bombing, or areas they did not want us to see. This was my first (and last) ride through Hanoi without blinders on! Our destination was the Gia Lam Airport, and to get there we had to cross the Red River. When we got down to the banks of the river, we saw that all bridges had been bombed out. The banks of both sides of the river had been freshly graded for several hundred yards in from each side and a mile or two along the banks. It was all very neatly smoothed over like freshly planted farmer's fields. There seemed little doubt that the object of smoothing over those many acres of ground was to eliminate all signs of bomb damage. Our crossing was very slow, across a float bridge typical of the ones assembled by army engineers in battle situations.

We traveled a bit on the far side, before coming to a stop on the side of the road. Several women came around with sand-wiches. I took one and looked inside, counting four pieces of pig fat in half a loaf of bread. "Are you going to *eat* that crap?" someone asked me.

"You bet your ass I'm gonna eat it! This may be my last chance to get a pig-fat sandwich, and I don't want to miss it!" At the airport, we pulled up near the terminal to wait out the low fog. If our planes were coming this morning, they would have to use their own radar on an instrument approach, because there were certainly no compatible instrument landing aids at Gia Lam.

On a signal from a Vietnamese we got off the buses, then slowly walked to a departure checkout desk set up at the edge of the aircraft parking ramp. One would think that the V would have had someone unknown to us at the checkout desk. But no, the hated Rabbit was there to do the honors! There were about a thousand Vietnamese gathered there, mostly women, watching out of sheer curiosity. After the Christmas bombing they had as much, or more, reason than we had to hope the war was over.

An hour after our arrival at Gia Lam, we heard the welcome sound of approaching aircraft. Looking toward the end of the runway, we could see a beautiful silver bird just touching down— it was a type I had never seen before, a four-engine transport called the C-141 Lockheed Starlifter. My feelings at that moment were more of a detached curiosity than anything else. The silver bird taxied to within seventy-five yards of us. The pilot turned the aircraft until the tail pointed toward us, and shut down the engines.

The cargo door at the rear of the 141 dropped to the ground to its position as a loading ramp. People started jumping down from the airplane, people I had forgotten existed, who looked to me like they were from another world. Yes, they were from another world . . . *our* world! The moment I saw those beautiful people, my feelings changed from placid curiosity to a state of such extreme excitement I became spatially disoriented. I wasn't aware of any of my fellow POWs, or what they were thinking, or how they were reacting. I was totally engrossed in my *own* feelings, my *own indescribable excitement!* I could hear my heart pounding in my chest. Several men with stripes on their sleeves rolled out a red carpet and went through some other moves, rapidly arranging things that I couldn't make out. They were very precise in every move, as though it were a drill. They looked sharp and neatly dressed in their air force blues, their shoes shiny as glass. They were so handsome! A couple of flight nurses and flight stewardesses walked toward us, smiling prettily. They looked like movie stars in their tight, very short blue skirts and their neat blouses with silver bars on the collars. They were all wearing cute overseas caps, nylon stockings, and high heels. What a beautiful sight they were! I glanced once toward the Vietnamese women, who were also taken by this scene. They had never seen this type of Caucasian woman, and I know they had never, ever imagined women as pert, pretty, and outwardly happy as these American girls.

The first military officer I saw alight was Lieutenant Colonel Dick Abel. Then walking alongside him came Colonel Al Lynn, who wore a chest full of ribbons, and who I figured was probably the overall mission commander. They kept a keen eye on the Rabbit and the checking-out procedures. As each POW checked through the out desk, he walked over to Colonel Lynn and saluted, then continued on to the airplane. When my turn came, I did the same. As I turned toward the airplane, a tall American civilian grabbed me around the shoulders. ''Larry,'' he exclaimed, ''Evelyn and the boys are doing great and can't wait to get you home!'' I was stunned, and suddenly felt a wave of weakness as my knees started to buckle slightly. The man steadied me, with a firm grip.

''Do I know you?'' I asked.

''No, you don't know me, but I know *you*! I'm Dr. Roger Shields, with the Department of Defense.''

'Do you recognize that person over there?' I said, pointing back to the Rabbit.

''No.''

''That's the Rabbit.''

''So that's the Rabbit! I've heard plenty about that son of a bitch.''

''What took you so long to get here?''

''We've been trying very hard, and for a long time, to get to you.'' Dr. Shields walked with me all the way to the cargo ramp, keeping his arm around me. I think he knew I needed it. I climbed aboard that beautiful airplane, the first of three now on the ramp. The nurses and stewardesses said things to me, but I couldn't make out what they were saying—my ears were ringing, and I couldn't hear anything over the pounding of my heart!

I don't know how many of us were aboard, somewhere between twenty and forty POWs. Steadier hands helped to strap us into our seats. Everything went off like clockwork—each person knew his or her job, and they did it well. As soon as the engines were cranked up, the pilot did a fast taxi to the end of the runway, as if he was trying to get us the hell out of there before we could be stopped or delayed by some unforseen incident.

As we rolled I thought, "I guess this time it's the real thing. . . . It looks like we're going. . . . " The bird shuddered as the pilot eased the throttles forward, but the brakes held it in check. He was making his last-second instrument cross-check. Then the four engines screamed at maximum power. . . . We held our breath, just barely exhaling . . . the pilot finally released the brakes. The bird surged forward, and in seconds we were racing down the runway; we were close . . . close . . . we all let out our breath in tumultuous screaming . . . yelling. . . . Tears of joy streamed down our faces. . . . We pounded the arms of the seats. . . . We could feel the nose lift, as the pilot eased back the stick. . . . The bird rotated and stood on its main wheels, as if perched on its hind legs . . . then it *leapt* into the air, and we all went completely crazy . . . screaming, yelling, "We're off . . . we're up . . . we're out . . . we're out of that rotten place . . . we're really going *home* . . . WE'RE FREE . . . FREE . . . FREE!!!!!"

Not to Be Forgotten . . .

During the period 1962 to 1975, American involvement in Vietnam and Laos cost us nearly sixty thousand dead and two thousand still carried as missing. Hanoi continues to play a cruel game with the minds and emotions of the families of the missing and stubbornly refuses to divulge information that could put many of the cases of the missing to rest for all time.

Those of us who shared the prison experience want to remember the names of those twelve men believed to have died in the camps, including the few who were known to be captured and died somewhere between the point of capture and the prison camp.

The second list of thirty-six names are my personal and family friends. Several are still carried officially as Missing, all the others were Killed In Action.

Ron Storz	J. J. Connell
Norman Schmidt	Ken Cameron
Edwin Atterberry	John Frederick
Earl Cobiel	Ed Burdett
Lance Sijan	Arthur Mearns
Ward Dodge	Wilmer Grubb
John S. Albright	Melvin Killian
David Allinson	Darel Leetun
John Armstrong	J. A. Magnusson
William Barthelmas	George McCleary
Frank Bennett	William Nelson
Dwight Bowles	Richard O'Keefe
Arthur Brewer	Dan Packard
Kelly Cook	Dean Pogreba
Dennis Crane	Jerry Pyle
Morgan Donahue	Robert Ronca
Wayne Ensminger	Ted Shattuck
Jack Farr	Charles Shelton
Wayne Ferguson	Richard Swift
Jack Fowler	Smith Swords
Wayne Fullam	Rainford Tiffin

Robert Greskowiak   Samuel Waters
William Hail   Don Woods
David Hrdlicka   Patrick Wynne

ABOUT THE AUTHOR

A retired U.S. Air Force Colonel, Lawrence "Larry" Guarino was born in Newark, New Jersey on Easter Sunday in April 1922. Growing up, his boyhood hero was Charles Lindbergh, and the young Larry always dreamed of being a flyer. His dream was realized soon after Pearl Harbor, when he joined the Army Air Corps, receiving his pilot's wings in 1943.

There followed an illustrious career as a fighter pilot, spanning three decades, and covering three wars—World War II, Korea, and Vietnam—flying everything from British Spitfires and P-51 Mustangs to F-105 Thunderchiefs. In World War II, as a young lieutenant, Larry flew cover for the Allied landings at Gela Beach, Salerno Bay, and Anzio, and downed several German Messerschmidts in air battles over Cassino, Italy. Later, with General Clare Chennault's famed 14th Air Force in China, he flew missions over south China and into the Hanoi area of French Indochina, as Vietnam was known at the time.

After stints in Korea, Okinawa, and Thailand, Colonel (then Major) Guarino was shot down on his 50th mission, captured by the North Vietnamese, and taken to Hanoi, where he spent nearly eight years as a prisoner of war, undergoing extreme deprivation and inhuman torture.

Repatriated in February 1973, Colonel Guarino was awarded more than fifty decorations including the Air Force Cross, the Distinguished Service Medal, and two Silver Stars.

He retired on July 4th, 1975, and now resides in Satellite Beach, Florida, with his wife of forty-seven years, the former Evelyn Gennell.

The couple has four grown sons, one of whom is following in his father's footsteps as a career Air Force fighter pilot, Colonel Allan Guarino.